James & Dolley
MADISON

AMERICA'S FIRST
POWER COUPLE

BRUCE CHADWICK

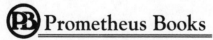 Prometheus Books
59 John Glenn Drive
Amherst, New York 14228

Published 2014 by Prometheus Books

Cover image of James Madison: *James Madison*, 1804, oil on canvas by Gilbert Stuart
(The Colonial Williamsburg Foundation)

Cover image of Dolley Madison: *Dolley Dandridge Payne Todd Madison,*
1804, oil on canvas by Gilbert Stuart (White House Collection, gift of the
Walter H. & Phyllis J. Shorenstein Foundation in memory of Phyllis J. Shorenstein)

Cover design by Jacqueline Nasso Cooke

Inquiries should be addressed to
Prometheus Books
59 John Glenn Drive
Amherst, New York 14228
VOICE: 716–691–0133
FAX: 716–691–0137
WWW.PROMETHEUSBOOKS.COM

18 17 16 15 14   5 4 3 2 1

Library of Congress Cataloging-in-Publication Data

Chadwick, Bruce.
    James and Dolley Madison : America's first power couple / by Bruce Chadwick.
        pages cm
    Includes bibliographical references and index.
    ISBN 978-1-61614-835-5 (hardback)
    ISBN 978-1-61614-836-2 (ebook)
    1. Madison, James, 1751–1836. 2. Madison, Dolley, 1768–1849. 3. Presidents—
United States—Biography. 4. Presidents' spouses—United States—Biography. 5. United
States—Politics and government—1809–1817. 6. United States—Politics and
government—1789–1815. I. Title.

E342.C47 2014
973.5'10922aB—dc23
                                                                                          2013036222

Printed in the United States of America

For Margie and Rory

CONTENTS

ACKNOWLEDGMENTS

*T*his book took a lot of time to research and write, but I was fortunate to have much help along the way. At New Jersey City University, many thanks to Dr. Fran Moran, Tim Stuckey, Allen Smith, and Elvis Emmanuel. Thanks to Tom Glynn—a librarian at Rutgers University, where I lecture—for his assistance in research. I had much help in obtaining photographs from Jeni Spencer at Montpelier, Andrea Ashby at the National Independence Historical Park, Elise Allison at the Greensboro Historical Library, Jamison Davis at the Virginia Historical Society, Marianne Martin at the Colonial Williamsburg Foundation, Jonathan Eaker at the Library of Congress, and Kathy Ludwig at the David Library of the American Revolution in Washington's Crossing, Pennsylvania.

Special thanks to Tiffany Cole, who helped me conduct research at Montpelier; and to Ralph Ketcham, the world's premier Madison scholar, who read the manuscript and made many useful suggestions. Thanks also to editor Steven L. Mitchell and copyeditor Jade Zora Scibilia at Prometheus Books.

AUTHOR'S NOTE

To make this book easier to read, I have taken some liberties with titles. The term *White House* was not applied to the president's home until the late 1830s and early 1840s. It would be difficult to continually refer to his residence as the President's Mansion or the Executive Mansion, as it was known when Madison was president. So I simply called it the White House.

The title of First Lady, to acknowledge the president's wife, was not coined until the death of Dolley Madison. Until then, the president's wife was called "the president's lady" or, in some cases, "the presidentress," or simply "Mrs. Madison." To make all of that easier, I just referred to Dolley as the First Lady throughout the book.

1
SAVING GEORGE WASHINGTON IN A CITY ON FIRE

*J*ust after sunrise on August 24, 1814, Dolley Madison stood on the roof of the White House, holding her hands steady around a spyglass in the balmy summer morning. She squinted with one eye and peered through the spyglass with the other, in a vain effort to find her husband, the president, who was said to be riding back to the White House from an army camp in Bladensburg, Maryland, about seven miles away, and spurring his horse to run as fast as possible down narrow dirt roads of the green countryside to meet her. She could see from her perch atop one of the two highest buildings in the city (the other being the still-unfinished Capitol) all of the wide thoroughfares and the side streets of Washington, DC. They were nearly deserted; most of the residents had fled the day before, after they read in the newspapers that the British Navy, with fifty-two ships in all and thousands of men, horses, and cannon, had landed in Maryland on Friday, after a brief trip up the Patuxent River from the nearby Chesapeake Bay, in the War of 1812.

It was a jolt; the news panicked the region. The capital attacked? Impossible. The editor of the *National Intelligencer*, the capital's leading newspaper, told his readers, "all citizens must join in the common defense."[1]

All were surprised by the landing. The war had been winding down. Peace talks were being held. Why should the British invade the Chesapeake? Washington? And if there was an attack, everybody expected the British to assault Baltimore, not Washington. The surprised residents of the capital now shuddered that the nightmare was about to come true, that Englishmen in their blazing red coats, carrying their muskets and pistols and lugging dozens of cannon behind them, would soon enter the city.

Wild rumors flew all over town. One had Dolley Madison surrendering the

White House to the British commander and begging him not to burn the city. Another had the British torching all of the government buildings but sparing residential homes. A third had all of the residential homes set on fire. A fourth put the British troop strength at sixteen thousand (it was closer to five thousand). Another said that the American defensive force was well over ten thousand troops (it was barely three thousand). Yet another had dozens of other enemy ships landing at different seaports on the Maryland shore.

The rumor about the torching of the capital raised eyebrows. Nearly a year and a half earlier, in the spring of 1813, that same rumor had floated through Washington and made everybody nervous. Dolley Madison wrote in that spring that she had heard that the British planned to land several hundred soldiers below Alexandria and attack Washington from across the Potomac in boats "so that they may be on hand to burn the President's house and offices." She told this to Edward Coles, who had just left as Madison's secretary. She added that she kept a sharpened Tunisian sword near her in the White House every day just in case the Redcoats did appear.[2]

In the previous day's edition of the *National Intelligencer*, General R. G. Hite, the commander of the military's tenth district, put out a call for volunteer troops. "To see their capital threatened by an insolent foe who insists upon dictating terms to them, after desolating their shores and sacking their cities," he cried, "the spontaneous efforts of the people are demanded." That same day, Washington James Blake, a physician serving as mayor of Washington, also begged for volunteers to defend the city and established a 10 p.m. curfew. "Every man will come forth in this glorious cause," he said.[3]

Dolley had become an enemy of the British, almost as much so as her husband. The feisty First Lady had sent off letter after letter to her friends in Europe that scalded the British and their armed forces as the war droned on. "The British on our shores are stealing & destroying private property, rarely coming to battle, but when they do are always beaten. . . . If the war should last six months longer the U.S. will conquer her enemies," she told a friend in Paris, writing the letter in positive tone in case someone else read it and forwarded it to the British.

She was hated by the British army, the British diplomats and the British press. British admiral Sir George Cockburn, head of the British Navy and one of its heroes in the Napoleonic Wars, had written Dolley a letter. In it, he told her that he planned to take the White House and have dinner there in two days. He urged her to flee because if he caught her there, the president's home would be "burned over your head." An insulted Dolley replied, "I do not tremble at this, but feel affronted that the Admiral . . . should send me notes that he would make his bow at my drawing room soon."[4]

Not satisfied with his threat, the cocky Cockburn then told America's First Lady that his men would capture her, put her on a boat, and take her to England, where she would be held hostage, imprisoned in a dark, dank jail, and then paraded through the streets of London in disgrace as hundreds of thousands of Brits jeered at her as her cart was hauled by.

Similar threats had been made by the British against Martha Washington during the American Revolution. She paid no attention to them. Martha told friends that she wanted to know when she would be paraded through the streets of London so that she could wear her best dress.

President Madison's wife of twenty years was a tiny figure on the roof of the President's Mansion that day. The oversized White House was one of the largest and most impressive buildings in the country. The sprawling, twenty-three-room building stood three stories high, with two upper floors reached by outside staircases and a ground-floor level with the street. It had lengthy, covered walkways on each side of it. The building sat near the Potomac River in the middle of a series of tree- and shrub-filled fields with no structures on them, making the president's home seem even larger. Pennsylvania Avenue, one of the capital's main thoroughfares, ran past the front of it. Several chimneys, one with a huge metal lightning rod, stuck up out of the roof. All of the rooms on all three floors had huge windows that overlooked the city.

President John Adams and his wife, Abigail, had moved in during the winter of 1800, when it was still incomplete. Abigail Adams complained bitterly that there was not enough wood to make fires and no bells to summon people, and that she had to hang her family's washed clothing on lines in the big rooms of the house to dry. She wailed that there was no yard, no fence, and few complete rooms. She warned her sister that she had to "keep all of this to yourself and when asked how I like it, say that I write you the situation is beautiful."[5] Even so, Abigail wrote upon leaving the home in 1801 that it was "a beautiful spot ... the more I view it, the more I am delighted with it." Eight years later, when Dolley became First Lady, her husband persuaded Congress to let her refurbish the entire interior of the building, making it as classy as any European monarch's home.

Of course, the building had its critics, such as the teenaged daughter of a politician who visited in 1808. "The President's House is surrounded by dark stone which looks very like the wall belonging to the state prison," she snapped.[6]

In 1814, Washington, DC, was not a large metropolis. The 1810 census showed that it had just over eight thousand residents. They lived on a series of streets connected in a huge grid designed by Pierre L'Enfant, the French architect who laid out the town over empty meadows and chopped down forests along the banks of the river. Most of the streets where people lived in 1814 con-nected to Pennsylvania Avenue, a very wide street filled with horses and car-riages all day long. They kicked up huge clouds of dust throughout the summer months. Most of the homes in the town were two stories high, although some were three. In 1814, Washington was still physically small in geography, and everyone was just a ten-minute horseback ride from everyone else. To give it even more distinction, L'Enfant had planted hundreds of high, green trees on the sides of Pennsylvania Avenue. They not only gave the street a majestic look, but also served to provide extra shade and cool spots in the town, which was oppressively hot in the summer.

L'Enfant had planned the capital with considerable help from the first pres-ident, George Washington, who wanted an imperial city whose large govern-ment buildings would make it, in just a few years, one of the most admirable capital cities in the world.

As Dolley stood on the roof of the President's Mansion that morning—a lone, tiny figure—servants, on her orders, were starting to set a large table and prepare a scrumptious dinner for dozens of generals, cabinet officers, the presi-dent, and friends of the Madisons who lived in the capital. Servants hurried from the kitchen and wine cellar to bring drink and food to the side tables in the dining room. Large ice buckets were prepared for the wine bottles that were expected to be used that night. Sets of candles were placed at various spots on the large table to provide light. Dolley expected all of those invited to meet there that night. She had assured her staff, friends, and the president that she would run the White House while the president was at the front, working with his generals in Maryland to battle the British, who were clashing with American forces in nearby Bladensburg. She paid no attention to the stories in the local newspaper that covered not only the imminent British attack at Washington but also the war in the Great Lakes, with lengthy American death and casualty lists.

She looked forward to the dinner party, as she looked forward to all the social events at the White House. It was not unusual for the president's house to host a dinner or party every night, sometimes two or three. The First Lady would wander through each, within minutes becoming a dazzling lightning rod of attention.

Those who met Dolley never forgot her. She was "a handsome woman, tall and majestic. Her manners were affable but a little affected. She has been very much admired and still fond of admiration. [She] loads herself in finery and dresses . . . her complexion is brilliant, her neck and bosom the most beautiful I ever saw. Her face expresses nothing but good nature. There is something very fascinating about her," wrote one woman who met her in 1808.[7]

"[She wore] a gown of brick colored silk with a train two yards long trimmed in white. On her head she wore a small cap with a large bunch of flowers . . . she moved with much ease and grace," another woman wrote of Dolley.

Her husband, the president, was nowhere in sight, so Dolley put down the spyglass. Just one day earlier, she was on the roof of the building and watched as panic spread through the streets of Washington when people learned that the British had landed and were marching toward the capital. The American army, really nothing more than a collection of badly trained militiamen, was not expected to stop them at any of the encounters they planned in the Maryland countryside. Thousands of Washingtonians packed up their belongings in carts, carriages, and buggies and sped out of town as fast as their horses could carry them. They all also fled at about the same time, so their huge numbers created traffic jams. They were headed for Alexandria, Virginia, or Georgetown, and had to walk or ride across the few bridges that crossed the Potomac to those destinations from Washington. The people fled as individuals, couples, and entire families. Many families went in large carriages or wagons, some with their children sitting in the backs of the wagons, waving to friends that they saw on their way out of town. Some brought their pets with them, and others left them at home. Cats purred and dogs barked as they fled, providing the exodus of residents with a cacophony of sound. Many fled past the slave market near the capital.

Some departed in long trains of carriages, with different members of families and servants in each one. They looked like any other nervous horde of refugees leaving their hometown in any war and headed for an unknown and dangerous destination. They comprised thick crowds pouring past the White House and the Capitol, all intent on getting as far away from the city as possible, and quickly. There was great worry that the British would seize and perhaps even burn the city to the ground.

Dolley waited, and waited, for her husband to return, long after everyone else had fled to safety. The hours and minutes ticked by ever so slowly. She used the spyglass to look north toward Bladensburg; east toward the American naval yard and its ships and warehouses; and northwest, to Georgetown. She could not spot him anywhere.

She had feared this day for over a month. At the end of July, she wrote Hannah Gallatin, the wife of Treasury Secretary Albert Gallatin, that "we have been in a state of perturbation here for a long time—the depredations of the enemy approaching within twenty miles of the city & the disaffected, making incessant difficulties for the Government." She was nervous. "Such a place as this has become I cannot describe it—I wish (for my own part) we were at Philadelphia."

She feared for the safety of her husband and herself, but not necessarily from the British. Americans, unhappy with the progress of the war, which the press had early on called "Mr. Madison's War," or lack of progress, had been threatening the Madisons with harm. "Among other exclamations and threats, they say if Mr. M attempts to move from this House, in case of an attack, they will stop him and that he shall fall with it. I am not the least alarmed at these things, but entirely disgusted and determined to stay with him," wrote Dolley.

Back then, in late July, she never thought the day would come when she, the First Lady, and her husband, the president, would be forced to leave the White House and flee for their lives. Now, on the hot morning of August 24, that seemed the most likely course of action. That afternoon, Dolley Madison did not even know where the people scheduled to dine with her were or if they were alive. No matter where she looked on the roof with her spyglass, she saw refugees and the landscapes of a war.

And she worried about her husband. "I am determined not to go myself until I see Mr. Madison safe, so that he can accompany me, as I hear of much hostility towards him. Disaffection stalks around us," she wrote with a chill that day.

She had been worried all day. "Since sunrise I have been turning my spyglass in every direction, and watching with unwearied anxiety, hoping to discover the approach of my dear husband and his friends, but, alas, I can descry only groups of military, wandering in all directions."[8]

She should have been worried. Madison had joined his troops in the rural countryside of Maryland and had given his generals a pep talk in order to get them to defend Washington. They were surrounded by several thousand American soldiers, mostly members of militia units, who seemed overwhelmed in their skirmishes with the British army. President Madison was misled by Secretary of War John Armstrong and General William Winder, who assured him that the British had no intention of marching on Washington. Thanks to that view, the governor of Maryland, entrusted by the president to protect his own state, had done little. He also had no intelligence on the British because neither the federal nor the state governments had bothered to set up a spy network. Madison, who rode about and walked through the bustling camp, greeting the soldiers, seemed bolstered by their promises and wrote a hopeful note to his wife.[9]

"I have passed the forenoon with the troops who are in high spirits and make a good appearance. The reports as to the enemy have varied every hour. The last and probably truest information is that they are not very strong, and are without cavalry or artillery and of course that they are not in a condition to strike at Washington. It is believed also that they are not about to move from Marlboro," he said.[10]

Madison was placing much of his estimate of the war in Maryland on the word of Secretary Armstrong, a controversial figure throughout the war. Madison's friend and fellow Virginian, Secretary of State James Monroe, who would succeed Madison as president, continually warned Madison that Armstrong was trying to use victories in the war to make himself president, putting the safety of his own men at risk to do so.

A few hours later, troops brought in two British soldiers who said they were deserters. Madison, taking more of a hands-on role as commander in chief, interrogated the men himself for quite some time. He learned that the British total force was just as large as he had feared and that men were still getting off large boats in the harbor in Maryland. An aide, Major Thomas McKenney, told the president that he now believed that Armstrong and Winder, a former Baltimore lawyer, were wrong. The British planned to attack and capture Washington itself, something everybody thought unthinkable. Madison was too late. All now looked hopeless. His generals told him that the Americans had to pull back from fighting the English in the field because they were poorly prepared, outnumbered, frightened, and, frankly, had no chance. "They will limit themselves to disputing the crossing of the eastern branch at Bladensburg, six miles from the capital," wrote the French minister that day.[11]

Madison, angry and tired from another long day in the saddle, now feared not only for the army but also for his wife, unprotected back in Washington. He sent her a note that she said later was an emergency letter to let her know that the British army was on its way toward her. It was, she said, "alarming." "He desires I should be ready at a moment's warning to enter my carriage, and leave the city; that the enemy seemed stronger than had been reported and that it might happen that they would reach the city with intention to destroy it," she wrote.[12]

The president ordered his generals to send men to the capital to protect it, and they did, but orders that went through Winder and Armstrong were misdirected and misunderstood. The next day, instead of having a strong fighting force ready to meet the British at the point where local roads would take them into the capital, the American forces were split in half. General Winder had bollixed his orders and that morning, the twenty-fourth, and had placed two armies, each consisting of 2,500 men, five miles apart from each other at river crossings. Both were tired and, at their size, neither were large enough to defend the city against a well-rested and heavily armed British force of nearly five thousand men.

Just before midnight that night, a worried President Madison received a frantic note from Monroe, whose scouts monitored every move the British made. "The enemy is in full march for Washington," read Monroe's short note, written shortly after 9 p.m.[13]

Monroe had worked hard since his arrival in Washington earlier. He found disorganization wherever he went and rode to the Maryland countryside as quickly as he could to help officers reorganize their troops in order to defend the area against the British. Monroe, who had fought with George Washington's army in the American Revolution, even changed battlefield assignments at the last minute.[14]

The next day, on a hot August morning, Madison sent orders for his forces to stop the English troops at the village of Bladensburg. He hoped that if they could do so, the British would give up the quest to seize Washington, turn around, and head back to their ships. No one had much hope that would happen, even the optimistic Madison. He was in charge of amateur soldiers and didn't even have enough of them. "Extensive and pressing calls have been made for militia and we hope they will be prompt," he wrote Monroe.[15]

They were prompt but could not stem the British tide. After an initial bold attempt to hold back the British, the Americans, few with any combat training, turned and fled southward. They fired a few cannon, a few hundred rounds with their muskets and pistols, and that was it. President Madison, using his own spyglass, watched them retreat. Locals joked that it was the "Bladensburg Races." General Winder winced. "Our force was principally militia and that of the enemy was all regulars and picked men," Winder told a newspaper editor in an effort to defend himself.[16]

The door to Washington was now wide open.

All of Dolley's friends had left town, accompanied by the troops who were supposed to guard the White House. "My friends and acquaintances are all gone, even Colonel C. with his hundreds, who were stationed in this enclosure," wrote the First lady as she looked around the White House.[17]

Dolley waited, a last sentinel in the White House, as the day progressed and there was no sign of her husband. Had he been captured? Killed? She heard the dull, muffled sounds of booming cannon to the north, and had been informed that the American army had been routed at Bladensburg. The soldiers had fought for a while, then given up and fled. The British were headed toward Washington and moving rapidly. They might be there by nightfall. Rumors flew. Couriers kept telling people to leave town. Friends sent each other messages with slaves and servants, who hurried through the streets of the city with their notes.

Everything was chaos that afternoon. Secretary Armstrong rode into town. He kept telling Dolley that there was no danger, that the British would not enter the city, but the mayor of Washington, James Blake, rode over to the White House twice to beg her to get out of town before the British arrived. She kept returning to the roof to look out on the desperate scene with her spyglass in a last-ditch effort to find her husband. Off in the distance, she could see hundreds of American soldiers fleeing the Bladensburg battle and walking down the roads toward Washington. Far over the treetops, she heard the last low blasts of British and American cannon as the Bladensburg battle died down. The American soldiers that she did see did not encourage her. They showed "a lack of arms or of spirit to fight for their own firesides," she wrote.[18]

She was right. Many of the men who did sign up to fight with the militia had little interest in the war and hated their American compatriots as much as they hated the British. The case of an unruly man dismissed from a Pennsylvania regiment just two weeks later was typical. An officer wrote that "there was a man drummed out of camp for disobedience of orders. He said he did not care a damn for all the officers [and] that he would be damned if he did not shoot some of them."[19]

Hastily written notes from friends and relatives arrived all day. Her sister Anna sent a slave running to the White House with a short letter. "Tell me for God's sake where you are and what [you are] going to do ... we can hear nothing but what is horrible there—I know not who to send this to—and will say but little."[20]

Dolley waited, and waited, for her husband. She had enormous confidence that he would return, that he would not be captured, and that, eventually, he would lead America out of this war. People who knew her husband shared that confidence. Former president Jefferson wrote a friend a few months earlier, "I say so with great satisfaction, when I contemplate the person to whom the powers were handed over. I have known [Madison] from 1779, when he first came into the public councils and from three and thirty years trials, I can say conscientiously that I do not know a man in the world of utter integrity more disinterested and devoted to genuine Republicanism, than himself. He may be seconded by others, betrayed by the Hulls and Arnolds of our country, for such there are everywhere. We shall only appreciate his true value when we have to give him up."[21]

Charles Carroll, a wealthy landowner, drove to the White House shortly after 3 p.m., his carriage horses kicking up large clouds of dust from the dirt street, to urge Dolley to leave the town and travel with him to his large estate at Bell Vue outside of the city. Several other men did the same. Everyone seemed to know that the president was with the army and that she was alone at the White House. They worried about her more and more as soldiers fled town and the city was wide open to an attack. Word that the British troops were approaching the city spread like wild fire.

Dolley told all of the White House staff except a few servants to get out of town and to find safety. A French servant named Jean Pierre Sioussat, a fifteen-year-old slave named Paul Jennings, and Dolley's trusty servant, Sukey, remained with her all day. By late afternoon, in a huge mix-up, there were no troops protecting the White House or the First Lady. Finally, in late afternoon, when there were reports that the British were on the outskirts of the capital, she finished packing. She had been loading boxes for over a day. "I have pressed as many Cabinet papers into trunks as to fill one carriage; our private property must be sacrificed as it is impossible to procure wagons for its transportation," she wrote her sister Anna.[22] She packed up her much-talked-about blazing-red drapes, a copy of the Declaration of Independence, several boxes of important government papers, some silver, a crate of books, and a small clock. She left a lot of government things behind, as well as personal possessions, such as her own wardrobe and the clothing of the president.

"It would fatigue you to read the list of my losses, or an account of the general dismay, or particular distresses of your acquaintance," she later wrote to her friend Mrs. Benjamin Latrobe.[23]

She and her servants carried everything to the wagon standing in front of the White House. On the way out, she passed the huge, eight-foot-high and five-foot-wide painting of George Washington by famed artist Gilbert Stuart that had hung on the wall of the dining room of the White House for more than twelve years, since Jefferson moved in. The painting had been purchased by the US government in 1800 for $800 and then secured on the wall shortly afterward. She stared at it. When she redecorated the White House in 1809, she had insisted that Washington's portrait be placed on that wall as the centerpiece of the room and that portraits of all succeeding presidents should hang on the wall of the room around it. Washington, she had told her decorators, as not just the centerpiece of the room; he was the centerpiece of the nation.[24]

In a flash, she saw the painting as symbolic of all that America stood for—the revolution, independence, equal rights, prosperity, and democracy. That stirring painting of George Washington, the father of the country, of her country, could not fall into the hands of the dastardly British. If they captured George Washington, they captured America. She could not let that happen. She told her servants that they had to take the huge painting with them. They begged her to forget about the painting and leave. There was little time left to save themselves. They reminded her that thousands of British troops were about to stream into the streets of Washington and that her life was in danger.

And then there was Carroll, there again with his carriages. He fumed at her delay over the painting. "Mr. Carroll has come to hasten my departure and is in a very bad humor because I insist on waiting until the large picture of General Washington is secured and it requires to be unscrewed from the wall," she wrote. She did not care about anyone; she took her time to get the picture down from the dining-room wall. As she did, precious minutes ticked away and the enemy moved closer and closer.[25]

Hatchets were apparently used by the doorman, servant Jean Pierre Sioussat, and one of the gardeners to break the large, heavy wood frame that held it. The portrait was to be rolled up, but then someone warned that doing so would cause the paint to crack. So it was carefully cut out of the frame with sharp knives by Dolley and others. She did not want their haste to ruin the treasure.

"It is done!" Dolley wrote triumphantly to her sister moments after she put her knife down and helped take the painting down from the wall.

Dolley and the servants then carried the painting out of the building as passersby shouted at her to flee, that British troops had been seen at the edge of town. She now had a second fear about the painting. It would fall into British hands if she herself was captured. She needed someone else to hide it. Dolley saw two New Yorkers she knew, Robert De Peyster and Jacob Barker, a ship owner and close friend of her husband, respectively, passing the White House on horses and asked them to take the painting and hide it somewhere safe so that the British could not grab it.

"Save that picture!" yelled Dolley to the two men. "Save that picture if possible. If not possible, destroy it. Under no circumstances allow it to fall in to the hands of the British."[26]

The men took the portrait and headed northwest. "Carried off, upheld whole in the inner wooden frame, beyond Georgetown, the picture was deposited by Barker in a place of safety. The presidential household got the image of the father of his country—by whom its chief city was fixed near his home, and by whose name it was called—was then snatched from the clutch or torch of the barbarian captors," wrote Charles Ingersoll later.[27]

Ironically, Barker found a wagon to bring some of his prized goods out of town and put the painting in the wagon. In letters, diaries, and journals, many Washingtonians later wrote that they saw the painting sticking up from Barker's furniture as he rode slowly out of town with everyone else. It seems that everybody except the British saw the portrait that day.

A few moments later, James Smith, a freed black man who worked as a courier for the president rode up and saw Dolley in the front yard. "Clear out! Clear out! Secretary Armstrong has ordered a retreat!" he roared.[28] Carroll soon returned in his coach, full of nervous family members, and picked up Dolley and her servants. He had her sister Anna and Anna's husband, Richard Cutts, with him. Their driver, Joe Bolden, then headed northwest and sped out of town, through deep, green forests, across Rock Creek, to the village of Georgetown, some five miles away. Another servant drove a second wagon full of trunks and a bed, the only piece of furniture removed, tied hard to the back of the wagon.

Dolley had one last mission. She told Frenchman Jean Pierre Sioussat to take her well-known pet macaw bird to Octagon House, a mansion owned by friends of hers, the Tayloes, but today temporarily occupied by French diplomats. She knew the handsome bird, a favorite for White House visitors, would be safe there.[29] As they left, Carroll told them that it would be a long journey to Bell Vue; he had reports from servants and friends that the thick string of refugees had clogged up all the roads. Mrs. Madison planned to stay for a short time at Bell Vue and then head south into Virginia, over one of the Potomac River bridges. Carroll told her that the crossing of the river bridges would be very time-consuming because of the crowds of refugees trying to get over them. He heard that families had spent an entire afternoon clambering their way across the bridge, jammed with carts, wagons, carriages, horses, and buggies, all piled high with trunks and boxes.

Dolley wrote just before she jumped up into Carroll's carriage, "I must leave this house, or the retreating army will make me a prisoner in it by filling up the road I am directed to take. Where I shall be tomorrow, I cannot tell."[30]

The events of the day raged within Dolley Madison for quite a long time. She wrote a friend later that year, just before Christmas, that she had been so depressed over losing the White House that she had not even mourned for the substantial invaluable losses she suffered in destroyed or stolen clothing and jewelry. And she was mad, too. Dolley wrote, "I was free from fear, and willing to remain in the Castle. If I could have had a cannon through every window; but alas, those who should have placed them there fled before me . . . my whole heart mourned for my country."[31]

The calm, cool behavior of Dolley in the middle of the panic in Washington impressed all and rekindled their admiration for her. "Mrs. Madison commanded the situation with grace and dignity," wrote Margaret Bayard Smith. "The most valiant soul in the White House, she remained at her post, guarding its treasures, as the President had admonished her to do when he set forth for Bladensburg. Unintimidated by the sight of friends and acquaintances making their escape from the city, of the officials of the State and Treasury Departments withdrawing with valuable papers, or even by the sound of guns, Mrs. Madison calmly awaited the return of her husband."[32]

As they disappeared from view northwest on Pennsylvania Avenue, a few dozen British troops began to move to within sight of the city. So did James Madison. He and his friends arrived from the battlefield at Bladensburg on horseback and had some refreshments a short time after Dolley left. Scouts told him of British troops throughout the countryside around the city and other troops that were only a mile or so behind him on the road he had traveled.

President Madison was not happy. He had waged a so-far-unsuccessful war against England. He had stuck with it for more than two years now, using a small, regular army and thousands of inexperienced and untrained militia, plus a largely untested navy, and the results were not promising. Even members of his own party, the Republicans, were angry with him. Many referred to him as "the little man at the palace."[33]

The British high command had boasted that it would capture the president and the First Lady and bring them back to England for trial as war criminals. They were intent on finding him and arresting him. Soldiers were out with specific orders to abduct him. He knew that and finished his drink quickly. He took off his holster with two pistols that he had been carrying for days and set them down gently on a wooden table. He sent off some military letters and then entrusted a note for his wife to a rider. He told his wife to meet him the next day at Foxall's Foundry in Georgetown. He gave it to the rider, then called him back. He wrote another note telling his wife to cross the Potomac the next day and meet him at Wiley's Tavern, an alehouse they both knew. Then he and his party rode away on horseback toward the Potomac River, barely in time, after he sent his wife yet another note that he would meet her the next day at a friend's home near Georgetown.[34]

The president rode out of town with his small entourage of military personnel, leaving his two pistols behind in the White House. He did not retreat in haste or in panic, but as the commander in chief should, full of confidence. A French minister still in town saw the president ride out that afternoon and wrote that he "proudly got on his horse and, accompanied by a few friends, slowly reached the bridge separating Washington from Virginia."[35] The British began to move in as Madison rode out. They had triumphed in the battle of Bladensburg, sending the American soldiers running away like scared rabbits, and now they had the capital of the United States lying at their feet.

Late in the afternoon, around 5 p.m., just a few hours after President Madison was seen riding toward the bridge to Virginia, the US Army fell into confusion. Several regiments were in the capital and several just outside of it, but no one seemed to know what to do. One regiment marched to the Capitol building, intent on defending it and expecting orders to arrive at any moment instructing them to do so. They passed hundreds of empty houses and some that were still occupied by owners who just could not believe that the British would attack. These residents also believed that the American army would protect the city, and them. They were angry about the war and angrier still that they were stuck in their homes. They had waited too long to flee and now faced the prospect of being seized by the British and held prisoner. Many moved in with neighbors in the same predicament. Every few moments, a rider would gallop through the streets, shouting at the top of his lungs for residents to evacuate immediately. "Fly! Fly! The Ruffians are at hand!" was a call heard often that afternoon.[36]

One of the first groups of American soldiers in the city, sixty cavalrymen on tired horses with their commander, Colonel Jacint Laval, all exhausted from a hard ride down from Bladensburg, trotted to the east side of the Capitol building. They stopped in front of the enormous structure, not yet complete, that sat amid large fields dotted with clumps of brush and a few trees. From there, they had a nearly interrupted view of the city. Laval thought he had orders to defend the capital but was not sure. If he did, then where were the hundreds of other troops who should be there to join him in what might be the final fight of the war? No one was there. Then he heard from a passerby who walked up to Laval, who was mounted on his horse, a rumor that the American troops had been ordered to leave the Capitol and to go down Pennsylvania Avenue to the President's Mansion to defend it when the long columns of British troops arrived. Laval and his men did the same, but when they arrived in front of the White House, they found no one there, either. It was eerie to see the usually busy home completely empty. He waited nearly an hour, with few sounds in the air except the distant retreat of scared residents across the bridges to Virginia. No other soldiers arrived. There were no military couriers. Nothing. He did not see any other soldiers in the city, either. Had they fled? Were they ordered out? "I could not, nor would not, believe that the city was to be given up without a fight," he wrote, adding that would cause "sorrow, grief and indignation for his troops."[37]

Men in the American regiments, apprehensive and frightened, broke ranks throughout the neighborhoods of the town. Many with permission and some without it left their regiments and visited friends and family to fill them in on the building disaster. Some returned to the army and some did not. Some could be found and some were missing. The departure of hundreds of men undercut whatever fighting strength was left in the army. "The idea of leaving their families, their houses and their homes at the mercy of an enraged enemy was insupportable," General Walter Smith said later.[38] "To preserve that order which was maintained during the retreat was now no longer practicable."

Within an hour, General Winder rode up to the Capitol, where some more troops had gathered after Laval's men left. Winder told them all that it was futile to make a final stand in the city; they were outnumbered and had been battered at Bladensburg. He ordered the American army to head for the heights in Georgetown, five miles away, where they would fight the British if necessary. The army had to abandon the city and leave it to the British. One regiment of seven hundred troops had finally been equipped that morning. They headed toward Bladensburg to fight but were turned back and told to defend Washington. At the Capitol, ready to give their lives, they met Winder, who ordered the troops, who had not yet even lifted their rifles, to flee once again— this time to Georgetown. The men in the regiment never fired a shot.[39]

Southeast of the Capitol building and the White House, loud explosions were heard late in the afternoon. It was the Navy Yard being blown up by Americans to prevent the British from using it. Destroyed were several entire ships, hundreds of carriages, and thousands of pounds of ammunition. Flames and thick smoke from the carnage rose quickly in the summer air and could be seen for miles on both land and sea. Residents of Baltimore, forty-five miles away, claimed they saw the smoke.[40]

Sometime in late afternoon, close to 6 p.m., seeing stores and homes evacuated and the rivers of residents on roads headed out of town, dozens of looters descended on the streets of the city. Residents still there reported groups of young men running into stores and emerging with armloads of stolen goods. Some even ran through the empty White House, stealing china, jackets, and other goods.

On a narrow street just north of the Capitol, the first British troops to enter town were fired upon by a resident taking sharp aim with his musket from a two-story house. The British dove off their horses and sought cover; none were hurt. They fired at will on the house, driving out the sniper. Furious, they set fire to the building, using their commander's philosophy that it was proper to burn down any structure, home, or barn, from which hostile fire had come. It was the first of many torches used on the nation's capital that day.

The British troops reached both the White House and Capitol building at about 8 p.m., as darkness was slowly falling on Washington. The decision had already been made by Admiral Cockburn and others to burn at least several government buildings in order to teach the Americans a lesson (he himself did not have orders to do that). The soldiers expected the torching to take place and were fully prepared for it, but many were reluctant to carry out those orders. They realized that the burning of the Capitol and/or White House would not only destroy the most important and lovely buildings in America but also enrage the American people. The invaders had captured the city; they did not have to burn it. To do so was a historical insult that would resonate for generations between the two countries.

"I had no objection to burning arsenals, dockyards, frigates, buildings, stores, barracks etc. . . . but we were horrified at the order to burn the elegant Houses of Parliament," wrote one young British officer.[41] Weeks later, the British press bitterly criticized the army for torching Washington, DC, and singled out Admiral Cockburn for their most vicious scorn. The *London Statesman* called him "a buccaneer" and wrote that "the cossacks spared Paris, but we spared not the capital of America." The *British Annual Register of 1814* called the burning of the capital "barbarism."[42]

The Capitol building was immense. It sat on a slight hill overlooking the rest of the town. The structure was three stories high. It was not finished. The two enormous wings, the Senate and House of Representatives, were intact, but to get to either, one had to take a wooden plank walkway that connected them. The dome above the building, soon to be one of the most famous in the world, was not there.

Troops entered through doors to the House of Representatives. Many said later that they were stunned at the beauty of the large chamber, with its elegant desks and seats and sixty-seven-foot-high ceiling. The British fired rockets into the ceiling, expecting it to burn, fall down, and set the rest of the chamber on fire. They did not realize that the ceiling was metal; it did not burst into flames. Then they piled up all the wooden furniture that they could find and made a large bonfire. The heat and flames from the bonfire ignited the desks and walls and the entire structure soon started to burn. Within a half hour, most of the building was engulfed in flames. It was a dark and cloudless night, and the sight of the rising flames, soaring into the night sky like crimson fingers, could be seen for miles. Those who had fled Washington watched from their safe houses in Georgetown or Virginia, miles away, and grimaced as the sky was lit bright orange with the flames.[43]

"You never saw a drawing room so brilliantly lighted as the whole city was that night," wrote Mary Hunter from her home in town. "Few thought of going to bed—they spent the night in gazing on the fires and lamenting the disgrace of the city."[44]

Nearby villages like Georgetown were overcrowded with refugees. "Night. Ten o'clock. The streets of this quiet village [Georgetown], which never before witnessed confusion, are now filled with carriages bringing out citizens, and baggage wagons and troops. Mr. Bentley's house is now crowded; he has been the whole evening sitting at the supper table, giving refreshment to soldiers and travelers. Every house in the village is equally full," wrote Margaret Bayard Smith, so stricken with fear that she told friends the government would have to abandon Washington and move somewhere else.[45]

At about 11 p.m., after the Capitol was set on fire, dozens of troops rode up to and walked into the vacant White House of James and Dolley Madison. They trudged through the house on an inspection tour and to survey the building in order to determine the best way to set it ablaze. They were astonished when they entered the dining room. They may have noticed that a large painting had been removed from the wall, but their eyes focused on the table. It was laid out for a dinner party for thirty or forty people, and a dozen or more bottles of wine lay in buckets of ice, all set earlier by Paul Jennings and other servants on the orders of the First Lady. The British had not eaten much all day, had been in combat, and had marched six long miles down the highway to Washington. They were tired and hungry. Dozens of them sat down in the dining room and enjoyed a delicious dinner and some of America's best wines. The spectacle enraged the American people.

Finished with their surprise dinner party, the soldiers went about their work to destroy the White House. First, the men looted the building, stealing everything they could find that marauders who went through it earlier had not taken. One man grabbed one of the president's hats and held it aloft on the tip of his bayonet. He said that if the troops were unable to capture "the little President," they could at least bring his hat to England. Another soldier stole the president's dress sword. Others took some of his clothing and jewelry that probably belonged to Dolley.

The mansion was still full of stacks of kindling wood for the many fireplaces. The troops spread the wood in front of wooden furniture, drapes, and other items that seemed combustible. Others simply set wallpaper, books, and drapes on fire in individual rooms and let them burn. Within minutes, all of the rooms in the building, the heart of American heritage and freedom, were on fire. The troops and officers, happy with their work, withdrew and watched the structure incinerate from the street. They were disappointed that the thick, sandstone walls of the outer structure did not burn, though, permitting reconstruction of the building much later.

That night, the troops, on orders, burned down the Treasury building, one block from the White House. They were going to burn the nearby War Department building, but the high command rejected that. There was an attempt to burn a local bank, but that was rejected, too. They were sometimes stopped by residents of the town, who begged them on the streets in front of the buildings not to destroy America's landmarks. William Thornton, an architect, ran to the Patent Office building to try to take art treasures out of it when he heard it would be burned. He encountered British troops in front of it and begged them to leave it alone. If they destroyed it, he told them, they "would be like the soldiers who burned the legendary library at Alexandria" two thousand years earlier. They did not. The British had certainly done enough work for one night, destroying America's Capitol building, its presidential mansion, and the Treasury building.[46]

One of the trips Admiral Cockburn made with his men that night was to the offices of the *National Intelligencer* newspaper, the paper of record for government activities. The editor had fled on news that the British were coming into town, and the offices were empty by the time the British soldiers arrived with Cockburn. First, he ordered them to burn down the building, but the quick arrival of four women who lived in houses that surrounded the newspaper halted that. They pleaded with Cockburn that the flames would leap to their homes and destroy them. He canceled the order. Then Cockburn told his men to take the hundreds of books and files in the newspaper's small library and pile them up in the street. They were burned. Cockburn then ordered them to destroy all of the printing presses and metal used to make letters for stories, and then trash the office. He wanted to make sure the city's most prominent paper did not publish for quite some time. "Make sure all the 'C's are smashed," he told them, "I don't want any more abuse of my name." (All of this did little good; the newspaper was printing again, in smaller-sized editions, one week later.[47])

Bad weather saved further depredations in the American capital. The next day, Thursday, the region was battered by terrible thunderstorms that dumped several inches of rain on Washington in wide, unending sheets of water. Small, fierce tornadoes, a rarity in the Chesapeake region, whipped through the area, knocking down buildings like they were made of paper, uprooting large, hundred-year-old trees, knocking over carriages, terrifying horses, and in one area of the city forcing an entire building to collapse, killing several British soldiers inside of it. The dreadful weather, reports of American soldiers still in the area regrouping for a fight, and the realization that they were some distance from their ships in Maryland convinced the British to leave the city and march back to the Patuxent River.[48]

On Wednesday, the night of the fire, the whereabouts of the president and First Lady were largely unknown. The president, some cabinet officers, two dragoons from the army, and a few servants rode around northern Virginia, evading British troops and seeking shelter. The president missed his wife. Madison's first stop was Wiley's Tavern, where he planned to spend the night and then reunite with his wife the following day. He was there only a short time when soldiers arrived with (untrue) news that British patrols were riding through northern Virginia, looking for him. He and his entourage then rode to the Great Falls of the Potomac, hoping to make a crossing and reunite with General Winder's army near Georgetown. The party was unable to cross the river, though, and turned back. One report had him sleeping in a grimy, old cabin in a forest, with most of the others sleeping on the grounds around it. There were other reports that he spent the night at Salona, a 466-acre estate owned by a friend, Rev. William Maffitt. It was a large, brick mansion only four miles from Washington.[49]

The president was supposed to ride to Wren's Tavern, in Virginia, to meet his wife. On the stormy Thursday, he arrived there when darkness fell, had some dinner, and then left after only one hour. He told his hosts he had to find his wife; he did not really know where she was. He was halted by the storm, though, and sought shelter at the Crossroads Tavern, where he spent the night. Dolley had gone on to Wiley's Tavern, an inn on the road from Georgetown to Leesburg, on her husband's orders. She received a harsh welcome. Men and women driven from their homes by the British and fed up with the war yelled at her when she arrived and blamed her and Madison for the war and the loss of their houses. Dolley spent the night in her room for safety.

The next day, she left Wiley's and drove to the home of George Minor and his wife, her friends. The house was jammed with refugees from Washington who knew the Minors. Dolley was not scorned there. She decided to spend her time there not as a bedraggled refugee on the run from the enemy, but as the First Lady of the United States. She wore her best gowns and her makeup, and carried herself with great elegance and dignity. All who spent the time there with her remembered the gracious way that she presented herself and spent her time with them.

There, at the Minorses', Dolley watched the fires rising in the sky over Washington. Matilda Roberts, a seven-year-old child at the house with her, was astonished by the sight. "I thought the world was on fire," she wrote later in her diary.[50] "Such a flame I have never seen since."

On Friday, President Madison, who had still not found Dolley, was riding in Maryland, trying to find General Winder's scattered army in order to rally them for an attack against the British troops holding Washington. When he received news that the British had left, he pulled hard on the reins of his horse, turned around, and rode back to the capital. The president of the United States, aged sixty-four, a man who had complained bitterly of physical ailments all of his life, including rheumatoid arthritis, had now finished nearly four entire days in the saddle, commanding troops in the field, making decisions about the war, and getting his wife out of Washington and himself into it between British regiments that planned to seize him if they could. His forces had been badly defeated and pushed back and his capital burned. None of the citizens of Washington, returning with him, thought the president had done a good job. Those who saw him on his horse during the attack and torching of Washington criticized him and even scolded him. Some angry men sketched vicious cartoons about him, and others wrote scathing poems about the president. Rumors flew that there were threats on his life by Washingtonians. His wife even feared that someone with a gun would shoot him if he saw him during those turbulent days.

President Madison was demoralized by what he saw in the capital, as was everyone else. Margaret Bayard Smith lamented in her journal, "The poor capitol! Nothing but its blacken'd walls remained. Four or five houses in the neighbourhood were likewise in ruins . . . but none was so thoroughly destroy'd as the House of Representatives and the President's House. Those beautiful pillars in that Representatives' Hall were crack'd and broken, the roof, that noble dome, painted realized that he had no army, no home and no wife and carved with such beauty and skill, lay in ashes in the cellars beneath the smouldering ruins. . . ."[51]

The president of the United States, Dolley's "great little Madison," leaned forward on his horse as he reached the front of the White House, looked at the charred building, and frowned. "Mr. Madison's War" had now become a disaster, personally as well as politically. That hot Friday afternoon, the fierce storms were gone a half day and the countryside was sot with rain, demolished buildings, and fallen trees, and the forlorn president realized that he had no army, no home, and no wife.

2

OPPOSITES ATTRACT

The Unlikely Meeting of James Madison and Dolley Todd

*Y*ellow Fever struck the city of Philadelphia, the largest in America, in the quiet, lazy summer of 1793. It arrived suddenly, without warning, as the Yellow Fever always did in colonial America, and attacked voraciously. Thousands died. Medical experts estimated that nearly five thousand people, or close to 20 percent of the residents of the community, were killed in the epidemic. So many people died each day, and their deaths were so well publicized around the nation, that betting-obsessed gamblers wagered tens of thousands of dollars on the final death toll, turning the Yellow Fever casualties into a macabre lottery.

Many people fled Philadelphia, traveling on horseback, by carriage, in wagons, or by whatever form of transportation they could find, led by President George Washington. The president was not afraid of medical catastrophe. He had not only stayed in the army when smallpox struck his troops, and parts of the country, in the winter of 1776–1777, but also invented a new way to vaccinate his troops, and thousands of civilians, by eliminating the preinoculation "rest" period of two weeks, long believed necessary by the medical profession, and inoculating people at once. Washington had been struck by smallpox at age nineteen and survived. He still had pockmarks on his face from the attack. The general told his soldiers what he wanted to do and then supervised town meetings, held in halls, churches, and large barns, to explain the new procedure to civilians who lived near his winter camp, and other winter army camps in America. His innovative practice worked; few of those inoculated right away died in the epidemic. Many who were not inoculated perished, and Washington and his soldiers had to bury them in grey village churchyards. General Washington had been praised throughout America, and in Europe, for his efforts and successes. The medically adept president did not feel he was any match for the tidal wave of Yellow Fever that swept over Philadelphia in 1793, though, and he fled the metropolis with his wife, Martha, and his servants to Mount Vernon, on the banks of the Potomac River in Virginia, hundreds of miles away.

American doctors did not know how Yellow Fever arrived, and they did not know how to treat it. They assumed, as doctors all over the world did, that it grew in contaminated water in overly hot weather and that anyone who drank the tainted water was susceptible to it. They also believed that it had been brought into Philadelphia from the Caribbean by sailors who had caught it there. They were also certain that it was contagious, that anyone could catch it, even those not in contact with someone sickened from it. The doctors offered rest periods and odd diets to fight it, but had no real cure. If anyone in a family came down with it, people in contact with them might be afflicted by it, too. There was no way to contain it, either; at least smallpox could be fought with quarantine. The fever had struck again and again in the United States throughout the eighteenth century, usually in warm-weather states. It killed a large percentage of those who contracted it and made another high percentage of people very ill. The Yellow Fever spread, and spread quickly. In the summer of 1793, it rolled through the streets of Philadelphia toward Dolley Todd, her husband, and her family.

Yellow Fever brings about an awful death. It causes high fever; chills; aching joints; intense stomach pains; jaundiced, yellow skin; liver failure; and black vomit. People struck by it can die within a day; some linger for a few days before succumbing, and some lucky victims survive it. Parents who were afflicted by the fever transmitted it to their children, who transmitted it to their friends, who then transmitted it to *their* parents.

Nearly half the population of Philadelphia fled along with the president, including Dolley. Entire families fled together, packing supplies and clothing into any carts, wagons, or carriages they could find and, horses struggling to pull the oversized loads of people and supplies, left town as fast as they could. It was a flight that took place in a near panic. Dolley's husband, John, sent her and the two children, one just a baby, to a community called Gray's Ferry, on the banks of the Schuykill River just southeast of Philadelphia, where he hoped they would be safe. Dolley was carried down the roads to Gray's on a litter amid what appeared to be a thick army of refugees, of all shapes and sizes, professions, ages, colors, and religions, seeking safe shelter from the disease. Dolley's two children went with her.[1]

Her husband did not. John returned to Yellow Fever–ravaged Philadelphia, a ghost town now with so many residents gone, dead, or dying, to take care of his parents, who had come down with the fever. He put himself to work trying to organize the care for neighbors stricken with the sickness, a bold but dangerous thing to do. He also helped others take care of business in the city, left unattended since so many clerks had left. He rode out of town on horseback every week or so to visit Dolley, who begged him not to go back. She was terrified that he would catch the fever, too. This went on for several months. He often wrote her affectionate letters. "I hope my dear Dolley is well & my sweet little Payne can lisp mama in a stronger voice than when his papa left him. I wish he was here to run after Mr. Withy's ducks. He would have fine sport," he wrote in July.[2]

Each time his visit with her and the children was over, Dolley would beg her husband to remain with them and be safe. She even tried to get her brother-in-law, James, to intercede to get John to join her permanently at Gray's Ferry.

"Oh, my dear brother, what a dread prospect has thy last letter presented to me," she wrote, adding that "love'd husband in perpetual danger." She told her brother-in-law that she had "repeatedly entreated John to leave home . . . but alas he cannot leave his father. . . . Is it too late for their removal? Or can no interferance of the earthly friends rescue them from the too general fate?"[3]

Her husband, John, and her son William both died from the fever on October 14, 1794. Dolley, who had been ill for weeks prior to their deaths, although not from the fever, was crushed. It was a dual tragedy, though, that would show her inner strength, a strength that would later save a nation.

Those who knew her felt badly that she had lost both her husband and her baby on the same day. They could see that she was not only staggering along physically but was emotionally distraught. As if to add insult to injury, right after the double burial, she was stunned by the reluctance of the Todd family to give her the inheritance that her husband had left her.

"My poor dear Dolley," wrote her mother, "what does she and will she suffer . . . the same day consigned her dear husband and her little babe to the silent grave," Mary Payne told Dolley's nurse. She added that with John Todd dead, her daughter had a grand total of only nineteen dollars to her name, and she owed that money for her husband's and child's funeral and other debts.

Mary Payne, fed up with Philadelphia, the Yellow Fever, and the Todds, left and traveled to Virginia, where she moved in with her daughter Lucy. Lucy had married George Steptoe Washington, the nephew of the president, and lived in grand style on a large plantation with servants. Dolley was left all alone in Philadelphia, sick, grief stricken, and penniless.

But she was determined. She wrote her brother-in-law, James, and demanded that he give her all of her husband's estate, money as well as property. Her brother-in-law refused. America in 1794 was a man's world, and a widow had little standing in the courts to sue. In most states, a widow could not sue; she had to hire a man to sue on her behalf. Much to her disappointment, her husband had thought too highly of her. John Todd knew that the men one usually hired to help a grieving widow were not needed for his wife. No man was as smart, competent, resourceful, and capable as she was, in or out of court. So, in his will, in which he clearly left her everything, he did not name any executors or aides to help her. She was left all alone to battle in court for an estate that clearly should have been hers. James knew all of this but did not know his feisty sister-in-law as well as he should have. She was relentless. Dolley started a nearly daily letter-writing campaign to James to get the estate. He refused.

Then, fed up with her letters and growing angrier by the day, James wrote her that he would agree to selling off parts of the estate, month by month, and sending whatever money came in from the sale to her. He would start by selling the books in John's library. Dolley was furious. "I was hurt my dear Jamy that the idea of his library should occur as a proper source for raising money. Books from which he wished his child improved shall remain sacred and I would feel the pinching hand of poverty before I disposed of them," she wrote.[4]

He was adamant in his plan to sell off the books and then the rest of the estate, piece by piece. She wrote him again. "I am constrained once more for request and if a request is not sufficient—to demand that they may be delivered this day," she said of the estate papers. "I cannot wait . . . without material injury to my affairs."

Her brother-in-law, probably with a smug look on his face, still refused. Then Dolley startled him; she retained a lawyer. She hired a friend of her late husband's, William Wilkins, to sue James Todd to get all of the property, house, and monies in her husband's estate. She meant business. Her brother-in-law, taken aback by the suit, the boldness of Dolley, and the angry demeanor of his sister-in-law and her lawyer, gave in. Dolley received everything from her husband's estate, and immediately. James did not get anything; nor did anyone else on her husband's side of the family.

The receipt of the house, property, and monies made Dolley a comfortable widow. She was twenty-five, in the prime of life, with a home. She would now slowly get back on her feet and try to make a life for herself and her baby, Payne. She took off her black grieving clothes and settled into her house again, and felt a very long way from her log-cabin beginnings in the thick forests of the Piedmont plateau in North Carolina.

The new and very lovely widow Todd was considered quite a prize for the men of Philadelphia, who could not resist looking at her every time she strolled down a city street. Distinguished merchants, lawyers, and bankers gawked at her as she walked by, a thin smile always on her lips. She was a very tall woman, nearly 5'8" in height, well proportioned, with a large bust and wide hips, and she possessed a beautiful and expressive face. She dressed well, attended Quaker meetings when she could, spent time shopping in the slowly reviving Philadelphia business district, went to plays and concerts, and met hundreds of men, many smitten with her good looks and vivacious personality. By this time, she had already made the acquaintances of many congressmen and government workers in Philadelphia, the nation's capital, through visits to her mother's inn, where many of them lived. Her lawyer, William Wilkins, was one, and another was Aaron Burr, the congressman from New York. Both had resided at her mother's inn in downtown Philadelphia for long periods of time and met Dolley there whenever she visited. She had become so close to Burr that she made him guardian for her son.[5]

One day, Burr, who would later become one of the most infamous figures in US history, took her aside. He told Dolley that a congressman who was a friend of his, James Madison of Virginia, one of the country's most renowned bachelors, would like to meet her. The two had never met, but Madison apparently knew a great deal about her. He had been investigating her, checking up on her family and talking to people who knew her to find out what she was like. She was reluctant to go. Some people had said admirable things about Madison, but others had criticized him. Many felt about Madison the way Washington Irving of New York did; Irving later wrote that Madison was "a withered little applejohn." A Washington socialite later said of Madison that he was "mute, cold and repressive."[6]

Dolley was charming and outgoing. She was, friends and relatives said, a person who could get along with anyone, regardless of their station in life. Madison, she knew, based on what she had read about him and what everybody said, was shy and low-key. She was twenty-five years old, and he was forty-three, an age considered quite old in that era. She was a flamboyant dresser, and he dressed in black, head to toe, nearly every day. She loved loud and raucous parties; he loved quiet moments in front of a fireplace. She was a Quaker, and he was an Episcopalian. She hated slavery, and his family owned dozens of slaves. She was a relatively uneducated girl from the woods of North Carolina; he was one of the most brilliant men in the world. She was an unknown, unaccomplished widow; he was the author of the US Constitution, a close friend of both Thomas Jefferson and George Washington, and one of the most important congressmen in America. She was one of the tallest women in America at 5'8" and had a shapely, buxom figure. He was one of the shortest men in America, at 5'4" and weighed only about one hundred pounds.

They had nothing in common at all. She said yes.

Dolley actually looked forward to meeting the very famous Madison, one of twelve children (only seven survived). Why would a man so different from her be interested in a meeting? There were so many women in Philadelphia who she thought were much better matches for him, older women and better-connected women. Why her? With a twinkle in her eye, she wrote her niece, Mary Cutts, "Aaron Burr says the great little Madison has asked him to bring him to see me this evening."[7]

Madison was transfixed by Dolley when he met her. Many men in the era married for convenience, but Madison, whom everyone thought was a lifelong bachelor, wanted to marry for love. He had been "engaged" twice to younger women with whom he was deeply in love. Both unceremoniously jilted him. "Kitty" Floyd, the teenaged daughter of a New York congressman, dropped him and married William Clarkson, a medical student. She hurt Madison by writing him a letter of departure telling him that she was completely indifferent to him. She sealed the letter with rye dough to show that her affections for Madison had "soured." A few years later, he fell in love with Henrietta Colden, a New York socialite, who broke off the engagement as well. Madison, who could talk with eloquence to men all over the world and by his writing through the ages, could not talk to women at all.

While Madison was not surprised by Dolley, she must certainly have been surprised by him. People had warned her that Madison was a chilly, frumpish man who was dreary in physical appearance, a hopeless hypochondriac, and, worse, dour in disposition and personality. She found him just the opposite. Dolley found him to be a man who was a delight to be with, once you got to know him. Everybody who knew Madison felt that way; those who did not know him accepted the erroneous sour public view of him.

No one expressed that sentiment better than bookseller Samuel Whitcomb, who met Madison late in life. "Mr. Madison is not so large or so tall as myself and instead of being a cool reserved austere man is very sociable, rather jocose, quite sprightly and active. . . . [He] appears less studied, brilliant and frank but more natural, candid and profound than Mr. Jefferson. Mr. Madison has a sound judgment, tranquil temper and logical mind . . . nothing in his looks, gestures, expression or manners to indicate anything extraordinary in his intellect or character, but the more one converses with him, the more his excellences are developed and the better he is liked."[8]

The "great little Madison" made up his mind to marry Dolley. He decided to win her affections by a carefully planned romance. He took her to lunches, dinners, musical concerts, and plays and spent an inordinate amount of time with her. She began to call him "Jemmie," a nickname only his friends used. To bolster his crusade to win her heart, he conspired with a cousin of Dolley's, Catherine Coles, to write letters to Dolley on his behalf, expressing his romantic feelings toward her. Young Coles thought it was a wonderful idea, a terribly romantic little game for her to play with him, full of love, and she plunged into the writing, turning out a string of fascinating love letters for Madison. The girl, quite a gifted author, wrote with gusto. Madison approved everything the girl wrote. In one letter, she wrote Dolley that "he thinks so much of you in the day that he has lost his tongue, at night he dreams of you and starts in his sleep a calling on you to relieve his flame, for he burns to such an excess that he will be shortly consumed and he hopes that your heart will be callous to every other swain but himself."[9]

Coles always reminded Dolley that Madison had read the letters and consented to all of them. In fact, she added to one letter, he did so "with sparkling eyes."

Coles's letters and James Madison arrived on Dolley's doorstop nonstop throughout the late autumn and the winter of 1793–94. The union between Madison and the widow Todd surprised all who knew them. There were merits to marrying James Madison for Dolley. He was a wealthy and important man who could instantly give her one of the most comfortable lives in America. He had also impressed her. Madison was, friends and associates knew, a very complicated man. He was somber and sober in public, but behind closed doors, with trusted friends, he was reportedly quite a storyteller and wit. He was a quiet man at most public social events but a bon vivant at private parties. Those who knew him slightly described his personality as chilly, but those who knew him well described him as a colorful character full of charm and resilience.

He was a man of two distinct faces. Mrs. Margaret Bayard Smith, a friend for more than sixteen years in Washington, wrote that "in public life and as a writer, James Madison was the most solemn of men. In private life he was an incessant humorist, and at home at Montpelier used to set his table guest daily into roars of laughter over his stories and whimsical way of telling them."[10]

But there were problems, too. He was much older than Dolley, his temperament was decidedly far cooler than hers, their entertainment interests varied greatly, and James would bring her back to his slave plantation in Virginia, very isolated from the world.

There was her religion. Because she married a non-Quaker, and might have done so within a year of her husband's death, the Quakers would probably exclude her from their meeting, a disastrous religious and social punishment. She knew that the Society of Friends did not care whom she married—she was marrying outside the religion. They had banished her younger sister Lucy from the Society because she married outside the faith—and she had married the nephew of the president of the United States, George Steptoe Washington. Dolley had little hope that the Quakers would keep her if she married Madison.

Her young child would have a father, well, a stepfather, forty-three years older than him. When her son, Payne, was twenty, his father would be sixty-three, a very old man in that era. Payne might have had friends in crowded Philadelphia, but there would be no one for him to play with at the mammoth plantation where she and Madison would live in the Virginia forests. Where would he go to school? Dolley worried constantly about the relationship between Payne and her prospective husband, any prospective husband. Dolley had lost her young husband and her other child; Payne was all she had left. Her boy needed a stepdad who would be a role model for him, spend a lot of time with him, play with him, tuck him in at night, have common interests, love him, and take care of him.[11] All widows felt that way about their second husbands. How could Madison, already forty-three, do that?

What she did not know, but later found out, was that Madison had delayed courting more women because he thought he might have epilepsy. He also declined to volunteer for the American Revolution as a soldier for fear he would suffer attacks while in the service. His brother-in-law said that he had physical tremors as a teenager that he thought made him an epileptic. He had "a constitutional liability of sudden attacks, of the nature of epilepsy."[12] Madison said that his seizures were "somewhat resembling epilepsy and suspending the intellectual functions." A Madison biographer, Irving Brant, wrote that it was "epileptoid hysteria." Thomas Jefferson believed that Madison was an epileptic and gave him a book by a French physician that covered epilepsy. The seizures did not return as he became an adult, though, as they might have if he had epilepsy (there were no medicines for it in that era). What he had might have been twitches of some kind brought on by temporary nervous disorders or stress, but it was probably not epilepsy. It might also have been another of Madison's minor ailments that he had, as usual, built up into some monumental disease. As he aged, he forgot about it.

Dolley was not disheartened, though. She studied Madison from many different angles. She had wanted to spend all of her life with her first husband, John. Now she wanted to spend her life with a second husband. Madison had to meet a lot of expectations from her, perhaps too many. One of them was that he play the role of stepdad. She had become convinced, in her months of seeing him, and spending much time with him alone, that he had the temperament to be a good stepdad. It was not enough for Dolley that Madison had a lot of money and lived on an enormous plantation. Money did not mean everything. It would provide comfort for Payne, but not love. The little boy needed a lifetime of love from her, and from a stepdad.

Dolley wanted to find out everything she could about Madison. She had very close friends investigate the congressman to see what he was really like. She feared that his fame would overwhelm people and that she would not receive an honest evaluation from most. Friends would give her an honest opinion and would be able to find out things she needed to know. She knew several men who were very close friends of Madison. One, William Wilkins, who had been her lawyer, knew Madison very well. He wrote Dolley that "Mr. Madison is a man whom I admire. I consulted those who knew him intimately in private life. His personal character therefore I have every reason to believe is good and amiable. He unites to the great talents which have secured him public approbation those engaging qualities that contribute so highly to domestic felicity. To such a man therefore I do most freely consent that my beloved be united and happy."[13]

Dolley also had a resounding, and quite surprising, character reference for Madison from a most unlikely source, the First Lady of the United States, Martha Washington. Dolley was invited to the President's Mansion one day in the summer of 1794 and was greeted warmly by Mrs. Washington. Her husband and Madison had been extremely close friends for years, as Dolley and everyone in Philadelphia knew, and Martha was intent on brokering a marriage between Madison and the Todd widow. "Do not be ashamed to confess it [love]; rather, be proud. He will make thee a good husband and all the better for being so much older [Mr. Washington and I] both approve of it; the stem and friendship existing between Mr. Madison and my husband is very great and we would wish thee to be happy," Martha said.[14]

Dolley left Philadelphia in the summer of 1794 for a visit with relatives in Virginia that was scheduled to last several weeks. Madison was crestfallen by her departure from town. He shook with worry. Kitty Floyd had broken up with him when she went on a summer vacation, too. It would happen again. To halt that chain of events, Madison and Catherine Coles kept up their steady chain of love letters (it is unknown how many Coles wrote). In a letter sent toward the end of that summer, Madison asked Dolley to marry him and dreaded receiving any mail after that, fearing that she would say no.

In mid-August, Madison received a letter from Fredericksburg, Virginia, in which Dolley agreed to be his wife. He was jubilant. "I can not express but hope you will conceive the joy it gave me. The welcome event was endeared to me by the style in which is conveyed," he wrote. Then Madison added, "If the sentiments of my heart can guarantee those of yours, they assure me there can never be a cause for [pain]."[15]

The pair were married on September 15, 1794, the wedding anniversary of James Madison's parents. The ceremony took place at Harewood, the estate of Dolley's sister Lucy and George Steptoe Washington, located near what is now Charlestown, West Virginia. Dolley wore a white, patterned, silk and lace dress, cut low in the neck and tightly fitted at the waist. She wore a headdress of orange blossoms. She wore heel-less white, satin shoes so that she would not tower over her much shorter husband. Madison, of course, dressed in black, as always.[16] Madison gave her a necklace and earrings of carved gems that were supposed to represent scenes from early Roman history. She smiled widely at the unique gift.

On the afternoon of the wedding, Dolley wrote a very personal letter to a friend, Eliza Collins Lee, who had married another Virginia congressman. In it, she said that she expected the marriage to bring her happiness. She wrote that "in this union I have everything that is soothing and grateful in prospect and my little Payne will have a generous and tender protector."

She signed the letter Dolley Payne Todd. Later that evening, as she prepared to send it off, she looked at her signature again, smiled, crossed it out, and with great joy wrote for the first time in her life "Dolley Madison! Alass!"[17]

3

THE HAPPY GROOM RETIRES FROM PUBLIC LIFE

*T*he new couple did not have time for a honeymoon. They spent a few days with Madison's sister Nelly; were in limbo for a week while Dolley fought off an attack of the flu; and then drove back to the nation's capital, Philadelphia, where Madison quickly returned to his duties as a congressman, political operative, and close friend to President Washington. Dolley and her son moved in with her new husband, as did her younger sister Anna, who would be with them for several years.

Madison had been a key player in the brand-new US government since its inception. He was one of the friends who urged George Washington to become the first president, despite his reluctance. Madison had Washington's ear right from the beginning of that first administration, which began in 1789 with Madison's best friend, Thomas Jefferson, as the secretary of state. Senator William Maclay of Pennsylvania wrote that Madison was "deep in the business" of helping Washington put together the government.[1]

The president also told Madison, Jefferson, and Hamilton that they could spend all the time they wanted in intellectual discussions about politics, but he could not. His job, he told Madison, was simple—keep the brand-new country together. If he could finish his term with a united nation, he knew he would have done a good job. He was walking, he wrote one man, "on untrodden ground."[2]

The first term of the Washington administration was a great success. For most of it, he headed up the only political party at the time, the Federalists, and they went along with his wishes as the chief executive. He was cheered and honored wherever he went, and his friends—such as Jefferson, Madison, and Hamilton—applauded, too. The new government established a new paper currency, assumed all of the state debts from the war, increased sea trade, established a sensible foreign policy run by the president, levied taxes, and filled the seats of the Supreme Court.

In his first four years, Washington achieved great success with the people and with Congress. The government, through import taxes, helped the nation achieve financial stability. The state governments became powerful because the federal government allowed them to do so.

Throughout this period of time, Madison operated as perhaps the most powerful congressman in the country. He wound up in Congress because an enemy, fellow Virginian Patrick Henry, used his influence in the state legislature to deny Madison the coveted US Senate seat he desired. Undaunted, the Montpelier intellectual won a seat in the House of Representatives. In Congress, he had operated as the "whip," or floor manager, for the new government, wrote and had passed the Bill of Rights, and became a close ally to President Washington and even closer to Thomas Jefferson.

He had been consulted by Washington on just about all the key pieces of legislation that were introduced, on both foreign affairs and domestic policy. As a bachelor, he had no domestic responsibilities to take time away from governmental work, and he was a hopeless workaholic.

Slowly, Madison became disappointed in both Washington and Hamilton. He had admired both as the founders of the new republic, but now, after a few years in office, they seemed determined to create a strong and monolithic federal government that might, in the future, overwhelm the states. They were creating a country that Madison had never wanted.[3]

He was also tired of Hamilton's frequent verbal abuse of him. In 1791, that same year he and Jefferson started their party, Hamilton told George Washington that Madison had unethically used the friendship between the two to help friends of his in Virginia. He said he had material that "furnishes proof of Mr. Madison's intrigues . . . an abuse of the President's confidence in him be endeavoring to make him, without his knowledge, take part with one cabinet officer against another," and that "Madison's character is the reverse of that simple, fair, candid one which he has assumed."[4]

Madison refuted these charges and said that Hamilton's accusations were political and stated to hurt the new alliance between Jefferson and Madison.

Madison had moved beyond the boundaries of Congress and had, in the summer of 1791, with Jefferson, started a major new political party, the Democratic-Republicans, with a states' rights focus, and worked hard to make it grow, and grow quickly. Within a year of its beginning, the Republicans had thousands of members. It started to field candidates for federal, state, and local offices. They began to win numerous offices in the elections of 1794 and by 1796 would be as strong as the Federalists.

The two men also started their own Republican newspaper, the *National Gazette*, to counterbalance the pro-Federalist *Gazette of the United States*. Jefferson gave editor and poet Philip Freneau a job in the State Department as a printer, hoping that would get him started with the new Republican newspaper, but Freneau did not earn enough money to launch it. Jefferson and Madison then obtained contributions and worked to build up a subscription list. In late 1791, the newspaper, opposed to Washington's administration, hit the streets. Madison was proud of it. He "entertained hopes that a free paper meant for general circulation and edited by a man of genius, of republican principles and a friend to the Constitution, would be some antidote to the doctrines and discourses circulated in favor of monarchy and aristocracy and would be an acceptable vehicle of public information I many places not sufficiently supplied with it."[5] A year later, an all-out newspaper war developed between the papers backed by the Federalists and the Republicans. Hamilton, under a number of pseudonyms, routinely blasted Jefferson in the columns of the Federalist paper, driving the pair even further apart.

Throughout the remainder of his life, Madison always continued his admiration of Washington, even after their friendship cooled during Washington's second term, and never believed the first president had much admiration for the second. He told friends that "the hotheaded proceedings of Mr. A are not well relished in the cool climate of Mount Vernon."[6]

Then Dolley Todd walked into Madison's life and everything changed. He saw his future entirely differently with his new, young wife and son. Now, finally, when his term ended in 1796, he could be a family man, a husband, a dad. He could return to Montpelier and become the farmer he had always dreamed about being—the planter, the well-dressed, high-society patron of Virginia—like so many of his friends. At the same time, Madison had lost Jefferson. His best friend had left Washington's cabinet, retired, and moved back to Monticello. And Madison was tired. He had been in public life since 1776, twenty long years, and was worn-out. He was exasperated, too, by the political fights in Congress and now, too, additional battles as one of the heads of the new political party. His numerous physical ailments returned and irritated him. He lost his zest for Philadelphia and government, ignored the advice of Washington, Jefferson, and others to stay in government, and retired.[7]

Madison was determined to leave the political stage and would not let anyone, especially Jefferson, talk him back into government.

Jefferson, surprised at the actions of his friend, pleaded with him to stay in government. "I do not see in the minds of those with whom I converse a greater affliction than the fear of your retirement," he wrote him.[8] In fact, Jefferson was so intent on keeping his friend in government that he told him he should not only remain in Congress but run for president. He said that Madison should be elected to "that more splendid and ... most efficacious post": the presidency.[9] He told him he would make a fine president and if his urging was not enough to help him retain his congressional seat, at least, he should ask Dolley "to keep you where you are."

This opposition to his retirement must have caused Madison to smile. After all, no one had extolled the virtues of retirement from political life more than Jefferson himself. He told friend Edward Rutledge that that he enjoyed retired living "like an Antediluvian patriarch among my children and grand children, and tilling my soil."[10]

He told Madison that he did not have to write a dozen political letters a day and never missed newspaper debates about politics. He was "so thoroughly weaned from the interest I took in the proceedings there ... that I never had a wish to see one [newspaper] and believe that I never shall take another newspaper of any sort."[11]

Madison told Jefferson he had no desire to be president and then turned the tables on him, telling him that he, Jefferson, should run for the office. "You ought to be preparing yourself ... to hear truths, which no inflexibility will be able to withstand," he wrote him.[12]

Madison would not be cajoled into a campaign for any office, either. He even wrote his father at Montpelier, "If Mr. Jefferson should call and say anything to counteract my determination; I hope it will be regarded as merely expressive of his own wishes on the subject, and that it will not be allowed to have the least effect. In declining to go into the Assembly ... I am sincere and inflexible."[13]

This stunned his friend Jefferson. The former secretary of state feared that his marriage to Dolley had taken his mind off government, politics, and everything else.[14]

The leading Federalists in the country did not believe Madison's retirement would last long. He would miss government, they charged, and he would especially miss public service now that his best friend, Jefferson, had been elected vice president in 1796. Newly elected president John Adams scoffed at Madison's departure from the political world. "Mr. Madison is to retire. It seems the mode of becoming great is to retire," Adams wrote his wife, Abigail, just after he took office.[15] "Madison, I suppose, after a retirement of a few years is to become President or V.P. It is marvelous how political plants grow in the shade."

Friends were surprised but understood. A lawyer, Hubbard Taylor, wrote him, "I am extremely sorry to find that you are about to quit the political theater, although we could not expect any one citizen to devote his whole life to public service and it is most certain you are not indebted to your country on that score."[16]

Jefferson's pleas, and similar pleas from dozens of others, did not change James Madison's mind. The congressman left Philadelphia in 1796 in a small train of wagons carrying his furniture and clothes, and returned to Montpelier amid its lush forests with his new wife and son, a man out of government for good.

Or so it seemed.

4

RETURN TO MONTPELIER, 1796

he only career James Madison had when he left Congress in March 1797 was that of a farmer. He had plunged into politics and the revolution as a young man and never looked back. The years flew by, some swift and some slow. He spent very little time at his family home at Montpelier, run efficiently and profitably by his aging father and over one hundred slaves. His father had built the plantation on 5,400 acres. From 1786 to 1793, Madison spent only seven months at Montpelier. From 1793 to 1796, though, he spent more than twenty months there, returning home whenever he could as his father's health declined and he was needed to run the plantation.

There were dozens of Madisons in Orange County, Virginia, all related to each other. James Madison had three brothers and three sisters living and residing nearby; his father, James Sr., had been a tireless patriarch of the Madison brood and, over the years, served as a pillar of Orange County, holding several offices, including sheriff. As he aged and became ill, he turned over more and more responsibility for the sprawling plantation to his son James, who enjoyed the work.

Madison's decision to retire from politics coincided with substantial change back in Orange County and at Montpelier. His brother Ambrose had died in 1793 and Ambrose's wife in 1798. Their teenaged daughter became Madison's ward, and she asked him to oversee the running of her family farm. Madison's brother Francis died in 1800, and his sister Nelly fell sick. His sister Fanny married Dr. Robert Rose. His father's health continued to decline. Madison, still working in Philadelphia, took on more responsibilities for the family as the years went by until he finally returned, for good, it appeared, in the winter of 1797.

He had started making business decisions for the plantation in 1793 and made more of them until he returned in 1797 to take over fulltime management. In 1794, with his father's blessing, he built a gristmill at Montpelier and made improvements on the lands and the family home. The gristmill was "particularly favorable to the interest of my brothers as well as myself," he wrote.[1]

He studied scientific farming, read farm journals, and corresponded with Jefferson about crops and harvesting improvements. He agreed with other Virginia farmers that the sharp increase in the grain market in Europe made it more profitable to grow wheat instead of tobacco, which had been Virginia's main crop for a hundred years. Madison not only ordered a general shift to wheat at Montpelier but also had slave workers plow his lands in different patterns to avoid soil erosion. He ordered slaves to ride horses less frequently and to take better care of them, fearful of illnesses and the early deaths of his steeds.[2] He gave more responsibility to black slave Sawney, who could read, put him in charge of large sections of the plantation, and gave him the power to order food, machines, and supplies. He gave orders to Sawney and other, white, overseers to treat the slaves as well as they could. "Treat the Negroes with all the humanity and kindness consistent with their necessary subordination and work," he wrote, and added that they had to make certain the slaves ate well and enjoyed good living conditions.[3]

Madison and his wife enjoyed an extensive social life in Orange County. They traveled to the homes of all of Madison's many relatives and friends for daylong visits and dinners and then invited all of them to visit Montpelier. Dolley spent much of her time running the domestic slave staff of twenty-three people that worked inside the mansion and assisting her new husband in running the plantation. She, like her husband, was the recipient of numerous letters from Thomas Jefferson and others on home-and-grounds construction and repair.

People in Orange County raised their eyebrows when they met Madison. He seemed a very changed man, changed for the better. He smiled more, seemed friendlier, and was more pleasant to be with. Now, unlike before, he was genuinely happy to meet people. They all attributed the substantial changes in his personality, which had seemed so set in its ways at the age of forty-three, to his new bride, Dolley. Everybody in Philadelphia had applauded the "new" Madison, too, and said it was all due to Dolley. "Mr. Madison has been married in the course of the last summer—which event or some other has relieved him of much bile—and rendered him much more open and conversant than I have seen him before," marveled Jonathan Trumbull, governor of Connecticut.[4]

One thing that took up much of Madison's time was the reconstruction and expansion of the large mansion itself. He and his wife, plus her sister, and their young son, Payne, now lived in the house with his mother and father and occasional relatives. They all needed more room. Madison sought advice from his father, who had not only designed and built the mansion but had built large homes for several of his friends in Orange County over the years. Madison also received advice from Jefferson, whose Monticello was already being acknowledged as one of the finest homes in the United States. To increase the size of the mansion and create more living space, Madison decided on radical reconstruction. He built a large wing on the north side of the house, leaving the original building as it was, with its center hallway. He added an elegant, white-columned portico with new front doors that took visitors to a small lobby inside the house (Jefferson's suggestion), with more doors that led into a large parlor. The windows on the parlor rose from the floor to the ceiling and could easily be opened at the top and bottom (another Jefferson idea). To the left of that, he built the new rooms and connected the downstairs and upstairs with a new staircase that had short steps to accommodate his wife's problems with her bad knees. There were several bedrooms upstairs.

From their upstairs rooms, the Madisons enjoyed one of the most sweeping, beautiful views in all of Virginia. The house was nestled into the Blue Ridge Mountains, which rose and fell gently round them and gave them an estate of rolling land with few level meadows. The house sat on a gentle ridge in the middle of thick forests full of trees that were hundreds of years old and meadows that were full of high, green grass. In the spring and summer mornings, large, white billows of thick fog that looked like high ocean waves rolled through the Madison farms, giving them an eerie and haunting look. "It is a wild & romantic country," wrote Anna Thornton, who visited Montpelier several times.[5] "[It is] very generally covered with fine flourishing timber and forest trees." The house, she said, had a "handsome portico of the Tuscan order, plain but grand appearance." Mrs. Thornton added, triumphantly, that when the Madisons were finally finished with the home, "It will be a handsome place & approach very much similar to some of the elegant seats in England."

Mrs. Mary Bagot, wife of a British diplomat, who seemed to detest everything about America, fell in love with Montpelier. "The house is more comfortable and better furnished than any other I have been in in this horrid country. It is wildly situated—surrounded by forest & with the Blue Ridge." Some visitors to Montpelier said they liked it more than the much more renowned Monticello. "Mrs. Sam[uel] Smith is might delighted with her excursion [to Montpelier]," wrote Anna Thornton in 1809. "She seems to admire your situation more than Mr. Jefferson's & indeed, I think myself it is capable of much greater embellishment."[6]

A lengthy row of slave huts sat within one hundred yards of the mansion at the bottom of a gently rolling hill and one of the larger tobacco fields. Between the slave quarters and the mansion was the narrow roadway that visitors used to arrive in their carriages or on horseback. The Madisons stood on their front porch and used a spyglass to discover who was arriving at the gate. Sometimes, for fun, the Madisons would conduct foot races against each other, and against guests, on the front porch of their home. A white-columned "temple," or large gazebo, was built a hundred yards from the mansion; Madison spent much time reading there in the summer months. The family cemetery was several hundred yards northwest of the home.

Montpelier was connected to the nearest town, Orange Court House, by a dirt highway that meandered through rolling meadows or tobacco and corn and thick forests of trees that in some places completely blanketed the mountainsides along the highway.

Madison had all of his furniture sent down from Philadelphia in wagons when he moved out of his home on Spruce Street. This included a dozen handsome Windsor chairs, mahogany chairs, and numerous boxes and trunks full of small items. The furniture did little to fill up the spacious rooms at Montpelier, though. When he arrived back home, he wrote his friend James Monroe in Paris and asked him to buy furniture for Madison and Dolley there. Madison was intent on breaking from the tradition of large landowners in Virginia to model their homes on Great Britain. He and his wife had started to use French furniture in Philadelphia and now ordered massive pieces of it.[7]

Monroe was happy to help. When he first arrived in France, he wrote Madison that "there are many things here which I think would suit you. I beg you to give me a list of what you want, such as clocks, carpets, glass, furniture and table linen—they are cheaper infinitely than with you considering I have advantage of the exchange."[8]

Through Monroe, the Madisons ordered a huge bed trimmed in crimson damask, a bedstead and mattress, silk curtains, two Persian carpets, and a chimney clock. They were happy to purchase beautiful furniture, curtains, and rugs directly from Paris, thanks to Monroe, and happier to buy them at prices, even including shipping, that were cheaper than it would cost to buy the exquisite French items at American stores.[9]

Friends gave the Madisons small pieces of furniture and other goods. The Monroes, as an example, sent two eighteen-foot-long table cloths, dozens of napkins, and two large mattresses. Jefferson sent goods from Monticello. They had farming and gardening advice from many friends and neighbors. Madison collected busts of famous Americans, including Jefferson, and had them on display in the parlor, the main room in the house. There was an electrical machine in the parlor, too, that Madison thought was great fun. He had guests stand around it in a circle, holding hands, and then used the machine to give them a jolt. Upstairs, in addition to the bedrooms, Madison created a large library with a window that overlooked the front fields of the plantation and the hills of the Blue Ridge in the distance. The library was stuffed with books. Tomes packed the shelves, filled extra shelves, and were piled high on the floor. He had close to four thousand volumes in the library. It was there, in 1786 and 1787, that Madison read hundreds of history and political books to prepare for the writing of the Constitution.[10]

Madison plunged into the renovations of the mansion. He wrote Jefferson and others for advice but was careful to redesign his home in his own way, ignoring numerous suggestions by Jefferson to make it look too much like Monticello. Madison either built or rebuilt the large front porch with its four white, wide columns and added a full-service kitchen, a large dining room, and a two-story addition to the main building. He personally supervised all of the construction and selected all the materials used, right down to the tiniest of nails.[11]

Visitors to Montpelier in those years saw a still-unfinished home and plantation grounds that were under construction and reconstruction. Some were annoyed by the slow progress. British foreign minister Sir Augustus John Foster wrote that the grounds were underdeveloped. There are "some very fine woods about Montpelier but no pleasure grounds, though Mr. Madison talks of some day laying out space for an English park, which he might render very beautiful from the easy graceful descent of his hills into the plains below." Other visitors felt the Madisons needed more time to finish the large job of renovating the home and farms. They all agreed on one thing, though. They all knew that the dour, sour public James Madison was, in private, a very friendly and animated man. Wrote Foster, "no man had a higher reputation among his acquaintance for probity and a good honourable feeling, while he was allowed on all sides to be a gentleman in his manners as well as a man of public virtue."[12]

Madison was consumed by the desire to fix up his home and grounds, but he did not spend all of his time at Montpelier. He traveled back and forth to Richmond, sixty miles away, by wagon and by carriage on shopping expeditions and visits to friends who lived in the state capital. Dolley often went with him. For example, in early January 1798, in the middle of winter, he spent two entire weeks in Richmond.[13]

And, as always, he was frequently ill. He had bouts of numerous ailments that laid him low for days and weeks on end. He wrote in 1799 of a weeklong confinement in bed from dysentery, which "left me in a state of debility not yet thoroughly removed."[14]

Dolley kept busy at Montpelier. In addition to raising her son, Payne, she became heavily involved in gardening and frequently sent friends jars of gooseberries, pickles, and preserves, and bags stuffed to the top with cherries. She took over the responsibility of running the mansion on a day-to-day basis from her mother-in-law. Early in the morning, usually before 7 a.m., Dolley met with a manager of the twenty-three domestic slaves who worked in the home to plan the day.[15]

They sweated from high temperatures in summer and shivered from low ones in winter. Madison wrote friends one winter that the temperature dropped all the way to ten degrees. He wrote Jefferson in May 1798 that the temperatures at Montpelier were still in the thirties and there were daily frosts that threatened to kill his crops. There had been little or no rain, he told Jefferson, and called the weather "the evil" (Dolley found the beauty in winter, though, as she did in everything, writing "our mountains are white with snow, the winter's wind is loud and chilling").[16]

The lack of rain and the chill had ruined his crops the previous autumn, too. At the end of 1797, he wrote, "The drought is also equal to the cold. Within the last eleven days, the fall of water has been but 1 ¼ inches only. Of snow there has been none. This cold and dry spell, succeeding the dry fall and late seeding, gives to the wheat fields the worst of appearances."[17]

The Madisons and everyone else struggled through a generally weak economy that lingered through the end of the 1790s. He complained to friends of high prices in Virginia, and friends complained to him of high prices where they resided. "A great stagnation in commerce generally," Jefferson wrote him from Philadelphia.[18] "During the present uncertain state of things in England, the merchants seem disposed to lie on their oars."

Madison continued his book buying, as he did wherever he lived. In August 1797, for example, he purchased James Callender's *History of the United States* (thirteen copies of it) from John Snowden and William McCorkle, two Philadelphia booksellers, who, upon finding out who the buyer was, promptly tried to get him interested in becoming an investor in their new newspaper (he declined).[19]

His wife continued to socialize throughout Virginia, never letting the boundaries of Montpelier tie her down. She traveled to the plantations of friends and the cities of Richmond and Charlottesville frequently, usually with her husband or younger sister. Her social network was ever expanding.[20]

By the end of his first full year as a retired planter, Madison took great pride in his work renovating his family home and farms. Dolley had established herself as the new leader of the Orange County social world. Dolley and her husband sometimes dined at the tavern in Orange Court House. She brought friends there when they visited. Anna Thornton was impressed with the village and the tavern, which was a notorious buyer of the moonshine whiskey produced just prior to the Whiskey Rebellion in 1794. "A large number of well-dressed and well looking boys and girls collected to their lesson in dancing at the tavern, which is almost the only tolerable looking house at the Court House," she wrote.[21]

Dolley also kept up a lengthy stream of letters with old girlfriends in Philadelphia. Many supplied her with juicy tales of gossip in and out of the government. One was Sally McKean, who had married a Spanish ambassador. She filled Dolley in on all the behind-the-scenes doings of her old friends in Congress and their wives, with names, places, and escapades. Another was Eliza Collins Lee, who also did a lot of Dolley's shopping for her when both lived in Philadelphia. Dolley also helped her husband run his huge library and supervised the lending of books to friends, acquaintances, and congressmen. Dolley traveled throughout Virginia from 1797 to 1800, building a network of friends. "I have found the place [Richmond] to my surprise, a most agreeable one. The society is delightful," she wrote a friend in January 1800. [22]

Yet, despite his much-publicized disdain for politics and government, Madison felt himself slowly drawn back into the national political wars. This began with a letter from James Monroe in which his disgruntled friend savaged the Adams administration in language that reflected Madison's own rapidly growing disenchantment with the national government. Monroe wrote Madison that "I have read the speech [by Hamilton] and replies and really begin to entertain serious doubts whether this is the country we inhabited 12, or 15, years ago: whether we have not by some accident been thrown to another region of the globe, or even some other planet, for everything we see or hear of the political kind seems strange and quite unlike what we used to see."[23]

Monroe's chagrin was triggered by the actions of President Adams, whom Madison intensely disliked. Madison had disagreed with some of Washington's policies but admired him enormously. Madison despised Adams, though. In comparing the two presidents, he wrote that "the one cool, considerate and cautious, the other headling and kindled into flame by every spark that light on his passion: the one scrutinizing into the public opinion, and ready to follow where he could not lead it, the other insulting it by the most adverse sentiments and pursuits. Washington, a hero in the field, yet overweighing every danger in the cabinet—Adams of the smallest disturbance of the ancient discipline, order and tranquility of despotism."[24]

To Monroe, Madison wrote of Adams and his friends, "let us hope, however, that the tide of evil is nearly at its flood and that it will ebb back to the true mark, which it has overpassed."[25] Similarly, Madison wrote Jefferson in 1798 that he agreed with Benjamin Franklin's assessment of Adams as being "always an honest man, often a wise one, but sometimes wholly out of his senses," and he added that Adams's speeches were "the old song" and that the Senate's answer to his policies "was cooked in the same shop with the speech."[26]

He had an equally low opinion of the followers of the second president. Madison wrote of them that "it is a pity that the non-attendance of the Adamsites is not presented to the public in such a manner [newspaper stories], with their names, to satisfy the real friends of Washington, as well as the people, generally, of the true principles and view of those who have been loudest in their hypocritical professions of attachments to him."[27]

In April 1798, as the snows around Montpelier melted, he wrote, "the President's message is only a further development to the public of the violent passions and heretical politics which have been long privately known to govern him."[28] Madison took Adams to task for everything. When Adams expressed ill feelings toward the brand-new capital at Washington, DC, Madison whipped him for that, too. "The discovery of Mr. A's dislike to the city of Washington will cause strong emotions," he said, and he added that the "magnificence of the President's house belongs to a man of very different principles from those of Mr. A."[29] Later, after reading a statement by Adams reprinted in a newspaper, he said that "his language . . . is the most degrading and abominable that could fall from the lips of the first magistrate of an independent people."[30]

His criticisms paled compared to his friend Jefferson's view of Adams. Jefferson called all of Adams's speeches "a national affront" and "follies."[31]

Madison slowly became consumed with Adams's misdeeds, as he saw them. He opposed any involvement in a war with France, was annoyed at the XYZ Affair (in which French ministers reportedly tried to bribe US officials to obtain a generous policy decision), and did not think that any of Adams's appointments were credible. His ire, and Jefferson's anger, with Adams and his Federalist cadre came to a head over the Alien and Sedition Acts, one of the most controversial pieces of federal legislation in American history.

For several years, beginning with President George Washington, Federalists had bristled under the lash of critical newspaper editors who worked for Republican-controlled newspapers. They went well beyond freedom of the press, Federalists claimed. Some were severe in their demands that the critics be silenced. The editor of *Gazette of the United States* wrote that one critic was "this scum of party filth and beggarly corruption, worked into a form somewhat like a man" and added that he "was entitled to the benefit of the gallows."[32] US Supreme Court Justice Samuel Chase agreed, saying that "a licentious press is the bane of freedom and the peril of society."[33]

They might have been offended by criticism, Republicans had argued, but the criticism was never treasonous or libelous. James Callender, for example, had called President Adams a "hoary headed incendiary" and wrote that "the reign of Mr. Adams has to be one of continued tempest of malignant passions . . . the grand object of his administration has been to exasperate the rage of contending parties to calumniate and destroy every man who differs from his opinions."[34]

Under the terms of the Sedition Act, anyone who criticized Presidents Adams or his administration could be imprisoned. The Federalists began to jail people quickly, too, sending several newspaper editors to prison and shutting down their papers. One newspaper editor was even sentenced to death for opposing the president (this sentence was overturned on appeal).

The Philadelphia *Aurora* printed long articles on the arrest of its editor, William Duane, with eyewitness accounts of people who saw Duane arrested, beaten, and bruised, while all the time yelling that he was being "murdered."[35]

The bills brought about a lengthy correspondence among Madison, Jefferson, and others that lasted for months. Madison saw a bright side to the bills, too, and that was the political repercussions they were sure to bring. He wrote Monroe, "the party which has done the mischief [Federalists] is so industriously co-operating in its own destruction."[36]

Newspapers throughout Virginia and the South were filled with stories about the acts. Madison was so angry about the two bills that he listened to friends who told him the best way to fight them was to figure out a way for the state legislators, under states' rights powers, to overturn them within state boundaries. To do that, they told Madison, he needed to get elected to the Virginia state legislature and work with other Republicans in Richmond to write bills to overturn the Alien and Sedition Acts.

Madison had not wanted to return to politics. He had been retired for only two years, and his home and farms still needed his attention. He and his wife, Dolley, were in the middle of constructing a happy social life for themselves. Yet he could not remain home as Adams and his cohorts circumvented the Constitution he wrote to blunt all criticism of their behavior. What was a free country without freedom of speech and freedom of the press? Adams and his aides were trampling on the Bill of Rights Madison had shepherded through Congress.

His return to politics was unusual. Ordinarily, the man running for office traveled to a few dinners and rallies to give speeches, alone, without his wife. Politics was in the male dominion in America in the waning years of the eighteenth century. Madison was different, though. He brought Dolley to his dinners and rallies. She did not sit in the rear of the audience, either. She sat in the front row on the platform, right next to her husband, and applauded madly when he made his campaign speeches. Soon, other wives joined their husbands on the campaign trail, and the look of the political world in America changed forever.[37]

He and Jefferson hatched a secret plan to blunt the federal acts. They would each write legislative bills for different states, Kentucky and Virginia, which called upon those state legislatures to overturn the federal acts. Jefferson was vice president and could not publicly do that, so he did so in secret, winning support from Kentuckians to carry on the fight for him. Madison did the same thing in the Virginia legislature, but publicly.

In Richmond, full of indignation for Adams and defensive about the Constitution and Bill of Rights he had authored, Madison took the floor of the legislature and, voice louder and more persuasive than usual, battered Adams over the Alien and Sedition Acts. He argued that the First Amendment guarantee of press freedom absolutely forbid federal-government infringements upon rights in any way, shape, or form. It would be "a mockery to say that no laws should be passed preventing publications from being made, but that laws might be passed for punishing them in case they should be made," and he added, "to the press alone chequered as it is . . . the world is indebted for all the triumphs which have been gained by reason and humanity over error and oppression."[38]

The Kentucky and Virginia Resolutions were not duplicated in any other state legislature. Madison and Jefferson, and their Republican friends, tried to gain support in other state legislatures, making herculean efforts to do so, but failed. The Kentucky and Virginia Resolutions, passed in 1799, had little consequence. They were no longer effective when Adams's term ended.

The battle over the Alien and Sedition Acts wound down right around the time the 1800 presidential election arrived. Thomas Jefferson, an exasperated vice president, decided to run for president against Adams. He was strongly supported in his bid by Madison, who joined one of the Virginia committees connected to the election to make certain that his friend received all of the electoral votes in his state, the largest state in the Union. The election campaign that followed drew Madison back into politics, with his wife's blessing.

Madison had other reasons to return to government, especially since the new federal capital was now located nearby on the Potomac River. His wife, Dolley, a social butterfly, had nowhere to fly in isolated northwest Virginia, especially in the winters when cold and snow set in. Madison's dream of living out his days as a successful lord of the plantation manor had not worked out that well, either. Running a plantation was hard work. He wrote in the spring of 1798, "It has now become certain that not half crops of wheat can be made, many will not get back more than their seed, and some not even that. We have lately had a severe spell of n.e. rain which in this neighborhood swept off at least 15 per cent of the [harvest] and from accounts in different directions it appears to have been equally fatal. We are at present in the midst of a cold n.w. spell, which menaces the fruit. The tops of the Blue Ridge mountains are tinged with snow and the thermostat this morning was at 31 degrees. It does not appear, however that the mischief is yet done. The coming night, if no sudden change takes place, must I think, be fatal."[39]

And on top of all of that, the man who was renting his house in Philadelphia, Stephen Moylan, told him that not only could he not pay his rent for a while, but that the house was in need of substantial, and costly, repairs.[40]

James Madison had put up with so much trouble from bad weather, irate workers, unhappy slaves, deteriorating homes, and nonpaying boarders that a job as secretary of state, where he had to worry only about wars with nations, must have looked very appealing.

5

MONTPELIER TO WASHINGTON, DC

The Making of a Public Man

When he was young, James Madison did not want to follow in his father's footsteps and become a planter at Montpelier. Running a large plantation farm, keeping books, and sweating in the heat and shivering in the always surprisingly cold Virginia winters were not for him. Shopping at the dreary, little, local general stores and supervising slaves had no appeal. What did appeal to the teenage James Madison were books, volumes of every size and kind—thick ones and thin ones, old ones and new ones. Madison dove into the pages of every book he could find, following the staid debates on governments throughout history in one book, and, in the next, the heroic exploits of the heroes of ancient Greece and Rome. He was just as fond of the warrior Achilles as he was of the writer Aeschylus.

The young Madison did not know exactly what he wanted to do in the world, but it was not farming. His father understood. James Madison Sr. had sent his son to study with a noted tutor, Donald Robertson, an instructor at the Innes plantation in King and Queen County, Virginia, for five years. There, he studied with the children of other wealthy and influential Virginia planters. He learned geography, languages, history, and mathematics. He came back to Montpelier at the age of sixteen to study more advanced work with another tutor, Reverend Thomas Martin. Then he was ready for college. Almost all of the college-aged young men of Virginia whose families had money attended the state's finest school, the College of William and Mary, but Madison resisted because of the oppressively hot climate in Williamsburg, which he was certain would ruin his always-precarious health. Instead, he traveled to Princeton,

New Jersey, to enroll at the College of New Jersey (later Princeton University). There, the slight, thin Madison, who rarely smiled, plunged into college work amid the tree-lined streets of the pretty campus. He jammed three years of academic study into just two, reading day and night, and then stayed at the college for another year to read more. He studied many of the governments of European countries, their history and structure, as well as those of Russia and Asia. His studies took him all the way back to the Roman Empire and the city-states of ancient Greece. This fascination with government would engage him all of his life.

In 1772, he returned to a Virginia that had been torn apart by political disputes between the British Parliament and the colonies. Virginia had been in crisis since 1765, when the British government imposed the Stamp Act on America, forcing the colonists to pay a tax on any printed material. The tax was imposed because Britain had decided that the enormous cost of the Seven Years' War, concluded in 1763 with British victory over the French and their Indian allies, had to be paid by the Americans. British citizens were already paying heavy taxes and should not be charged even more fees, Parliament leaders believed and, besides, that war had been fought to protect the colonies on the eastern seaboard. So, naturally, they had to pay for it. The colonists disagreed, and loudly. The British fought that war, colonial political leaders and newspaper editors argued, to solidify and expand its empire in North America. Victory had given Britain nearly half the continent. The British would reap the profits from the war, so Americans believed that the British should shoulder the cost of it. Colonial representatives from nine colonies met at a special Stamp Act Congress in New York and drew up a formal statement of protest. Colonial leaders agreed to "non-importation agreements," a boycott of British goods. Women made homespun clothing to replace the expensive dresses they had been purchasing from fancy London shops as another protest. Men of all ages who had merely watched politics unfold in their cities now jumped into the political wars, angrily siding against the Crown. The Sons of Liberty and Daughters of Liberty, which would become powerful revolutionary groups a few years later, were formed as protest organizations. Newspaper editors, taxed on their newspapers, railed about it, some even predicting that it would end freedom of the press in America. There were parades and public rallies against it. Raucous protests, which included physical attacks on tax collectors, took place in many villages and cities. British merchants complained bitterly to Parliament that their shipping, half of which went to America, and sales had been crippled by the protests. These much-publicized efforts finally forced that tax to be overturned a year later, but the British Crown came back with more taxes.

Nobody understood more than Madison that the taxes came to a set of colonies that had developed into their own country over the past 150 years. Americans had become one of the world's most important trading partners. American court systems, modeled after the British tribunals but with changes, were efficient; crime was low; and business was good. The colonies had become a country within the British Empire.[1] There was one more, deep, wrinkle to that portrait—virtue. During the last half century, Parliament and other British governing agencies had been crippled with very public corruption scandals. The British government, Americans believed, was no longer virtuous. Lobbying for liberty grew everywhere in James Madison's Virginia in the 1760s and 1770s. Nowhere was it better expressed than in a soaring speech by Virginian Patrick Henry. Henry would go on to be a six-time governor of Virginia and ardent political foe of Madison. He told the House of Burgesses, the Virginia state legislature, that the taxes would "destroy American freedom." In soaring language, hands and arms flying about him, he shouted, "If this be treason, make the most of it." (Madison's friend Jefferson, in the hall that day, said Henry showed "torrents of eloquence.")[2]

Madison felt like Washington, whom he would meet later, that the colonies had suffered much. Later, Washington wrote, "We had borne much; we had long and ardently sought for reconciliation upon honourable terms, that it has been denied us, that all our attempts after peace had proved abortive, and had been grossly misrepresented, that we had done everything which could be expected from the best of subjects, that the spirit of freedom beat too high in us to submit to slavery and that if nothing else could satisfy a tyrant and his diabolical ministry, we are determined to shake off all connections with a state so unjust and unnatural."[3]

There in Williamsburg, legislators developed the Committees of Public Safety. These were secretive citizen groups designed to gather information about Crown activities and share it with committees throughout the colony and in other colonies. Each colony had several committees.

Madison, aged twenty-three, joined the Orange County Committee of Public Safety. It was his first official political position. He was then elected as a county delegate to the state convention in Williamsburg and a year later, in 1776, was elected to the state assembly, the House of Burgesses. There, in its somber chambers in an elegant brick building, he met and became a close friend of Thomas Jefferson, one of the most brilliant men in America. Madison had witnessed fierce persecution of Baptist ministers in Virginia and in the legislature worked on measures to guarantee religious freedom. In just the three years that he served as a delegate to the House of Burgesses, Madison had been deeply immersed in the anti-Crown politics of Virginia and America, befriended the leaders of the various tax disputes, served on anti-Crown committees, and written anti-Parliament letters. The Virginia state legislature sent him to the Continental Congress in Philadelphia in 1780 as a state delegate when he was twenty-nine. He was an easily recognizable figure in Philadelphia because he almost always dressed completely in black and, wherever he went, he carried armfuls of thick books. His small room in Philadelphia was crammed full of books.

In Congress, he visited the army camp, dined with Washington on several occasions, and met with Washington whenever the general visited Congress to deliver reports on the progress of the war. In Philadelphia, Madison debated and befriended just about all of the delegates, who represented colonies he had never even visited. He got bills passed in several areas and even convinced Virginia to give up part of its lands to form a brand-new geographical region, the Northwest Territories, governed by Congress.

Few people in America had been so exposed to American political thought, and action, as the radical Madison. Few had interacted with so many political figures from so many colonies. Few had met and spent time with so many generals and officers of the Continental Army. Few Americans, ever, had been so exposed to every nuance of colonial politics or understood the politics of England, both on the battlefield and in philosophical debates. James Madison was, as Edmund Randolph said, "a child of the Revolution."[4]

He was a successful congressman but not, at first, a successful politician. Madison hid behind his books, reading long into the night, and never developed the political skills necessary for dealing with other congressmen. His writings were dry; they did not soar with the lyrical prose of other public figures. He was a low-key public speaker whose speeches were barely audible; his voice did not soar with eloquence like that of other Virginians, such as Henry. He was effective, but not a leader. One Massachusetts congressman wrote that Madison was "a man of sense reading, address and integrity" but "a little too much of a book politician and too timid in his politics."[5]

But he was effective.

The great political change in Madison came after the war, in the fall and winter of 1787–88 and in the spring and summer of 1788, when, with John Jay and Alexander Hamilton, he lobbied to get all of the thirteen colonies to ratify the brand-new Constitution, the Constitution he wrote. To do that, George Washington warned him, he had to step back from his long-held image as a political theoretician and put on the coat of a political arm twister. He needed to engage in hardscrabble politics to win views and get votes. Madison needed to make friends and make deals. That was the only way the Constitution, objected to by many, was going to be ratified in each state. Madison listened to Washington, and others who offered him the same advice, and changed his ways. His voice never grew louder or stronger, but the way he delivered speeches improved. His ability to talk others into agreeing with him, and to rebut the arguments against the Constitution and to refute powerful speakers, increased dramatically in just a single year.

Another bit of advice Washington told Madison was that his fellow Virginian had to make better use of the country's newspapers to gain support for the Constitution. He had to court editors and make them a part of his campaign. Later, just like Washington, Madison began the practice of reading every newspaper he could find so that he knew what the media and the people thought of his policies.[6]

One Georgian congressman, William Pierce, said of him later that "every person seems to acknowledge his greatness. He blends together the profound politician with the scholar . . . he is a most agreeable, eloquent, and convincing speaker . . . he always comes forward the best informed man of any point in debate. In the affairs of the United States, he perhaps has the most correct knowledge of any man in the Union. He was always thought one of the ablest members that ever sat in Congress."[7]

Massachusetts senator Samuel Otis wrote of him that he had "the endowments of a great statesman and a fine scholar, in the study of men and books, possesses a cool, deliberate, cautious judgment [and] writes his friends in Congress in terms very encouraging."[8] Others said that he combined the skills of the statesman and politician, that he not only had ideas but also could do the difficult work needed to bring those ideas to fruition. Brissot de Warville, a French statesman, wrote that "he distinguished himself particularly well at the time that the conventions met to vote on the new Federal Constitution. For a long time, Virginia hesitated to join the Union, but by his logic and his eloquence Mr. Madison persuaded the convention to favor acceptance . . . he looked tired, perhaps, as a result of the immense labors to which he had devoted himself recently. His expression was that of a stern censor; his conversation disclosed a man of learning, and his countenance was that of a person conscious of his talents and of his duties."[9]

Madison had not only designed the Constitution but implemented the document's ideas into his everyday job as a congressman. He was not rash or flighty; he thought before he spoke; and he always expressed his appreciation of every view on a subject, as well as his own. New Hampshire senator William Plumer said of him that "no man was more tenacious of his opinions than he was—he would die sooner than give them up, but then no man was more ready to save for the present the applications to existing circumstances.... Something of this disposition is no doubt seen in most men, but was remarkably characteristic of Mr. Madison, and forms the true explanation of his conduct in more than one important transaction."[10]

A friend who was a Virginia historian, Hugh Grigsby, said of him that "Madison was more elaborate in his argumentation [than Jefferson]. It is difficult to cull from the papers or even the speeches of Madison written purely on party topics, an adage or a maxim or even a pointed phrase, as a weapon to be used in the existing contest."[11]

⟨∽∞⟩

When he returned to Philadelphia with his new bride, Dolley, Madison was even more of a political dynamo than when he had left. He had learned in his courtship of Dolley that two of her sisters had married congressmen. They, and Dolley, knew as much about American politics from their husbands as most congressmen. The women kept their knowledge of domestic and world affairs and the working of the political game quiet, as women did in that era. Their friends knew of their political wizardry, as did their husbands. No one else did, though, enabling the sisters, especially Dolly, to enjoy a much-appreciated persona of the lovely women above politics when they were, behind closed doors, immersed in the political landscape of America.

Dolley found her family a new home and furnished it. Then she resumed her friendships with various women she had known in Philadelphia and, rather quickly, met many more at receptions she attended with her husband. By the fall, she had started friendships with President Washington, members of his cabinet, and dozens of congressmen. She hosted numerous parties at the home she now shared with her husband; dozens of Philadelphia couples invited them to their homes for dinners and parties. Everybody wanted to meet James Madison's vivacious new wife, who, socially, took Philadelphia by storm.

Madison found himself in another storm upon his return to the nation's capital—the Whiskey Rebellion. Hundreds of men in western Pennsylvania who produced whiskey refused to pay taxes on their brew. General Washington raised an army of fifteen thousand men, larger than any he had commanded in the American Revolution, and marched across the state, determined to defeat the whiskey rebels; Alexander Hamilton served as Washington's chief general. The rebels surrendered before Washington's army arrived, but the Whiskey Rebellion sparked a national debate on federal versus states' rights.

And to Madison it was yet another attempt by Hamilton, whom he and Jefferson by now despised, to create a monolithic federal government that would rule over the states and the people by imperial force. Hamilton had hinted at that in letter to Rufus King. In it, he said that the whiskey rebels were "outlaws." He added that "this business must not be skimmed over. The political putrefaction of Pennsylvania is greater than I had any idea of. Without rigor everywhere our tranquility is likely to be of very short duration and the next storm will infinitely rise [more] than the present one."[12]

Madison wrote James Monroe that "if the insurrection had not been crushed in the manner it was I have no doubt that a formidable attempt would have been made to establish the principle that a standing army was necessary for enforcing the laws."[13]

What really annoyed Madison, though, was that he believed Washington and Hamilton were scheming to blame the Whiskey Rebellion on the various Democratic-Republican clubs of his new party. He criticized the president's annual message to Congress, which contained veiled criticism of the clubs. "The introduction of it [reference] by the President was perhaps the greatest error of his political life. . . . The game was to connect the Democratic Societies with the odium of the insurrection—to connect the Republicans in Congress with those societies—to put the President ostensibly at the head of the other party, in opposition to both—and by these means prolong the illusion in the north and try a new experiment on the south."[14]

Madison was a great champion of the various democratic societies because they supported the party he had started with Jefferson and because they offered people a choice at election time. The society heads nodded knowingly. "The collision of opposing opinions produces the spark which lights the torch of truth," wrote the head of the Patriotic Society of Delaware.[15]

The seemingly endless disputes between Madison, Hamilton, and President Washington all stemmed from the creation of the Democratic-Republican Party by Madison and Jefferson in 1791. The new party satisfied Madison and Jefferson because it provided a choice for voters, represented states' rights, and gave both men a platform upon which to express their views in addition to the halls of Congress and the newspapers. President Washington was astonished that a second party emerged, aghast that his friend Madison helped form it, and fearful that this new political-party system would plunge the country into ruin.

Washington told friends that he was of "no party" and that he was a man "whose sole wish is to pursue with undeviating steps a path which would lead this country to respectability, wealth and happiness." He scalded political parties in his farewell address, at the end of his second term. "Parties," he wrote, "may now and then answer popular ends, [but] they are likely in the course of time and things, to become potent engines by which cunning, ambitious and unprincipled men will be enabled to subvert the power of the people and to usurp for themselves the reins of government; destroying afterwards the very engines which have lifted them to unjust dominion." He added that parties were "the worst enemy" of popular government.[16]

Madison and the "Madisonians," as his allies were starting to be called, began to oppose Washington and his administration more and more. They were against the Alien and Sedition Acts. Madison was against a treaty engineered by Chief Justice John Jay with England that attempted to gain better political and business relations with Great Britain. He saw the Washington administration pushed farther and farther toward a despotic government by Alexander Hamilton, whom Jefferson hated. His own, new, party was still a minority in the Senate and Congress and while a threat, had no real power yet.

The new Republican Party, struggling to gain power, should have been weakened when Jefferson quit the cabinet and went home to Monticello, but it was not. The cofounder, Madison, took up the reins and ran it very smoothly from Congress. He took over quickly, too. Congressmen saw him as the leader right away. "[He is] the great man of the party," said Massachusetts politician Theodore Sedgwick in 1794, who would be Speaker of the House five years later. A few weeks later, Senator Samuel Smith referred to the upstart political organization as "Madison's party." The Virginia congressman, in touch with Jefferson constantly, kept the party growing and running smoothly for three more years, until Jefferson's return to government as vice president.[17]

He not only ran the party but also quickly defined it as not just another party but a party needed to blunt the force of the Federalists. He told all that the two parties were very different, with different supporters and different goals. The Federalist Party "consists of those who from particular interest, from natural temper or from the habits of life are more partial to the opulent than to the other classes of society . . . having debauched themselves into a persuasion that mankind are incapable of governing themselves, it follows with them of course that governments can be carried on only by the pageantry or rank, the influence of money and the terror of military force," he wrote in one newspaper. In another, he argued that the Republicans had always supported the constitutional government and that history had already shown that the country did not have three branches of government just at the federal level, but at the state level, too, giving the people a second set of checks and balances.[18]

Back in Philadelphia, the Madisons lived in a comfortable home on Spruce Street, a cobblestoned, tree-lined avenue with fashionable brick sidewalks in the heart of the affluent residential district. The Madisons hosted many parties under the skilled leadership of Dolley, who invited not only the rich and powerful but also friends and people in the arts. They attended numerous private parties and the frequent, large public affairs, such as Washington's birthday celebrations, already a national holiday.

Dolley was asked to join the Philadelphia City Dancing Assembly, one of the most prestigious social groups in the city. She attended just about all of their meetings, dances, and dinners. Everyone was glad to see her at the events. Men and women alike crowded around her when she arrived. As always, James Madison, eyes wide in admiration, trailed alongside her, glowing in her glory, never envious and loving every minute of it.[19]

Dolley Madison assumed her place in the busy social season just as women's fashions took a dramatic turn. Started in Paris, there was a new trend in women's dresses—low-cut necklines, bare arms, and no lengthy trains for gowns. They were smart, they were sexy, and they were a scandal to many. Abigail Adams was enraged by the new dresses. "The style of dress . . . is really an outrage upon all decency . . . most ladies wear their clothes too scant upon the body," she wrote.[20]

Adams and her conservative friends also complained that the new dresses were cinched in such a way as to show off even more bosom than intended. Even the commonly accepted practice of placing a handkerchief between the breasts in such a dress did not hide much, they protested.

And the amply endowed Dolley Madison? She loved the new, low-cut dresses so much that she not only wore them in public all the time but had one of her official portraits painted of her in one of the dresses, with, of course, no handkerchief to be seen. Frances Few, Albert Gallatin's niece, gushed about Dolley that "she had the most beautiful . . . neck and bosom . . . I ever saw."[21]

Change was everywhere. The new wife of Emperor Napoleon Bonaparte, Josephine, had started to wear daring, low-cut, form-fitting dresses that caused quite a scandal. Dolley had to get one as soon as she read about it in the newspapers. She bought one at a Philadelphia shop and put it on, all ready for a formal dance and dinner at the City Dancing Assembly. She did not think she looked quite right, so she picked up two brightly colored plumes and stuck them into her hair and smiled.

Many women were outraged by her dress. Abigail Adams thought Dolley looked like a tart. "Since Dolley Madison and her sisters adopted the new fashions and seemed in every way delighted with the French-influenced manner of Philadelphia society, we may assume ex-bachelor Madison enjoyed fully the 'luxuriant' feminine displays," she wrote.[22]

Dolley caused an absolute uproar at the dance, and the next day, all of her critics rushed out and bought their low-cut gowns, too. She did not accept change after it was in place; she accepted it right away. Dolley not only greeted fashion changes warmly, but immediately, within days, she changed her own dress and led the new fashion charge. She did this easily, as she did everything easily, and that skill enabled her to maintain her position as the nation's social lioness.[23]

She became such a fashion queen so quickly that right after her portrait painter, William Dunlap of New York, met her, he described her in his diary as "the wife of the Secretary of State and leader of everything fashionable in Washington."[24] Everyone who met Dolley liked her. Even truculent, grouchy John Adams was smitten by her. "I dined yesterday with Mr. Madison. Mrs. Madison is a fine woman and her two sisters (Anna and Lucy) are equally so," he wrote his wife in 1796.[25]

The parties and receptions that made up the social life of Philadelphia, "the season," featured and were run by what locals called "the young set" of women, married and unmarried, living in town. The leader of the "young set" was Dolley Madison. Her marriage to the influential Madison had made her an instant social leader, and her style and personality added to her social power. Everyone wanted to have Dolley, and her husband and her sisters, at their party. Women in Philadelphia kept in touch with Dolley and her sisters when they were back at Montpelier, too.

One year, Sally McKean, daughter of a Pennsylvania political leader, wrote Dolley's sister Anna a letter in which she urged her to return to Philadelphia as quickly as possible to meet all of the handsome, very eligible, young men in the city. "For heaven's sake, make as much haste to town as you can for we are to have one of the most charming winters imaginable."[26]

Dolley Madison was one of the best-dressed women in America. She dressed well because she understood that well-dressed people make a greater impression than others. She and her husband had the money to dress elegantly, and so they did. Mrs. Madison, though, always went an extra step in her fashion pursuits. It was never enough for her to be one of the best-dressed women in the social world; she had to be *the* best dressed. To achieve that end, she spent enormous amounts of the Madison money on clothes. She had friends keep an eye out for attractive dresses, bonnets, shawls, and shoes for her. Friends in New York and Philadelphia, who knew her sizes, would purchase clothing for her and send it on to Washington. Dolley had other friends in London and Paris who did the same thing. The dresses and hats usually fit; sometimes they did not. It was the chance all American women took who bought clothes from abroad. If she saw someone else in a new style dress, she told friends to find one for her immediately. She purchased to excess. For example, following the approval of federal funds to redecorate the White House, she added, at her own expense, two dozen pairs of white kid gloves; one dozen pairs of black, silk stockings; two dozen pairs of white stockings; one dozen pairs of shoes with heels; one dozen pairs without heels; four Merino shawls; a large, white shawl "with a rich border"; and one dozen more snuffboxes. That was just one of hundreds of clothing orders while she was First Lady.[27]

Dolley could be fussy. She would return clothes that did not fit her as well as she assumed they should. She once had several pianos ordered for the White House, had someone play them, judged them out of tune, and sent them all back. She continued to do that until one was delivered whose music she enjoyed.[28]

In 1809, she decided that coasters that could hold three glasses at the same time were just what the White House needed and told decorator Benjamin Latrobe to buy some. He looked all over America only to discover that nobody made them. Dolley was very disappointed. Then she asked him to buy a piano for the White House and he went on another national search, turning down one piano after another until he found one for $530 (about $9,000 in today's money) that he assured Mrs. Madison he could get for $450. "It is of such superior tone, in strength and sweetness, that I would be by all means recommend its being taken at that price," he gushed to her. She bought it. Latrobe and his wife worried themselves sick that they could not please the First Lady. A few months later, they were unable to find French china sets with cups and saucers for her because they were not manufactured that way. They spent days finding marvelous-looking cups and saucers made in Nanking, China, and prayed that Dolley would use them. She did; they were relieved. Just a week later, Latrobe was sweating again because he could not find the type of cloth Dolley wanted for the interior of two new carriages he was decorating for her. "I have been obliged to have recourse to second cloth of somewhat a darker tint, but of the same character of color. The color of your carriage will be a very beautiful reddish brown, according to your wish," he wrote.[29]

Her efforts, and those of her friends, not only permitted her to be a fashionista of the first order, but a trendsetter. Her trends were not only unprecedented but daring. People often went to parties just to see what Dolley Madison was wearing that night. The next day's conversation would be consumed with talk about her clothes and hats, plus her extravagant guest list.

Later, in Washington, Dolley created a colorful social life for her husband and those he and she entertained. "The frank and cordial manners of its mistress, gave a peculiar charm to the frequent parties there assembled," wrote Margaret Bayard Smith.[30] "All foreigners who visited the seat of government, strangers from the different states of the union, the heads of departments, the diplomatic corps senators, representatives, citizens, mingled with an easy freedom. A sociability and gayety, to be met with in no other society . . . never was a woman better suited to the task."

One thing that Dolley was intent on doing was leading American women out of the drab, somber look in their clothing. Following the American Revolution, the simple look became popular as a contrast to the upper-crust British royalty look and the exaggerated dress of the wives of diplomats and rich merchants. Simple was Republican and patriotic. Dolley, though, believed that it was a new century that demanded new fashion rules—and she would set them. She also felt that, as the unofficial hostess in the White House and then First Lady, it was her solemn obligation not only to help eradicate the old fashions but also to lead the charge. She never flinched in her new dresses and her dazzling new look.

One night, she stunned people with a dress that Frances Few wrote was a "gown of brick coloured silk with a train two yards long trimmed with white—on her head a small cap with a large bunch of flowers." That ensemble was nothing. Shortly afterward, partygoers saw her in an over-the-top ensemble that would have made the royals of Windsor Castle blush. A friend wrote of Dolley that "her Majesty's appearance was truly regal—dressed in a robe of pink satin, trimmed elaborately with ermine, a white velvet and satin turban, with nodding ostrich plumes and a crescent in front, gold chains and clasps around the waist and wrists."[31]

Dolley was extremely careful in her dress, and did not simply throw on the latest dresses from Paris. She always made certain that while she showed plenty of cleavage, it was not too much. She wanted to look like the finely dressed women at Washington parties, but not *exactly* like them. She wanted to look European, but American too. One huge issue was her jewelry. She wore many rubies, emeralds, and pearls, but never diamonds. Americans did not like diplomats or First Ladies in diamonds. Mrs. Elizabeth Merry, wife of the British ambassador, was roundly criticized for wearing a diamond necklace to a White House party and Dolley understood, right away, that diamonds were the symbols of the rich. She never wore them.[32] The Dolley Madison look, though, was not just her new and expensive dresses and her exotic turbans. Her look included her makeup, the way she glided from room to room never making a false step, her laugh, and her smile. Altogether, it was an irresistible combination. She, like Washington earlier, had created a very royal look that was not quite royal, a very elegant look that was not quite elegant, and a very wealthy look that was not quite wealthy. What she had done, like Washington, was create a distinctly "American" look. It was new and different, and he and she exemplified it. And, too, she always remembered the words of her husband on fame, "be always on your guard that you become not the slave of the public, nor the martyr to your friends."[33]

Dolley also had the rare ability to talk to anybody about anything. She knew something about whatever region her guests were from, knew some of the people they knew, and encountered some of the problems they had endured. "We remarked on the ease of which she glided into the stream of conversation and accommodated herself to its endless variety. In the art of conversation she is said to be distinguished," said one White House guest.[34] Another said that she always exhibited "a willingness to please."

The people loved her for doing it and rarely criticized her for reveling in it. Danish minister Peder Pederson put it best: "I have, by turns, resided in all the courts of Europe, and most positively assure you, I never have seen any Duchess, Princess or Queen whose manners, with equal dignity, blended such equal sweetness," he said.[35] "She looks like a Goddess; she moves like a Queen."

She was a fashion lioness with style, though. People expected her outrageous dress, wanted it, and, when they saw her in those clothes, loved her for it. A woman who met Dolley at a party wrote that "she had on a pale buff colored velvet made plain, with a very long train, but not the least trimming, and beautiful pearl necklace, earrings and bracelets. Her headdress was a turban of the same coloured velvet and white satin (from Paris) with two superb plumes, the bird of paradise feathers. It would be absolutely impossible for anyone to behave with more perfect propriety than she did. Unassuming, dignity, sweetness, grace. Such manners would disarm envy itself and conciliate even enemies."[36]

6

A NEW WORLD

The Madisons Arrive in Washington

*T*he Washington, DC, that greeted James and Dolley Madison upon their arrival on a quiet day in the spring of 1801 was a small country village with some gargantuan public buildings dotting its streets and meadows and enormous, uninhabited stretches of land. The huge structures soared into the sunlit morning sky and cast lengthy, dark shadows on the uneven lawns around them. The sprawl of land within the city's borders was mostly empty, and a bit foreboding, when they made it to town that May. Washington was a brand-new city, the new national capital, under construction on the banks of the wide, easy-flowing Potomac River. The community had fewer than ten government buildings finished and opened that spring, including the Capitol (which was still unfinished, without its dome and with a combination of two large buildings connected by a narrow, mostly wooden center) and the President's Mansion (later named the White House). Streets that would become famous in history, such as Pennsylvania Avenue, were just wide stretches of dirt, mud, and holes that horses, carriages, and wagons had a hard time traversing. Parts of the lengthy avenue, one of the city's main thoroughfares, ran through a very wet, murky, mosquito-infested swamp that no one seemed able to drain. There were unfinished structures everywhere, from half-completed stone walls to the wood frames of houses and warehouses. No matter where you looked, you saw piles of stone, lumber, sand, and bricks that workers were using to finish public buildings, as well as residential homes and boardinghouses. Wooden ladders rose alongside buildings, and from early morning until dusk workers toiled, nailing thick, freshly cut wood beams together; lifting large grey stones; and finishing roofs, all amid a loud clamor of noise. Horses could be heard shifting about in their newly constructed stables, and servants repaired carriages that sat in new coach houses or under slowly blooming trees. People walked down the streets and marveled at the way that homes and boardinghouses were built, often able to see construction completed from the skeleton wood frame to finished homes with lighted living-room candles. Workers put up houses as quickly as they could and then moved on to the next home, the new row, the next block, the next neighborhood. Once-vacant blocks filled up quickly with houses, and uncut meadows became green, alluring backyards. Fully completed blocks and neighborhoods stood next to huge, vacant lots in what was an odd panorama for foreign visitors so used to large, populated, and very completed European capitals such as London and Paris.

"The houses were very low and far in between," said Mary Cutts, Dolley's niece, who arrived in town later. "In many places the roads not opened, the beautiful square in front of the President's house not distinguishable from the open commons, many original trees still growing in the midst of this new city. In bad weather, the roads were almost impassable."[1] Madison slave Paul Jennings grumbled that "the city was a dreary place."

The local newspapers were filled with ads run by people who were selling either finished homes, houses under construction, or vacant lots. The house ads were not just for Washington, either. Dozens more were for sale in neighboring Georgetown and Alexandria, Virginia.[2] There were several dozen streets that had become home to boardinghouses for government officials, senators, congressmen, and judges. Residential structures, large and small, had been opening their doors over the last several months. Some buildings were constructed as clusters and given names like "Six Buildings," which was a tightly built row of six large, brick homes that included the offices of the secretary of state. Architect William Thornton, soon to become a close friend of the Madisons, supervised the construction of "Six Buildings" as well as several other handsome homes in town. Thomas Law oversaw the construction of nine houses on a single block near the Capitol. There was also Carroll Row, with more than a dozen homes within its confines. Wide and unoccupied lots, many with tree stumps, large boulders, ravines, and narrow creeks that ran through them, sat next to many government buildings, such as the White House. Some of these lots were so large that people went horseback riding on them. President Jefferson oversaw the planting of poplar trees along the sides of some city streets. City parks were unfinished, bridges not yet built, outhouses still common, and a press corps not yet founded. Foreign dignitaries settled into crude quarters that were a far cry from their opulent palaces back in Europe (and that they complained about endlessly).

Businesses in the nation's capital were scarce. The city in 1801 was home to just eight boardinghouses, one tailor, one shoemaker, one printer, a washing woman, a grocery shop, a pamphlet-and-stationary shop, a small dry-goods shop, and an oyster house. There was a liquor store, though, called Alexander Henderson and Co. and located at Merchant's Wharf, that had a sale on Madeira wine (with "moderate" prices).[3] The capital was designed in three sections: the Capitol area, the White House neighborhood, and the village of Georgetown, several miles away (Alexandria, Virginia, was across the Potomac). Each bloomed independently of the other.[4] Visitors complained that the houses that had been completed in such record time were constructed poorly and were barely inhabitable. Altogether, there were 108 brick buildings and 253 made of wood. The last year that Congress would spend any money on improvements in Washington was 1801; and the city, still struggling with untrained self-government and unable to raise much money, became a ramshackle capital full of water-filled meadows and muddy streets. Tom Moore, an Irish poet traveling in America, wrote a sarcastic poem about the capital:

> This famed metropolis where fancy sees,
> Squares in morasses, obelisks in trees,
> Which traveling fools and gazetteers adorn
> With shrines unbuilt and heroes yet unborn.[5]

Some did not mind the debris. Others loved the city despite its faults. On an 1803 visit, Hetty Ann Barton of Philadelphia said that "the romantic city, rising in splendor out of the forests all combined, formed a picture as beautiful as can well be imagined in the happy mixture of an endless variety of objects."[6] She added that the city and its surrounding villages looked their best from the roof of the White House, where she stood with President Jefferson. "The Potomac in all its grandeur and serenity as far as the eye could reach, in the distance just visible, the town of Alexandria enveloped in a fine blue mist, yet glittered in the sun, just playing on its spires. The number of beautiful country seats in every direction, the fine scenery along the bank of the river."

Even foreigners who seemed to despise everything and everybody they met in Washington, such as Mrs. Charles Bagot, the wife of a British minister, fell in love with the Potomac. "I was much struck with the beauty of it & particularly with the opposite shore of Virginia which is thickly wooded & the light green of the trees . . . intermixed with the dark pines & cedar trees had a beautiful effect," she wrote one day; and then, on another day, when she visited Potomac Falls, she added, "the scenery at the little falls is as wild & romantic as it is possible to conceive. On each side of it are rocks of a grey kind of stone which on the right side are immensely high & raggy & covered with every beautiful description of American forest tree which appear as if they sprang from the rocks themselves."[7]

It was an ever-expanding city, though. In 1801, on the day the Madisons arrived, Washington was home to only 3,200 residents.[8] By the time Madison became president in 1808, that number would jump to 8,208 and to 13,117 by 1820, just after he would leave office. The whole area, including Georgetown and Alexandria, had fourteen thousand residents in 1801 and thirty-three thousand in 1820. The town was constantly growing and no matter where you walked or rode in those years you went past construction or road improvements of some kind. There were dirt piles and shovels everywhere.[9] The government had begun construction of a large wooden barracks for the Marine Corps and spacious warehouses and offices at the Navy Yard, on the Potomac, where new ships would be built and old ones repaired. In the summer and fall of 1801, new boardinghouses began to open along different city streets with new dry goods, grocery, and clothing stores nearby. Pontius Stelle's hotel on capital square, the first in the city, opened its doors. Construction was started on Mechanics Hall, a large rooming house for working men, in Georgetown. Its purpose was to house the hundreds of laborers working on government offices and residential housing in the area. Several well-appointed inns, with large stables behind them, opened on Pennsylvania Avenue, all affording a grand view of the half-finished Capitol to one side and the three-story-high President's Mansion on the other. By the end of 1801, 599 houses were owned or were rented or served as inns in the community.

"No town in the Union has advanced so rapidly," wrote the editor of the *National Intelligencer.*[10] It was a city of potential. President Adams said in his last State of the Union message that "in this city may ... self government which adorned the great character whose name it bears be forever held in veneration."[11]

Others sneered. Critics charged that the nation's capital was a dark, unlit, dangerous town. There were few oil lamps to guide people and horses through the streets at night. The newly laid-out streets were not only narrow but badly maintained. Ruts and potholes were frequent, and sometimes tree stumps under the roadways were uncovered by a hard rain. The rain turned streets to mud; and in summer, with little precipitation, the dry dirt turned to dust and drifted about town when a steady gust of wind blew down the streets. It was routine for visitors upon arrival at their destination to first say hello and then flick dust off their clothes.

It was "both melancholy and ludicrous ... a city in ruins," wrote the unhappy congressman of Connecticut, Richard Griswold, to his wife back home.[12] Gouverneur Morris wrote sarcastically that "we only need here houses, cellars, kitchens, scholarly men, amiable women and a few other such trifles, to possess a perfect city."[13]

The brand-new city had little entertainment, and this annoyed not only diplomats from capitals in Europe that were full of music and theater but also American officeholders who had enjoyed concerts and plays in their home cities. Washington only had one legitimate stage, the Washington Theater, and it was open for just two months a year when a traveling acting company from Philadelphia made it their home. The theater did not stage full dramas, either, but only shortened Shakespearean plays and new one-act plays by British authors. The actors who worked there always considered the theater inferior to the one in Williamsburg, Virginia. Smaller, one-room theaters opened for a few weeks throughout the year and offered entertainment and acrobats. There were no concert halls or opera houses, no art galleries, and no salons in which philosophers and intellectuals could gather. The only recreational area that was popular was the racetrack, the Jockey Club, where wealthy Washingtonians who owned well-bred horses raced them during a short season of three meets in good weather. The races seemed to attract everybody, and many wagered on the finishes. A lavish ball, with an orchestra and finely dressed servants, was held at the beginning of the Jockey Club's racing season and was said to be as impressive as those held in other major cities.

Wealthy residents, such as James Tayloe, owned several racehorses and traveled with them to different tracks in the Chesapeake area, such as those in Annapolis and Richmond. The Jockey Club's social life pleased many Americans, but some of the wealthier residents of Washington scowled at them and referred to them as public circuses. At the club's track, "persons of all descriptions from the president and chief officers of state, down to their Negro slaves . . . collected together, driving full speed about the course, shouting, drinking, quarreling and fighting," snorted Dr. Samuel Mitchill, a leader of the town's social set.[14]

The Marine Corps band began to play concerts each Saturday afternoon in spring and summer, but President Jefferson did not think they were very good. He tried to hire a dozen Italian musicians to join them, but immigration paperwork was snarled and only half of them ever played with the band.[15]

The plans of Pierre L'Enfant, the architect who designed Washington, DC, called for a fabulous city full of wide avenues and lovely neighborhoods with river vistas, parks, and elegant private homes, but that city remained sitting on his blueprints, gathering dust. Right then, in the spring of 1801, Washington was a city of the future, of the far future, a city of promise. It was a town, though, even in its infancy, that would grow as the federal government grew and, with it, as the Madisons grew.

The town's fully developed newspapers offered one bright spot on the otherwise-under-construction horizon. In addition to the brand-new *National Intelligencer*, and its weekly version, the *Universal Gazette*, the Washington area was home to several papers. The *Washington Federalist*, the *New York Weekly Museum*, and the *Cabinet* were printed in Georgetown; and, across the river, the *Alexandria Advertiser*, later named the *Alexandria Gazette*, and the *Expositor*. The three Georgetown papers expired after a few years, as did many newspapers in Washington in the nineteenth century, but the *Intelligencer* and the *Alexandria Gazette* had a long life.

The arrival of the new secretary of state and his wife, Dolley, on May 1, 1801, was a quiet one. They were over two months late because Madison's father had died on February 27. The new secretary of state, deep in mourning, had to bury his father and take care of his affairs at Montpelier. His father left a complicated will and had named James Madison as his executor; unraveling the will was time-consuming. Madison had overseen his father's last days while battling a bout of rheumatism. Then, right after he and his family buried James Madison Sr., Madison came down with another illness and was bedridden for four days and unable to travel to Washington. It was so debilitating, he told Jefferson, that it "has not yet permitted me to leave the house."[16] Further delays were caused by inclement weather that turned highways into muddy roadways that could not be traversed. Jefferson, well aware of his friend's chronic medical ailments, had Attorney General Levi Lincoln serve as his stand-in on the job until Madison arrived.[17] The president also consoled him on his sickness, as he had always done throughout their long friendship. "[I have] learned with regret that you have been so unwell," he wrote him in condolence.[18]

Even though he was stuck at Montpelier and sick, Madison did a fine job as an absentee secretary of state, working from home. Lincoln ran the office, met with Jefferson, saw foreign diplomats, and sent out voluminous correspondence, but Madison read all of the letters from ambassadors and foreign diplomats and kept abreast of foreign conflicts, such as the touchy situation with the Barbary pirates and the leaders of Tripoli. He kept up a steady stream of correspondence, oversaw Lincoln's work, and did almost as much at Montpelier as he might have done in Washington in those early days of Jefferson's first term. The only chore that Madison did not do was interview job applicants and read résumés. Lincoln did that and he was overwhelmed by them. He wrote Jefferson on April 26 that "it is much to be regretted that Mr. Madison's indisposition continues." No one was happier to see Madison and his wife arrive in Washington than was Lincoln.[19]

The Madisons had driven down over five days and were still sore from the road bumps and holes their small carriage had pounded through. Traveling in 1801 was not only time-consuming but dangerous. Virginia was a southern state, but in many winters it snowed in parts of the state, and the melted snow brought about ruts in the dirt roadways (it snowed on February 11, the day on which the House of Representatives started its special election to select the new president, and snow remained on the ground for a long six weeks after that as the weather remained chilly throughout the Washington, DC, and northern Virginia area).[20] Trees fell. Some roads were flooded out. Others, particularly in the hillier section of the state where Jefferson and Madison resided, were extremely steep and hard for a carriage to climb. Yet others ran for miles before there was any stop for food or water. Inns that offered accommodations to travelers were small and miles apart. For Madison and his wife to travel almost eighty miles in five days was an accomplishment. Dolley wrote of one journey, "In truth my limbs yet tremble with the terror & fatigue of our journey . . . difficulties and danger . . . our horses had no chance but to swim."[21]

Accompanying the pair were Dolley's younger sister Anna and several servants. People who saw them arrive that day had a pretty good glimpse of what they would be like. James Madison, aged fifty, the secretary of state and the cofounder of the Republican Party with President Jefferson, was clad in black and sported a dated revolutionary ensemble of clothes. He was very short, dour-looking, unsmiling, determined, and blandly dressed. One man said that he looked like "a schoolmaster dressed up for a funeral."[22] His wife, Dolley, aged thirty-three, was just the opposite. She was a tall, buxom, beautiful woman whose dark-brown curls fell gently over her forehead. She was well dressed, even for a long and arduous carriage ride. Dolley was "still young, happy, hopeful and very beautiful," her sister wrote. Mrs. Madison's eyes beamed as she looked over her new hometown, a city that, although she did not know it, would be home for most of the rest of her life and would see her rise from a barely known new arrival to one of the most famous women in the world.[23]

The Madisons would live in Washington for the next sixteen years. They arrived in a slow-moving parade of wagons and carriages, the mode of transportation in the day, but in 1817 they would return home by stepping onto a fast-moving steamboat that would take them up the Potomac River. The transportation revolution would be just one of the epic transformations in the United States during their time in power.[24]

Madison arrived in the capital to serve as secretary of state in Jefferson's cabinet after the new president was elected chief executive over Aaron Burr by the House of Representatives in a historic vote after the Electoral College was unable to decide the contest. Electors had mistakenly voted for both Jefferson and Burr, who was running for vice president, creating a tie (Madison had gone along with Burr as the vice presidential nominee and helped to start all the trouble, after his political colleagues in Pennsylvania assured him that Burr had support everywhere).[25]

Jefferson had already established a brand-new look for the presidency. He had stayed at a local boardinghouse while Congress thrashed about in its unprecedented election of the chief executive and, after the vote, remained there for two weeks, dining with everyone, as usual, and immediately creating the image of the "ordinary man." He luxuriated in the support of his friends, such as Madison. His new secretary of state had never wavered in his support of Jefferson for president or his belief that the House of Representatives would elect him in its extraordinary vote. "I can scarcely allow myself to believe that enough will not be found to frustrate the attempt to strangle the election of the people, and smuggle into the Chief Magistracy the choice of a faction. It would seem that every individual member who has any standing or stake in society, or any portion of virtue or sober understanding, must revolt at the tendency of such a maneuver," Madison wrote.[26]

Afterward, when he moved to the White House, Jefferson answered the front door when people arrived, which startled many (in fact, one visitor thought he was a servant). He went horseback riding around town, waving to residents as he passed them on the street. He wore ordinary clothes, favored slippers and not shoes at work, never wore a wig, and rarely powdered his blazing red hair.[27]

His newfound "man of the people" manners pleased Americans but annoyed diplomats, who had met kings and queens dressed in their regal best at royal balls. Many complained that Jefferson did not seem to care what he looked like when he met them and often appeared unshaven, with his hair uncombed. Anthony Merry, the British minister, was aghast when he was first introduced to Jefferson at the White House. Jefferson, Merry complained, was dressed in "an old brown coat, red waistcoat, old corduroy small clothes much soiled, woolen hose and slippers without heels."[28]

In addition to all of that, Jefferson framed his election, and the roaring rise of his political party, as a new era in America, an era dramatically different than that which he said ended with the administration of New England Federalist John Adams. "The revolution of 1800 was as real a revolution in the principles of our government as that of 1776 was in its form," he later wrote proudly.[29]

The election of 1800 was seen as a bellwether election by the Republicans; the common people agreed with Jefferson that a political revolution had taken place and that America was headed in a new direction. Most of the Federalists whom the Republicans despised had been swept out of office and had left town. The first president, Federalist George Washington, had died a year before. The second Federalist president, Adams, was back in Massachusetts. Alexander Hamilton, the influential Federalist secretary of the treasury, was not just out of office but also out of politics entirely. Many of the original Federalists elected with Washington twelve years earlier had retired or died. Now, in 1801, as the new century bloomed, America was run by a different party, the Republicans, whose belief in small government, states' rights, and people's rights would move the nation down a new path.

The change in politics was enormous in many ways. The brand-new Republican Party made America a two-party system, something no one anticipated when the revolution ended. Within a few months, the busy city scenes of the national capitals in New York and Philadelphia were long forgotten, and the huge, sprawling, wide-open Washington, DC, was the backdrop for the nation's political story. The old presidents' mansions, elegant homes in New York and Philadelphia, had been replaced by the gargantuan President's Mansion in Washington, one of the most magnificent homes in the world, a building that towered over every other structure in Washington except the Capitol. All of the traditions of the President's Mansion, and the president living in it, were new. The social calendar at the White House was brand-new; the social lions, new; and the sites of all the parties, new—and very different.

Importantly, too, the new capital, thanks to a tricky political deal between Jefferson and Federalists, was now located on the banks of the Potomac, just about halfway down the eastern seaboard. It was now centrally located and not a northern capital, as were those in Philadelphia and New York. It was a southern capital within the boundaries of the new District of Columbia, but that was within the boundaries of Maryland, a southern state.

In just the twelve years since the passage of the Constitution, America had sped through one political era and entered another.

Jefferson had been elected by the House of Representatives, but he certainly did not see himself as a compromise president or a minority president. A confident leader, he saw himself as a powerful new president who had majorities in the House and Senate behind him. He would take steps to get rid of many Washington and Adams appointments to the judicial bench and government offices; ally himself with Republican state and city officeholders; draft editors for brand-new, influential Republican newspapers; push manufacturing in the northern states and farming in the southern states; embrace the new Industrial Revolution; and try, when possible, to enlarge the physical size of the United States (particularly with Spanish-held Florida). Jefferson would chart a new and different course for the United States and do it as the leader of a government that he saw as a merger of the state and federal governments, unlike the top-heavy federal government of Washington and Adams.

Both Jefferson and Madison loathed Adams. "The conduct of Mr. Adams was not such as was to have been wished, or, perhaps, expect. Instead of smoothing the path for his successor, he plays into the hands of those who are endeavoring to strew it with as many difficulties as possible and with this view, does not manifest a very squeamish regard for the Constitution," wrote Madison just before Adams left office.[30]

Madison had yet another reason to cheer his friend's election as president. The election process proved, despite its critics, that the new form of democratic government Madison had devised with the Constitution worked. Referring to the force frequently used in European transitions of power, he wrote, "What a lesson to America & the world is given by the efficacy of the public will when there is no army to be turned against it!"[31]

Jefferson was buoyant. He wrote his friend Madison of Washington, DC, that "we shall have an agreeable society here."[32] To his son-in-law Thomas Mann Randolph, Jefferson said of the city that "we find this a very agreeable country residence . . . good society and enough of it and free from the heat, the stench and the bustle of a close built town."

Jefferson was thrilled to have Madison in his cabinet because the two men were such good friends. Madison's slave said they were "like brothers."[33]

The new president had significant experience in foreign policy. He had been the minister to France in the late 1780s and served as Washington's secretary of state until 1794. He knew, as he took office, just how foreign powers saw him and his new government. They understood the advances the United States had made during its first twelve years and understood the changes he wanted to make in the country. They understood, too, that the new, red-haired president, who could play his violin as well as pass his legislation, was tough. He was not a compromiser and would get what he wanted in foreign policy. He took office at a stormy time. The United States had been involved in a police action against France, dubbed the Quasi War, just a year before he moved into the White House; the French and British were often battling each other; and the pesky Barbary pirates, based on the coast of northern Africa in Tripoli, were harassing shipping in the Straits of Gibraltar and in the Mediterranean.

Jefferson had brought Madison to Washington with him as his secretary of state because the men were close personal friends and cofounders of the Republican Party, but there were other reasons. No one understood the workings and promises of the American government more than Madison. Madison knew everybody in government from his years of service in the House. He was a smooth and clever politician who could help Jefferson write legislation and get bills passed (he had been nicknamed "the Big Knife" for his ability to cut through problematic areas and move legislation through the halls of Congress). Madison's views on foreign policy were the same as his, and Madison could always rely on the president, a former secretary of state himself, to understand what he was trying to do in his job.

They were a good pair. "The mutual influence of these two mighty minds upon each other is a phenomenon, like the invisible and mysterious movements of the magnet in the physical world," John Quincy Adams said of them.[34]

Republicans were happy to see Madison back in government. His friend James Monroe told him that he was a sterling choice as secretary. "His [Jefferson's] outset is as favorable as it could have been. His admin. is formed of characters that will draw to him an increased portion of the publick [*sic*] confidence, and in other respects give him all the support he could expect from one. So that on the whole I think you all have a fair prospect of promoting the welfare of your country, and of being rewarded for the service by a due acknowledgement on the part of the people," he wrote Madison.[35]

A veteran New York politician, Samuel Osgood, wrote that both Madison and Jefferson "promote to the first Office in our republican government the man who has so richly merited the confidence of his country; who, regardless of the torrents of slander & abuse, has so ably supported the genuine principles of civil liberty, as delineated in our excellent constitution. Malevolence and slander are still using every effort here to defame and blacken the characters of the virtuous and upright in politics, but their edge is very much blunted."[36]

Madison worked diligently, arriving at his office early and remaining past nightfall. He was a good overall manager and fine micromanager. "Mr. M. is overwhelmed with business—the British, French & Spanish—infringements are all under his pen—M wishes to write Col. C but has not a moment," his wife once wrote.[37]

The Madisons stayed at the White House as the president's guests for three weeks. Jefferson was thrilled to have them. The only other person who lived in the White House with the president was his secretary, Meriwether Lewis. The two men felt like they were walking through the halls of a large museum. The irony of their condition is that living in the mammoth White House was one of the enticements the president used to lure Lewis to the job. After telling him why he should take the job, the president wrote Lewis, "you would of course save also the expense of subsistence and lodging as you would be one of my family."[38] Jefferson wanted more friends there with him, and, at least for three weeks, he had them.

After their short stay in the White House, for two months, the Madisons settled into one of the connected houses that comprised the "Six Buildings" complex.[39] Following that, they moved to a much larger home that architect Thornton had located for them at 1333 F Street NW, just a few blocks from the White House. The Madisons liked their new home. Madison was the secretary of state and had to live like one. He needed a home where his wife could host parties, hold receptions, and socialize with all the men and women in Washington. It had to be a home where people could mingle in rooms throughout the entire first floor and hallway, or tumble out into the backyard in the hot spring and summer months. A small apartment, even a large apartment, would not do. This new home was a three-story-high, brick residence topped by a handsome cupola. There were four bedrooms on the third floor, and plenty of rooms for offices and social receptions on the first two floors. There were servants' quarters, a stable for four horses, a coach house, and several outbuildings to the rear of their house. The building had a large wine cellar. They were both very comfortable living in it and would remain there for eight years. It would soon be home to Dolley and what everybody in Washington began to call her "young set."[40]

Dolley, dazzled by the city, which looked different every day as streets were finished and buildings erected, found herself in a very unusual spot when she arrived. President Jefferson lamented the living conditions in the still-under-construction White House. His predecessor, John Adams, and his wife, Abigail, found them appalling. People who walked through the President's Mansion thought the home resembled a large, drafty barn rather than the home of a head of state. Jefferson hired teams of carpenters and asked them to finish the White House as quickly as possible. He had another, larger, problem, though. He was a widower, had no romantic interest in any woman in Washington, and spent his nights in the White House alone. He had no woman to serve as an official hostess for him, as a president's wife, or as a "First Lady." He needed a First Lady badly to set the social calendar for the White House and to serve as the feminine side of the new administration.

The role of First Lady was not mentioned in the Constitution. No one planned for the arrival of a First Lady. Martha Washington invented the job when she arrived in New York in 1789. She had managed a busy social calendar at Mount Vernon for years, one in which Washington felt comfortable, and proceeded to do the same thing in the new president's mansion in New York. It worked. Most applauded her for establishing the role. Some, such as Albert Gallatin, were critical. "She was Mrs. President not of the United States but of a faction," he said.[41]

Martha, and Abigail Adams after her, quickly became the First Lady of the land (although the term was not used officially until the 1840s). Normally, a president's wife had to organize a social life for the chief executive; throw parties; send out invitations; schedule receptions, lunches, breakfasts, and dinners; plan a daily menu; supervise cooking; socialize with the wives of public officials and foreign diplomats; talk to members of the press; serve as a liaison with the ladies of Washington; support causes; and, through her good works, build up an admirable image that reflected well on herself—and the president.

Jefferson did not have a wife or companion to do all of that for him. But he did have Dolley Madison. The president had liked Dolley from the first time he met the vivacious wife of his best friend. On the personal side, he thought she was a superb companion for James Madison. He recognized, as did all, that the Madisons were as alike as night and day. He saw, too, as everybody saw, that opposites did, indeed, seem to attract. She was gorgeous, socially oriented, very friendly, and at ease with men and women of any background, and she was a great conversationalist. Dolley was also a fine head of his household, of anybody's household. She was completely in charge of meals, social events, receptions, and an army of servants. She got along with everybody and seemed to have an easy way with workers at the White House. Her husband slept late, but Dolley was usually up at 6 a.m., and began arranging the day, and everybody's work in it, before the sun had risen very high in the Maryland sky. Everybody liked her; so did the president.

Dolley was the perfect First Lady. She had all of the social strengths needed to be the First Lady and the administrative skills to fill the job. She just wasn't his wife. Fortunately, that was not an obstacle to overcome in 1801 Washington. She was the wife of his best friend, the secretary of state. It seemed natural that, not having a wife, the wife of a cabinet member should help him put together a social calendar and greet people as an unofficial hostess at the White House. So he asked Dolley to be his hostess. She agreed. No one objected.

Dolley Madison had been asked by Jefferson to serve as his hostess just after he was inaugurated. In the third week of March, he began to tell foreign diplomats that Mrs. Madison would formally greet them on his behalf when she arrived in Washington.[42] Dolley was glad to do so for several reasons of her own. First, her husband was Jefferson's best friend. Second, Jefferson was her friend and said he needed her assistance. Third, the president needed someone and she knew that she could do the job better than most women. Fourth, she and her husband were newcomers in town. What better way to meet people? To meet everyone? And, too, she thought to herself, what better way to help her husband's career than to act as First Lady and spend all that time in the White House, with her husband there with her?

Jefferson also needed her because he rose early in the morning, worked hard all day in his office, and had no time to plan parties. "[Work] keeps me from 10 to 12 and 13 hours a day at my writing table, giving me an interval of four hours for riding, dining and a little unbending," he wrote; and he always referred to work as "a steady and uniform course."[43]

Jefferson wanted someone to devise a social life for the White House and just tell him when to show up and what to do. Dolley understood how he thought, was familiar with his moods through several years of friendship, and served him well in that capacity.

She probably did not know how busy the role of First Lady would make her, or perhaps she relished the job precisely because it did keep her so busy. Abigail Adams had done little in Washington as First Lady because the White House was still being constructed and she lived there for just one year. She complained bitterly to family and friends that it was a large, cold, airy place and that there were no bells to summon servants and no wood to throw into the many fireplaces to keep the rooms warm. Most of the rooms were still incomplete when the Adamses lived in the White House. "The house is made habitable but there is not a single apartment finished and all within, except the plastering, has been done. We have not yet fence, yard or other convenience, without and the great unfinished audience room I make a drying roof, to hang up the clothes in. The principal stairs are not up and will not be this winter," she wrote.[44]

Now, there was so much to do. Dolley did not want to replicate what Abigail did. She used Martha Washington's active social life as a model but expanded upon it. Martha had hosted four receptions a week at the president's mansions in both New York and Philadelphia. Dolley discontinued that schedule, but, in a new and different way, expanded upon it and increased its size.

Dolley's forte was the large, elegant dinner parties, public receptions, and balls that she designed. Elaborate planning went into each. She used accepted protocols of the day—who should sit next to whom and at what time different things should happen—but enhanced them. She took the view that she was the president's hostess and this was the White House, so she could do whatever she wanted—and did.

No cost was spared. Servants drove the White House wagon from Pennsylvania Avenue out to the shops in Georgetown, where they purchased the food Dolley had ordered. They went over bumpy dirt roads to Georgetown just about every day and brought back expensive bills that were passed along to Dolley, who passed them on to Jefferson, who signed them and then promptly forgot about the cost.

Dolley entertained several dozen people at each dinner at the White House and twenty or more people at "quiet" dinners at her own home.

"He always thought twenty five thousand dollars a great salary when Mr. Adams had it. Now he will undoubtedly think twelve thousand five hundred enough," the editor of the Federalist *New England Palladium* newspaper wrote sarcastically of her expenses in 1801.[45]

Mrs. Madison also dressed in whatever fashion she desired. She did not feel that she had to look staid or conservative just because she represented the president and secretary of state at social events. *Somber* was not a word in her vocabulary. Dolley and her husband were a sight to see. Madison, as always, wore all-black suits and had his powdered hair pulled back and tied behind his head. He never wavered from his conservative, dreary, and a bit outmoded, dress. His wife, though, was a rainbow. Dolley brought down all of her ballroom gowns from Montpelier and bought many more. The women's style of dress in the era was the wide skirt, tight waist, and low-cut bodice, a style that really only worked well for full-busted women. Dolley was one of them. She also had beautiful shoulders and soft, white skin, all shown off nicely by her gowns with their deeply plunging necklines. The dresses accentuated all of her admirable physical features but were of splashy colors that stood out no matter where she was standing in the White House. Her dresses were of many colors and designs, and she wore so many different ones that many Washingtonians swore that she never wore the same clothes twice. She often wore a French beret, a radical look, and loved wandering about the floor of an official reception with it tilted buoyantly on her head. Sometimes she replaced the beret with high, brightly colored feathers that could be seen throughout whatever building she was in. All the talk of the capital the day after a reception at the White House was about what Dolley Madison wore.

She had a unique style at parties and balls that no one had encountered before. Dolley had the rare ability, those who saw her at parties said, "to move from place to place, room to room" to meet each and every guest at the White House parties, which were quickly named "Mrs. Madison's levees." She did this very smoothly, very nonchalantly. "It became evident, in the course of the evening," one partygoer wrote, "that the gladness which played in the countenances of those whom she approached was inspired by something more than respect . . . we have not forgotten how admirably the air of authority was softened by the smile of gayety; and it is pleasing to recall a certain expression that must have been created by the happiest of all dispositions, a wish to please and a willingness to be pleased."[46]

Other levee guests enjoyed the tours of the White House that Dolley relished giving. "Then through the house we sallied forth from one end to the other, Mrs. M seemed quite at home here, and in fact appeared to be mistress. She took us from room to room, in her usual sprightly and droll manner," said one. As an added treat, she loved to show them the dumbwaiters that Jefferson had invented to carry food and wine from the basement to the dining room and all of Jefferson's carefully designed apparatuses upon which to hang his clothes.[47]

But there was far more to Dolley and James Madison at parties than mere dress. It was a time, Dolley understood, to let her husband shine, and to help him shine. The public view of Madison was that he was a quiet, laid-back, pale-skinned, doughty, boring, tiny man who had little to say—and when he did, he said it very softly and without much conviction. She knew, and Jefferson knew, that Madison was not like that at all. He had a rapier wit, was conversant about all the topics in the news, and was a persuasive man who could carry on conversations with anybody, from counts to congressmen, and tell marvelous stories. Dolley engineered her receptions so that many people got to meet her husband under the best of circumstances and came away with a good impression of him. She arranged seating plans so that he could shine in conversations during dinner, always talking to a different group of people each night. He was funny and told humorous stories, or engaged in colorful conversations with Jefferson's guests. She often positioned him at one place in a room at a reception or ball and then, in a subtle way that few recognized, casually brought people over to meet him and chat with him. He could glow as both the very public secretary of state and the private Mr. Madison, with Dolley helping along via her party work and dinner planning. People who had only read about Madison or only knew him slightly came away with a whole new, and better, opinion of him at these parties, thanks to his wife.

Edward Coles, a young Virginian neighbor of Madison's who later became his secretary, had the same negative opinion of Madison when he first met him, as did many others. Outlining the dour secretary of state, he began,

> I never knew him to wear any other color than black; his coat cut in what is termed dress fashion; his breeches short, with buckles at the knees, black silk stockings, and shoes with strings or long fair boot tops when out in cold weather, or when he rode on horseback of which he was fond. His hat was of the shape and fashion usually worn by gentlemen of his age. He wore powder on his hair, which was dressed full over the ears, tied behind, and brought to a point above the forehead, to cover in some degree, his baldness. . . . [He had] a small and delicate form, of rather a tawny complexion, bespeaking a sedentary and studious man; his hair was originally of a dark brown color; his eyes were bluish, but not of a bright blue; his form, features and manner were not commanding.

Then Coles changed his tone. "But his conversation [was] exceedingly [commanding] and few men possessed so rich a flow of language, or so great a fund of amusing anecdotes, which were made the more interesting from their being well timed and well told. His ordinary manner was simple, modest, bland and unostentatious, retiring from the throng and cautiously refraining from doing or saying anything to make himself conspicuous," he finished.[48]

One thing Madison did accomplish at parties was to renew acquaintances from old political wars. He became friendly with John Quincy Adams, the son of his archenemy, President John Adams. A friend told John Quincy Adams in 1805 that "Mr. Madison had expressed himself in very favorable terms of me . . . it was his wish to employ me on some mission abroad, if I was desirous of it."[49]

And, of course, too, Dolley worked very hard to give President Jefferson the chance to socialize with as many important people as possible and to show off his many skills, which ranged from a sharp sense of humor to a far-ranging intellect (she also cautioned Jefferson that it was perfectly all right to wear his slippers when he met people during the day at the White House, but he could not wear them at receptions, balls, and dinner parties). Dolley worked with a large staff of servants to make certain that the parties featured fine food and lots of it, served in covered dishes. Guests ate everything from steak to ice cream, with plates of nuts (George Washington loved nuts and had bowls full of them all over the President's Mansion and at his home in Mount Vernon). Jefferson had brought a famous French chef over from Paris to be the full-time White House chef, and this impressed all. Small musical groups and orchestras played at the receptions. Everybody danced to the music that wafted through the president's home until the late hours of the evening (except Dolley, who did not dance).

Friends told Dolley that she was overdoing it as the official White House hostess. There was no reason to work so hard to aid Jefferson in his official life. Her long hours and hard work would wear her out and make her ill, they insisted. The more they criticized her work habits, the harder she worked. Dolley did not like being told what to do or how to do it. "I have had a lecture from S.L. on seeing too much company, and it brought to my mind the time when our Society [Quakers] used to control me entirely, and [kept] me from so many advantages and pleasures. Even now, I feel my ancient terror revive in a great degree," she wrote.[50]

Some, especially the British, hated Dolley's parties. Mrs. Mary Bagot, who arrived with her husband, the British minister, after the War of 1812, wrote that "the women usually sit stuck around the room close to the wall. The men— many of whom come in boots & perfectly undone & with dirty hands & dirty linen—stand mostly talking with each other in the middle of the room Tea & coffee & afterwards cld punsh [*sic*] with glasses of Madeira & cakes are handed around & by ten o'clock everyone s dispersed," and she added after another party that Mrs. Madison was "very stupid and very much stared at."[51]

Mrs. Bagot did not have much love for anyone in America. She was invited to an elegant dinner party at the home of James Monroe, and she wrote that it was "the dullest dinner I ever was at. Mrs. Monroe gives herself the airs of a fine lady without succeeding in being one."

But Mrs. Bagot went to them all and was impressed at the number. She wrote home that the White House levees run by Mrs. Madison were packed with partygoers who seemed to have a wonderful time, even if she did not. The Washington party schedule, she wrote, "ran from twelve at noon to 12 at night without intermission—tired to death."[52]

The gourmet dinner tables that Dolley set were famous throughout the country. Dr. Samuel Mitchill, a guest, described one meal in his diary, "dined at the President's ... rice, soup, round of beef, turkey, mutton, ham, loin of veal, cutlets of mutton or veal, fried eggs, fried beef. A pie called macaroni, which appeared to be a rich crust filled with the stribbions of onions or shallots ... tasted very strong and not very agreeable, ice cream very good, crust wholly dried, crumbled into thin flakes ... very porous and light, covered with cream-sauce—very fine. Many other jimcracks, a great variety of fruit, plenty of wines, and good."[53]

Congressman William Plumer said that Dolley's tables in the White House were filled with delicious sweet meats and, he added with great enthusiasm, very fine French wines. He laughed that Dolley's French wines were far more successful than Jefferson's French politics.

Another enchanted guest, Dr. Mannassah Cutler, a congressman from Massachusetts, wrote of Dolley's parties, "an excellent dinner. The round of beef of which the soup is made is called boulli. It had in the dish spices and something of a sweet herb (basil) and garlic kind, and a rich gravy. It is very much boiled and is still very good. We had a dish with what appeared to be cabbage, much boiled, then cut in long strips and somewhat mashed; in the middle a large ham ... the dessert [was] apple pie in the form of half of a muskmelon, the flat side down, tops creased deep and the color a dark brown."[54]

She was also adamant about serving American food in an American setting for dinners with foreign diplomats. If they wanted to know America and Americans, she contended, they needed to know how Americans ate.

She was criticized by one diplomat, British minister Augustus Foster, for a meal that he sneered at for being "more like a harvest home supper than the entertainment of a Secretary of State." She snapped back, with a little smile on her lips, socialite Margaret Bayard Smith wrote, "as profusion so repugnant to foreign customs arose from the happy circumstances of the abundance and prosperity of our country, she did not hesitate to sacrifice the delicacy of European taste for the less elegant but more liberal fashion of Virginia." (Not everyone was pleased. New Hampshire senator Jeremiah Mason dined with the Madisons and wrote to his wife of Mrs. Madison that "she by no means answers my ideas of a high-bred, courtly woman.")[55]

The Madisons also made friends at casual visits to homes on weekend afternoons. The Madisons and their hosts would sit outside in good weather, lay in hammocks, eat apples and other fruit, chat about events and friends, drink tea, and later go inside for a casual dinner, sometimes in a formal dining room and sometimes in a kitchen, where a large table would be set up. Sometimes, in late spring and summer, people would eat a makeshift dinner at a picnic table in the yard.[56]

Or a woman would invite seven or eight women to her home in the afternoon for drinks and then, later, a dinner. Informal afternoon and evening soirees, with just a dozen people, were also popular. Many Washingtonians would go to the local military barracks on weekend afternoons to listen to bands play. They would go with other couples or meet other couples at the concerts.

Dolley re-created Washington's social world back home at Montpelier in the summers when they lived there, hosting long strings of parties, receptions, and balls, and inviting dozens of people to stay over at their home for as often as they wanted. British foreign minister Foster, as an example, stayed for an entire week one summer. She wrote at the end of the summer of 1807 that "we have had, my dear, a constant round of relations and neighbors to visit us, so that I have been unable to steal an hour for writing."[57]

People loved to go riding on horseback, or in carriages, because the new capital was such a beautiful place, a newly carved, bucolic Garden of Eden along the Potomac. "Conrad's boardinghouse . . . was on top of the hill, the precipitous sides of which were covered with grass, shrubs and trees in their wild uncultivated state. Between the foot of the hill and the broad Potomac extended a wide plain, through which the Tiber wound its way. . . . Its banks were shaded with tall and umbrageous forest trees of every variety, among which the superb Tulep-Poplar rose conspicuous; the magnolia, the azalea, the hawthorn, the wild rose and many other indigenous shrubs grew beneath their shade, while violets anemonies and a thousand other sweet wood flowers found shelter among their roots, from the winter's frost and greeted with the earliest bloom the return of spring. The wild grapevine climbing from tree to tree hung in unpruned luxuriance among the branches of the trees and formed a fragrant and verdant canopy over the greenward, impervious to the noon day sun," wrote one resident.[58]

The idea of a "dancing assembly," or club, so popular in both New York and Philadelphia, caught on, too, and hundreds of Washingtonians joined the one that opened there in 1802. The dances were usually held in public rooms of the new hotels. They were run by Captain Thomas Tingey, an audacious naval officer. Dolley ran them with Tingey and tried to make them as lively as the ones she attended in Philadelphia.[59]

Being the president's hostess was not an easy task. Jefferson paid little attention to the women of Washington when he took over the reins of government. He held dinner parties that were attended almost entirely by men. It wasn't until the second year of his first term, at the urging of Dolley, that he began to invite women to his dinners. Those dinner parties that Dolley supervised for men were a struggle for her, too. To fit his egalitarian image, President Jefferson insisted that all of his dinner parties be held at a round table so that no one in attendance would feel socially slighted by where he sat at a rectangular table. Jefferson invited only Federalists to one dinner party and only Republicans to another to avoid the same kind of arguments and rancor that existed in the halls of Congress. The dinner ordinarily started in late afternoon, but after the meal, guests lingered, at Jefferson's insistence, and talked diplomacy and politics well into the night, all under the watchful eye of Dolley and the White House staff.

Dolley was the official hostess at all the dinner parties, whether all-male or mixed company. In addition to being at the dinner, she met guests before and after the meal to fraternize. "[We] sat in the drawing room with Mrs. Madison and her sister, whose social disposition soon made us well acquainted with each other," said one woman guest at a White House dinner.[60] She also served as hostess each New Year's Day, when Jefferson, with her husband at his side, flung open the White House doors for a day-long reception for anyone in town who wanted to socialize with the president. It was "a festal day in high style," wrote Congressman Cutler. "Mrs. Madison wore a headdress like a white turban."[61]

Another problem Dolley had at the beginning of Jefferson's term, and in her own household, was that few of the congressmen brought their wives to live with them in Washington. In many years, there were only twenty or thirty congressional wives in town. In 1801, just seven congressmen of 130 representatives and 34 senators brought their wives to the capital. The women stayed for the fall and winter and went home with their spouses in the spring. Dolley had to make certain that all of them were invited to the White House, and the Madisons' home, as frequently as possible and that she befriended them so that they would feel comfortable in this new and growing city far from their own homes, family, and friends. It was not easy.[62]

Dolley also went out of her way to create a large social community in Washington that included not only elected representatives, government workers, and diplomats but also local residents, regardless of their line of work. She had maps drawn of residential areas and made up long lists of citizens whom she invited to different parties. She and her husband were seen throughout Washington. They rode around town in an easy-to-spot, elegant, horse-drawn, dark-green coach with silver monogram *Ms* on each door, glass windows, and venetian blinds, plus candles for nighttime traveling. They stopped at the homes of different friends, traveled to Alexandria and Georgetown, and made social connections everywhere. Dolley was convinced that merging the residents, government officials, and visiting diplomats was the best way, the only way, to create a vibrant social life in the nation's capital.[63]

She enjoyed acting as the president's hostess but, always with an eye to friendship and diplomacy, moved aside when Jefferson's daughters were in town. Whenever his girls, "Patsy" (Martha) and "Polly" (Maria), visited the White House, Dolley had them join her as hostesses for the evening, stepping back whenever the president introduced them to friends, permitting the president's family to shine.

Dolley liked the president's two daughters, whom she had met after her marriage to Madison, and renewed her friendship with them as soon as they visited Washington. The girls, used to the quiet life of Monticello and its environs, were overwhelmed by the high society of the capital, with its well-dressed diplomatic corps and army of lobbyists. They were nervous at meetings with people and at dinners and balls they were invited to, so Dolley decided to take them under her wing and went everywhere with them. She introduced them to everyone she knew, took them on tours of Washington and nearby Georgetown, and with her grace and charm enabled the girls to feel as comfortable as if they were home on the lawns at Monticello. Mrs. Madison went further. She told the girls that if they needed any shopping done in Washington, if they needed anything at all in the capital, she would be glad to do it for them. It was the least she could do for old friends, she told them, and she was never annoyed at their letters seeking clothing, jewelry, or other amenities. Merchants often talked of her happily shopping for the girls and then sending goods to them at Monticello via couriers or by carriage.

The process was simple. The girls wrote Dolley Madison directly, or they wrote their father. In the fall of 1802, for example, Martha Jefferson wrote the president, "Dear Papa ... will you be so good as to send orders to the milliner—Madame Peco, I believe her name is—through Mrs. Madison, who very obligingly offered to execute any little commission for me in Philadelphia, for two wigs of the color of the hair enclosed, and of the most fashionable shapes." Dolley was always glad to do it, no matter where she was living. In 1805, when she was recovering from knee surgery in Philadelphia, Jefferson's daughter asked her to buy some things for her there. She did not send any money, so Dolley just paid for them herself.[64]

Jefferson never thought twice about asking Dolley to go shopping for his family. When Virginia, the president's granddaughter, was going to be married, he asked Dolley to shop not only for her wedding gown and other garments but also for jewelry, trinkets, and clothing for the entire Jefferson family. She and a servant spent several days in shops in Georgetown and Washington completing the job.[65]

All of this work never kept Dolley from her family life. She took care of her husband and took extra care of her rambunctious teenaged son, Payne, who, like his father, always tended to be sickly. Midway through Madison's two terms as secretary of state, in July 1804, the worried Dolley took her ill son, upon whom she had doted all of her life, back home from Washington, hoping that the fresh air and forests of their plantation at Montpelier would help him recover from his latest malady. "We go to Montpelier this week. Payne continues weak and sick; and my prospects rise and fall to sadness as the precious child recovers or declines," the very worried mom wrote her sister.[66]

Dolley usually arranged three or four dinner parties a week for the president with a dozen or so guests, in addition to receptions and balls. Jefferson was criticized for his numerous and elegant dinner parties, but he ignored his critics. He saw his many parties as instrumental in creating relationships with government officials, diplomats, and politicians that were outside the staid and somber hallways and chambers of the Capitol building: "I cultivate personal intercourse with the members of the legislature that we may know one another and have opportunities of little explanations of circumstance which not understood, might produce jealousies and suspicions injurious to the public interest," he said, defending his dinners.[67]

Dolley's events were quite popular, and the president, and the Republicans, urged her to host more. She did. By the end of that first year in Washington, she was hosting some event just about every night at the White House and sometimes as many as three events during a single day. She was also always at the White House for state dinners, official visits, and holidays. She kept busy and kept smiling through it all, no matter how arduous the work became. She wrote her sister with a smile, "The Fourth of July I spent at the President's, sitting quite still, and amusing myself with the mob."[68]

Everybody was charmed by her. Dolley dressed well and was intelligent, witty, well read, and politically attuned to whatever issues were being debated at dinners or parties. There was something more to her success, though. One man summed it up best when he said that "there is something very fascinating about her—yet I do not think it possible to know what her real opinions are. She is all things to all men."

The women loved Dolley even more than did the men. She held numerous soirees just for women at the White House and at her home. These were soon called "dove parties," and the highlight of each was a lottery in which a woman holding the lucky number won a prize. Then, as the women departed, each received a personal gift from Dolley that they treasured.

The capital's cleverest politicians listened carefully to everything she said and to what people reported that she said to them. They were impressed. Dolley Madison talked as easily about foreign-trade problems as she did about the latest fashions, yet did it so casually that years later, President Martin Van Buren said of her that "Mrs. Madison's talk at dinner is free on any matter."[69] John Quincy Adams was equally enchanted. He wrote of Dolley that "she was the most beautiful lady in America . . . the liveliest, endowed with the greatest charm, and possibly was the most sensible."[70] Mrs. Margaret Bayard Smith added that "Mrs. Madison was a foe to dullness in every form, even when invested with the dignity which high ceremonial could bestow."[71]

And Mrs. Madison got along with everybody. She found it just as easy to befriend people from Philadelphia as from Washington and from France as from America. She wrote her sister about her relationship to a French woman she had just met in 1805, "She is good natured and intelligent, generous, plain and curious—we ride, walk together and visit sans ceremony. I never visit in her chamber but I crack my sides laughing—I wish I could tell you on paper at what. She shows me everything she has and would fain give me everything." Later in life, she explained her personality traits to her niece. "I might fill a volume in favor of always sustaining a sweet and gentle character."[72]

One of her strengths as a hostess for the president, and hosting her own parties at the Madison home, was her exuberant fashion styles and her height. At 5'8", she was taller than almost all of her party revelers. She also loved to wear high, brightly colored feathers stuck into a turban or a speckled band that wrapped around her forehead. The feathers made her appear to be seven feet tall and her height, and the feathers, made it easy to find her. This was critical in large parties in which several hundred people mingled. Where was the hostess? She was right there, over to the right, in the orange feathers. It helped her maintain her status as the capital's social lioness.

In addition to the parties at the White House, Dolley was invited to dinner parties all over town, along with friends, such as Margaret Bayard Smith. The editor's wife wrote that in just a single two-week period, she dined at the White House twice, three times at the home of the French minister, four times at the home of the Navy Yard commandant, and once at General John Mason's. She also wrote that she had tea at someone's home three or four times, went to several balls, and declined invitations to others. Yet Dolley's social card was even more active than Smith's.

Dolley met people who arranged their invitations within the hour. Thomas Jefferson's son-in-law was one of them. He had been to numerous rather-loud parties and teas on a visit to Washington before visiting Mrs. Madison, alone, in her home. She relaxed him completely. He told his wife he had been charmed by the "sweet simplicity of Mrs. Madison's conversation."[73]

Dolley understood that her work as hostess made it possible for Jefferson to succeed as president and for her and her husband to win over many Washingtonians as new companions. They had many friends—government workers—when they arrived because Madison had been his friend Jefferson's chief political adviser in setting up the new government. Jefferson had appointed most of the people whom Madison had recommended, and Madison knew these men as officials and as friends. Once the Madisons arrived in Washington, they made more friends.[74]

Dolley also learned the talent of gliding out of an awkward situation. One night the White House threw a party for the chiefs of Native American tribes. She was upstairs in a lounge when she saw, in a mirror, the image of one of the chiefs, staring at her. She simply moved to the side of the room and pulled on a bell chain to summon an aide. He arrived and learned that someone had given the chief, who was very apologetic, the wrong directions to find a room, and he wound up in Dolley's. She thought nothing of it and told friends it was a fine "frolick." She always spoke fondly of the chiefs and referred to them as "the Kings and Princes."[75]

She socialized in unpleasant circumstances, too, such as the time after Aaron Burr, the vice president, shot and killed Alexander Hamilton in a duel. She wrote about the duel "with horror" in several letters and told friends her husband and the president had been badly shaken by Hamilton's violent death.[76]

No one knew more than Dolley that James Madison was not an easily lovable man, on the surface. He was a "gloomy, stiff creature," said one woman. Another woman who met him said he was "mute, cold and repulsive." British minister Foster wrote that he found James Madison "a little man" and a "disputatious pleader" on issues.

Dolley's job was to get them to see the man she loved or, through osmosis, to like him because they liked her. It worked. British minister Foster, for instance, did not care for Madison but was astonished by his wife. "[She is] a very handsome woman and tho' an uncultivated mind and fond of gossiping, was so perfectly good tempered and good humored that she rendered her husband's house as far as depended on her agreeable to all parties."[77]

Dolley Madison also arrived on the public stage at the time of the demise of the Republican woman, the wife who ran her husband's farm or business, an important job, for years during the revolution and then was returned to the domestic sphere when the conflict ended. Without power or influence once again, the Republican woman faded from the footlights and turned to the new job of raising her children as worthwhile members of the "new" democratic country. By 1800, when Dolley arrived in Washington, that era had ended. Women had changed by then, and Dolley's activities at the center of the public stage did not cause anyone to denigrate her, as they might have twenty years earlier. Mrs. Madison was also not just a well-dressed, bejeweled, wealthy woman, a natural source of envy to ordinary women. Dolley had become so opulent, so ostentatious, that she had soared well past all the boundaries and was beyond envy. She had become a dazzling, iconic figure, something special. And, very carefully, she did all of that in the guise of an ordinary woman, a loving wife, reflecting the glory of her husband and never seeking it for herself. Everyone liked that about her. It was a skill that she carried all of her life.

Mrs. Madison's gossiping helped her. She had the same gasping astonishment at scandalous news as many of the other women in Washington and chatted about salacious news she heard with many. This had started when Madison was just a congressman in Philadelphia. An older diplomat had been caught in bed the wife of a servant. Dolley wrote friends that the husband had "caught the old goat, with his wife, and in not the most decent situation. So the fellow very politely took him by the nose and saluted him with kicks [at] the corner of the street."[78]

In another example, Dolley led the critics of French minister general Louis-Marie Turreau, a bald, red-faced man with a prominent moustache and a reputation for brutality in the French Revolution. He had a lovely wife whom all admired and felt sorry for because of the gossip attached to their marriage. Dolley chortled about Turreau and his wife. She said she heard "sad things" about the marriage and "that he whips his wife and abuses her dreadfully. I pity her sincerely; she is an amiable and sensible woman."[79]

But the talkative Mrs. Madison usually had nothing but good things to say about members of the diplomatic corps. She saw all of them as both men and women and as diplomats, and she joined her fellow Washington ladies in admiring them. She was one of the first to be smitten by the new diplomat from Prussia, Baron Freidrich Alexander Von Humboldt. Like everybody else, she thought he was just dazzling and was not afraid to say so. "We have lately had a great treat in the company of a charming Prussian Baron," she wrote. "All the ladies say they are in love with him, notwithstanding his want of personal charms. He is the most polite, modest, well informed and interesting traveller we have ever met with," she wrote her sister.[80]

But she could raise an eyebrow as fast as anyone in Washington when women appeared in extremely revealing dresses. An example of this was a ball at which Dolley saw Betsy Patterson Bonaparte of Baltimore, the American wife of Jerome Bonaparte, Napoleon's nineteen-year-old brother. Betsy wore a very revealing gown with a plunging neckline that was the talk of the town. Mrs. Bonaparte also enjoyed walking back and forth in the window of her bedroom during the day, with little on.

Even women thought that she was gorgeous; Phoebe Morris wrote, "I think I never beheld a human form so faultless," she said, and she added that Mrs. Bonaparte reminded her of Venus de Medici. "She is truly celestial, it is impossible to look on any one else when she is present."[81] One of the doyens of Washington society wrote that the ladies of the capital would have nothing to do with Mrs. Bonaparte until she "promised to have more clothes on."[82]

Dolley joined in the chorus of critics, nodding her head up and down in agreement with the conservative women who harangued the dazzling, young Betsy about her clothing, or lack of any. Dolley did this even though she, herself, was often admonished for her famous, daring, low-cut dresses and her absolute refusal to stick a handkerchief into the neckline of her dresses to cover herself up. And then, to show just how much she despised Betsy, she became one of the girl's best friends.

Dolley also gossiped about sad events, such as slave attempts to force Martha Washington to give them their freedom, promised by President Washington before he died. "Mount Vernon has been set on fire five different times & tis suspected some malicious persons are determined to reduce it to ashes. Oh, the wickedness of men & women," she wrote her sister.[83]

One thing Dolley also did as the wife of the secretary of state and the hostess of the president, which she rarely talked about, was put up with two seemingly hopeless medical hypochondriacs. Jefferson was famous for his migraine headaches, either real or imagined. He could be bedridden for a day with a headache, or promptly quit work at nine or ten in the morning to lie down for hours until his headache passed. Dolley's husband was the same. He appeared in good health, although very thin, but he complained endlessly about different ailments he claimed that had made him ill. If it wasn't a headache, it was a stomachache or malaise or aching joints. If everybody else had the flu, he soon had the flu. If a cold was infecting many Washingtonians, Madison suddenly came down with a cold. He would wake up in the morning and announce his daily ailments to his wife.

His friend Jefferson had been aware of his supposed and actual health problems for years. Madison had delayed or canceled visits because of his ailments. Madison was notorious for cancelling meetings because of headaches and colds that might not have been as severe as he described them.[84]

William Thornton wrote Madison just before his arrival in Washington that "the President . . . wrote me that you had long experienced delicate health and he even feared a change of climate might finally be requisite," and then, to make him feel better, he bragged that "I do not think I ever enjoyed such health as since my residence in this place . . . you will have cause to pronounce it one of the healthiest places in the world."[85]

An example was January 1800, a few months before Madison traveled to Washington to become secretary of state. He wrote that morning that "my health still suffers from several complaints, and I am much afraid that any changes that may take place are not likely to be for the better."[86]

Dolley did her best to put up with the medical ailments, and sudden moods, of both men. Their ailments upended many of her plans and sometimes threatened to unravel her composure. She once wrote her sister in frustration that her husband was suffering from yet another bad cold and was unable to work. Sick, he still wanted to visit Jefferson, but, Dolley said, the president was sick with one of the headaches that many claimed were psychosomatic.

Whenever either man was ill, it was Dolley's job to rearrange the schedules of the State Department or the White House that day.

Dolley realized that Washington was a brand-new town in a vast, quiet countryside, a long ferry ride across the Potomac from the nearest community, Alexandria. The social life she was building at the White House, with its receptions, dinners, luncheons, and balls, was really the only social life most Washingtonians had. The social bashes were also a way in which they could meet each other and then invite each other to their own parties and dinners. She encouraged foreign ministers to host balls and parties (all learned the latest Russian waltz at a Russian embassy ball). Mrs. Madison also encouraged the leaders of the new Navy Yard to throw large parties. Dolley held it all together. These were mostly people who had moved to Washington from somewhere else to work in the federal government. They did not know anybody in the capital, except Dolley. Through Dolley's effort for Jefferson at the White House and for her husband at their residence, they got to meet each other and make friends. She was building a vast social network that would grow as the years went by and help everybody who moved to the nation's capital.

Why did she, a new arrival, have this opportunity when it had been denied to women for hundreds of years in national capitals? The answer was timing and the wide wave of change, change of all kind, that was sweeping across America. Dolley and her husband moved to Washington when it was a brand-new city, just a little over a year old. Unlike New York's and Philadelphia's societies, it had no social traditions or prominent hostesses. Anyone who wanted to work hard to be anointed the leading social queen of Washington could do so; Dolley did. That convergence of her willingness to work hard to be the social queen, and the vacancy at the top of the social hill, combined to make her the unquestioned leader of Washington society. She recognized that the new capital needed a social life. The social life that worked well in New York and Philadelphia did not work that well in Washington. It needed change, and she brought that. Socializing in Washington was sometimes accomplished outdoors because the spring, summer, and fall seasons were warmer in Washington than in New York and Philadelphia. New buildings housed new parties. New homes were the residences of new social queens. As the city grew, the social life grew, and it grew in the fashions of the new city on the northern banks of the Potomac. Dolley not only recognized that but also helped lead the growth of the social world. She and "her set" were in charge of the social universe for sixteen long years and made that world the new social life of the American capital. It was enormous change in Washington, and in the United States, and Dolly was there to not only organize it but also engineer it.

She was always at President Jefferson's beck and call, any hour of the day. Once, she was sitting at home and received an urgent message, delivered by a runner, that the president required her and/or her sister Anna to rush to the White House right away to help him entertain a group of people that had women in it and whose arrival he had never anticipated. She was there in a few minutes, looking lovely, and she charmed everybody.

In those first years in Washington, as the town was growing quickly, many congressmen and senators brought their wives, sisters, and daughters to the White House to meet Jefferson, who was always eager to see them; and each time Dolley was summoned, literally on a moment's notice, to greet and mingle with the women and arrange entertainment for everybody. She loved it and they loved her.[87]

The Madisons met everybody through the president. Many of these people became political allies and friends. An example was Samuel Harrison Smith, a journalist. Jefferson recruited him from Philadelphia and brought him to Washington to become the editor of the capital's first Republican newspaper, the tri-weekly *National Intelligencer*. Smith arrived with his wife, Margaret Bayard Smith, a social gadfly, and his cousin. The Smiths were well connected. He was the son of a member of the Continental Congress and a hero of the Revolutionary War, where he saw service as the colonel of a Pennsylvania regiment. Editor Smith's wife was the daughter of a revolutionary hero, member of the Continental Congress, and speaker of the Pennsylvania Assembly. Her cousin was James Bayard, a US senator from Delaware. She was a writer who contributed stories to several magazines and later authored two novels. She and her husband had become extremely close friends of Thomas Jefferson when he lived in Philadelphia as vice president. The pair was devoted to making Jefferson a success as president and Washington socialite. They had money, lots of it, and spent it to create a far-flung social life for themselves that included Jefferson and his political associates. Mrs. Smith was the head of the Washington social set outside of the White House and had enormous influence in town.[88]

The Smiths were among Washington's social elite. They lived in a large home, drove a handsome carriage, had a stable full of horses, and bragged about their large wine cellar. Dolley and Margaret, with many common interests, became fast friends. One of the reasons the two women were such good friends was the fact that Margaret had been married just seven months when she met Dolley. She was a newlywed. Mrs. Madison herself had been married for only four years when they met. Each woman also saw the other as a social butterfly who could help them meet hundreds of new friends in Washington. The Smiths were close to the president, too, and often dined at the White House. The editor and his wife also visited Monticello numerous times as Jefferson's guests during his two terms as president. Samuel Smith, in his newspaper columns, always supported the Jefferson government and Madison's work as secretary of state. He was a hopeless cheerleader for the president and the Republican Party and had famously written that "the triumph of Republicanism is the triumph of principal."[89] The editor ran the election results in any race in which Republicans were victorious. In 1801, he hailed George Clinton's election as governor of New York as a "demonstration of complete triumph of Republican principals [in New York]."[90] Smith's columns on the strength of the Republicans were numerous, and when he was not clapping his hands for it, other writers were.[91] Smith also made it a practice to reprint pro-Republican columns from other newspapers to buttress his own support of the party. In 1801, for example, he ran a column from the *Examiner* in which the pro-Republican editor urged party members not to be complacent about the upcoming elections just because in recent years they had achieved electoral dominance over the Federalists.[92]

And, again and again, year after year, he reminded his readers that the Republican Party had been created to protect them against ogres like the Federalists. "Republicanism rests in equal rights for the people . . . [the party] represents their will" was a well- and often-used line of his.[93]

When Smith tired of those bombasts, he would find statements he did not like in Federalists' speeches or newspapers and attack them as treasonous. He wrote of one newspaper editorial, "a more naked condemnation of the Republican structure of government cannot be found."[94]

Mrs. Smith was enchanted by Dolley, as all seemed to be. "I have become acquainted with and am highly pleased with her; she has good humor and sprightliness, united to the most affable and agreeable manners," wrote Mrs. Smith, who knew everybody, and knew them well.

The Madisons also socialized with cabinet members, who introduced them to top-ranking government workers. They met senators from one state who introduced them to senators from another state. Congressmen, especially those who knew Madison from his years in the House of Representatives, flocked to the Madisons' home, bringing their friends.[95]

In just a few months in Washington, Dolley Madison had become a very famous and important person, the flamboyant wife of the secretary of state and the hostess for the president. No one expected her to create or fulfill either role. She not only met the social challenges but also met them in her own style, making the role of the president's hostess, the First Lady, an important one in the country. She was an important cog in American life. By the end of the spring of 1801, Dolley's first at the capital, people treasured her.

In Dolley, they had something new and different, someone who was exciting. She was the fashionable wife of the secretary of state and the president's more-than-capable hostess, all at the same time as she was an intelligent and sociable woman whom all enjoyed being with and a fashion plate like no one else in the United States. Dolley worked very hard at her new roles and succeeded. She had become special, and quickly so. By the time Christmas 1801 arrived, Dolley was an established part of Washington, just as the Supreme Court or Congress, but a lot more fun.

7

THE MADISONS AS SOCIAL LIONS

hile Mrs. Madison had to overcome social barriers, her husband had to establish himself as secretary of state, which was not an easy task. He had to work with the president on foreign matters, think like the president, and yet offer advice that the president often did not want to hear. He was the foreign-policy face of the administration in an era in which interest in foreign policy dominated discussions between public officials and the people and took up much space in newspapers (most newspapers devoted their entire first news page to foreign news). At the same time, though, Madison found himself practically drowned by the ordinary details of his job, the mountains of paperwork he had to sign and the seemingly endless meetings, at the office and at home, with the never-ending stream of officials whose letters he had to read and people whom he had to meet.

The secretary not only met with foreign ministers but also had to read hundreds of reports and letters from diplomats, American ambassadors abroad, and American politicians; write and sign letters; hold departmental meetings; and meet with the president, just about every day. He worked in a very small State Department that, including him, had only nine employees. His offices were enlarged as the summer of 1801 began, when Jefferson moved the State Department and the War Department into a new building just one block from the White House and two blocks from Madison's home. Madison let one of his eight clerks go in a budget move and had to run the foreign policy of the United States with only seven aides. Some worked hard, and some did little work and infuriated him. Most were holdovers from the days of Adams's secretary of state Thomas Pickering and did not care for Madison, but he kept them on.[1]

The stress of the job, he told his wife and colleagues, threatened his very weak physical constitution: "I find myself in the middle of arrears of papers, etc. etc. which little accord with my unsettled health," he wrote one man. Two months later, he used the work as an excuse for not keeping up correspondence with a friend. "Having brought with me to this place a very feeble state of heath, and finding the mass of business in the department at all times considerable, swelled to an unusual size by sundry temporary causes, it became absolutely necessary to devote the whole of my time and pen to public duties, and consequently to suspend my private correspondences altogether, notwithstanding the arrears daily accumulating," Madison said.[2]

And, on top of all that, he remained President Jefferson's closest friend and chief political adviser. He was, with Secretary of the Treasury Albert Gallatin, a member of a small "brain trust" given the responsibility of both helping the president navigate through the often-treacherous waters of congressional liaisons and presenting a positive and productive image of the president to the public. In this capacity, Madison saw the president regularly, dined with him, attended parties with him, and socialized with him at every opportunity. Then, when both were at home in the hills of central Virginia during the oppressively hot Washington summer, they continued to see each other because they lived only twenty miles apart. The two men had one of the closest relationships in United States history. Politicians and newspaper editors of the early nineteenth century generally agreed that Madison was just a cabinet officer to the rather glorious, at times, President Jefferson. The president disagreed, and told everyone, upon leaving office in 1809, that the presidency Madison was inheriting was one that he himself had carved out with equal hard work, and grace, as the president himself.

There were drawbacks to his success, though. Madison was under enormous political pressure on all sides from diplomats, senators, congressmen, and members of the press. Everybody lobbied him for something and at parties he was constantly accosted by people looking for a favor. It drove him and his wife crazy. At the start of the summer of 1804, tired of the politics, Dolley wrote, "I feel now very impatient to be in Montpelier."[3]

Jefferson's other close adviser was Gallatin of Pennsylvania, an economic wizard. Gallatin, who came to America from Switzerland in the 1780s and had a slight French accent, was a controversial figure. He had at first supported the very unpopular Whiskey Rebellion in 1794, earning the condemnation of George Washington and Alexander Hamilton. He was later elected to the US Senate, but the Federalists hated him and conspired to get rid of him by convincing the Senate that Gallatin had not been in the United States long enough to hold a Senate seat. Gallatin seemed to have proved that he had lived in Pennsylvania for over fourteen years, but the Federalists had documents that seemed to show it was just nine years. There was a furor over the issue, and the Federalists finally ousted Gallatin from his seat by a straight party vote of 14–12 in the Senate chamber. The angry Gallatin came back a year later as a congressman and served three terms before Jefferson named him as his secretary of the treasury. While in Congress, Gallatin convinced that body to establish a special committee on finances that exists to this day.

His primary job as head of the Treasury Department, Jefferson told him, was to reduce US debt from its staggering $80 million. He would do that. Along the way, though, Gallatin became a vital part of the Jefferson team, working with Madison and others to promote foreign policy, internal affairs, and, in 1803, both the Louisiana Purchase and the fabled expeditions of Lewis and Clark. His wife, Hannah, the daughter of wealthy Commodore James Nicholson, became a close friend of Dolley Madison's.

Thomas Jefferson saw his election in 1800 as a dramatic new chapter in American politics. The party that he and Madison had created nearly a decade ago had been quite successful in both elections and public policy. They had ousted the Federalists after twelve years of dominance, and now they were a new party in a new capital. The Republicans quickly dismissed campaign charges by Federalists that Jefferson's election would bring on "Civil War . . . [where] murder, robbery, rape, adultery and incest will all be openly taught and practiced, the air will be rent with the cries of distress, the soil will be soaked with blood and the nation black with crimes."[4]

It was a significant step in the political world. The changeover from Federalist to Republican government not only showed that new ideas were acceptable to the people but also that shifts in government could be achieved without the bloodshed that usually accompanied them in other countries.

Late on the morning of his inauguration, March 4, 1801, Thomas Jefferson dressed and then left the boardinghouse where he had been staying for two weeks to go to the Senate chamber to be inaugurated as the third president of the United States. This time, under the Republicans, there was little pomp and ceremony. Both George Washington and John Adams had arrived at their inaugurations in expensive carriages following long processions through large crowds. Jefferson was different. The new president walked from the boardinghouse several blocks from the capital, accompanied by an escort of Alexandria militia, a group of congressmen, and two of John Adams's outgoing cabinet officers. As he approached the Capitol building, a squad of local militia fired off a series of cannon to honor him. He arrived, the *National Intelligencer* said, "plain, dignified and unostentatious."[5]

The speech itself was delivered in the Senate chamber, jammed with onlookers for the occasion. Those there estimated that nearly one thousand government officials, senators, congressmen, judges, and members of the general public were in the semicircular hall, with its vaulted roof, to hear the address. Many had to stand along the rear walls, pushed tightly against each other. Men wore their finest suits and ladies their most expensive dresses. Those there felt they were not only a part of politics but a part of history. Mrs. Margaret Smith wrote that she had "this morning witnessed one of the most interesting scenes a free people can ever witness. The changes of administration, which in every government and in every age have most generally been epochs of confusion, villainy and bloodshed, in this our happy country take place without any species of distraction or disorder."[6]

Jefferson was pleased with his speech and the reception of it by the loudly cheering crowd of people in the Senate. Cannon had boomed again when he walked out of the Capitol. "We can no longer say there is nothing new under the sun," he wrote Joseph Priestley.[7] "For this whole chapter in the history of man is new. The great extent of our Republic is new. Its sparse habitation is new. The mighty wave of public opinion which has rolled over it is new. But the most pleasing novelty is, it is so quickly subsiding over such an extent of surface to its true level again. The order and good sense displayed in this recovery from delusion, and in the momentous crisis which lately arose, really bespeak a strength of character in our nation which augurs well for the duration of our Republic; and I am much better satisfied now of its stability than I was before it was tried."

When Jefferson took office, he told the nation, in a lofty inaugural address, that the government he headed would work for everybody. "We are all Republicans; we are all Federalists," he said.[8] "If there be any among us who would wish to dissolve this union, or to change its republican form, let them stand undisturbed as monuments of the safety with which error of opinion may be tolerated where reason is left free to combat it." He added, too, that the change was radical: "The revolution of 1800 was as real a revolution in the principles of our government as that of 1776 was in its form; not effected, indeed by the crowd, as that, but by the national and peaceable instruments of reform, the suffrage of the people," he said.

Jefferson had started his administration on a high political road, forgiving his enemies and optimistically hoping for universal support in his programs. It was a dream, but a dream worth having, he wrote friends. "The mass of our countrymen who call themselves federalists, are republicans . . . to restore the harmony which our predecessors so wickedly made it their object to break up, to render us again one people acting as one nation—should be the object of every man really a patriot. I am convinced that it can be done."[9]

No one was prouder of the address than his best friend, Madison. He was "the chosen one," the hand-picked successor to Jefferson. The two men had started a new, Republican government that would last for sixteen years and, with their friend James Monroe, for eight more years following Madison, a total of twenty-four years.

Jefferson was proud of Madison. He wrote Madison of his selection, and of his entire cabinet, that "my association in those whom I am so happy as to have associate with me is unlimited, unqualified, and unabated. I am well satisfied that everything goes on with a wisdom and rectitude which I could not improve [on]. If I had the universe to choose from, I could not change one of my associates to my better satisfaction."[10]

His soaring inaugural address pleased many, especially since Jefferson heralded a new moment in American history—the transition of the federal government from one political party to another. He received hundreds of notes of congratulations, but perhaps none pleased him more than one from a man writing on behalf of friends in Providence, Rhode Island. "It is with no common joy that we behold at the head of the American administration a man whose uniform political integrity—whose correct and extensive information and affectionate concern for the happiness of the human race will add to the splendor and secure the stability of [government]," it said.[11]

Maybe Jefferson was both a Republican and a Federalist, but others were not. The country was split into two political groups, attached to one party or the other. That brought about the first problem Madison faced with Jefferson, and that was job patronage. Jefferson was bombarded with requests for federal government jobs from relatives, neighbors, and friends. Without shame, people with no skills at all even sought out judgeships and cabinet posts. All took the view that when the Federalists were in power, the Federalists were awarded all of the government jobs, so now Republicans, in power for the first time, should have all the jobs. This is exactly the mind-set that Madison and Jefferson wanted to change, but they quickly found that they could not.

Shortly after his inaugural address, Jefferson wrote James Monroe that he would get rid of Federalist leaders "whom I abandon as incurables and will never turn an inch out of my way to reconcile." His chest beating was encouraged and applauded by the editors of Republican newspapers, who howled for the heads of Federalist officeholders. The editors wanted them all fired.[12] Yet the president saw no need to fire men who did their job well. "Good men, to whom there is no objection but a difference of political principle, are not proper subjects of removal," he said.[13]

Jefferson told Madison that he wanted to boot out of office anyone President

Adams had named after he learned he would not be reelected, especially judges he had appointed in his last days, the "midnight" appointees. Following that, men found to be grossly incompetent had to be removed. Jefferson also wanted to remove hundreds of federal marshals from lower-ranking jobs in states and cities. Jefferson removed all Federalist district attorneys. He felt good about his work on the federal level and was surprised to see that Republicans at lower levels were far more bitter about Federalist officeholders there. Jefferson was deluged with letters from Republicans in cities and even tiny villages in which party members complained that their work was curtailed by the enemy—Federalists still in office. Those men, the Republicans insisted, had to be replaced with people from their own party and right away. These complaints came from both individuals and the media. The New York *American Citizen* called the remaining Federalists in state and county jobs "culprits" and urged the president to fire them. "If this should not be the case, for what, in the name of God, have we been contending?" the editor asked.[14]

This was Jefferson's dilemma. Just as he was opposed to the Federalists running the government without any Republican help, he was opposed to that same practice by his own party, now in power. In theory, a government with all Republicans was politically ideal. In practice, it was not. In the first few months, Jefferson, and Madison at the State Department, fired about 10 percent of the Federalists and replaced others who retired over the next eight years. At the end of two years, about half of the Federalists had been let go. In 1803, 158 of the 316 jobs in Jefferson's control were held by Republicans. The Federalists held onto 132, and 26 independents were awarded the rest. It was nearly an even split in patronage and, when it was done, Jefferson was pleased. Madison, in charge of a much smaller State Department, fired one Federalist, kept seven, and hired Republicans when jobs opened up over the next few years.

Madison had personal problems, though, that took up much of his time. He was the stepfather to a temperamental, impulsive, wasteful, and unambitious son, Payne, whom Dolley loved with her whole heart and soul. The reckless and irresponsible Payne caused endless problems for his parents. Dolley did nothing about them, leaving discipline and guidance to her husband. Payne was a handful. The Madisons sent him off to boarding school, hoping that a strict academic and living environment would help him. It did not, and Madison always fretted about him. Right after his first term as secretary of state ended, he wrote his wife, back at Montpelier for a visit, a veiled letter in which he told her that "Payne is well, and I am endeavoring to keep him in some sort of attention to his books."[15]

Payne would be a problem for the Madisons all of their lives. His tempestuous behavior knew no bounds, and he never had any regrets about what he did or whom he hurt. Boarding schools did not help. Life in the White House did not help. Nothing helped. Payne's problems would grow in frequency and seriousness as he aged. He could not maintain relationships with women, had few friends, and fell prey to alcoholism and gambling. He felt no sense of responsibility and never worried about trouble because his mother would always come to the rescue. The Madisons' problems with their son lasted a lifetime and grew worse.

The secretary of state had become an important cabinet office right away in the first Washington administration. The new American government had to design its foreign-policy goals, pick sides in disputes between countries, fund an army and navy that had to be expanded, and, on many levels, assure the people that the United States could not only defend itself in another war but also prevail if one broke out.

America was seen as a huge and powerful international political player because of its size, its trade, and its trading potential, and because of the universal respect it had earned for its conduct during the revolution. It was not just an extra country on the globe; it was big and it was special. It was unprecedented, too, because of its unique new system of democratic government and officials elected by the people. The United States was, right away, a colossus in world affairs.

Thomas Jefferson had served as an effective first secretary of state during Washington's administration. Washington had taken a bold step in 1793, turning down a plea by France to join it in its war with England, which was rapidly becoming one of the greatest conflicts in European history. Washington issued the "neutrality proclamation," that stated that while he would like to help out France, in this particular instance he chose not to do so. As a former general, he knew that European wars lasted decades, and he did not want the brand-new United States tied up in a long conflict. Wars were costly and the United States was just getting on its financial feet after the imposition of a new tax system. Great Britain, not France, was America's major trading partner, and to declare war against the British Empire would be harmful to the American economy; it might be crippled for years. He also understood that when you choose one side in a war, you gain the other as your enemy. He did not want that. The president especially did not want England as his enemy. He did not want ten thousand or more young American men pulled into a war far from home, for goals that did not involve the United States.

Washington's refusal to go to war caused great controversy at home, where many Americans favored the French and still hated the British from the revolution. Washington was castigated by many. He held his ground, though, and the uproar subsided and the United States remained free of any foreign involvement.

In his farewell address, Washington again warned Americans against all "foreign entanglements." Yet, just several years later, the United States was nearly plunged into the French-British war by President John Adams. France had been harassing US merchant ships, so Adams asked the French to cease. They did not. Adams, unwilling to commit the nation to a large war, then sent a small flotilla of frigates to protect American shipping. They became involved in a shooting war with French ships that attacked the merchant ships on the Atlantic Ocean, in the Mediterranean Sea, and in the Caribbean Sea. One battle on the high seas followed another; ships were sunk and men were captured or killed.

Adams, pushed hard by the British to do something against the French, then called up nearly ten thousand troops to form a new army that he might need to send to France to fight the French on their soil. He asked George Washington to come out of retirement to lead the new army; he did. Washington, then sixty-five years old, insisted that his Revolutionary War chief of staff, Alexander Hamilton, be named his top aide to help him run the army. Adams agreed. All of this was quickly termed the Quasi War, a war without a real war. This started a firestorm because Hamilton, the former secretary of the treasury, was a key player in national politics. The controversy amounted to nothing, though, when the Quasi War ended. Adams did not really want to send an army to France, and Napoleon saw no real purpose in fighting skirmishes on the seas with little reward. A peace treaty was signed that pleased most Americans and the French.

The Quasi War had lingering effects, though. It pulled the United States into a small war in defense of foreign-policy goals. It showed the nation, and the world, that the American government had no hesitation to call up a large army and go to war. It showed, too, that the next administration would have its hands full in trying to forge an alliance with its former enemies of Britain and France. America was now suspicious of France. Would the French retaliate for the Quasi War? Would they send ships and troops to their Caribbean holdings, such as the island of Santo Domingo, as a jumping-off point for a war with America? What would England's stand versus the United States be now? How would America view this new, and very large, step into world affairs?

This was the mood of the State Department that Madison inherited. With the president, he had to work with French ministers, British ministers, and others to maintain commerce with both nations and all the other European countries. They had to keep up tenuous relations with both countries and guard themselves against intrusions by each in the Americas. England and France had possessions in the Caribbean; both coveted the port of New Orleans, now in

Spain's hands, and the Mississippi River valley. If either gained control of New Orleans, it could bottle up American transportation on the Mississippi and in the Gulf of Mexico, which was not an endearing prospect.

Madison's job was to steer the country through what could be perilous waters in foreign policy that kept changing. Every country's policy changed as new monarchs took over, dictators seized power, and governments fell. Napoleon, especially, had huge goals in Europe and did not hesitate to start wars against other countries to gain them. (Jefferson never trusted Napoleon and as late as 1809 told then president Madison that the French emperor was not a reasonable man. "His policy is so crooked that it eludes conjecture," he said.[16]) England had to protect its far-flung world interests within its wide empire. Countries in northern Africa had strengthened themselves to participate in trade with European countries and America. Nations in Central and South America were getting stronger and testing their own policies with the United States to the north and Europe to the far east. The international political world that Madison stepped into was full of hot rivalries, old feuds, and new troubles. The new secretary of state, who had to lead the country into this very large world in his tiny new offices a block from the White House with just a handful of aides, would have his hands full.

In his first year in office, Madison found himself thrust into the middle of a testy political dispute in the Caribbean. Black political leader Toussaint L'Ouverture had led a successful revolt that ended the institution of slavery there and forced the French forces in Santo Domingo to abandon the island (over twenty thousand troops died from diseases in the conflict). It was a brutal rebellion. A resident there said that there was "murder everywhere" and that victims had "eyes pulled out . . . others had their eyes and ears cut out," and that the French fought "tigers and not men."[17]

The war sent the Caribbean into panic. The governor of the nearby island of Trinidad, Thomas Picton, declared a national emergency. He said that his island had "imported numbers of slaves from other islands, that operates to increase an evil which already gives cause to serious alarm" and asked US ships to bring food and supplies to his island.[18]

The United States favored the end of French power on the island but did not favor further slave revolts, fearful that they would set an example for slaves in America. So Madison decided to steer a neutral course concerning Santo Domingo. He established American neutrality there, defended American shipping in the area, and worked to keep the French happy but nervously happy. The real fear Madison had was that France, under the leadership of the aggressive Napoleon, would now move on to a treaty with Spain and somehow wind up with the city of New Orleans. Since the late 1790s, it had been rumored that Spain had ceded New Orleans back to France, but the deal had been kept secret.[19] French ownership of land in the American south also raised the specter of Napoleon attacking America from that position and drawing the country into another war. Madison could not know that through an incredible turn of events soon to transpire, the secret deal between Spain and France would lead to the Louisiana Purchase and the doubling of the size of the United States.

The new secretary of state became involved in a dangerous foreign-policy dispute at his very first cabinet meeting, May 15, 1801, just two weeks after he and Dolley had arrived and unpacked their bags. Under President Adams, America had paid $80,000 a year in tribute to the Barbary States in north Africa, headquartered in Tripoli, whose armed pirate ships patrolled the Mediterranean Sea and the Straits of Gibraltar. The money was to help the pasha of Tripoli restrain pirates in the area from attacking American shipping. The pasha told Jefferson that he was enraged that America had paid Algiers more than him and upped his fee to $225,000. Jefferson, furious at the shakedown, refused to pay and convened his cabinet to discuss the issue. He wanted to go to war with the pirates, but in such a way that the United States was not dragged into the Napoleonic Wars. He could, of course, have followed George Washington's example and declared war on the Barbary pirates in his role as commander in chief of American armed forces, but he decided that including his cabinet in the decisions was a better idea.

Jefferson's bold plan was to send a fleet of warships to the Mediterranean to protect any US merchant ships sailing those seas from the Barbary pirates. If attacked, the American ships would attack back and sink them. Madison agreed completely with Jefferson's policy; the United States could not be pushed around, and especially by a pasha whom the pair saw as a third-rate military gadfly. All in the cabinet agreed, and within weeks, a fleet of thirty warships set sail for the Mediterranean. By the beginning of summer, six frigates were sailing alongside American merchant ships past the Rock of Gibraltar and through the Mediterranean, past fleets of Barbary pirate ships that did not attack—for now.

Madison was careful in his work with the Barbary pirates. He saw them as not only an incendiary group that would engender deep passions in the United States but also a group that could cause the United States to overstep its policy boundaries in its treatment of them. He had warned Jefferson about heated foreign-policy issues in 1798: "the management of foreign relations appears to be the most susceptible of abuse, of all the trusts committed to a government, because they can be concealed or disclosed, or disclosed in such parts and at such times as will best suit particular views and because the body of the people are less capable of judging and are more under the influence of prejudices, on that branch of their affairs, than of any other. It is perhaps a universal truth that the loss of liberty at home is to be charged to provisions against danger real or pretended from abroad," he said.[20] The disputes with the Barbary States would grow and become even more heated over the next few years, though, bringing Jefferson and Madison to a critical decision about the pirates later.[21]

At the same time that Madison worried about Napoleon and the island of Santo Domingo, he went about the rather ordinary business of meeting different ministers, conferring with other cabinet members, and finishing the work of the State Department. He labored to build good relations with the powers in Europe, such as the always-testy Great Britain and France, and worked with African countries, plus Spain and Portugal, to keep American shipping prosperous.

Madison read the letters that poured in from all over the country. One day, he received an explosive letter from Virginia newspaper writer James Callender, who fumed in heated and insulting language that President Jefferson had refused to give him money to pay a fine that he had incurred during the Adams administration, when the federal government under Adams brought him to trial and had him jailed under the volatile, anti-press Alien and Sedition Acts. Jefferson had promised to pay his fine, but had not. Where was the money, Callender asked. Why had Jefferson abandoned him? He was angry. Madison read the letter, shrugged, and did nothing about it. Later, an angry Callender would become involved in one of the great scandals in American history, a scandal that would target Jefferson and question his morals.

Madison also worked with Jefferson and the cabinet to keep America out of foreign wars, did not sign treaties that might bring the nation into conflicts, and was eager to establish good relations with key countries. Jefferson and Madison, remembering Washington's noninvolved foreign policy, and its success, said they were determined, like him, to make certain that America never became an international bully or was dragged into foreign wars through overly friendly ties with some nations.

With its shores protected from foreign attack, and free of costly wars, the United States could move on to prosper at home. Madison and Jefferson sought favorable trade agreements, reasonable import taxes on foreign goods, and a brisk export-and-import trade with foreign merchants. Jefferson's new federal government, eager to give states and cities more power and to limit the power of the federal offices, flourished.

Madison could sit back, as he did later, and write of any nation (Spain, in this instance) "that she dreads ... the growing power of this country and the direction of it against her possessions within its reach. Can she annihilate this power? No. Can she sensibly retard its growth? No."[22] He added that any country that tangled with America would bring on itself "prematurely the whole weight of the calamity which she fears."

At the end of his first year in office, James Madison had built a strong and productive State Department, served his friend the president well as a political adviser, and, thanks to his wife, become one of the most sociable figures in all of Washington.

Life was good for the great little Madison.

8

THE LOUISIANA PURCHASE

America Becomes A Giant

*T*he deplorable condition that Napoleon's army found itself in following the Yellow Fever epidemic in Santo Domingo led French military advisers to suggest a second army be sent to put down the slave revolt, but this new force had to be just as large as the first. A frustrated Napoleon, overwhelmed with affairs in Europe, declined. What was the loss of one island, anyway? He still owned just about all of the middle third of North America and was about to gain New Orleans from Spain, and perhaps Florida, too.[1]

James Madison and Thomas Jefferson worried about Napoleon. Madison had studied the history of French government over hundreds of years. Napoleon was aggressive and had proved that again and again in his wars in Europe and in the Caribbean. Madison did not want Napoleon on the American doorstep. It made no sense for Napoleon and France to retain that land; it hampered a substantial amount of good that America could do in that area; and it completely stifled American growth.

A substantial amount of American shipping went down the Ohio and Missouri Rivers to the Mississippi, and then down to New Orleans and the Gulf of Mexico. France could bottle that up in New Orleans. Since the end of the revolution, tens of thousands of Americans had migrated into the Mississippi valley and saw that area as their new, permanent home. Many of them wanted to keep on moving west. They did not relish having the French there as their neighbors, either.

And Jefferson had never trusted the French emperor and tended to side with whoever was opposed to him. He wrote Ambassador Robert Livingston in 1802 that "we must marry ourselves to the British fleet & nation."[2] He told the ambassador that "it appears evident that an unfriendly spirit prevails in the most important individuals of the [French] government towards us."

Jefferson had the American press on his side. Some Republican newspaper editors even urged Jefferson to declare war on France rather than have them sit in the Midwest.[3]

One editor asked readers why Napoleon wanted to hang onto Louisiana anyway. "Its cultivation will be carried on by slaves . . . felling all those trees and forests is hard work and [not suited to slaves]," he wrote, adding that the only real resource to be obtained in Louisiana was lumber. The thousands of slaves needed there would also drive up the price of slaves throughout the South.[4]

Many in America, like Jefferson and Madison, did not trust Napoleon. One American diplomat at The Hague reminded newspaper readers that Napoleon had kept eleven thousand French troops in Bavaria long after he had promised to withdraw them. His attack on Switzerland worried many, too. "The recent attack made by Bonaparte upon the liberties and independence of the Swiss cantons here naturally made a strange impression on the inhabitants of this country," the diplomat wrote.[5]

Napoleon did not trust the Americans, either. For years, his ministers, speaking for him, complained that Americans, public and private, had helped the rebels defeat the French in Haiti. French minister to the United States general Louis-Marie Turreau, wrote Madison in 1806, "but it was not enough for some citizens of the United States to convey munitions of every kind to the rebels of St. Domingo, to that race of African slaves, the . . . refuse of nature; it was moreover necessary to injure the success of the ignoble and criminal traffic by the use of force. The vessels destined to protect it [rebellion] are constructed, loaded, armed in all port of the union under the eyes of the American people and the federal government itself and that government does not forbid it."[6]

President Jefferson, who intended to buy New Orleans with money secretly authorized by Congress, was careful, though, not to provoke a confrontation with the always-edgy Napoleon. "We are endeavoring [with Congress] . . . to obtain by friendly negotiations a reasonable redress of the injuries," he wrote of one dispute with France.[7]

Madison was a pit bull in his determination to rein in French ambition in the Louisiana Territory. In 1802, he warned through the French ambassador that "France cannot long preserve Louisiana against the United States." America would ally itself with Great Britain against any aggression by France in the Americas. Madison told the French ambassador, who relayed the message to Napoleon, that Americans were swarming into the Mississippi region. Already, in just fifteen years, the population of Kentucky alone had leaped from 60,000 to 250,000 settlers. More were on the way. Pioneers were traveling across the mountains to the Mississippi region from the east in lengthy parades. They came by wagon, by horseback, and on foot. There were single men, married couples, and families, large and small. They set up tiny villages and soon had churches, general stores, and newspapers. They were there to stay, and when they looked west, they did not want to see the French staring back at them. It was not a tiny trickle of people; it was a tidal wave. The new settlers included slaves, merchants, riverboat captains, sailors, farmers, and new waves of immigrants. The American government could not possibly rein in that horde, and they were restless people. They would create their own country in those territories, and France would not be able to handle them, Madison insisted. He wanted to annex New Orleans, but he also wanted to stop bloodshed in any uprising that the Americans who lived there already might start against Napoleon and any army the French emperor brought to the region.[8]

Besides, Madison felt just like his countrymen who lived there. He had been a champion of the Mississippi region as part of America all of his life. Nearly twenty long years earlier, he had written James Monroe that "the use of the Mississippi is given by nature to our western country, and no power on earth can take it from them. Whilst we assert our title to it therefore with a becoming firmness, let us not forget that we cannot ultimately be deprived of it and that for the present war is more than all things to be deprecated [for it]."[9]

Madison told Napoleon that France, concerning Louisiana, had "to be resigned to [America's] future power, to conciliate them and acquire the merit, useful in other respects, of acceding to that which the force of events will give them in spite of us."[10] That force of events, Madison knew, had helped to bring about the rapid population of the huge French territory in the plains west of the Mississippi by Americans. Who else would move there? How long would it take until hundreds of thousands of Americans began claiming land and building homes in the territory, regardless of what the French claimed?

Added to all of that was Florida. France had been trying to purchase Florida from Spain for a year. If France owned Florida, and its ports, it could increase its trade in the Caribbean and surround America west and south. Spain was in no hurry to sell Florida to France, however. It was not willing to sell the peninsula to the United States, either, despite repeated offers. For the next sixteen years, American politicians would argue that if the United States had the Louisiana Territory in the west, it had to have Florida in the South to be complete. One New York newspaper letter writer said that the only tract of land the United States received from Napoleon was New Orleans. He said the

Americans needed to purchase Florida, too, and that "a few millions of dollars will be appropriated for another bargain."[11]

Secretary of State Madison kept up his pressure on Napoleon throughout 1802 and 1803, and also bitterly condemned the Spanish for shutting the port of New Orleans for a period of time and halting the export of American goods that had been carried down the Mississippi by hundreds of boats. To Madison, there was no future with either Spain or France in charge of New Orleans.

The Secretary of State told the US ambassador to Spain Charles Pinckney that the Mississippi was "everything" to merchants who shipped their goods on it. "It is the Hudson, the Delaware, the Potomac and all the navigable rivers of the Atlantic States formed into one stream."[12] He let ambassador to France Robert Livingston know that he wanted to be tough with Napoleon. He asked him to warn France that Napoleon had to watch out not only for official American anger but also for anger by the large militia forces in the Mississippi region, which the US government could not control. "There are now ... not less than 200,000 militia on the waters of the Mississippi, every man of whom would march at a moment's warning to remove obstructions from that outlet to the sea, every man of whom regards the free use of that river as a natural and indefeasible right and is conscious of the physical force that can at any time give effect to it. France [needs] to cure the frenzy which covers Louisiana."

By the spring of 1803, opposition in America to French power in the Mississippi area had become fierce. The newspapers were filled with stories that the militias might take matters into their own hands. One congressman even demanded that. He rose in the House chamber and said that President Jefferson should raise an army of eighty thousand militiamen, paid for with a $5 million appropriation from Congress, and that they should, as soon as possible, march on New Orleans and seize the city.[13]

There were stories, too, repeated again and again, that the British Navy might sail to New Orleans and occupy it, an act that would start a war with France. In the middle of all this, Madison, at Jefferson's request, sent officials to Paris to purchase the city of New Orleans from France.

The negotiators, which included James Monroe, loaded down with lengthy and detailed instructions from Madison, were startled when French foreign minister Charles Talleyrand offered to sell them the entire Louisiana Territory, the whole one third of what is today the continental United States. The previous day, as they were preparing for the meeting, an angry Napoleon, disgusted with defeats in Santo Domingo, pressured from England, and squabbling with the United States, in particular with Madison, became fed up with Louisiana. At the same time, he knew that he needed money, and quickly, to fight a war that he foresaw breaking out with England. Talleyrand and his other ministers turned down the American offer for New Orleans and suggested it buy the entire territory. The Americans did not have high regard for Talleyrand; few did. The British duke of Argyll said he was "the most disgusting individual I ever saw. His complexion is that of a corpse considerably advanced in corruption."[14] They had to do so right away, the French insisted, or Napoleon, known for his flighty behavior, might withdraw the offer.

Monroe wrote Madison that he was not only stunned by the offer but also certain that Jefferson could buy the whole territory for very little money. In the end, the sale price was just $15 million, an average of just four cents an acre.

How could the United States buy the territory, though, and how? There was nothing in the Constitution that enabled the president to purchase land. Jefferson assumed that Congress could do so, but that would consume months of talks and committee meetings, and Napoleon might withdraw the offer. The president wanted to buy Louisiana by himself, but thought that he needed a constitutional amendment to do that, which would be a very time-consuming process. He sought the advice of Madison, who wrote the Constitution. He agreed that an amendment was required. Others did not. Several people told them that this was the same thing as a treaty, and George Washington's assumption of foreign-policy and treaty-making powers gave Jefferson the right to buy Louisiana. It not only was perfectly legal but also would speed up the entire process and set a good precedent for future purchases and/or acquisitions of land for the United States.

John Quincy Adams, who studied the Louisiana Purchase, wrote that what Jefferson did was open the door to permit the United States to purchase territory "to the two polar circles and from the straits of Hudson to the Straits of Magellan."[15] He added, though, that he admired Jefferson for doing it. "The merit of its accomplishment must ever remain as the great and imperishable memorial of the administration of Jefferson." Another critic, the loquacious John Randolph, bristled at the entire idea but admitted to others that the president had the power to buy the territory. "Foreign relations, every matter short of war and even the course of hostilities, depend upon him [the president]," wrote Randolph of executive power.[16]

Jefferson also believed that the Constitution was a flexible document, meant to be interpreted as the years went by. So he built upon Washington's "implied powers" of the Constitution to give himself the power to consummate the deal to buy the Louisiana Territory from France. The Constitution, he felt, was a document that had to change as the American people changed and circumstances changed, and it had to protect and preserve the rights of those people. That came later. Others insisted that the Constitution was a large house with many rooms, and designed for many additions. It was meant for the people it served, no matter when they lived, and was not a legal shrine for the ages, hopelessly stuck in time. When John Jay lobbied for passage of the Constitution at the New York State ratifying convention in 1788, he told opponents of it that it could always be changed, with amendments, when the people did not like it. He told the head of the opposition group that, as a mother would tell her children about food, "try it, you'll like it." If they did not like it, Jay assured opponents, they could change it with amendments. It could be changed, too, by interpretation by the president and Congress. Now, Jefferson believed that he could change it, and he did. He loathed those who "look at Constitutions with sanctimonious reverence and deem them like the Ark of the Covenant, too sacred to be touched."[17]

Madison, like everybody else, was ecstatic that the United States was able to buy all of Louisiana and double its size with one stroke of the president's pen. He told Monroe, "the purchase of Louisiana at its full extent . . . is received with warm, and, in a manner, universal approbation. The uses to which it may be turned render it a truly noble acquisition. It may be made to do much good, as well as to prevent much evil."[18]

Settlers began to arrive in New Orleans and the rest of the purchase lands immediately, and in great numbers. Hundreds of vessels began to call at New Orleans as a port, Haitian planters moved there, followed by freed blacks from that country. The port thrived. Within five years, New Orleans would double in population and the rest of the territory would grow at a rapid rate.[19]

Jefferson dispatched his aide Meriwether Lewis and William Clark to explore the new Louisiana Territory with a team. The pair conducted an extensive and harrowing exploration of the region, taking their crew all the way to the Pacific Ocean. The historic Lewis and Clark expedition not only gathered much material for the future development of the region but also garnered enormous positive publicity for the Jefferson administration. It was seen as a tremendous accomplishment for the country by the people, regardless of their party.

The acquisition of New Orleans, the Mississippi valley, and the plains of the Midwest also satisfied the growing yen for more territory. In 1803, Americans were in the early stages of an obsessive need to consume their continent, to seize all the land and natural resources they could, by any means necessary, in a feeling of manifest destiny that at times knew no limits. The opening up of the vast Louisiana territory gave all of these people a "second" country to roam through and live in. It also gave America, now twice as large, a wider window on the west. The west was filled with Mexico and its territories, such as Texas and

California. Now, with Louisiana, the United States could look out at what was left of the rest of the land that led to the Pacific Ocean.

All of that dreaming was made possible by the acquisition of Louisiana. It was not only a deal that dramatically increased the size of the nation but also a deal that set the nation on a new course of exploration and occupation, a new course that would eventually lead to the Texans' war with Mexico and their freedom and entry into the United States as a state, and the 1846 war with Mexico that gave America the rest of Texas, New Mexico, Arizona, and California. All of that was due to the acquisition of Louisiana, and that was due, in a large measure, to Madison and his State Department.

The Americans were not responsible for the Louisiana Purchase; Napoleon was. If the French emperor did not need money and did not have a war on his doorstep, he would not have sold the land. The Americans, though, were responsible for acting swiftly to make certain the deal did not fall through. Madison, in particular, got much credit for forcefully explaining to the French that they had no realistic future in America and should get out of the country, if they could. He opened the door that Napoleon soon jumped through.

Madison did not lose a breath in discussing the enormity of the Louisiana Purchase; he wanted to expand upon it. He agreed with opinions from Albert Gallatin around that same time that the nation should buy Florida. The large peninsula of land, then owned by Spain, plus Louisiana, would spread the boundaries of the United States from Maine to the Caribbean Sea and westward to the plains territories and Rocky Mountains, making the nation huge. "If West Florida can alone be purchased, it is certainly worth attending to," Gallatin wrote.[20] "The possession of West Florida ... is extremely important and that if it can be obtained, it ought expressly to include all the islands within twenty leagues or such distance as to include those which are marked on the map."

Throughout all of this, Madison and the Republicans were sometimes under attack by the Federalists, who chortled at every party victory they achieved. "The election of four Federalists to Congress was certainly a great mortification to the plotting of the [Republicans] of Virginia," snickered one Federalist Party leader after elections in 1803.[21] The Federalist newspapers constantly blasted the president. "Mr. Jefferson, however, has gratified his ambition! Our devoted country has lost her honor! Honest men will judge the lesser evil," wailed the editor of the *Washington Federalist* newspaper.[22] And, of course, the Federalists never considered the Republicans as a party at all, just political interlopers. "Federalism is Patriotism," snapped a Federalist editor.[23]

Jefferson, who had insisted the press could say whatever it wanted when he attacked the Alien and Sedition Acts just five years previously, now bristled at

Federalist newspaper attacks on him and Madison. "The artillery of the press has been leveled against us," he wrote. "The offenders have therefore been left to find their punishment in the public indignation."[24]

9

THE VETERAN
SECRETARY OF STATE

he social life at the White House had improved considerably by the spring of 1805 and the beginning of Jefferson's second term. By then, hundreds of new women, married and unmarried, had moved to Washington permanently. These were married women who wanted to be with their husbands, married women who worked for the government or for companies that did business with the government, or single women out to find husbands. Most lived in Georgetown, just a few miles from the White House. The single women helped to balance out what had been an overwhelming ratio of men to women in the capital and made it easier to run parties. More diplomats brought their wives, and also their children, to town with them from overseas cities. More taverns opened and prospered. Men enjoyed gambling and drinking, just as they did back home. More small orchestras and bands were available to play at White House functions, and Dolley hired all of them. They also played at the many more outdoor concerts that different governmental and civic groups had authorized. Music seemed to continually waft over the Potomac. There were more shops, in Washington as well as in Georgetown, where food could be purchased and dresses and suits of the latest fashion were available.

Dolley's love for her husband grew during her years as White House hostess. Everyone respected the deep admiration they had for each other, and few gossiped about all the time she spent entertaining men at the White House and the considerable time she spent with Jefferson. Her love for "the great little Madison" was exhibited in numerous notes she wrote him. In one, after she recovered from an illness, she wrote that "to find that you love me, have my child safe and that my mother is well, seems to comprise all my happiness."[1] She told him in 1805 that "your charming letter has revived my spirit & made me feel like another being—so much does my health, peace & everything else, depend on your affection and goodness."

Madison's love for his wife was evident to all. During Jefferson's second term, Dolley's knee was infected by a lump that soon burst open. Bandages did no good, and it was suggested that she go to a Washington doctor. He could not help her. So she went to a second doctor, and then a third, and then a fourth. None could treat her knee, which she suspected was affected by rheumatism. "Never had I more extreme pain in sickness," she wrote her sister.[2] "Dr. Willis bled me and mother Madison nursed and waited upon me with great attention and kindness." She was laid up in bed. "I write to you from my bed, to which I have been confined for ten days with a bad knee; it has become very painful and two doctors have applied caustic with the hope of getting me well, but heaven only knows. I feel as if I should never walk again," she wrote her sister in early summer. It was then suggested that Mrs. Madison travel to Philadelphia to see one of America's most respected surgeons, Dr. Phillip Syng Physick. She wanted to go alone, but Madison insisted that he accompany her and stayed with her for a month in Philadelphia, their old home, as she recovered from a unique treatment of caustics that saved her knee. He ran the State Department from their rooms. Part of the treatment was putting her injured knee into a splint for several weeks. During this time, Philadelphia was hit with another epidemic of the Yellow Fever, the same disease that had taken the lives of thousands in a previous scourge in 1793. Madison, remembering the tragedies of that epidemic, immediately moved his ailing wife out of their house and found quarters in a neighborhood on the far outskirts of the city, a long distance from the areas where residents were being laid low by the fever. "I feel as if my heart was bursting—no mother, no sister—but fool that I am, here is my beloved husband sitting anxiously by me and who is my unremitting nurse," Dolley wrote. She worried about her husband more than herself, even though it was Dolly who was sick. "One night on the way he was taken very ill with his old complaint, and I could not fly to aid him as I used to do. Heaven in its mercy restored him the next morning," she said. Dolley was also pleased that in every letter President Jefferson wrote to her husband, he always ended it with a line expressing his deep concern for her health.[3]

While they were in Philadelphia, the Madisons were deluged with well-wishers. "I have had the world to see me, everybody of every description. We have invitations from one dozen gentry," wrote Dolley.[4]

A few weeks later, after her husband returned to Washington to resume his work in the government, Dolly, still stranded in Philadelphia with her bad knee, wrote in her journal how much she missed him. "What a sad day! I found myself unable to sleep, from anxiety for thee, my dearest husband. Detention, cold and accident seem to menace thee," she said, and she added that in a dream she saw Madison sickly, lying in bed, and wanted to reach out to him to make him better.[5]

Back in Washington, Madison spent time at the State Department and also spent considerable time trying to get their always-troublesome son, Payne, enrolled at a prep school in Baltimore run by Bishop John Carroll. He had seen the bishop and written him several letters. He thought the bishop's school would help discipline the rambunctious and irresponsible Payne. "A berth seems at last to be secured for our son & I hope it will prove a fortunate one," he told Dolley, ever hopeful.[6]

He wrote to her often. Madison fired off one letter as soon as he read in hers that she was blue. "The low spirits which pervade [you] affect mine," he said.[7] His love for her was constant. Once, when after returning to the White House in a crisis and leaving her behind, Madison wrote Dolley, "everything around and within reminds me that you are absent, and makes me anxious to quit this solitude . . . God bless you and be assured of my constant affection."[8]

Madison expressed his love to Dolley often; sometimes he wrote her the same day that he was back in Washington. An 1826 letter is a good example. He had been detained on business and wrote her that "it appears now not to be certain that I shall be able to get away even tomorrow. Every exertion however will be made to effect it . . . I cannot express my anxiety to be with you; I hope never again to be so long from you, being with devoted affection ever yours."[9]

Those who observed them saw it, too. Margaret Smith sat at the Madisons' table at the dinner following his inauguration as president later and marveled at how much the pair liked each other. They sat directly across from each other, she wrote, and dazzled the table.[10]

Dolly and her sisters, away from Washington, did not always enjoy the adulation of the public, which grew as the years passed. They sometimes found themselves with people they did not like who engaged them in social activities they did not enjoy. For example, Dolley's sister Anna Cutts visited Mrs. Henry Knox in Boston, the aging wife of Washington's secretary of war, and a chess fanatic whom she found "haughty" and hardly bearable. Mrs. Knox insisted that Anna play chess with her, morning, noon, and night. She "pins me to her apron strings," Anna wrote Dolley, and said playing chess with her was "doing battle."[11]

Dolley was forced to stage formal dinners at the White House, but at home she and her husband hosted casual dinner parties at which people stood and walked from room to room, mingling with whomever they found. Many political figures felt freer to talk at the Madisons' home. John Quincy Adams, who would be president himself one day, wrote that he found himself bored at many of Jefferson's dinners but enjoyed life at Madison's house. He said that he and James Madison enjoyed "considerable conversation . . . on the subjects now most important to the public" and that he found Madison friendly and accessible.[12]

Editor Smith and others all agreed that Dolley's idea of the open party and an invitation list that included as many Federalists as well as Republicans was a good one. Smith wrote his wife once that he enjoyed the mixed company, different policy discussion, and, he noted with pride, the seemingly inexhaustible supply of champagne.

Dolley's parties were so fabled that people who invited the Madisons to their own parties often apologized that they were nowhere near as wonderful as Dolley's. In 1807, Dolley wrote back to one apologetic hostess, "I must scold you my dear for doing such injustice to the interesting little party of last evening, as well as for supposing me unable to appreciate such society. During five hours I did not breathe a wish for a single addition to it, so learn to think better of your friend another time."[13]

Those who knew them in Washington agreed, though, that the Madisons were not one-dimensional, party-hearty stick figures whose lives consisted of dances and drinking. Dolley was a very compassionate person and grieved with others when they lost loved ones. Jefferson's daughter Maria died in 1804, and Dolley was crestfallen. "A letter from the President announces the death of poor Maria, and the consequent misery it has caused them all. This is among the many proofs, my dear sister, of the uncertainly of life. A girl so young, so lovely! All the efforts of friends and doctors availed to nothing," she wrote. She was jolted even more by the death of her young niece Dolley in 1806, telling her sister Anna, "I can hardly write you, so sick with grief [and] apprehension is my whole frame."[14]

Dolley mourned over loved ones who moved away from her. She was delighted that her sister Anna, to whom she was closer to than anybody except her husband, was married to Richard Cutts of Maine in 1804, but she missed her terribly. "One of the greatest griefs of my life has come to me in the parting for the first time from of sister-child," she wrote after the wedding, attended by Dolley and her husband. She wrote Anna a few weeks later, "to trace you and your dear husband in that regretted city [Baltimore] where we have spent our early years, to find that even there you can recollect with affection the solitary being you have left behind, reflects a ray of brightness on my somber prospects."[15] Dolley was so upset at her sister's departure that she literally shut herself up in her house for several days, until her husband convinced her to take a carriage ride with some friends. Each morning, relatives or friends visited her to console her on the loss of her sister, as if Anna had actually died.

And she was filled with joy when those in her family were happy. She was ecstatic over the birth of her sister Anna's daughter. "Joy! Joy! To you, my beloved brother and to you my dearest Anna ... I claim her as my pet, my darling daughter, I wish Payne could marry her at once to put it out of doubt her being my own," she said.[16]

Any small thing that her son, Payne, accomplished was heralded by the Madisons to all. They hovered over Payne in Washington, as they did at Montpelier, trying the best they could to restrict their rambunctious son. Their praise of him was endless and criticism minimal, even though his behavior seemed outrageous to many.

One thing Dolley did through Madison's first term as secretary of state was stick by her husband as American foreign policy continually encountered rough seas. Right from the start of his days as secretary of state, Madison had to worry about the Barbary pirates, sea-bound villains who seized American ships and crews in the Mediterranean Sea off the coast of northern Africa near Algeria, Tunis, and Morocco. They had been doing so since the 1780s, and the American government initially paid a ransom to get them back. Then the pirates, working under Algerian authorities, demanded yearly tribute to prevent attacks, and America paid one million dollars annually until Jefferson took office. The new president and the secretary of state refused to pay tribute and convinced Congress to assign a small fleet of six frigates to protect American shipping in the Mediterranean. The pasha of Tripoli promptly declared war on the United States.

The United States found an ally in the Kingdom of the Two Sicilies, King Francis, who offered American ships ports and supplies for the conflict. The Americans sunk a warship from Tripoli in the Mediterranean in 1801, but the Barbary pirates captured the American vessel USS *Philadelphia* in 1803 and held it. Forces led by Lieutenant Stephen Decatur sailed quietly into the harbor of Tripoli one night in 1804 and set fire to the *Philadelphia*, rendering her useless to the enemy. Several other attacks followed as the faraway war heated up. Then, in the spring of 1805, in a daring move, a force of US Marines, joined by Greeks and some mercenaries, marched across northern Africa from Egypt to Derna, a city in Algeria, and captured it in a surprise attack. Faced with an invasion of Tripoli itself by the marines and a plot to install his brother on the throne, Pasha Yusuf Karamanli hurriedly signed a peace treaty. Captured American sailors were released, the war ended, and peaceful American sailing in the Mediterranean was guaranteed, for the time being. Jefferson and Madison were hailed for their ability to win a war far from American shores, make substantial use of both the marines and the navy, and do all of that without getting American tangled up in the Napoleonic Wars just across the Mediterranean in Europe.

At home, the new secretary of state luxuriated in the victory while at the same time applauding the rapid growth of Washington, DC, and the safety of the city in which he and his wife lived. One of the reasons why people flocked there was the lack of crime. Despite its muddy streets, swampy backyards, and oppressive summer heat, it was a good place to work, live, and bring up children. Nobody was afraid to walk the torch-lit streets of the city after dark. The reason for that was the newness of the town, which just a few years ago had been a forest on the Potomac's banks. The criminal element had not yet had time to settle in. It gave all Washingtonians, especially the social-minded Madisons, the opportunity to create new lives for themselves, unencumbered by street crime, gambling dens, taverns, or brothels. Washington was not a city infected by sin, such as New York or Baltimore. For the time being, it was relatively pure.

People who lived there and worked there appreciated that innocence, that newness, because in the years 1800 to 1816, the Madisons' time in Washington, nearby cities had turned into colonial-era Sodoms and Gomorrahs with their murders and robberies. A perfect example was Richmond, Virginia, just ninety miles away, visited often by the Madisons and Jefferson. Richmond, on the banks of the James River, was, like Washington, exploding in size. It had become the capital city of Virginia in 1779 and had grown rapidly ever since, thanks to sea trade and the surrounding tobacco empire, doubling its population every ten years. In 1810, just after Madison became president, it had ten thousand residents. By then it had become a hotbed of crime. There were so many felonies that as early as 1782, local officials had petitioned the federal government for help in fighting crime. The officials cited the "nocturnal depredations and robberies which have been lately so much practiced among us."[17]

Richmond had been invaded by houses of ill repute, taverns, and gambling casinos, all legal at the time, and their operators preyed on local residents. There were several dozen houses of prostitution, where pretty, young women seduced men for money. The brazen prostitutes not only strolled on sidewalks to solicit business but also walked through the town's theaters, too. They plied their trade at local dance halls and casinos and convinced men to spend their winnings on them. The neighborhood that housed the whorehouses of Richmond, just off the main street in town, which ran along the James River at the bottoms of the city's hills, was nicknamed "Pink Alley," and there was so much crime there that a Richmond newspaper said of the area later that it was "so notorious in the police annals of Richmond as are the Five Points in the city of New York."[18]

Richmond was home to more than one hundred taverns. There was so much drinking in the city that someone even opened up a local brewery to meet the overflow needs of bar patrons. It was not uncommon for men of that era to drink seven or eight beers a night. It was neither prostitution nor drinking but gambling that led to the downfall of many in Richmond, though. There were more than one hundred storefront-style casinos in town and elegant casinos in the large hotels on Main Street. Cardsharps from around America invaded the casinos to take advantage of amateur gamblers and made a fortune off of them. The city also sported "lottery parlors" where residents could purchase tickets for the hundreds of lotteries in Virginia (New York City had two hundred lottery parlors by 1820), many of which were advertised in the local newspapers. Gambling was frowned upon by civic leaders and church officials, who successfully lobbied to get numerous bills forbidding it passed in the state legislature; they were all ignored. Constables refused to shut down casinos where inside they found military officers, wealthy merchants, ministers, and public officials playing cards and rolling dice.

The drinking, gambling, and prostitution in Richmond brought on a crime wave, spearheaded by robbers who beat up and killed their victims on the dark streets of the city. From 1802 to 1806, among Madison's first years as secretary of state, the number of crimes in the streets of Richmond quadrupled to nine hundred felonies a year, and it was estimated that 11.3 percent of the city's residents were victims of a crime each year. The newspapers wrote that three crimes were committed in town each day and a violent crime every other day. The crimes in Richmond reflected the crimes in all other American cities; critics said America was creating a "criminal class." In Pittsburgh, a newspaper editor even wrote that "we have in the very midst of us a population of the most abandoned kind."[19]

There was so much crime in Richmond that the city not only had to build a large city jail in 1800 but in addition constructed a large state prison, too. If you add up all the murders, robberies, and other crimes and divide that into the overall population of Richmond, in 1809, the crime rate in the year Madison became president was just as high it would be in the early years of the twenty-first century. Crime was rampant; it scared everybody.[20] One exasperated visitor to Richmond in that era threw up his hands and said "O! The wickedness and abomination of the little city."[21]

The story of crime in Richmond was little different than similar stories of crime in other urban areas, but crime had not yet reached the brand-new town of Washington, DC. Its taverns had just opened, its racecourse so far had a relatively short season, and gambling casinos had not yet arrived as a force. They would, as they did everywhere, but Washingtonians had time to create a workable and safe, pleasant society without looking over their shoulders for criminals. It gave the residents of Washington time to flourish properly—and they did.

And so did James and Dolley Madison.

10

THE BATTLES WITH BRITAIN

*T*he British government had plunged into a war with Napoleon and France and decided that no neutral nation could help supply France, its mortal enemy, with guns, ammunition and supplies, especially the United States. It ordered all France-bound ships from America to stop off at British ports first for inspection before continuing on to seaports on the French coast. The British did this under a little-used 1756 order passed by Parliament that permitted the search and seizure of any ship thought to be supplying an enemy. In a lengthy two-hundred-page memo, Madison decried the searches and seizures and, in what many believed to be irrefutable research and logic, brilliantly put together a pamphlet that proved the 1756 British orders illegal under international law. The British, of course, ignored him. In his 1805 inaugural address, Jefferson feared a war with England. He asked for increased fortifications at US seaports, more gunboats, the restoration of existing gunboats, a larger army, and the construction of more warships.[1] By 1807, Madison, within the administration, was calling for tough military action to stop the search and seizure of American ships and impressment of American sailors. He knew, though, and Jefferson knew, that the United States had a tiny navy, a small army, and little funds for military activity and could not engage the mighty British Empire in a war. In fact, a congressmen reported in 1810 that of the alleged nearly two thousand troops in New Orleans, just 950 were left—the rest had died, had deserted, or were too sick to fight. Madison learned from Naval Secretary Paul Hamilton that the navy was in no condition to fight anybody because Congress kept cutting its budget and forbid not only the building of new ships but also the repairing of old ones (the 1810 budget of $450,000 for ship repairs was cut down to $150,000).[2]

Constant US entreaties on seizures of American seamen and the stopping of ocean-going ships by the British fell on deaf ears. American officials were furious. If a war could not be fought, then what to do?

The answer was an embargo.

James Madison had embraced nonmilitary protests, especially trade embargoes, as successful means of retaliation against nations as far back as his college days. A scholar of military and monetary policies covering two thousand years, he told friends that the government could do more harm to opposing governments by restricting trade than it could with the firing of a thousand cannon. Hit them in the pocketbook.

He had been a firm supporter of the nonimportation acts of the colonies against England prior to the revolution, embargoes that did not last because the colonists realized they needed—and wanted—British goods. Madison was certain that if the colonists had stuck to their good intentions on the embargo, they would have prevailed. The colonists never did, though, so there was no supreme test.

Madison continually insisted that an embargo would hurt England, and hurt her badly. It would put tens of thousands of shipping business laborers out of work, kill the profitable business that Great Britain did with America, and, as icing on the economic cake, curb the economy of British islands in the Caribbean, which Madison claimed desperately needed American goods because so many essential goods there were imported.

The test he had hoped for in the 1760s would come in 1808. He convinced Congress to support an embargo on goods sold to England, confident that the economic wallop of the embargo would force Britain to leave American shipping and sailors alone. At first, most supported the embargo. Tens of thousands of people all over the country attended meetings to pass resolutions for it. In New York, Mechanics Hall was jammed with an overcapacity crowd of seven hundred people. Hundreds of additional attendees were packed into the lobby of the building and filled the staircases. Hundreds more shut down the city street in front of the building as they formed a large crowd to discuss the embargo.[3]

There was support in other places, too. Several Federalist newspapers even supported it. The *Washington Federalist*, used to criticizing Jefferson and Madison, backed them on the embargo and even ran a mathematically arranged formula, with tonnage charts, to show that Britain needed American goods far more than America needed British goods. The Maryland state legislature voted to support it and said that it was "a measure strongly characteristic of the judgment and wisdom of our national councils."[4]

Abroad, Ambassador Pinckney wrote to Madison from London that the early embargo was having its effects on England, where people realized they needed to import goods that could only be found in America, such as cotton and machines. The British press worried about the embargo, and so did some members of Parliament. He told Madison that the embargo was a great idea and that it would soon bring England to its knees.

Fueled by Pinckney's letter and Jefferson's support, Madison became even bolder. He told Congress that England had to stop its shipping policies immediately and that anyone who did not support the embargo, such as merchants in New England, were unpatriotic. He wrote several colleagues that the embargo would also prevent war.[5]

Gallatin, Madison's close friend, had his doubts, though: "Governmental prohibitions do always more mischief than had been calculated and it is not without much hesitation that a statesman should hazard to regulate the concerns of individuals as if he could do it better than themselves . . . as to the hope that it may . . . induce England to treat us better. I think it entirely groundless."[6]

Madison received a letter from friend Wilson Nicholas that contained warnings about the plan, too. "If the embargo could be executed and the people submit to it, I have no doubt it is our wisest course; but if the complete execution of it and the support of the people cannot be counted upon, it will neither answer our purpose nor will it be practicable to retain it," he said.[7]

Madison, the political theorist and "Big Knife" dealmaker, overlooked the most obvious problem of the embargo. Americans still wanted to buy British goods and sell them goods of their own. They saw the embargo as entirely separate from political and military foreign policy. Worse, many, especially those in New England with Federalist ties and connections to the shipping industry, a huge business there, saw it as illegal pressure by the federal government on their ability to maintain their livelihoods. The Republicans were supposed to defend states' rights, and the rights of the people to earn a living, yet with the embargo, the federal government was doing just the opposite. Not only that, but the federal government, mostly Republicans, was doing it to New England, where most residents were Federalists. It was political, they argued, and it was wrong.

An outraged poet William Cullen Bryant, just thirteen years old at the time, savaged Thomas Jefferson in a poem on the embargo that ripped the president's recently revealed (alleged) relationship with slave girl Sally Hemings and called for his resignation.

> And thou, the scorn of every patriot's name,
> Thy country's ruin and thy country's shame!
> Go, wretch! Resign the Presidential chair.
> Disclose thy secret measures, foul or fair . . .
> Go scan, philosophist, thy [Sally's] charms,
> And sink supinely in her sable arms.

But quit to abler hands, the helm of state.
Nor image ruin on thy country's fate![8]

Others wrote songs about the embargo. One popular New England ditty went as follows:

Our ships all in motion once whitened the ocean;
They sailed and returned with a cargo.
Now doomed to decay they are fallen a prey
To Jefferson, worms and EMBARGO.[9]

To thwart the embargo, people began to smuggle British goods into the United States. The Canadian border was a sieve to trade; hundreds of small-time entrepreneurs smuggled goods over the border to Boston and other New England communities. Congressmen warned Jefferson that the only way to make the embargo work was for the federal government to become very aggressive in prosecuting people it suspected of violating it. In addition to all of that, Madison had underestimated the need of America to sell its exports. The business was bigger than he thought. He also pushed his plan through Congress and into law too quickly. The embargo permitted "special permissions" to be granted to some shipping companies. This meant that instead of no ships sailing to Europe in 1808, more than six hundred did. Imports were viewed the same way. Dispensations for certain European goods were allowed and others were brought in with them, finding a quick market. During 1808, for example, European shipping business at the port of Philadelphia did not drop by 100 percent, as Madison predicted, but by only 25 percent. In the Caribbean, Napoleon, busy with his wars, simply ignored the embargo. British islands seemed to shrug it off and continued with their daily lives. In England, merchants had huge surpluses of cotton and other goods bought from America before the embargo went into law, so they did not suffer. The Spanish markets in South America opened their doors to British merchants, too, and the increase in business to South America made up for the loss of business in the United States. The embargo was a failure with other nations, too. The more Madison insisted that others understand it, the more they did not and saw it as a desperate measure by a country unwilling or unable to find other means to reach its diplomatic goals. And, no matter how often the secretary of state said that it was a practical tool, everybody saw it was a cold, political gamble and nothing less. Madison would not let it go; everybody overseas blamed its failure on him.

Another complaint raised in the United States was that the government had led the people to believe that it was a short, temporary measure, but, in fact, it had seemed to become permanent. "They will now have to acknowledge that the predictions of the Federalists were too true. The federal editors declared long ago that the embargo was intended to be permanent . . . if Madison succeeded to the Presidency, it would continue during his reign. It is now found from experience to be a useless measure," wrote an editor at the *Washington Federalist.*[10]

One man wrote that by the end of 1808 everybody knew "the ravages that the embargo is making throughout the whole country" and said that it was not just shippers and merchants who were suffering, but farmers, too.[11] Newspapers from Maine to Georgia ran long lists of the profits from pre-embargo days to embargo days, noting the catastrophic declines in them. The Federalists framed the issue as one of submission, claiming that the United States turned to the embargo because England and France forced the country to back down when they demanded checks of American shipping. They were, the federalists charged, moving away from the nation's long-cherished revolutionary principals and scraping their knees to England and France.[12]

Congressman Matthew Lyons said that the embargo "cannot fairly be said to possess a single republican feature—it may be compared to an apoplexy; it stops the circulation of the blood in the commercial system and extends its baneful influence to the agricultural body; repeated fits will produce convulsions and death in the political as well as in the physical world. It is a weapon which never fails to wound those who use it."[13]

And many said that the embargo was the wrong weapon to use. If Jefferson and Madison wanted weapons, they argued, they should have obtained real ones. "To permit our merchants to arm, under proper restrictions, and to equip, man and send out our public ships to defend those maritime rights which are clear and indisputable is not war, nor will it necessarily involve us in war. Every nation on earth would respect us for defending our natural rights," argued Connecticut senator James Hillhouse.[14]

And in the middle of all this, Madison's wife became very sick. She had fainted at a reception at Montpelier and was put to bed. It was another bout of inflammatory rheumatism, which she had suffered before, but this was the worst. "Never had I more extreme sickness & pain. Dr. Willis bled me & gave me medicine. Nelly and Mother M nursed & waited on me with great attention and kindness. No language can give you an idea of the poignancy of my misery. I was never before in such a situation," she wrote her sister.[15] It was one of many encounters with rheumatism and other ailments that plagued Dolley all of her life. She had complained of weak and sore eyes since her twenties. Her knee, taken care of in 1805 by Dr. Physick, never fully recovered. From time to time, she felt parts of her face go numb, often in stressful situations. She also had great fears of the epidemics that spread throughout the country. She wrote alarmingly of a cholera epidemic that just missed relatives in Kentucky. In 1805, she wrote with great fear of yet another Yellow Fever epidemic. "I enquire every day & they tell me there is not a single case. Mr. M goes out a great deal & does not tell me he hears of it . . . I am often in miserable fears for *his* health."

By the beginning of the winter of 1808, most people in America thought there was going to be a war. "If by mid-summer [of 1809] the [embargo] does not occasion a relaxation in the belligerents a war will be substitute. The people are quite up to the war," wrote Congressman Joseph Story.[16]

The press predicted war as well. "As in all affairs that are human no god is without the ally of evil," wrote the editor of the *Aurora*, the pro-Republican newspaper in Philadelphia, of the British just prior to Madison's inauguration.[17]

The editor was not the only American convinced of the inevitability of conflict; so was Dolley Madison. She wrote bluntly to her sister early in 1809, "It is likely there will be a war."[18]

James Madison, too, felt that war was inevitable. "Few are desirous of war, and few are reconciled to submission, yet the frustration of intermediate courses seems to have left scarce an escape from that dilemma," he said on New Year's Day 1810.[19]

Some people had thought that more than ten years earlier, when Jefferson took office. "There is a mass of violence and passion in the party which seems to me disposed to press on to war . . . [the administration] will use all means to excite the resentment and the hate of the people against England," wrote John Marshall in 1801, before he was chief justice.[20]

Even Jefferson foresaw war as the embargo failed. "War will become preferable to the continuance of the embargo after a certain time," he told Madison at the end of 1808.[21]

The rage against the embargo was so great that a small group of unhappy residents in New England tried to get their states to secede from the United States in order to protect their economy. "If the patriots of the revolution had refused to submit to privations equal to [that] of the embargo what would have been the condition of America now?" wailed a writer in the *Aurora*. The editor of the Lexington, Kentucky, *Reporter* reminded all that "the federal papers in the eastern states are openly an unblushingly advocating a dissolution of the union."[22]

Instead of seeing this as a telltale sign that a growing portion of the people were against the embargo, Secretary Madison only saw those against it as traitors. Instead of dealing with them in a diplomatic way, he excoriated them publicly and called them names. He said he could not believe that there was "so much depravity and stupidity" among the New Englanders. He vented every time he had the opportunity. On threatened secession, he railed that "such a project may lurk within a junto ready to sacrifice the rights, interests and honor of their country, to their ambitious or vindictive views."[23]

He had fumed to everybody that the embargo was the right policy. He wrote Pinckney in the spring of 1808 that the embargo was correct and that most Americans supported it, which they did not. He told Pinckney that public opinion in Great Britain would overwhelm the government. It faced "the distresses of the West Indies, the discontents at home [and] the alienation of [American] habits from their manufacture."[24]

He was wrong.

To the day it was repealed, Madison never admitted that he had made a catastrophic mistake. "If it failed, it was because the government did not sufficiently distrust those ... whose successful violations of the law led to ... its repeal." he wrote.[25]

And, too, there were always organizations or politicians he could point to as supporters of the embargo and a major reason he had embraced it and held onto his support of it. After all, President Jefferson had supported it every single day that it was law. The problem with Jefferson, though, critics said, was that he was in favor of it because he never took time to try to understand why so many were against it. Madison was delighted with a letter Jefferson received from a large group of citizens in Maryland, in early February 1809, that offered continued support for the embargo as a way to strike back at England. Jefferson had responded by telling the Marylanders that "the aggressions and injuries of the belligerent nations have been the real obstructions which have interrupted our commerce and now threaten our peace ... embargo laws were indispensable."[26]

Surprisingly, one of the few people in the American government to realize the failure of the embargo was Dolley Madison, who had lectured her husband on it without success. Dolley, who feared the embargo would not work and that war would follow, and who listened to her husband explain it but also listened to her diplomatic and business friends denounce it, said that "the President and Madison have been greatly perplexed by the remonstrances from so many towns to remove the embargo ... the evading it is a terrible thing. Madison is uneasy."[27]

Madison's error in supporting it went back to one of his own fundamental warnings about democratic government, that no government is without fault and the legislator or cabinet officer was not born who did not make mistakes—and refuse to admit it. "The problem to be solved," he believed about democracy, "is not what form of government is perfect, but which of the forms is least imperfect."[28]

The embargo had been imperfect, and so had Madison.

11

MISTER PRESIDENT

*T*he inauguration of James Madison as the nation's fourth president was a day full of music, cheering, and wild celebrations in every nook and cranny of Washington, DC. When the sun rose early that morning, everyone in the capital knew it was a special day because the big artillery guns at the Navy Yard and at nearby Fort Warburton roared out a loud, smoky welcome to the city as a reminder of the inauguration. Troops of smartly dressed, uniformed soldiers from Georgetown and Alexandria marched to Washington to accompany President-elect Madison and his wife, Dolley, to the House of Representatives chamber, where he was sworn in as the fourth president of the United States. Thousands, some who had driven for miles for the event, packed the parade route taken by the soldiers and the Madisons. "The House of Representatives was very much crowded, and its appearance very magnificent," said John Quincy Adams, who was there.[1]

The morning gossip was full of news about that night's upcoming inaugural ball and the recently repealed embargo, a congressional move in February that saddened Madison but gave most in the country much relief. The House galleries were jammed with men and women attired in their finest suits and dresses. Madison, a slight man dressed in black, smiled a bit as he looked out at the crowd that pushed its way into every available square foot of space in the chamber and placed his hand on the Bible. The oath was delivered by Chief Justice John Marshall, who towered over Madison and dominated the scene with his huge frame and deep, black, penetrating eyes.

Looking back, Madison's election seemed easy even though it did not appear that way just a few months before the process began. There had been some stiff opposition to his elevation to the presidency. The hatred of the Embargo Act was considerable, especially in New England, and even worse was the public anger at Madison, and Jefferson, for clinging to it after so many charged that it was a calamity. Most of the Senate's business in the last few months had been the debates over the successful repeal of the embargo, and they had filled the front pages of most newspapers.[2] Ironically, Republicans who loved Jefferson refused to blame him, their sainted hero, for the embargo, so they blamed Madison instead.[3]

The Federalists opposed to Jefferson charged that Madison's administration would just be an extension of his; they were best friends. Some joked that if they were in a law firm, Jefferson was the senior partner and Madison the junior partner. New England electors were vehemently against him from the start of the campaign. All of the Federalists were opposed to him. Many did not want the line of Virginia presidents to continue and were against Madison for that reason. In his own party, eccentric Virginia congressman John Randolph, who had hated him for years, mounted a campaign to get James Monroe elected and even started his own, small political party, the "Quids," to do so. The Quids loudly rallied around Monroe.[4]

Randolph never fretted about President Madison's animosity toward him and his years-long campaign to derail Madison's career. "When the President has done well, I will claim the right of approving him and I would say 'well-done thou good and faithful servant' and in so doing I am permitted to say 'ill done thou bad and faithless servant.' Where we have a right to praise, we have a right to dispraise," the arrogant Randolph said in Congress.[5]

Randolph was one of the Congress's more colorful members. A scion of the wealthy and influential Virginia Randolph family, John was an elegant dresser in and out of Congress and took his two pet dogs everywhere, including the congressional chamber. He never wore a wig or powdered his hair and kept his light-brown hair short. He suffered a childhood disease that damaged his throat; his voice remained high-pitched all of his life.

Over the last few years, Randolph aroused controversy wherever he went. He was chosen as the chief prosecutor in the Senate impeachment trial of Supreme Court Justice Samuel Chase, who caused controversies with his antipress rulings in Alien and Sedition trials, and he bungled the attack on the justice, who was acquitted. Worse, he insulted those who questioned his authority at the trial and publicly humiliated others. He always had a hard time controlling his temper. A year after the Chase trial, angry that the administration did not do something the way he suggested, he took a sudden vacation and went home, stranding the Ways and Means Committee without its chair and making it impossible for any Senate business to be completed. Shortly after that, enraged at both Jefferson and Madison over misdirected plans to purchase Florida, Randolph scorched both men, and others, in several House tirades.

Senator Samuel Smith wrote that "Randolph expects that ... a public explosion of our views and plans will render abortive this negotiation and render the Executive and poor little Madison unpopular. ... However, he spares nobody and by his conduct has compelled all to rally around the Executive for their own preservation."[6]

Years before, just after Jefferson's first election, Randolph had criticized Jefferson and Madison and suggested that everything they did was not to benefit the country but to make it possible for Madison to succeed Jefferson as president.

Both Samuel Smith and John Randolph were members of a powerful Senate and House political faction nicknamed "the Invisibles" because they were publicly together on many issues but split, and "invisible," on others. Other members of the group were Secretary of the Navy Robert Smith, Samuel's brother; Jefferson's friend Wilson Nicholas; William Giles; Dr. Samuel Mitchill; and Michael Leib.[7]

Senator Smith scorned Randolph, Madison, and all of the Republican Virginians, whom he saw as part of the "House of Austria," as denouncers referred to Virginia politicians. Smith accused them of scheming to line up Jefferson, Madison, Monroe, and perhaps others to permit Virginia control the country forever. Many others felt the same way.[8]

Madison's presidential aspirations benefited from having Jefferson's blessing and being in the heavily favored and ever-growing Republican Party. The Federalist Party had just about collapsed during the previous four years and had little strength left on either the national or the state level.

Congressional delegations met to decide party candidates in that era, following popular votes in some states that were seen by congressmen as barometers of the people's views. Some states held caucuses (just to show his true strength, Madison defeated Monroe handily in the Virginia caucus and, in a popular vote, defeated him in a landslide, 14,665 to 3,468).[9] The Madisonian Republicans were so strong in Virginia that they also controlled seventeen of the twenty-four seats in the Richmond city council. Madison was nominated as the Republican candidate along with ailing vice president, George Clinton, who died soon after the election, and Federalist candidate Charles Cotesworth Pinckney.

The Federalist newspapers were against Madison (he was often called "an accommodating trimmer" and said to be antibusiness and a weak leader), and the Republican newspapers were for him. The Federalists saw him as an extension of Thomas Jefferson, and they loathed the third president. Jefferson was accused of "shameful doings" and Federalist editors were glad he was leaving office so he could no longer "deceive the people." These editors saw a Madison presidency as "gloomy and alarming."[10] The editor of the *Washington Expositor* quoted a critic who charged that the congressional caucus that nominated the secretary of state did so unfairly and its actions were "in direct hostility to the principles of the Constitution and a gross assumption of power not delegated by the people."[11] In another issue, a writer using a pseudonym in the *Expositor*, who supported George Clinton, the longtime New York politician who was famous for his bushy eyebrows, argued that Madison was going to be president because he could cajole the congressional caucus into selecting him, ignoring the wishes of the people. Another writer in the *Expositor* said the idea that anyone would serve more than two terms after Washington had set that as a limit was ridiculous.[12]

Impressment of sailors was an important election issue. Everybody wanted Jefferson, and now Madison, to do something to stop the constant kidnapping of American seaman by the British, even those who did not favor the embargo. Across the country, dozens of large and glamorous balls were staged to raise money to help the families of seamen sitting in British prisons or forced to work on British ships. Studies, including one ordered by Madison, showed that since impressment of American sailors had started in 1803, nearly three thousand had been taken and put aboard British ships, and were still there.[13]

One reason for Madison's election, Senator Mitchill told friends, was the ability of his glamorous wife, Dolley, to make her husband look "presidential" at her many soirees and the inability of either Pinckney or Clinton to do the same. "The former [Madison] gives dinners and makes generous displays to the members [of Congress]. The latter [Clinton] lives snug at his lodgings and keeps aloof from such captivating exhibitions. Mr. M is going greatly ahead of him," he said.[14]

The Madisons clearly understood that they had to use their social skills as well as their political skills to win over members of the congressional caucus who would nominate men for president, and they did. Neither Madison nor his wife ever actually discussed the upcoming election at their parties, but that was the clear goal. They wanted everybody to see Madison as a likable and skilled man, someone you wanted to run the country. It was subtle and it was powerful, and it was all carefully, and skillfully, managed by Dolley. She had been doing this work for her husband as secretary of state for eight years and had been very successful at it. This effort to get him the presidency was just one more step in her social/political program.

Another reason for his election was that Jefferson and Madison had talked up Madison's succession as a fait accompli for more than six months. The thinking in Washington, too, was that young Monroe could wait his turn to be president, and in the coming four or eight years gain even more experience with which to be a good chief executive. With Madison following Jefferson and Monroe next in line, the Republicans lined up three presidents in a row. One writer who supported Monroe gave up hope and said that "Mr. Madison would be acquiesced in" and that this "had been understood and agreed upon by the friends of both parties."[15]

There were more than twice as many Republican newspapers as Federalist, and their editors pushed Madison's candidacy everywhere. The *Aurora* wrote that "since the [Revolutionary] war, Mr. Madison has been in public life discharging a train of successive trusts with uniform superiority of talents and uniform purity of character."[16]

Madison had his supporters. British minister Foster, who knew him well, said of him that he was "social, jovial, and good humored companion full of anecdotes and sometimes matters of a loose description relating to old times, but oftener of a political and historical interest ... he was a little man, with small features but occasionally lit up with a good-natured smile."[17]

National Intelligencer editor Smith, his longtime friend, went to a number of parties with Madison and remembered him as a cheerful companion. He always told friends the story that at one party, the usually solemn Madison recommended that everybody drink champagne all night. "[He said that] more than a few glasses always produced a headache the next day. This was the very time to try the experiment, as the next day being Sunday would allow time for a recovery from its effects. . . . So, bottle after bottle came in."[18]

There were politicians, such as John Quincy Adams, who believed Madison was right in his embargo, even if had not worked. Adams felt that Madison's new Non-Intercourse Act, a watered-down bill passed after the embargo was eliminated, was a good idea, too. "Our intercourse with foreign nations ... requires live oak hearts and iron or brazen mouths to speak that they may be distinctly heard, or attentively listened to, by the distant ear of foreigners," he wrote.[19]

And, of course, Madison had his detractors. John Beckley, the clerk to the House of Representatives, represented them all. "Madison is deemed by many [to be] too timid and indecisive a statesman, and too liable to a conduct of forbearance to the Federal party which may endanger our harmony and political safety," he said.[20]

John Randolph was always against Madison. When all of his protests against the president failed, Randolph always retreated to Madison's retirement from Congress in 1796. "In the hour or terror and persecution, he deserted his post and sought in obscurity and retirement a shelter from the political tempest," he wrote, and he added that Madison had been retreating from the Republicans' old principals.[21]

Randolph was said to be the author of a statement signed by seventeen angry Republicans against Madison. It read, "We ask for energy and we are told [Madison's] moderation. We ask for talents and the reply is his unassuming merit. We ask for his services in the cause of public liberty and we are directed to the pages of *The Federalist. . . .* We ask for that high and honorable sense of duty which would at all times turn with loathing and abhorrance [*sic*] from any compromise with fraud and speculation. We ask in vain."[22]

As early as 1803, during talks about the proposed sale of the Louisiana Territory from France to the United States, Randolph was criticizing Madison in Congress. He said that he was not a tough diplomat, but that his friend Jefferson always made him out to appear that way.[23]

The Jefferson administration, and Madison, also suffered from the 1807 treason trial of Aaron Burr, the man who killed Alexander Hamilton in a duel in 1804. Chief Justice Marshall, who served as the sole arbiter at the trial, ruled that the prosecution had to prove in its case that Burr had actually started a physical movement to overthrow the government, not that he planned to do so. The trial ended in an acquittal for Burr. A large group of angry residents in Baltimore stuffed dummies of Marshall, Burr, and others into a cart one night and drove them down a dirt road to a gallows and hung them in effigy.[24]

Most Americans were certain that Burr was a villain. "Burr's party fights hard, but it is the general conviction that he will be convicted," wrote Dolley Madison of the man who introduced her to her husband, who added that he was "evil."[25]

There were unhappy Federalists who might have supported Madison but changed their minds. "We found ourselves insulted and maltreated by all and perceived no assurance on which we could confidently rely that the political system which has been adopted would be changed by any of them [Republicans]. The superior talents of Mr. Madison would probably have placed us in his scale had not recent events induced the opinion that his prejudices with respect to our foreign relations were still . . . incurable," wrote John Marshall just before the election.[26]

The growing feud between the United States and Great Britain, fueled by the 1807 British attack on the American frigate USS *Chesapeake*, which killed or wounded twenty-one sailors, also turned public opinion against Madison, who handled all the dreadful negotiations with the recalcitrant and unrepentant British as secretary of state.

Congressmen were livid over the bombardment of the *Chesapeake*. "The conduct of Humphries, the captain of the *Leopard*, in attacking the *Chesapeake* was . . . an assault upon our sovereignty," said Congressman William Plumer, who added that the United States should have declared war on Britain right after the first shot was fired.[27] Many agreed with him. Right after the attack of the ship, several thousand residents of Baltimore signed up for local militia companies and began military drills, held parades, and were reviewed by local officials. "The attack on the *Chesapeake*, while it excited the indignation, awoke also the slumbering military spirit of the country," wrote the angry editor of the *Washington Federalist.*[28]

Many avid Republicans did not think that Jefferson or Madison were radical enough in their policies and that the Jefferson administration, and prospective Madison government, had turned from champions of states' rights into just another branch of the nationalistic, big-government Federalist Party.

Madison suffered because he followed Jefferson into the White House. The flamboyant and often-charming Jefferson was quite popular. He possessed a charismatic personality, was always at home in social settings, and was a brilliant writer. Madison still had a difficult time mingling socially, struggled through parties, and was a mundane writer. Jefferson took stands and never backed down from them; Madison always seemed to be reassessing his position and looking for the middle ground in any dispute. And Madison, upon becoming president, was still finding it difficult, despite his wife's ceaseless work to reframe his image, to shed his dour personality in public and to improve on his quiet, unmoving speaking voice. His wonderful demeanor in private, admired by all, and sure handling of policy, remained hidden from the great masses. Madison insisted that he could not be someone whom he was not; his aides and wife assured him that he could be. Wasn't that a brutal definition of politics?

And Madison could not understand why he did not have the support of all the people. He wrote in 1787 that "all men having power ought to be distrusted to a certain degree."[29] But, when people distrusted him as secretary of state and president because of his power, he did not understand their feelings and was demoralized.

He understood, though, that he was never going to be judged fairly by Federalist newspapers, just as he was never going to be criticized by Republican papers. The opposing parties controlled their newspapers, and politicians of all parties knew the kind of coverage they would get in each journal. "Could it be so arranged, that every newspaper when printed on one side should be handed over to the press of an adversary to be printed on the other; thus presenting to every reader both sides of every question, truth would always have a fair chance," he wrote.[30] He knew that he, like every other president, simply had to live with the press, whether it was friend or foe.

The Federalist press continually sniped at him during the presidential campaign. Editors wrote columns against him, and numerous anti-Madison letters to the editor were printed. Anybody who ever had an unhappy business transaction with Madison somehow scribbled a letter that found its way into the papers.

Madison had problems in his own party, too. Ever since the birth of the Republican Party, longtime, devoted members found fault with Jefferson and Madison as they slowly moved away, they charged, from rock-solid Republican principals of states' rights, individual freedom, and small government. Their number did not grow until Jefferson's second term, so the leaders of the group found in Madison's election hopes a wide target at which to level criticism. Even people in Madison's home state, Virginia, such as the highly respected judge from Virginia, Edmund Pendleton, opposed him.[31]

Madison's friend the president countermanded all of them, though, with a brilliant idea. He had all of Madison's official papers read in Congress, a job that took six long days. Republican newspapers then printed some of the speeches and, especially, the letters. Jefferson gave the country a never-before-seen view of behind-the-scenes workings at the secretary of state's office. The secretary shone in the papers. He exhibited a genuine grasp not just of his office but also of the workings of the entire federal government. The papers showed him as a good boss, a fine negotiator, and a partner to the president. Most of all, though, they showed that he was tough. He was tough with the British and the Spaniards, and he was especially tough with Napoleon Bonaparte. The people liked that.

For example, at the beginning of 1809 he sent a lengthy report to the president, which was leaked to the press and widely reprinted, in which he listed the insults and outrages of Great Britain against America and bluntly said they were "belligerent decrees, orders, and proclamations." More than anything else, the public readings of the papers enabled Madison to become president.[32]

The unpopular embargo, which should have hurt his chances to be elected, did not. Opposition to the embargo was strongest in New England, and New England was dominated by the Federalists anyway, so it made little difference in the vote there. In the end, too, the embargo was neutralized as an issue because enough Americans supported it or at least put up with it, in different regions to overcome its enemies in New England.

But there was another factor that was overlooked at the time. James Madison and his wife, Dolley, had become political animals. Madison was a good listener. One of the momentous moments of his life was listening to George Washington tell him in the winter of 1788 that he had to put aside political theory and get his hands dirty with rough-and-tumble politics if he wanted to succeed in the political world. He did that. In the first Congresses, he was a major dealmaker.

During Jefferson's election as president in 1800, he had served on the main election committee and provided Jefferson and others with state-by-state, city-by-city, and even town-by-town vote totals and analysis that he demanded from local political leaders. Madison did the same with various gubernatorial races a few months later. He had given Jefferson probably the best analysis of why he was elected president by the Congress. He knew how politics worked, and so did his wife. In 1808 and 1809, the pair put all of their skills to work to map out a successful election campaign.[33]

George Clinton, ill, stayed at home and campaigned very little. Pinckney, who did not even know he might be a candidate until he was nominated, began his campaign in a burst of enthusiasm, rallying the party faithful and reminding all that the Federalists were the first party and a good one. "The spirit of Federalism which is bursting forth to the north and east of the Susquehanna must have an advantageous effect on our public affairs," he said, but he lost his energy as numerous groups of his own Federalists criticized him and abandoned him during the fall. Pinckney also had little support outside of his own region of the country.[34]

The election of the president by the Electoral College, held publicly then in Congress, was an elegant affair. Spectators jammed the House of Representatives chamber in Washington for the counting of the electoral ballots in a two-hour-long meeting. Madison won, gaining most of his strength from the South and the West plus New York, New Jersey, and Pennsylvania. He had 122 votes. George Clinton had 6, and Charles Pinckney had 47. It was a surprisingly easy victory. He was proclaimed officially as the President-elect, and his wife, Dolley—her friends bragged everywhere,—was the "Queen-elect."

Their friends were pleased. Eliza Collins Lee wrote Dolley that "you are about to fulfill a character the most dignified and respectable in society. . . . I feel no small degree of exultation in knowing that the mind, temper and manners of my Philadelphia Quaker friend are peculiarly fitted for the station, where hospitality and graciousness of deportment will appear conspicuously charming and conciliating."[35]

One thing Madison did worry about as the new president was the power of public opinion and the people in America, a country that was practically doubling in population every ten years (3.699 million residents in 1790, the year of the first census). "The larger a country, the less easy for its real opinion to be ascertained . . . the more extensive a country, the more insignificant is each individual in his own eyes. This may be unfavorable to liberty," he wrote earlier, in 1791, and he believed it more fervently when he was elected to the nation's highest office.[36]

He remembered, too, that regardless of his high office of president, his eight years as secretary of state, and his many terms in Congress, he was, at heart, a rebel. "Every nation has a right to abolish an old government and establish a new one. This principle is not only recorded in every public archive, written in every American heart, and sealed with the blood of a host of American martyrs, but is the only lawful tenure by which the United States hold their existence as a nation," he firmly believed.[37]

He was now finally in charge of a government he had designed in 1787, and a government that he saw as the pride of the world. He had written in a newspaper column that the United States was "a government deriving its energy from the will of the society and operating by the reason of its measures, on the understanding and interest of the society. Such is the government for which philosophy has been searching and humanity been sighing, from the most remote ages. Such are the republican governments which it is the glory of America to have invented and her unrivalled happiness to possess."[38]

He later told the marquis de Lafayette, whom he had befriended during the American Revolution, that the strength of the US democracy was its system of checks and balances: "A government like ours has so many safety valves, giving vent to overheated passions, that it carries within itself a relief against the infirmities from which the best of human institutions cannot be exempt."[39]

Madison was not a powerful speaker. In his inaugural address, he told the packed crowd at the House of Representatives that he sought neutrality in foreign relations (he and all others had remembered how Washington had steered the United States away from a war in Europe with a neutrality proclamation ten years before) and prosperity at home. In one long-winded sentence, he told the gathering, too, that he wanted to

> foster a spirit of independence too just to invade the rights of others, too proud to surrender our own, too liberal to indulge unworthy prejudices ourselves and too elevated not to look down upon them in others; to hold the union of the states as the basis of their peace and happiness . . . to respect the rights and authorities reserved to the states and to the people as equally incorporated with and essential to the success of the general system . . . to promote by authorized means improvements friendly to agriculture, to manufactures and to external as well as internal commerce.[40]

He also promised freedom of religion, freedom of the press, and aid to Native Americans.

Hundreds of people met the Madisons at their home (Jefferson was still living in the White House) following his swearing in at the Capitol. The house was packed. The chilly streets outside were filled with elegant horse-drawn carriages, well-dressed men on horseback, and thousands of people walking on foot from all over town. Inside the Madisons' home, every room was filled with people, as were the wide, high hallways and the sprawling lawn both in front and in back of the building. The president and Mrs. Madison met all of their well-wishers on a lengthy receiving line. All were glad to meet the new president, who greeted them in his soft voice, and were very happy to meet the effervescent Dolley. "She looked extremely beautiful," wrote Margaret Smith. "[She] was dressed in a plain cambric dress with a very long train, plain round the neck without any handkerchief, and beautiful bonnet of purple velvet and white satin with white plumes. She was all dignity, grace and affability."[41]

That night, in yet another precedent-setting change, the first inaugural ball in Washington was held as a formal activity at the new, large Long's Hotel in the downtown area of the city. Over four hundred dignitaries and local residents attended. Mr. Madison arrived a bit late with Dolley on his arm. She was radiant in a long gown of yellow velvet, her neck and arms adorned in pearls. She wore a turban on her head with an outrageous bird-of-paradise plume sticking out of it. All eyes were on her as she entered and the orchestra played. "She looked like a queen . . . dignity, sweetness, grace," wrote a woman there.[42]

Dolley stood out, as she always did, but now, in the winter of 1809, there were far more well-dressed women in Washington than there had been when she arrived in town in 1801. There were many more women's clothing stores in Washington and the nearby towns, and newspapers now wrote about ladies' fashion, and Dolley's example had spurred many women to dress up. No one had to fear criticism for opulence; after all, the First Lady dressed that way.

The hall in the hotel where the inaugural ball was held was overheated, and the temperature rose as more and more guests arrived. Everybody at the ball began to get uncomfortable. There did not seem to be a way to drop the temperature, so the clerks finally broke the glass windows to permit air to flow in from the capital's night sky. After that, the guests breathed easier and danced all night.

While the inaugural ball did wonders for Dolley's reputation, as did everything, it hurt the new president's image. The ballroom of the hotel was very crowded, and the short Madison often became lost in the crowd. He was trying to draw attention and had to contend with the dynamic Jefferson, there at the ball to say good-bye to everyone. And Madison, working all day on his inaugural address; delivering it; and then spending the rest of the day with receptions, celebrations, and parties, was tired. Even his friends frowned on his appearance.

Margaret Bayard Smith said he looked "spiritless and exhausted" and added that he "looked as if could scarcely stand."[43] He told all around him that he wished he could go to bed. And he did. He and his wife left the party while the revelers continued to dance and drink—and talk about the new president's very early departure.

Madison could not, at first, escape withering criticism from some, even supposed "friends." Frances Few, Albert Gallatin's sister-in-law, scalded Madison when he took office. "Mr. Madison, the President-elect, is a small man quite devoid of dignity in his appearance—he bows very low and never looks at the person to whom he is bowing but keeps his eyes on the ground. His skin looks like parchment—at first I thought his appearance was occasioned by the small pox," she said.[44] Alexander Dick wrote that President Madison was "a very small man . . . he seems to be incapable of smiling but talks a great deal."[45]

Joseph Story, soon to be a Supreme Court judge, went to several of the Madison receptions. He thought the president felt like a duck out of water at social events. He said that Madison at parties "has grace and sober character and retired life lead him far from the pleasantries of a coterie." Many who met him described him sarcastically. "She looks like an Amazon; he like one of the puny knights of Lilliputia," sneered one.[46]

Historian Gaillard Hunt, who edited Madison's papers and probably knew him better than most scholars, agreed. "He was an old, sour eyed man" when he became president, Hunt wrote. "There was never any dash or fire of youth in him." But yet, Hunt said, as everybody who knew the president when he was in office remarked that there were two James Madisons.

"His charm was unassailable," Hunt wrote, and he added that he had hazel eyes that twinkled and a voice that could be very animated. Madison was, to those who knew him well, "an inexhaustible mine of information, frank, communicative." And, too, they all added, he had "good teeth" and a "nice smile."[47]

Catharine Adams, the wife of John Quincy Adams, met Madison just after he was inaugurated. She was struck by his size, like everybody else. "Mr. Madison was a very small man in his person, with a very large head," she said, but quickly added that he was an unassuming man with a "lively, often playful conversation."[48]

Part of his problem, too, some said, was that his wife was so charismatic, so stylish, and so personable that whenever she was in the room with the president, she always overwhelmed him. That was fine with her husband, but it made it difficult for him to establish himself when in a crowd with his wife. Mrs. Adams noticed that, too. "There was a frankness and ease in her deportment that won golden opinions from all, and she possessed an influence so decided with her little man," she said.[49]

And, too, Madison followed Jefferson into office. Jefferson was leaving in glory as the man who annexed all of the Louisiana Territory and defeated the Barbary pirates. The end of his second term had been trouble-free and peaceful, and Madison was coming into a term that might lead the nation into a war with England. British writer Harriet Martineau, who met Madison years later, wrote that if he had not followed Jefferson in office, he might have been considered a great president.[50]

Friends scoffed at the criticism. "If he does not guide the helm successfully, the requisite qualifications for that station cannot be found on earth," snapped brother-in-law John Jackson.[51]

When he took office, the town's and nation's newspapers wondered how he would do. The editor of the *Washington Expositor*, like many, told him not to listen to his advisers and do what he thought was best for the nation. He wrote that "you will either be at once proclaimed by shouts and hosannas as the second savior of the liberties of the United States or you will stand charged and justly loaded with all the evil consequences upon that state of public affairs which shall shake the very existence of the union and overwhelm the peace and happiness of the country . . . like all men going into power, your virtues are now trumpeted forth and there are not wanting characters, and a good many of them, who are prepared to assure you that you are transcendentally great."[52]

The Federalist press was critical, but Madison paid little attention to them. Jefferson had ignored them, too, but in private he admitted that the criticism hurt. One had to expect "the extreme of their wrath," he wrote Levi Lincoln in 1801.[53] "The laws of the present day withhold their hands from blood, but lies and slander still remain to them."

President Jefferson told Madison that he would be a fine president and told all Americans with confidence that "what man can do will be done by Mr. Madison." His beaming smile at Madison's swearing in, and congratulations to him at the ball, reminded all of their deep friendship. "I do believe father never loved son as more than he loves Mr. Madison," wrote Margaret Smith.[54]

Jefferson left town shortly after the ceremonies. The third president simply saddled a horse and headed home to Monticello. He left Washington amid a torrent of praise and thanks from Republican newspapers. "As members of a great and flourishing nation, over which you have so illustriously presided, your virtue, talents and service commanded their esteem, admiration and gratitude," wrote Robert Brent in the *Aurora*.[55]

Thomas Jefferson and his friend would keep in close touch over the coming years. They were so friendly that Jefferson would ask Madison to bring him clothes that he had left in the White House the next time Madison visited him at Monticello. Few people in American public life were as close as the pair. They were so attached that Dolley was at Monticello when Jefferson's alleged illegitimate son with Sally Hemings was born in 1803. The story went that Sally asked Dolley if she could name the boy Madison, after her husband. Dolley approved heartily (another version of the story has Jefferson just doing it and telling a delighted Madison later). Madison said that he had known Jefferson as "a luminary of science as a votary of liberty, as a model of patriotism, and as a benefactor of human kind. I have known him … for a period of … years … during which there was not an interruption or diminution of mutual confidence and cordial friendship, for a single moment in a single instance."[56]

Jefferson was glad to be back at Monticello and as far away from Washington as his horse could carry him. His party had fallen into infighting among different factions, and the oppression of Britain against American merchant ships on the high seas had increased during his last two years in office to the point where it was insufferable. Now he could have breakfast at Monticello, take a walk, look down over the forested valleys that surrounded him, and ignore the rapidly growing problems of Washington. "Never did a prisoner, released from his chains, feel such relief as I shall in shaking off the shackles of power," he said of his retirement.[57]

President Madison faced a world that had changed considerably since he wrote the Constitution and lobbied to get it ratified by writing most of the essays in the Federalist papers and campaigning with Alexander Hamilton and John Jay to have it approved in all the state conventions. Now, in the winter of 1809, Napoleon Bonaparte was wreaking havoc with his wars in Europe, the government of the Caribbean-island nation of Haiti had been overthrown in a slave revolt, the Russian oligarchy grew, and England had started to harass American shipping once again. At home, the invention of the cotton gin and the profitability of farm products had brought about a dramatic increase in slavery in the southern states. The size of the country had doubled with the Louisiana Purchase; two political parties now ran the country, with the Federalists in decline and the Republicans on the rise; newspapers had increased by tenfold, and many of them were controlled by Federalists and were highly critical of the Jefferson/Madison government; hundreds of political clubs of all kinds had started to appear; the Supreme Court was feeling its power; cities had exploded in population; and the Industrial Revolution had started, pitting farmers against manufacturers. Young men and women had started to leave their families and farms to find jobs in the burgeoning cities. The failed embargo had pitted many American business and interest groups against the federal government.

America was, in 1809, settling in as a country of many factions struggling to succeed individually and, together, as a nation. It was exactly the kind of country Madison had envisioned when he wrote the Constitution and the kind of diversified population, driven by religious, social, and political factions he had foreseen. His Republican government, on paper, had been realized. All of these factions, no matter how loud or aggressive they became, would push hard against the fabric of democracy, but not tear it. He was certain that a large government, designed to represent everybody, would hold up under the pressures of many new and very vocal opponents.

It was a stressful time to become president. The embargo had failed, Britain had continued to impress seaman, and now, it seemed, the United States had no means by which to stop them from establishing draconian rule of the sea. "Aversion to war, the inconveniences produced by or charged on the embargo, the hope of favorable changes in Europe, the dread of civil convulsions in the East and the policy of permitting the discontented to be reclaimed to their duty by losses at sea," Madison wrote, telling friends that these all contributed to the weakness of the new Non-Intercourse Act.[58]

He had written Jefferson in 1787 that those who believed that all Americans had the same interests were wrong. "We know, however, that no society ever did or can consist of so homogeneous a mass of citizens. . . . In all civilized societies, distinctions are various and unavoidable. A distinction of property results from that very protection which a free government gives to unequal faculties for acquiring it . . . [there are also] differences in political, religious or other opinions, or an attachment to the persons of leading individuals," he wrote.[59]

Madison had said the same thing in his essay "Federalist #10," when he told newspaper readers that a large government would function like a big tent, expansive enough to cover all, no matter what their political and social beliefs. The government would change as the people under the tent changed, too, so it would always work well.

Now Madison was in charge of the government itself and the head of it at a time when there were far more factions than he had ever anticipated and more acrimony between the factions than he had ever envisioned. Now he had to hold it together. He could do so not with his starry-eyed dreams but with practical political skills. It would be a challenge for him just as it had been for Jefferson, Adams, and Washington.

His critics said he made one great mistake as president. Madison had misread the British from the day he became secretary of state back in 1801. They were not going to back down over anything, and he never realized that. And, too, his archenemies said, he was a president of a struggling country who had absolutely no administrative experience. He had been a long-term congressman and a long-term secretary of state, but he never actually ran anything like Jefferson, who had been a governor, and Washington, who had run the army for eight long years.[60]

What kind of a president was America getting? James Madison had been a figure on the public stage since the 1770s, and yet few truly understood him. Critics had numerous complaints about him. In public, they said, he seemed a quiet and staid figure, soft-spoken, reluctant to give speeches, happy to bathe in the glory of his wife and not take center stage himself. Many thought he was not able to make decisions and, when made, would not stand by them. He was good working for somebody else, but not good at being in charge. He was a magnificent counsel but not a capable leader. He was cold and cheerless. He took a very long time to make a decision. He did not want to offend anybody. Madison seemed to rely more on his aides in the State Department than on himself. He never stepped forward and always remained in his friend Jefferson's shadow.

Yet those who knew him well saw an entirely different James Madison. To them, he was not only a brilliant man but also a man who, in small circles of people, sparkled. He told jokes and long, funny stories. He poked fun at other politicians and foreign diplomats. He may have taken a long time to come to a decision, they said, but that is only because he weighed the consequences of every issue and person involved. He was a good administrator, and those who worked for him liked him.

Some saw him as man caught between both personas. Senator William Plumer wrote that Kentucky senator John Adair, for instance, said that Madison was a superb secretary of state and adviser to Jefferson, but that when he stepped out into spotlight he was a weak an ineffective politician. "I considered Mr. Madison an honest man, but too cautious—too fearful and timid to direct the affairs of this nation," Plumer quoted Adair as stating.[61]

Others saw steadfastness but reluctance. Senator Plumer wrote that Madison would make up his mind on an issue, such as the embargo, and tell everyone it was right. Then he would backtrack and say, well, I am right but what do you think? I am right, but let's not be hasty. I am right, but we should wait and see what happens later. "Something of this disposition is seen in most men, but it was a remarkable characteristic of Mr. Madison and forms the true explanation of his conduct in more than one important transaction," Plumer lamented.[62]

Secretary of the Treasury Gallatin, who knew him well, shrugged his shoulders when describing the new president. "Mr. Madison is, as I always knew him, slow in taking his ground, but firm when the storm rises," he said.[63]

So was he the boring, timid thinker or the bold, animated warrior? America would find out as soon as Jefferson departed and Madison moved into the White House.

Madison understood people and their motivations very well and was an excellent judge of both character and ambition. He knew what people were looking for when they talked to him, and he conducted conversations with them in such a way as to not let them know what he was really thinking about their goals. For example, he wrote his friend James Monroe in 1803 that he always cast a skeptical eye on the cantankerous longtime minister from Britain, Anthony Merry. "He appears to be an amiable man in private society, and a candid and agreeable one in public business," he wrote Monroe. He told his friend that Merry and his wife had recently caused a stir in social circles over a snub, or a snub as they saw it, from President Jefferson at a White House dinner. Madison explained to Monroe that the Merrys made much of social troubles, but that did not affect the minister in his public responsibilities. They did, he believed, simply like to "make noise" to draw attention to themselves.

The temperamental Elizabeth Merry drove Dolley crazy. Dolley complained of Mrs. Merry's "airs" in 1805. "The other evening she came in high good humor to pass three hours with [me] when Merran [a servant] called in and mentioned that General [Turreau] and his family were walking near the house. Mrs. Merry instantly took the alarm and said they were waiting for her to depart in order to come in, seized her shawl and in spite of all I could say marched off with great dignity and more passion. You know when she chooses she can get angry with persons as well as circumstances."[64]

In 1804, exasperated by her, Dolley wrote her sister, "Mrs. Merry is still the same strange lass. She hardly associates with anyone, always riding on horseback."[65] Dolley's favorite way to get back at Mrs. Merry was to shower her with gifts in order to completely confuse her.

James Madison had told Anthony Merry that James Monroe would see him on the problem of the impressment of American seaman by British ships. "His ideas appeared to be moderate and his disposition conciliatory I am not without hopes that Mr. Merry sees the business in a good degree in the same light, and that his representations will co-operate with your reasonings on it," he said.[66]

Madison had no qualms in participating in schemes to bring in people who he thought might help the United States in a touchy situation or to remove people who were hindering the chances for American success. One man was Juan Morales, the former "intendant," or mayor, of New Orleans when it was held by the Spanish. He was trouble and threatened to cause problems in the new Louisiana Territory that the United States had just purchased from France. In a private letter, Madison told William Claiborne, the new governor of Louisiana, that Morales was "a mischievous member of society" and that "his removal to some other part of the United States, where he would be unimportant and harmless would be agreeable to the President." He told Claiborne to charm Morales and explain to him that he would face nothing but opposition in New Orleans, but have nothing but support from all if he moved to another part of the country. It was backdoor politics at its best and showed the Madison had mastered the art of cutthroat diplomacy.[67]

Madison's political shrewdness was shared by his wife. One foreign diplomat said, now that she was First Lady, that she would be assaulted by flatterers and needed to be prepared for false adulation. By 1809, Dolley was not surprised by anybody or anything. She had expected false adulation for years. She had learned politics from a master, her husband, plus President Jefferson and other skilled political players. Her eight years as the "unofficial hostess" at Jefferson's White House and director of her husband's busy social life had taught her all there was to know about national politics and the social world. She was just as savvy as her husband and, like him, able to cover up her Svengali-like knowledge of politics with a happy public persona. She wrote that Madison had always warned her of political pitfalls in the public world and false friends.[68]

And her husband taught her to be discreet. She could talk about anything she wanted to him, and express all of her opinions to him, positive or negative, but to no one else. She followed his advice, too, and would not even confide in her beloved sister. She wrote Anna in the spring of 1804 that "there is so much I could tell you about these new French people [Napoleon's ambassador and his wife, whose marital troubles were the scandal of the year in Washington], things that could not fail to divert you, but I must forbear, and am learning to hold my tongue well."[69]

The Madisons kept their friends close when they moved to the White House, and those friendships sustained them. Dolley had many friends from her days living in Philadelphia. One was Phoebe Morris, whom she knew for years, a young woman who adored her. A few months after Madison was inaugurated, Morris wrote the First Lady, "Those who formerly enjoyed the pleasure of your acquaintance, retrace the lines, features and expressions of a face and form on which they had gazed with delight; & those who have not been so favored gratify an anxious and amiable curiosity, in beholding a just resemblance of them in whose virtues they also claim an interest, as the dignified representative of our sex in very female virtue adorned with all her sex's beauty, grace and loveliness."[70]

And they constantly invited family to stay with them for as long as they wanted, especially Dolley's sister Anna, who had moved away when she married Richard Cutts. Dolley was ecstatic to learn Anna was visiting in 1810. "It is almost my first wish in this world that you should be happy & well & I will certainly advance it on every way that I can. Come then, with spirits & hope. I will have a fire made in your room and all prepared for your reception, with a sparkling bottle & warm hearts."[71]

Madison had been a good secretary of state. He not only had to advise the president but also make hundreds of decisions himself on US relations with dozens of foreign nations. He kept up a brisk correspondence with US ambassadors abroad, met regularly with foreign ministers in Washington, kept up a steady stream of letters to world leaders and ministers, and ran the State Department, which, small as it was, took considerable skill and time. He was cognizant of the views of all diplomats whom he talked to, and he knew the history of their countries and the history of their relations to the United States and the political situations they found themselves in. He knew how to deal with them and understood that events and decisions of world leaders would derail the best-made plans. He knew all about previous American dealings with foreign countries and could always, in his head, figure out the motives of foreign officials. His days as secretary of state were filled with decisions on matters in the new Louisiana Territory and in dealing with Spanish officials still there. He wrote Governor Claiborne at one point that he and Jefferson wanted the governor to strike some sort of deal with the Spaniards to give them post offices, but to suggest that they might be more pleased without post offices. It was that kind of clever dealing that made Madison successful.[72]

In international decisions, Madison exhibited the same shrewd understanding of politics and people. When he had to recall Charles Pinckney as ambassador to Spain, he told his successor, Monroe, that he had to be very careful about what he said about Pinckney. "I could not permit myself to flatter him, and truth would not permit me to praise him. He is well off in escaping reproof for his agency has been very faulty as well as feeble. Should you find him in Madrid, he may, however, give you some clues that may be useful."

He shrewdly added in his letter to Monroe that certain Spanish politicians ran the court, not those whom everyone believed ran it. To those people, Madison told Monroe, he had to pretend that the United States wanted a strong alliance with France in order to obtain a stronger one with Spain.

To become involved in such international political intrigue, Madison had to know his own ministers, know the foreign diplomats, have information from others on both, and use all to obtain his goals. He had to instruct his ministers on how to play their political cards as well as they could to get what he and Jefferson wanted. He also had to comb through dozens of newspapers to find out information about them. Madison was probably the best-read man in the country when he was secretary of state. He would preface his marks to many, "I have read in the newspapers . . ."[73]

He had a broad understanding, too, of the United States' place in the world and how both foreigners and Americans saw that place. It would be foolish to gain one goal at the price of losing another, greater goal. Foreign victories might be small if brought about by domestic losses. He bluntly told a Maryland man that "national degradation as the only calamity which is not greater than those of war. To avoid, if it be possible, amidst the unbridled passions which convulse other nations, both of these alternatives, is our true wisdom, as well as our solemn duty."[74]

He had also done a stellar job as a political analyst for Jefferson, constantly discussing how each party and every member of it saw an issue and how the actions of all were good or bad for the Republicans. He had, in his head, complicated analysis of politics at the national, state, county, city, and even village level. He had served as a political mastermind for years and now, as he assumed the presidential office, he was better at it than ever. James Madison was, in 1809, uniquely qualified to be president, and his politically and socially savvy wife made him even more qualified.

Now that he was president, Madison remained faithful to his Republican principles, as had his predecessor. He firmly believed that the country, and its government, belonged to the people, and that the president, and his party, had to represent all of the people. That's why he hated the now quickly disappearing Federalists; he believed they served a single, small faction of the American people. He also believed that it was the government's responsibility to rule fairly and not charge off on unnecessary domestic campaigns or foreign wars in order to build power. In a speech way back in 1792, when he was a congressman, he told his countrymen that each generation should not be burdened with the costs of the mistakes of previous generations. Americans are citizens, not caretakers. He argued, too, in that era, that a big government did not have to act in a big way.[75]

He understood, too, after a lifetime of friendships with politicians of both parties, that human nature and personal interest governed all politics. "In all . . . assemblies . . . passion never fails to wrest the scepter from treason. Had every Athenian citizen been a Socrates, every Athenian Assembly would still have been a mob," he wrote in 1788.[76]

James Madison the new president was not much different than James Madison the secretary of state or the founder of the Republican Party or the congressman or the architect of the US Constitution. He was, as friends and political allies said, an even-tempered man who never became exceedingly angry and saw all, despite their station in life, as equals. He was, his secretary Edward Coles said, "the most virtuous, calm and amiable of men, possessed of the purest heart and the best temper with which man was ever blessed."[77] Coles added that he never heard Madison "utter one petulant expression, or give way for one moment to passion or despondency . . . nothing could excite or ruffle him."

These were virtues that would serve him well when the War of 1812 began and he had to serve as commander in chief and political leader of his country at the same time. Charles Francis Adams, a historian and the son of John Quincy Adams, said that "foreign war and domestic discord came together upon him in a manner that would have tried the nerves of the strongest man," and yet he did not flinch.[78]

When he took office on March 4, 1809, Madison had advice from everyone. A correspondent who called himself "the old soldier" wrote just after his inauguration that it was time for tougher measures than an embargo. "[Only] if we could, for a moment, forget the insults and murders of the British and suppress our passions we should prefer this inoffensive mode of making war," wrote one man to a Philadelphia newspaper.[79]

Nobody had to tell him to watch the British; no one was more aware of Britain's truculence and duplicity than President Madison. In the winter of 1809, he still smarted from the complete lack of remorse by Britain for firing on the ship *Chesapeake* nearly two years earlier. "Every view of what had passed authorized a belief that immediate steps would be taken by the B. Govt. for redressing a wrong, which the more it was investigated appeared the more clearly to require what had not been provided for. No steps have been taken for the purpose," he wrote in the autumn of 1808. In a second letter on the *Chesapeake*, he ranted that the lack of any British apology was "evidence of hostile inflexibility on rights which no independent nation can relinquish" and that it would drive the United States "into an armor."[80]

Regardless of his talents and shortcomings, most American wished him well when he took office. Residents of Newark, Delaware, enthusiastically toasted him at a town gathering. "May we always be happy in celebrating the fourth of March to the memory of the virtues and wisdom of his administration," they toasted and cheered.[81]

President Madison was on his way.

12

A NEW ADMINISTRATION
AND A NEW COUPLE

*W*hen James Madison took over the presidency, he wanted to give it a different appearance. Jefferson had run the country for eight years and achieved great success. Madison wanted to leave his own thumbprint on the presidency. He wanted to do it in foreign affairs, in domestic issues, and with judicial appointments. But he also wanted to change the entire look of the federal government and saw the White House as representative of that. Madison wanted people to "see" the brand-new administration that he was talking about, and there was no better way to do that than to create a new White House.

There were numerous changes at the White House in Madison's first term. Madison asked for and was given five thousand dollars to permit his wife to redecorate the White House, which she claimed looked shabby. Jefferson did little upkeep during his eight years there. In 1809, under Dolley, the drawing rooms were furnished with new curtains and forty new pieces of furniture, highlighted by bright-yellow sofas and chairs. A huge mirror with a rising sun over it was placed on the wall. Dolley's own drawing room was now upholstered in yellow satin with stiff sofas and high-backed chairs. The long windows were hung with damask. Huge mirrors adorned the walls of different rooms. She purchased a new set of silverware from Philadelphia. There were yellow-fringed drapes over the windows. Chairs were set up in small semicircles throughout the room. Tables in it, and in nearby rooms, overflowed with cakes, meats syrups, ice cream, and hot pastries. Waiters brought around glasses of wine and cups of steaming hot coffee. It was there in the newly refurbished drawing room and other parlors that Mrs. Madison entertained guests. Now that she was the official First Lady, she went out of her way to raise the level of elegance at the President's Mansion.[1]

Within two years under the Madisons, the White House had become an elegant and richly furnished home. Visitors entered the front door and were at once in a large hall, which was used as an entry. Pillars of immense size were dispersed through this entry. It was handsomely furnished and had large lamps throughout. "The President's house is a perfect palace," said Elbridge Gerry Jr., the son of the late vice president.

Four large rooms were off the main entry hall. One was the dining room, said to be three times the size of any in America, and it was richly appointed. Dolley's sister said the sideboard was so large it would fill the entire parlors of most large American homes. Mrs. Madison's drawing room was off of the first-floor hallway, and it led to a larger, official drawing room that was oval and filled with large chairs and had portraits on the walls. A door opened from the drawing room to a terrace from which the Madisons could see the Potomac River. The enormous windows were the height of the drawing room and had silk-and-velvet curtains made of fabric that cost four dollars per yard (an astronomical sum for drapes in those days). The White House parties were held in the drawing rooms. The first floor also contained a parlor for the president and another for Mrs. Madison. Nearly half of one side of the rest of the first floor was taken up with a cabinet room and offices.[2]

Dolley upgraded the look of the First Lady and the president in a White House that seemed to see change everywhere. She ordered a new carriage, decorated by Benjamin Latrobe, with a huge, blazing letter *M* on each door; but this one was drawn by four horses and not two. Madison declined to have a six-horse carriage, as the Washingtons had. The carriage had expensive, English, lace curtains inside of it. Latrobe even consulted an Englishman who made carriages in London. Dolley approved everything before it was put into the carriage.[3]

Dolley expanded her circle of friends to include new arrivals in both politics and business. Her husband's close friend James Monroe was soon the secretary of state and lived in town, so the Madisons saw him and his wife frequently, entertained them at the White House, and visited their home. When the Madisons spent their summers back at Montpelier, they visited the Monroes, who lived nearby. John C. Calhoun arrived from South Carolina in 1811, and the Madisons saw him as a political leader right away and included him in their social circle.

Dolley continued to follow the latest fashions, such as wearing hats and bonnets as often as possible. She continued to do much reading, played the piano, and tended to her pet macaw. The bird was kept in a cage near a window in the White House, as it had been at the Madison's home, and Dolley fed it regularly. The president said hello to the bird when he could, and visitors spent much time looking at her. The macaw was as much an attraction at the White House as the Madisons. People who knew Dolley had a pet bird insisted that she needed more pets and sent them over. The biggest surprise was a large box of tiny, white mice.

James Madison, as president, could not visit Congress or the Supreme Court except on official business, but his wife could. She had done that for years and continued to do so as First Lady. She and a group of girlfriends would sit in the gallery and listen to the Senate and House debate and sit in on announcements of Supreme Court rulings. She was always well dressed, as were her friends. They drew such attention in Congress that sometimes upon their arrival a speaker who had just finished an address would stand up and deliver it again, for their benefit.[4]

The president smiled at that. He spent as much money as he could on Dolley, providing her with an enormous wardrobe and fine carriages. "Let me know how much [money] would be serviceable to you for your Philadelphia purposes. Let me know without reserve and I will do all I can in that as in all cases to evince the happiness I feel in giving proofs of my unlimited affection & confidence," he wrote her in 1805, when she was convalescing in Philadelphia.

When they traveled, they always stayed in the best inns. He was upset when he could not find superior lodgings for his wife. Once, when he had taken rooms for them in Richmond, he wrote sadly that "I found at Mr. Watson's a room prepared for me, and an empty one immediately over it, but they are both in a style much inferior to what I had hoped. You must consequently lower your expectations on this subject as much as possible before you join me," he told her.[5]

Mrs. Madison began the job of finding a cause to which she could devote her time. First Ladies over the next two hundred years followed her lead. Causes and charities are perfect tasks for First Ladies. They give the presidents' wives plenty to do, but the work is nonpolitical and does not draw negative attention to themselves or their husbands. She decided to become the head of the City Orphan Asylum, which grew as the population of the city expanded. Dolley did not merely lend her name to stationary letterheads, though; she plunged into the work of the orphanage, chairing meetings, raising money, donating her own money, and even designing and cutting clothes for the children. "I never enjoyed anything so much," she told a friend.[6]

She also had to fend off a surprising number of people, mostly Federalists, who hated the brand-new Washington and staged an early effort to move the capital of the country back to Philadelphia (they would try again in 1814). They argued that Washington was not a fit place to live. It had a sparse population, a thin social scene, little public entertainment, few parks, few public schools, and small libraries, and it was made up of people who were all from somewhere else. Philadelphia had been a fine capital, a complete, large city with residential neighborhoods, a large entertainment scene, and an established social life.[7]

Dolley and her husband, working with others in a heated behind-the-scenes movement, halted the efforts to move the capital back to Philadelphia. The decision had been made to build a new capital, but to put it in the middle of the country and to make its governmental buildings large, bold, and impressive. The new capital was the center of America's political universe and would be for hundreds of years. They had to stay put. And they did.

Madison read letters from editors in just about every American paper telling him that now that he was president, and not secretary of state, he had to do any number of things, and right away.[8] And he had to continually refute charges that he was a sick man and, as such, would be a weak president. A man wrote in the *Natchez Chronicle* that Madison was "a weak, debilitated man, greatly affected by fever" and "unable" to do his job.[9]

There were critics, too, who, despite the Republican electoral advantage, saw them as the devil incarnate. A man wrote in a local newspaper that since they were going out of office with Jefferson's retirement, it was time to judge them as "weak" and "foolish" public officials who had left the world worse for their eight-year reign.[10]

And Madison still had to deal with members of Congress, such as John Randolph, his archenemy, who had spent the last year lambasting him over his embargo. "I never said the carrying trade was not incentive and a profitable mode of employment for our ships [but I] do not think it of sufficient importance to be retained at the expense of a war," said Randolph.[11]

That had been just the latest Randolph tirade. In 1807, in a three-hour-long speech in Congress, Randolph had sneered at Madison for his 200-plus-page pamphlet against British impressment policy, shredding it page by page. Then he accused Madison of ruining Jefferson's cabinet. He finished off his scalding blast by accusing Madison of bribing the French to get them to help the United States obtain all of Florida, stunning the members of the House. Madison smiled when he heard of the criticism. Republican congressmen cringed at Randolph's abusive language, and even his friends told him he had gone too far. One told him that when all was said and done, years from then, history would overlook his vicious criticisms and consider Madison a great man. Randolph scoffed.[12] Less than a year later, Randolph called Madison "a polecat," sending even more shudders throughout the political world.[13]

The problems Madison faced as president were compounded by the "success" he had gained with his policies as secretary of state. As an example, he had always been a strong advocate of the migration of hundreds of thousands of Americans from the eastern seaboard to the Mississippi valley region. He was pleased by the invasion of settlers, but that fertile Louisiana world soon had troubles of its own. Attracted by the new traffic, small bands of robbers began to appear on all the dusty dirt roads in the area, which caused enormous distress to travelers and increased law-enforcement costs. Sales of land were in the tens of thousands of acres, and purchasers discovered that they had bought land that several hundred people already lived on—and refused to leave. That dispute went to local state courts and then all the way to the White House, where a disgruntled Madison had to order the forcible eviction of the squatters.[14]

At the same time that he was running the country, Madison was also still running his plantation back in Montpelier. His manager, James Dinsmore, whose only concern was the farm and not the president's overload of responsibility, constantly wrote him letters asking for decisions on mundane items such as bookshelves (the president had to decide whether or not to make the windows smaller to accommodate the larger bookshelves or keep the windows wide and get smaller book shelves).[15]

Personal tragedies beset him, too. Just one day after the bookshelf dispute at Montpelier, he learned that Meriwether Lewis, Jefferson's aide who, with William Clark, had headed up the landmark Lewis and Clark expedition into the newly purchased Louisiana Territory, which had gained worldwide attention, had committed suicide. He then had to investigate the sad end for the famous explorer, and that took time. Then he had to tell his friend Jefferson about it. On the home front, Madison continually struggled with his brother-in-law John Payne's alcoholism. It had depressed his wife, Dolley. Finally, Madison gave John Payne a job as a clerk in the minister to Tunis's office in Africa, hopeful, as his wife wrote friends, that new scenery would curb his drinking. It did not. A few months later, Lucy Washington was writing to her sisters Anna and Dolley that their brother John had resumed his drinking in Tunis. Lucy wrote her sisters, "I know not what to say or do, but greatly fear for him. It seems to me impossible his sisters can render him any essential service without ruin to themselves and then perhaps it may answer no good and—heaven help him I pray."[16]

Dolley wrote her brother and invited him to move into the White House with her, her husband, and other members of the family. "You promised to return to us long before this and I hope and trust that if you are disappointed in our prospects where you are, that you will not suffer those weak reflections [drinking] on yourself, which affect me, in your letter, to stay you one moment from my arms & heart, that are open to receive you. You would return to sisters & brothers that love you & whose happiness it would be to do everything for you, if you required."[17] She also asked him to give her power of attorney so she could sell his lands and wrap up his failed business ventures in America. She told him, too, that she and her husband would pull strings to get him a better job in the foreign service in Europe if he so desired. Unbeknown to him, she also sent letters to people in France and Africa who might see him to remind them to discreetly tell him to report for jobs and do what was required of him.

One month later, the president learned from officials that the Marine Corps was broke. Federal allocations of money were not enough to cover the expenses of repairing naval ships, whose costs came in much higher than anticipated. How does a country's Marine Corps go broke, he had to wonder.[18]

The Madisons had sad family tragedies, too. Dolley grieved at each one. She wrote her sister about the passing of a relative that "I can scarcely write you, so sick with grief, apprehension, is my whole frame." Then, just months before Madison took office, Dolley's mother died at the end of 1808 following a series of sudden strokes. Dolley had been very close to her mother and almost always mentioned her health in letters to family. In the spring of 1804, she added in a letter to a friend that "I have just received a long letter from Mamma, who is well." Dolley was deeply shaken by the loss of her mother. Then, a few months later, her sister Mary, who had cared for her mother, suddenly passed away. Mary's husband wrote that the mother's death killed Mary. "The shock which her sickness and death produced upon the health and spirits of my poor sick wife has been alarming in the extreme," wrote John Jackson to Dolley.[19]

The double tragedy crippled Dolley emotionally. "Eliza," she wrote friend Eliza Collins Lee, "I cannot write 'tho I wish to communicate everything to you; when I trace the sad events that have occurred to me, I feel as if I should die, too."[20] Later, she added that all of the love of the different women in the Payne and Madison families together could not help her overcome her grief. "What in this world can compensate for the sympathy and confidence of a mother and a sister?"[21]

The loss of her mother and sister drove her further into the arms of her husband, the president, for love and solace. She asked herself in a letter what could help her and then said that "nothing but that tie that binds us to a good husband, such as ours, and we ought to be satisfied."[22] Madison was there, for her, too—every day—despite all of his hard work as the president. He grieved with her for her mother and sister Mary and took care of her.

In all of her letters to her husband, Dolley expressed her deep love for him. She wrote him just after he returned to Washington in 1805, "A few hours only have passed since you left me, my beloved, and I find nothing can relieve the oppression of my mind but speaking to you in this the only way . . ." A few days later, she ended her letter, "Adieu my beloved. Our hearts understand each other, in fond affection thine . . ."[23]

All was not pleasant for the Madisons in Washington. Just about every week, the *National Intelligencer* and other local papers ran ads in which slave owners were asking area residents to catch their runaway slaves and return them to their plantations. From time to time, the Washington city sheriff would announce that he had captured runaways and was holding them in his jail so that their owners could ride to town and retrieve them. Dolley, who disliked slavery, must have flinched. Madison, who owned dozens of slaves but never liked the idea of slave ownership, must have been uncomfortable, especially since the *National Intelligencer*, which made money off the ads, was run by his friend Samuel Smith (Smith even worked as a middleman to reunite runaways with their masters at his newspaper office). Other ads, in all of the capital newspapers, were straight "for sale" ads to get readers to purchase slaves. Many promoted the sale of not only individual slaves but also whole families. For example, one ad featured four or five different families in one large sale of thirty-six people.[24]

The Madisons, and everybody else in the capital, had to read official letters in newspaper columns from Toussaint L'Ouverture, the spirited and cocky new leader of Haiti, who had led the slave revolt to kick the French out of his island country. He insisted that Haitian blacks in the United States who were enslaved had to be returned, free, to their homeland. It was "an act of piracy" to hold the free blacks from Haiti, a free country, he wrote with heated anger.[25]

President Madison was handcuffed by politics. One severe mistake Madison made early in his first term was to back down from fights with political opponents in forming his cabinet. He had worked well with Swiss-born Albert Gallatin in Jefferson's cabinet and wanted Gallatin to be his secretary of state. Influential Republican senators and editors urged him to give Gallatin some other job, though, because he was foreign born and too close to Jefferson. He had become the object of substantial vitriol for many. William Duane, the influential editor of the *Aurora*, wrote that Gallatin was guilty of duplicity and cunning and was hopelessly self-centered. "Mr. Gallatin will drag him down for no honest man can support an administration of which he is a member," he wrote.[26] Other Republicans joined him in crucifying Gallatin.

Madison worried about congressional approval of his entire cabinet, and he should not have. He won the election easily, followed a popular president, and, thanks to his wife, enjoyed the friendship of all in Washington except the most hardened Federalists. Yet he was nervous. Madison did not want to fracture his party. He decided to work with a representative cabinet with members from each region of the country, a noble, democratic idea that works on paper but rarely in practice. He turned down Senator William Giles as secretary of state and selected Robert Smith, Jefferson's secretary of the navy and the brother of Senator Samuel Smith of Maryland, whom he knew little about. He had to let Gallatin go in that post and was also barred from naming his longtime friend, James Monroe, because, his aides said, Monroe had run against him for president. Besides, he could always run the department himself if Smith was weak, he thought. No one thought much of Smith. Even Madison critic John Randolph sneered and said of Smith that "as he can spell he ought to be pre-ferred to Giles."[27]

He should have named Monroe. He and his fellow Virginian had been friends for years, and Monroe had served him well in the State Department. Monroe was a close friend of Thomas Jefferson, too. Jefferson had met Monroe during the American Revolution and in the early 1780s had taken him in as a clerk when Jefferson was the governor of Virginia. Jefferson had vouched for Monroe all of his life. Monroe had botched the election, and his relation-ship with Madison, because he never really thought things through. He did not realize the implications of what he did, and friends realized this. Lawyer William Wirt said of Monroe that "nature has given him a mind neither rapid nor rich, and therefore he cannot shine on a subject which is entirely new to him."[28] Wirt added, though, that once Monroe was sure what to do, he did it well. Wirt said he had "a judgment strong and clear and a habit of application which no difficulties can shake, no labours can tire."

Political aides talked the president into ignoring Monroe because of the election squabble. His friend Jefferson had scoffed at that idea and was angry that Madison did not name Monroe. Jefferson summoned Monroe to Monticello, as his friend, and had long talks with him there. Then he cagily wrote Madison that Monroe "had dined and passed an evening with me … he is sincerely cordial and I learn from several that he has quite separated himself from the junto which had got possession of him." He added that Monroe had split with Madison's enemy John Randolph and that "his strong and candid mind will bring him to a cordial return to his old friends after he shall have been separated a while from his present circle." It was the start of a fervent campaign to get Monroe back into government. It was an uphill campaign because, in addition to the political miscue, Monroe had angered both James and Dolley Madison by breaking off all social contact with them during the election and had remained distant from them ever since. There were a number of letters from Jefferson to Madison over the next few months, and at any news of Monroe, Jefferson would write Madison, reminding him of his long friendship with Monroe. A year later, in the spring of 1810, he heard that Monroe had visited Washington. He fired off a note to Madison: "There appears to be the most perfect reconciliation and cordiality established towards yourself. I think him now inclined to rejoin us with zeal. The only embarrassment will be from his late friends. But I think he has the firmness of mind enough to act independently as to them." His campaign worked.[29]

Jefferson had helped to heal a rift between two friends that never should have occurred. Whether he listened to political advisers or not, Monroe should never have run against Madison and never continually suggested, right until the end of the campaign, that all he wanted to do is put two Republicans on the ballot. Nobody believed that, and the aborted short campaign made Monroe look bad in Madison's eyes.[30]

Monroe took the secretary of state job when it was offered for a few reasons: he knew that there was no one more qualified to hold the office; it got him back into government and renewed relationships; and it would lead to the presidency. One friend, John Taylor, told him that "our foreign relations seem to be drawing to a crisis and you ought to be in the public eye when it happens, for your own sake, independently of the services you can render your country."[31] Monroe, who had just been elected governor of Virginia three months earlier, took the job heading up the State Department right away.

⁂

The Madisons held more receptions, parties, and dances at the White House; used more food and drink; and employed more help than had their predecessors. They doubled the number of full-time servants working in the White House to thirty, led by Jean Pierre Sioussat, a Frenchman who ironically had worked for their social archenemies, the Merrys of England. A cousin, Edward Coles (as secretary) and several of their personal slaves, such as Dolley's favorites, Paul Jennings and Sukey, worked there, too. There were more elegant carriages and more horses kept in the stables out back. More and diverse guests were added to their party lists, and the important ministers of foreign countries found themselves sharing drinks with local store owners. More orchestras, each larger than the previous, were hired to provide music for dances. The circle of the Madisons' friends grew in size and diversity, too, and more society women from all over the United States became their friends. The wives of key women from the diplomatic corps, such as the wife of Jerome Bonaparte, and the wife of

James Monroe, said to be two of the most beautiful women in America, became close friends of the Madisons. Dolley expanded her practice of asking all visitors to the White House to leave their calling cards, and she kept enormous boxes of them to create guest lists for her parties. The more the merrier.

Guests regularly marveled at the wide array of different foods at the receptions. They dined on ice cream, almonds, raisins, peaches, and baskets filled to the brim with apples and pears. There were dozens of trays full of small bags of candy.[32]

Dolley had plenty of help in the Executive Mansion, too. Her younger sister Anna, married to Congressman Richard Cutts, lived a few blocks away. Sister Lucy, now a widow following the death of George Steptoe Washington, moved into the White House with Dolley. A dozen relatives lived in the White House from time to time, too, making it a very busy home. The three Payne sisters, dubbed "the Merry Wives of Windsor" by the social crowd, shared entertainment chores at the White House. The three, led by Dolley, now had eight years of experience as hostesses in the Jefferson administration and were used to the work. Now, in 1809, they were professionals at it. Everybody who came to a party at the White House was greeted by the First Lady and then passed around the room in smooth order. Of his first White House visit at a reception, "Here I was most graciously received," wrote author Washington Irving, who would later write the short stories "The Legend of Sleepy Hollow" and "Rip Van Winkle." He continued, "[I] found a crowded collection of great and little men, of ugly old women and beautiful young ones and in ten minutes was hand and glove with half the people in the assemblage." And, like everyone, he was impressed by Dolley Madison. "Mrs. Madison is a fine, portly, buxom dame, who has a smile and pleasant word for everybody," he said.[33]

At her dinner parties, Dolley made certain that her husband's talkative and charming secretary, Edward Coles, her cousin, sat across the table from her so that the two of them could keep the conversation flowing. When Coles was not there, she made certain she sat a personable wife of a guest in that seat to achieve the same purpose. Everything about Dolley's balls, parties, and dinners was carefully orchestrated.

Coles helped the Madisons in many ways, in addition to working as the president's secretary. He stayed close to the president during parties and brought him over to people Madison needed to see for political purposes, making the meeting seem very casual. Coles was sent to parties at foreign ministries to mingle with guests and pick up political news. He was asked to befriend as many important people in the capital as he could to gather information for the Madisons and to spread it for them. Some men kept Coles on their regular, once-a-week dinner list, and others had his name on their regular party list. Young Coles, aged twenty-three, also worked with Madison in patronage appointments and was befriended by many congressmen because of his power to find jobs for their friends and relatives. He met famous men, such as steamship inventor Robert Fulton, who fumed to him about his woes with the US Patent Office. Coles was "a thorough gentlemen and one of the best-natured and most kindly affectioned men it has ever been my fortune to know," wrote William Preston, a guest at the White House, as a young man.[34]

The president liked Coles. He decided early on to use him as a liaison between political foes and allies in different states. He sent him on one trip to Philadelphia and another to Boston to listen to political figures and give them presidential messages. On his Boston trip, at the special behest of Madison, he even visited former president John Adams in Quincy to give him a message from his enemy, Jefferson, about the disputed election of 1800. Adams then wrote Jefferson. The two became friends, and their famous correspondence began. Later, Madison sent Coles on a sensitive mission to Russia.

All of the guests at the White House noted that the guest list had grown considerably since Madison was inaugurated and the parties were far larger than those when Jefferson was president and those at Madison's private home when he served as secretary of state. Before Madison became president, Dolly hosted two or three parties a week at their home or at the White House and attended three or four more at the homes of friends or at foreign embassies. It was not unusual to attend six or seven parties in a single week. Many residents called Dolley's White House parties her "squeezes" because of the size of the crowds (you had to "squeeze" your way in). Phoebe Morris and her brother went to a party there in 1812 when they arrived in town and were startled at the number of people in attendance, all dressed in their finest clothes. "It was a great day there. The house was crowded with company from top to bottom, the chambers and every room was occupied with Ladies and Gentlemen and all descriptions of persons," said Phoebe.[35]

William Preston, who lived in the White House for a while, had the same impression. He wrote that "there was a multitude of carriages at the door. Many persons were going in and coming out, and especially many in grand regimentals. Upon entering the room there were fifteen or twenty people ... around the room was a blaze of military and naval officers in brilliant uniforms."[36]

Dolley's social life extended to the Washington racetrack, built by her friend the architect William Thornton. He and her husband were the co-owners of a horse named Wild Medley. Other Washingtonians owned horses, too, some of which cost them $10,000 to purchase. The racing season took place in the autumn, as in other major cities. Thousands of people gathered for the races and bet heavily on the outcomes. Many parties were held around the racetrack, where fans gathered on horseback and in carriages. Evening parties were held at the clubhouse at the racetrack, too. The Madisons thoroughly enjoyed each racing season. "The whole ground within the circus was spread over with people on horseback, stretching round full speed, to different parts of the circus, to see the race . . . between 3,000 and 4,000 people . . . black and white and yellow, of all conditions, from the President of the United States to the beggar in his rags, all ages and both sexes," wrote one regular race goer.[37]

The First Lady was seen as a literary light, and authors continually sent first editions of their works to her at the White House. Writers dedicated books and poems to her. "Your character was not unknown to him. Of the greatness of your heart, he has heard much; but of the faculties of your mind he has heard much more. Always an admirer of intellectual worth and mental excellence, he would experience an unspeakable gratification in having an opportunity to evince the admiration he feels for your character," wrote one poet to her of a friend.[38] Writer David Warden not only dedicated his new book to the First Lady but also sent over a copy for her library. One playwright dedicated his latest drama to her.[39]

Her husband had been absorbed with books all of his life, but few knew of Dolley's own passion for reading. She had her own library when she was married to John Todd, and she brought all of her books with her to Montpelier. Over the years, she and her husband had expanded their library into one of the largest private libraries in the country. Her sister Mary wrote that the Montpelier library was not "only lined with bookcases, but the center so filled with them that there was only just room enough to pass among them. Books and pamphlets were piled up everywhere, on every available chair and table."[40]

Dinner guests and friends were always surprised at the number of books Dolley had read at Montpelier and in the White House, in addition to all the newspapers she consumed. Dozens of people in Washington had loaned her books and had notes back from her that showed she had read them. She was, by the time she became First Lady, one of the best read people in the country. Sarah Gales Seaton, whose husband followed Samuel Smith as the coeditor of the *National Intelligencer*, pulled women aside at White House dinner parties to tell them about lengthy conversations she had had with Dolley about books.[41]

Joseph Dennie, a magazine editor, put Dolley on one of his covers and told a friend that he could not believe the easy way that she slid into conversations on any topic about books. Guests at the White House always noticed that when she arrived at a party, she always had a book in her hand (*Don Quixote* was her favorite). Later, a statue erected in her honor at the Smithsonian Institution showed Dolley holding a book. Dolley also was a member of a small book club with her sisters and relatives. They exchanged favorite volumes with each other all of their lives. She asked her son, who traveled extensively, to buy books for her in European capitals, and sometimes she sent him a list of specific titles she was interested in. She asked friends to do the same.

The First Lady was the recipient of an enormous string of gifts from public figures, Washington residents, merchants, and their wives. Interior decorator Latrobe's wife was always buying Dolley new turbans in whatever city she visited and mailed them to her in Washington. Betsy Patterson Bonaparte, one of her social friends, bought hats, stockings, and dresses and sent them to the White House as gifts. Dolley received gifts from very prominent people, too, such as John Jacob Astor, who forwarded to her expensive fur hats. One of the strangest gifts she received was a fourteen-pound beetroot plant from France stuffed in a wooden crate, which was sent by Ambassador Joel Barlow, who called it her "oddest present ever." People did not give her gifts for favors; they did it because they liked her. A woman who gave her a cap told her that "I hope that you will wear it if only once & think of one that always thinks of you with great affection."[42]

She also became famous for always carrying snuff with her. It annoyed many, though. "Mrs. Madison is still pretty, but, oh, that unfortunate propensity to snuff-taking!" complained Aaron Burr.[43]

That combination of intellectual achievement, ebullient personality, and social graces made Dolley an extraordinarily successful First Lady. Harriet Martineau wrote that "for a term of eight years she administered the hospitalities of the White House with such discretion, impartiality and kindliness that it is believed she gratified every one and offended nobody. She is a strong minded woman, fully capable of entering into her husband's occupations and cares; and there is little doubt that he owed much to her intellectual companionship, as well as to her ability in sustaining the outward dignity of his office."[44]

One problem Dolley encountered in 1809 was her weight. After eight years as both hostess for her husband and the president, she had wined and dined guests at well over a thousand parties and dinners, all featuring gourmet meals and a never-ending stream of exotic desserts, such as multiflavored ice creams. She had put on twenty pounds or so in those years and now, in 1809, found herself more careful in picking out clothing that hid her weight. Two years later, she started to lose some of her hearing. In a panic, she wrote her sister that "the deafness continues & distresses me beyond anything that ever ailed me."[45]

Mrs. Madison stayed clear of any public connections to politics, preferring to lobby for her husband and his causes at home. She told a friend, "the mornings are devoted to Congress. where all delight to listen to the violence of evil spirit. I stay quietly at home (as quietly as one can be who has so much to feel at the expression for and against their conduct)."[46]

At home, though, behind the closed doors of the White House, Dolley was a full participant in national politics. She advised her husband on the issues of the day and, more important, helped him pick cabinet members and government workers, always reminding him to look at a man's total background, not just his political bent. Thanks to her, Madison wound up with a hardworking team that did not stir much controversy in the early years of his term. James Blaine, who would later become secretary of state, wrote "Mrs. Madison saved the administration of her husband, held him back from the extremes of Jeffersonism and enabled him to escape from the terrible dilemma of the War of '12."[47]

Dolley always knew what was going on in the political world through her husband. She often asked him to tell her more about politics in his letters to her and, in nearly all of them, reminded him that she would not reveal anything he said—and as far as one can tell, she was true to her word. "I wish you would indulge me with some information respecting the war with Spain and the disagreement with England which is so generally expected," she wrote. Then she added in the next breath, "you know I am not much of a politician, but I am extremely anxious to hear (as far as you think proper) what is going forward in the cabinet," she wrote the Madison in 1805. She wrote about politics to sister Anna, too, and Anna kept her views secret. For instance, at the end of the summer of 1808, when the embargo against England was a hot national issue, Dolley wrote her sister, "the President and Madison have been greatly perplexed by the remonstrances from so many towns to remove the Embargo. You see they refer to Congress, and the evading it is a terrible thing. Madison is uneasy."[48]

Dolley smiled broadly to all, but behind that smile could be petty grudges that she held against people, even longtime friends. For example, there was a feud she and her husband tumbled into with architect Thornton, who sold them their first house in Washington, introduced them to the capital social scene, and for a time co-owned racehorses with the president. The Madisons drifted from him, though. In March 1817, just after the Madisons left the capital when James's second term ended, Thornton wrote the president that "I have long had to lament a marked distance and coldness towards me, for which I cannot account, and am the more affected by it, because we once enjoyed the happiness of being considered as among your friends. It would have been kind to have mentioned any cause of dissatisfaction rather than wound us by exhibiting to the world our misfortune in the loss of your friendship and esteem."[49]

Sometimes Dolley snapped responses to questions and let her true feelings out. At one party, she was involved in a discussion with several women about the character of a woman no one seemed to like. Something was said to Dolley and she sneered, "Oh, she's a hussy." She would tell others that certain people were dull, were tedious, or bored you with endless "instructions" on how to live. She said of one woman that "it is in her power to be kind and perhaps useful to you, but if she is ever offended in any way she is bitter. It is best for us, my dear, to beware of 'most everybody' as I have often said."

Dolley could be biting. She had a sharp tongue, and pen, and she had used them since she was a teenager. In 1788, as a young woman, she wrote a friend about Philadelphia that "this place is almost void of anything novel." She told Anna Thornton of Thomas Jefferson's grandson that he was "a fine one, but as cross as you could wish anything to be." She wrote her husband in 1805 from Philadelphia that the impression of French ambassador Louis-Marie Turreau "was a sad one. He is the fighting husband. [Friends] said the Americans hate him."[50]

The gossip of her friends was just as scathing as her own. Sally McKean, who married the Spanish ambassador, told Dolley that "Harper has made the most ridiculous speech in the world ... the fool." About President Adams, she wrote that "old Adams' speech, or rather Old Beelzebub's, many people who went to hear him were so amazed at it that they scarce believed their own ears." McKean could be acidic. She said of an acquaintance, "that old, what shall I call her, with her hawk eyes, gave out that the weather was too warm and it would affect her nerves ... she is not young and confounded ugly." She added that the woman's family was eager to have a fuss made over them in Boston, "for, dear knows, they have had none made over them here." Another friend of Dolley's, Dolley Cole Beckwith, told Mrs. Madison that "I can almost see and hear Mrs. Duvell set shuffling her cards with her turban and frieze slipped to the back of her head and her false jaws working."[51]

Dolley would engage several people to help her conduct lengthy investigations into the lives of people whom she felt were being unfair to her and her husband or causing unnecessary trouble. She once utilized Edward Coles, Madison's secretary, for that purpose, sending him on trips to visit members of the family of General Alexander Smith to discover why the Smiths were involved in a vendetta against the Madisons. They had, Dolley charged, spread false rumors about the president and First Lady and, she said, written a pamphlet and slanderous newspaper articles about them in journals such as the *Whig*. A friend asked her if she laughed about the articles and pamphlet. She said her husband did, but she was furious at the Smiths. She vowed revenge, too. "It was too impertinent to excite any other feeling in me than anger. He will be sick of his attempt when he reads all that will be replied to it," she wrote.[52]

Coles visited the Smiths, dined with them, and drank with them in an effort to get at the truth. He also discovered that the scurrilous newspaper articles about the Madisons signed "Timolean" were actually written by George Stevenson, a nephew of one of the Smiths. These inquiries were not only meant to discover some secret but also to let the targets, and everyone else in Washington, know that Dolley Madison was going to investigate them. It was a powerful warning from the First Lady of the United States.[53]

Dolley gossiped continually with friends. She wrote Phoebe Morris in 1813: "You remember the Judges. They have been some time amongst us, and are as agreeable as ever. They talk of you continually, particularly [Supreme Court Justice] Joseph Story "[54]

Dolley's high-paced social life at the White House spurred others to host parties, too, officially and unofficially. The embassies of countries, such as France, England, and Turkey, all held receptions, dinners, and parties at their official houses, and the Madisons were always invited. "We had a breakfast at the French Minister's which was quite pleasant, a small party & profusion of fruit," wrote Dolley of one. Diplomats, congressmen, and Washington residents held dinners and receptions at their homes—very unofficial—and the Madisons attended those, too. By the time her husband's first term as president was over, Dolley had significantly increased the social world of Washington, and it all radiated from the White House.[55]

The parties did not just attract the beautiful and powerful. They attracted many people, including egotistical men and women who used the gatherings to showcase their looks and grace, sometimes looks and grace that they no longer possessed. Some were convinced that gowns and diamonds would cover up their age, wrinkles, and physical shortcomings. They were the targets of much behind-the-scenes talk. Congressman Joseph Story joked to his wife that the parties were filled with "some aged damsels, flirting in the gay undress of 18 and antiquated country squires assuming the air of fashionable beaux."[56]

When her husband became secretary of state, Dolley's signature headgear was the French beret that she wore casually over her hair. French fashions waned after a few years, though, and she replaced the beret with her own invention—the turban. She created the dazzling-looking turban, which looked like the headgear of Turkish princes, by simply wrapping a three- or four-foot-long piece of silk or other material around her hair in a wide cone. The turban was not just stylish but also enabled her to wrap up her uncombed hair in a few seconds. Women loved it because it also covered one's head and prevented the need, at the time, to powder one's hair. Women also did not want to spend endless hours combing their hair. And it was fast and simple to wrap the turban.

Dolley decorated her turbans with jewels and pins, making them quite stylish. Dolley first wore a turban at a White House ball, and hundreds of women in Washington began to wear it the following week. The turban then swept through America and overseas. It found its way to France, where Josephine Bonaparte began to wear it.

The turban also added another foot or so to Dolley's height, making her 6'8" tall when she walked through her parties, a wandering beacon of a hostess in blazing color, easy to find and easy to talk to about anything. James Madison never liked the turbans. Before each party he would tell her how much he disliked them and how they detracted from her natural beauty. They would argue a bit and then Dolley would spin around, wrap her hair in the turban, and walk to the party. Her husband, the president, would grumble and follow her.[57]

Dolley copied the daring French dress styles of the day, too. At one party, the belle of the ball was the rather daring, voluptuous, young American wife of Jerome Bonaparte, Betsy, whom Emperor Napoleon Bonaparte refused to meet and who seemed to dress for the sole purpose of creating scandal. She always wore low-cut, tight dresses that showed much cleavage. She looked like she had been poured into them. Betsy knew what she looked like, too, and she moved her body to show it off. She was so shapely that the *Baltimore American* newspaper even published a poem devoted to her physical beauty. Betsy had her own full-time hair dresser, too.

"Mobs of boys have crowded around her splendid equipage to see what I hope will not often be seen in this country, an almost naked woman . . . her back, her bosom, part of her waist and her arms were uncovered and the rest of her form visible," wrote one woman.[58]

Men certainly enjoyed the new, daring women's dresses. One man at a White House party wrote that "the ladies were not remarkable for anything so much as for the exposure of their swelling breasts and bare backs."[59]

Women out-dressed each other. Mrs. Anthony Merry, the British ambassador's wife, arrived covered in diamonds, from bracelets on her wrists to a necklace to a diamond tiara at one party. Then, fashionably late, the president and his wife arrived. Dolly was dressed in a beautiful, tight, ivory satin gown with a plunging neckline. On her head she had one of her turbans, decked out in jewels and, to top it all off, two large, flamboyant ostrich plumes stuck up out of the turban. All gasped; Dolley smiled.

Ambassador Merry and his wife were a constant problem for both Jefferson and the Madisons. The Merrys were thin-skinned and overly socially conscious. Success in Washington's social world seemed as important as success on the international front. At one White House party, the Merrys felt they were official invited dinner guests and that protocol dictated that the president, without a companion, should offer his arm to Mrs. Merry and escort her in to dinner. Instead, Jefferson turned to Dolley Madison and gave her his arm. She demurred and told him he had to take in Mrs. Merry. Jefferson smiled wryly, tightened his grip on Dolley, and led her into the dining room. Mrs. Merry, furious, followed them in the official procession. A week later, the Merrys felt similarly disrespected at a party at the Madisons' home and left early, offending everyone. Madison later explained to Merry that American dinner-party rules were quite loose, unlike those of England, and that no snubs were intended. The Merrys were still angry. Mrs. Merry steamed about the snubs for months and, with her ambassador husband, made it a huge social issue in the capital. No one in Washington paid much attention to the Merrys, and, Madison learned through snoopy gossips in London, neither did the British.[60]

On another occasion, Dolley invited the Merrys to a party and insisted that it was very unofficial and very informal. The president escorted Mrs. Merry into dinner on his arm, as required by social and political protocol. There, the smiling Merrys were introduced to the guests at the dinner. Then, at the end of the table, Mrs. Merry was introduced to a local haberdasher and his wife, invited by Dolley because she thought both were quite funny and would liven up the political dinner. Mrs. Merry was aghast. British legation chief Augustus Foster wrote his mother that America was "indeed a country not fit for a dog."[61]

It was that same Foster who also paid Dolley one of the finest backhanded comments she ever received. After a visit to Montpelier, Foster said of her that "she was a very handsome woman and tho' an uncultured mind and fond of gossiping, was so perfectly good tempered and good humored that she rendered her husband's house as far as depended on her agreeable to all parties."[62]

Mrs. Madison shone at Montpelier, where she reigned as the First Lady of both the United States and Orange County. She hosted numerous parties each summer, and each one was larger, louder, and gaudier than the other. On the Fourth of July in 1816, she outdid herself, throwing a party for ninety guests outdoors on her lawns. "The dinner was profuse & handsome," she said, "and the company very orderly . . . the day was cool & quite pleasant."[63]

As his first year as president ended, Madison told friends that the government he ran, and the country that he represented, had turned out well and functioned as a smooth-running union of states. His party retained its strong majority in Congress, Republican newspapers were solidly behind the administration, and the nation's farming and business was good. The people were happy. "With a union of its citizens, a government thus identified with the nation may be considered as the strongest in the world; the participation of every individual in the rights and welfare of the whole, adding the greatest moral, to the greatest physical strength of which political society is susceptible," he wrote at the end of 1810.[64]

It had been a tough first year, filled with international problems and political infighting at home, but he was satisfied with it. Those who saw him when he was not in the president's office said that the burdens of office were not wearing him down, as many feared. "When he can disengage himself for a moment from the [chores] attached to the painful honor of being Chief of a republican government, the wrinkles smooth out of his face, his countenance lights up, it shines then with all the fire of the spirit and with a gentle gayety; and one is surprised to find in the conversations of the great statesman . . . as much sprightliness as strength," wrote Baron de Montlezun, a diplomat.[65]

Madison had become a strong and resourceful chief executive after his first year in office. He had stepped out of the shadow of Thomas Jefferson and become his own man, his own president.

13

THE NEVER-ENDING DISPUTE
WITH GREAT BRITAIN

rom the first day he arrived at his office in the White House until the end of his administration, James Madison was crippled by the British. His embargo and subsequent Non-Intercourse Act had not succeeded, and neither had the diplomatic missions of any of his State Department envoys to London, all sent there to end the British search and seizure of American ships and impressment of American sailors. The British were determined to stop American ships wherever they found them, whether in the English Channel, the high seas of the rolling Atlantic Ocean, or the faraway ports of the Caribbean. They captured sailors whom they claimed were British Navy deserters and also grabbed Americans. They threatened to fire upon and sink American ships, and, in fact, had done so in American waters off the coast of Maryland in 1807 when, after a dispute over their right to board the ship to search for British deserters, they opened fire on the USS *Chesapeake*. Three American sailors were killed and eighteen wounded.

British diplomats resisted every effort by Americans to talk them out of their policies. The Brits argued that under a 1756 law, they had the right to stop the ships of all countries trading with a wartime enemy, and that enemy was France. The British had every reason to suspect, too, that—like so many European wars—the conflict with Napoleon and France might last many years. They could not permit America to trade with Napoleon. The Americans argued that they were a neutral nation and were sending only commercial goods, not arms, to Napoleon. The stone-faced British refused to listen.

John Quincy Adams even argued that Britain's action betrayed its own history and Constitution. "[It] is justified on the plea of necessity which being above all law, claims equal exemption from responsibility to the tribunal of reason," he wrote, adding that he cheered Madison's tenacity.[1]

183

That tenacity never wavered. Madison was, and would remain throughout his entire presidency, furious with the British. He wrote Jefferson in 1809 that the new British ministry was laden with "quackeries and corruption." He said it was going from bad to worse and he saw no change for the better in the future. Jefferson, as angry as he, wrote back that he could not believe the British public went along with its government on their anti-American policies. "They are on the point of being blown up and they still proceed with the same madness and increased wickedness," he wrote.[2]

Madison's conversation and correspondence was dominated by his woes with England. The time and energy he had to spend on the British trouble left him little time to address domestic problems that grew each year.

Why should the British be interested in any agreement, British supporters asked. Britain ruled the high seas; had the largest navy in the world; were officially at war with France; and had the right to stop neutrals such as the United States from aiding and abetting its enemy.

There was another reason, though—revenge. England continued to smart from its catastrophic defeat in the American Revolution. The empire had lost the war to George Washington and his armies and also had been forced into fighting a far-ranging and very costly world war for eight years. The American Revolution had cost Britain nearly twenty thousand soldier and sailor lives and tens of millions of dollars. The British had been embarrassed. It was a defeat that would be remembered throughout hundreds of years of their history. They never forgot the debacle.

In the winter of 1810, Robert Livingston, writing from London, reminded President Madison of that: "The King & the people of [England] hate, dread and envy us. And that they will do so until the memory of our having been rebel colonies is entirely lost and till the sordid spirit peculiar to a nation of merchants and tradesmen from the days of Carthage to the present era is extinguished by some great calamity."[3]

The Brits had refused to shut down their northwest forts in America, which was agreed upon in the peace treaty of 1783, for more than ten years. They had become involved in complicated negotiations over money owed to British merchants during the war and from the years prior to it. Now, in 1809, they would use their powerful navy to both interdict American shipping and humiliate America. They would do it for years, too, under the guise of the 1756 laws and the argument that they were always at war, somehow, someway, and needed to curtail American shipping for that reason.

If America did not like that, well, British officials shrugged their shoulders, do something about it. America did not. It continually submitted; it constantly backed down.

The president was only in office a few months when he fired off an angry note to the Republican Meeting of South Carolina. "The very unexpected and inauspicious turn given to our relations with Great Britain by the disavowal of the friendly arrangements concluded by her accredited minister, [do] not fail to excite a lively sensibility among a people conscious of their own just purposes and satisfied of the reasonable views and good faith, which have been evinced by their own government," he told them.[4]

England was not Madison's only problem, though. The French navy was just as bad as the British when it came to stopping American ships and seizing cargo and sailors. Madison's ministers had complained to Napoleon about his search-and-seizure policies, done under the same guidelines as the British, but the French emperor dismissed them. His attitude inflamed Madison. "The late confiscations by Bonaparte comprise robbery, theft and breach of trust, and exceed in turpitude any of his enormities not wasting human blood," he wrote.[5]

He began to get pledges of support for military action by local militias in different states. He wrote one that "with every allowance for the extraordinary course of events in Europe, the violent and unprovoked conduct of the principal belligerents towards the U.S. justifies the feelings which it has existed in all good citizens."[6]

He wailed about the British to his ambassadors. He told William Pinkney that "the British government continues to be equally ignorant of our character" and that "it is impossible not to see that the avowed object is no longer to retaliate on an enemy, but to prevent our legitimate commerce." He concluded his note to Pinkney by asking, "How can a national expect to retain the respect of mankind whose government described to so ignoble a career?"[7]

And he exploded in a letter to Jefferson late in his first year in office about "the extremity to which things must rapidly proceed under the quackeries and corruption of an administration headed by such a being as [Spencer] Perceval [the new primate minister]?"[8]

In a long letter, William Duane, the editor of the *Aurora*, told Madison that he should consider military options and that the people would support him. The British, he told the president, were so tied up in their European wars that they paid no attention to any American pleas on impressment. "The course which is best adapted to the interests and policy of the United States, though it cannot be very well mistaken by men of sober minds, is not so easily pursued directly, as it would be were the attacks upon the nation open instead of insidious—or by other weapons than those of diplomacy and intrigue," Duane told him.[9]

Madison was also told by many that he should not get involved in any war with Britain, and that if he did, he could not win. An ambassador, John Jackson, wrote him in the autumn of 1809, "I would now as soon attempt to move the rocky top of the Alleghany to battle as make war with G B for existing differences without some new crisis to aid me. We . . . must play a cautious game."[10]

Near Christmas, Pinkney wrote back that Madison should push the British government harder and added that the people of England did not loathe Americans as their government did. Peace could be brokered by a public-relations blitz. "They [British people] seem to have awaked for the flattering dreams by which their understandings have been so long abused. Disappointment and disaster have dissipated the brilliant expectations of undefined prosperity which had dazzled them into moral blindness," he said.[11]

Madison was livid against England in his first Annual Message to Congress, delivered at the end of November 1809. He told the congressmen that America was, in fact, already involved in a "disastrous and protracted war, carried on in a mode equally injurious and unjust to the U.S."[12]

As the new president he was happy, as Jefferson had been, that not only Congress but also various state legislatures had passed proclamations supporting the administration in its troubles with Great Britain, such as the Pennsylvania Assembly, whose proclamation read "we have the fullest confidence in the wisdom, the patriotism and the integrity of the administration of the general government and we pledge ourselves to co-operate with them to maintain . . . our national rights."[13] Similarly, the North Carolina legislature sent him a message agreeing with his stand and said that it agreed with "unqualified and unanimous approbation of the course which you have pursued . . . in times portentous and alarming as the present . . . citizens of the United States, unassisted by that firmness, wisdom and patriotism which have characterized your public conduct would, indeed, have much to fear . . . support with energy and at the risk of our lives and fortunes such measures as the government shall think proper."[14]

War was in the air. Even former president John Adams, who despised Jefferson and Madison, wrote lengthy letters to newspapers espousing war over embargos or further diplomatic maneuvers. "I think a war would be less evil than a rigorous enforcement of the embargo," Adams wrote, and he added that "no nation under the sun" would put up with the indignities that England had hurled at America. In a second letter, just as strident, Adams wrote that in the late 1790s he, as president, had assurances from French diplomats that they would never put into effect stringent sea laws as they did just a few years later. Adams wrote that he now felt betrayed.[15]

Throughout these years, Madison's men stood by him with loyalty and fierceness. Albert Gallatin, in a long letter to the *National Intelligencer*, wrote that the British were continually trying to rewrite history by misquoting American officials and party leaders. He told British ministers in strong language that there was no difference in American policy toward England in the Madison administration than in that of Thomas Jefferson. He warned the Brits, too, that they must listen to Madison and not opposing party leaders. "The groundless accusations of foreign bias and influence have been generated solely by the virulence of party spirit; and they were adopted abroad as an apology or pretense for unprovoked aggressions," he wrote.[16]

President Madison was tough with the British, and the longer they ignored him, the tougher he became. In late May 1809, as the temperature rose in Washington, the temperature rose in Madison's writings. He sent a message to Congress on May 23 that outlined a massive American buildup for war, including the spending of millions for national defense, the creation of a system of militia and a military call-up plan, plus the moving of all US gunboats to form a stronger navy. His message was clear. If Britain's leaders wanted war, Madison was happy to give it to them.[17]

So were many Americans. Congressmen rallied around Madison, and newspapers pledged their support. Robert Price, the head of the Washington and Jefferson Artillery Company, a militia unit in northern Virginia, said that his men were "ready to march at a moment's notice" to wherever the president needed them for a war with England.[18]

All over the country, political clubs at their meetings toasted Madison and, shortly afterward, the American seamen who were the object of the British searches and seizures. Newspapers began running letters from disgruntled seamen held in French or British ports or serving on British ships. One impressed American sailor wrote that "no man has ever yet writhed under the tyrant's lash without wishing to breathe the murmurs of his spirit and enlist the world in his cause."[19]

Each search and seizure on the high seas or at a British port wound up described in American newspapers. The editor of the Philadelphia *Aurora* complained that the British were "disregarding the petty obligations of oaths and bonds, and other legal restraints, to swell the coffers of their principals."[20]

During these years, Madison solidified much presidential power. He agreed with Gallatin's view that the presidential power Jefferson exercised in purchasing the Louisiana Territory could be used by him, or succeeding presidents, to purchase parts of or all of Florida.[21] He also understood that Britain might be scheming to gain rights not only to Florida but to Cuba, too. Jefferson told Madison that the United States should buy Cuba from Spain, but, to calm down those who would think America too aggressive, put up a monument on the southern shore of the island that would state the United States would not buy or take any islands south of Cuba. Madison declined.[22]

All of America breathed a sigh of relief at the end of April when Britain's foreign minister announced that he had reached an amicable agreement with the United States to end the practice of the impressment of seamen on the Atlantic and the policy of stopping American merchant ships. There would be no war. Madison had won. The news was so momentous that the *National Intelligencer* even put out its very first special edition to announce the details of the agreement. The special edition even carried the official letter from British minister D. M. Erskine that outlined the policy. "I have the honor to inform you that I have received His Majesty's commands to represent [England] to the government of the United States that His Majesty is animated by the most sincere desire for an adjustment of the differences which have unhappily so long prevailed between the two countries."[23]

In its next edition, the editor of the *National Intelligencer* praised the British for ending their practices. "The British orders have been rescinded so far as they respect the United States. On these happy results, together with the consequent renewal of amicable intercourse between the two nations, we most sincerely congratulate our fellow citizens."[24]

At Monticello, Jefferson, who had battled the British prior to his retirement, was happy. Jefferson believed that the English had changed their minds because of reversals in their policy in Spain. He also told Madison that he was right for sticking with the embargo and perhaps the British change of heart was, in a great part, due to that policy. "I sincerely congratulate you on the change it has produced in our situation. It is a source of very general joy here."[25]

Little did he know what lay ahead.

As soon as British leaders back in London learned what the headstrong, impulsive Erskine had done, they announced that he had overstepped his boundaries. Nothing he said or wrote meant anything, they said in tough language. British sea policy was firm and would not be changed. It was like an iron door that slammed between America and Britain.

Madison was livid. He said that England's behavior was "fraud and folly" and told friends that he had been double-crossed by George Canning, Britain's secretary of foreign affairs. Jefferson was aghast. "Canning's equivocations degrade his government as well as himself. I despair of accommodations with them because I believe they are weak enough to intend seriously to claim the ocean as their conquest and to think to amuse with embassies and negotiations until the claim shall have been strengthened."[26]

Attorney General Caesar Rodney was angry over the reversal of policy.

"The very unexpected and inauspicious turn given to our relations with G.B. by the disavowal of the friendly arrangement concluded by her accredited minister [does] not fail to excite a lively sensibility among a people conscious of their own just purposes," he told Madison.[27]

All of America's diplomatic efforts had failed. Politics had failed. History had failed. America was right back where it started, and Britain would continue to bully her. A corner had been turned, though. Now Madison and all Americans saw the British as duplicitous. They were not only never going to change their policy but also would slap down anyone, even their own minister, who even suggested that they might.

A summer darkness fell over James Madison's White House.

THE EVER-CHANGING AMERICA

*M*adison ruled over a country filled with extensive change, a nation in which something new seemed to be happening all the time, a society in high-speed transition. These changes, combined with the actions of the president and the people in his administration, contributed mightily to the "new" America that was rapidly developing.

It was a country whose life was distinctly different from that in nations in Europe, Asia, Africa, and South America. The United States had changed much since the first days of the revolution in 1775, but now, in the early 1800s, change was lightning fast. Everything seemed to be in flux, yet Americans adapted easily to all of it, no matter how crazy it became.

Madison was responsible for most of it or harnessed it and let it help him shape his government. The period of 1800 to 1836, which began with Madison's appointment as secretary of state and ended with his death, saw monumental differences in the United States.

James and Dolley Madison were well aware of the social revolution taking place when they arrived in Washington. The pair had adapted to dozens of changes in their own lives and had found that they were able to turn as the lives of the people turned. They were not stuck in the past, unable to look at their new country with new eyes, like so many of their friends in the colonial era, but instead they were constantly on the move. Madison had gone to college when the nation was part of the British Empire; served in Congress during one of the world's bloodiest revolutions; wrote a new Constitution for America; lobbied to have it ratified; served two terms in the new United States Congress; helped George Washington construct America's first government; and was now, in 1801, the secretary of state in a party that no one ever heard of a decade earlier. In his personal life, he had spent forty-three years as a bachelor and then suddenly turned around and married. More than that, he had married a much

191

younger, dazzling woman. His new wife introduced him to new friends and a brand-new life.

Dolley Madison had been born in a log cabin and now lived in a palatial mansion on one of the largest plantations in America. She had married happily as a young woman, lost her husband, and then married again. She had been accepted into and then booted out of the Quakers. In a few years, she had gone from a young woman who had just a handful of dresses to the fashion queen of America. Dolley had transitioned quite easily from an unknown girl in Philadelphia with few friends into the most famous woman in the world. Change? The Madisons knew all about it.

It was everywhere. The national change was no better represented, perhaps, than in the transportation revolution. In the early 1800s, the local Washington newspapers were full of advertisements looking for workers and heralding the success of the construction of the new Potomack Canal, one of the first lengthy canal waterways in America.[1] The canal, which went around the Great Potomac Falls several miles west of Washington, was the brainchild of President Washington. He had first sailed up the Potomac in 1754 when he was an officer in the Virginia militia, attached to the British army in the French and Indian War. His original purpose was to see what the possibilities were for the movement of British military troops up the river by boat into the Ohio territory. He immediately saw a controlled waterway, a canal. "I doubt but you will readily concur with me in judging it more convenient, least expensive and I may further say by much the most expeditious way to the country," he wrote James Innes in the summer of 1754. Later, in 1783, he went further, writing French diplomat Chevalier de Castellux that "I shall not rest contented until I have explored the west country [via canals]." He added that canals would give America "a new empire."[2]

Washington did not discover canals. The controlled rivers had been used by Montauk Indians on Long Island since the early 1600s. Massachusetts pilgrim leader Myles Standish proposed building a canal through the isthmus that connected the Massachusetts mainland to the lengthy Cape Cod peninsula in 1623. In 1690, William Penn talked of building several canals to connect Philadelphia to different Pennsylvania rivers. In 1724, Cadwallader Colden, a surveyor in New York, outlined a canal project from the Great Lakes to the Hudson River. In Pennsylvania, Benjamin Franklin proposed a canal between several rivers and the city of Philadelphia.[3]

John Ballendine started a company to build a Maryland canal. Ballendine and several associates traveled to England to study some of the successful canals there and decided it could be done in Maryland. In 1774, Ballendine said that he would begin excavating the areas around the Great Falls. The Potomack Canal idea grew in fits and starts from that announcement, but the revolution held up progress. It was in 1784 that Washington pulled his friend James Madison into it.

He saw Madison as his chief catalyst to get something done by the Continental Congress. Washington sent Madison copies of letters from Virginia officials supporting the canal, petitions from people in both Virginia and Maryland, and a copy of a bill to legalize the Potomack Canal Company. Madison liked the idea and, along with several congressmen, ushered the bill through Congress. Washington, ever the politician, told Madison that both the Virginia and the Maryland legislatures had to approve the idea. "Would it not be highly expedient, therefore, as the session of both assemblies must soon draw to a close, for each to depute one or more members to meet at some intermediate place, and agree upon an adequate bill to be adopted by both states?" he asked, adding that both states could make strong claims as to why their rivers were more important. Madison agreed. Both legislatures met and approved the canal.[4]

George Washington told Madison, and others, that in the end, the canal would be worth it to all. "We should do our part towards opening the communication with the fur and peltry trade of the Lakes and for the produce of the country which lies within and which will . . . be settled faster than any one ever did, or any one would imagine," he said, and he added that colonists in the western areas might align themselves with the French or the British there rather than the [English] colonists on the seaboard if there was no transportation connection.[5]

By 1791, work had started on the locks used to lift and lower boats on the Potomack Canal. Construction continued through 1801, when Madison arrived in Washington to serve as secretary of state. At the end of 1801, the Great Falls canal locks were completed and boats began to sail through.[6] Madison became hooked on the idea of canals. In 1786, he met with Benjamin Franklin and Benjamin Rush to begin the building of a canal from the Philadelphia area to the Chesapeake Bay. Their idea later became the Chesapeake and Delaware Canal, opened nearly thirty years later. As secretary of state and later president, Madison watched over the Potomack Canal and others (the Potomack project never grew beyond its original small stretch).

Madison convinced Jefferson of the importance of canals in expanding America and increasing business. In his second inaugural address, Jefferson called for Americans to turn their eyes "to the great purposes of the public education, roads, rivers, canals." He told the country that canals would help to unify regions, too. "New channels of communication will be opened between the states . . . the lines of separation will disappear, their interests will be identified and their union cemented by new and indissoluble ties."[7]

Jefferson and Madison were both aware, too, that population patterns in America were changing. Now, as the nineteenth century started, there were nearly one million American settlers in the Mississippi region and more were arriving by foot, on horseback, and in the large Conestoga wagons every day.[8]

Stirred by Jefferson's message and Madison's interest, Congress asked Albert Gallatin to design a system of new canals and roadways across the country. He and his aides spent months on the project. Their final system included dozens of intrastate and interstate canals, as well as lengthy new highways. The plan never went into effect, though.

In 1801, when he moved to the capital, Madison, like Washington, saw canals as a way to create easy transportation that would help coal-mining regions in western Virginia and Pennsylvania prosper. It would spur on the slowly growing manufacturing industry and permit southern states like Virginia to pursue new industries and leave farming, and slavery, behind. Madison realized that the South, with a large manufacturing component and its seaports would challenge the northern states for economic supremacy and enable southern manufac-turers and farmers to become larger trading partners with Europe.

Madison's support of canals to help manufacturing showed his ever-evolving thinking processes and the way that he changed as circumstances did. In the late 1780s and early 1790s, Madison had been a champion of farming. In a speech to Congress in 1789, he called agriculture "the staple of the United States" and admired the "manifest preference it has over every other object of emolument in this country." In an article he wrote for the *National Gazette* in 1792 he said of farmers "the great proportion of this class to the whole society, the more free, the more independent and the more happy must be the society itself." His friends, such as Jefferson, considered Madison, who was a neophyte to the fields, as a remarkably good farmer. "[He] is the best farmer in the world," said Jefferson of his friend in the 1790s. Now, changing with the times, Madison saw the promise of industry and transportation as well as farming through canals.[9]

The canal revolution receded with the advent of the railroad, which grew in gargantuan proportions from 1830 to 1880. The railroad could deliver goods cheaper and more swiftly. By the time the canal era, sponsored so enthusiasti-cally by Madison, ended, the nation had thirty-three major canals, ranging from the vast Erie in the North to the Chesapeake and Delaware Canal in the South, plus small waterways such as the Chemung Canal and Chenango Canal.[10]

Top Left: Dolley Madison and her niece Annie Payne Cutts—who took care of her during her later years in Washington, DC—in an 1848 daguerreotype by Matthew B. Brady. (From Greensboro Historical Museum Archives.)

Top Right: Dolley in an 1848 daguerreotype by Matthew B. Brady, one of the very last images of her. (From Greensboro Historical Museum Archives.)

Bottom Left: Portrait of Dolley Payne Todd Madison, ca. 1850, attributed to John Vanderlyn after a portrait by Gilbert Stuart. (From Greensboro Historical Museum.)

Bottom Right: Payne Todd was the reckless, impulsive, sociopathic son of James and Dolley Madison. The president had to bail him out of jail on several occasions and pay about $1 million to cover his debts. Payne, who never married, ruined the Madisons financially in later life. Watercolor on ivory by Joseph Wood, ca. 1817. (Currently held at the Metropolitan Museum of Art, New York.)

The government gave President James Madison free lifetime franking, or mailing privileges, and, as an act of courtesy, extended them to Dolley when the president died. (From Greensboro Historical Museum Archives.)

The British army burned down the US Capitol, which was still under construction, when it attacked Washington, DC, in the summer of 1814. Hand-colored aquatint by William Strickland (engraver) and George Munger (artist), 1814. (From the Library of Congress.)

Not content with burning the Capitol, the British army moved to the White House. There, soldiers first ate a dinner set for American diplomats who had fled, and then they torched the building. The act enraged the American public. This lithograph by R. Farnham depicting the aftermath was completed in 1848. (From the Library of Congress.)

The naval heroes of the War of 1812 were turned into historical legends by the media, as shown in this large portrait of some of them by Currier & Ives, completed by N. Currier in 1846. (From the Library of Congress.)

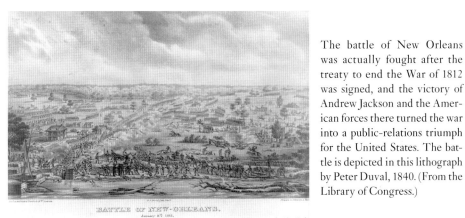

The battle of New Orleans was actually fought after the treaty to end the War of 1812 was signed, and the victory of Andrew Jackson and the American forces there turned the war into a public-relations triumph for the United States. The battle is depicted in this lithograph by Peter Duval, 1840. (From the Library of Congress.)

The US frigate *United States*, commanded by Stephen Decatur, defeated the HBM frigate *Macedonian* in the War of 1812. Painted by Thomas Birch and engraved by Benjamin Tanner, 1813. (From the Library of Congress.)

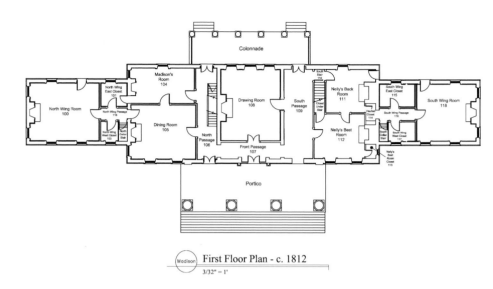

First Floor Plan - c. 1812

3/32" = 1'

Madison lived at his Montpelier mansion most of his life. In 1797 and in 1809, he renovated it. The first floor was changed by Madison to provide more room for his new wife and her sister when they arrived with him in 1797. A new front door (to the left on the map) was installed to offer access to the new wing of the home. He expanded the number and size of his mother's quarters on the right side of the floor, too. (Courtesy of Montpelier, a National Trust Historic Site.)

Second Floor Plan - c. 1812

3/32" = 1'

The second floor included more living space and terraces built on the roof of the first floor. Guests filled the terraces at parties. (Courtesy of Montpelier, a National Trust Historic Site.)

For decades, the original Montpelier building was buried beneath a larger structure. This is the actual plantation home, finally restored in the early 2000s. (Courtesy of Montpelier, a National Trust Historic Site.)

Left: President John Adams and Madison were at first rivals, but Adams later became Madison's friend and lent him his full support when the War of 1812 began. Painting by Charles Willson Peale, ca. 1791–1794. (From Independence National Historical Park.) *Right:* Alexander Hamilton and Madison lobbied together to have the US Constitution ratified in 1788, but they split over political differences during George Washington's second term as president. Painting by Charles Willson Peale, ca. 1790–1795. (From Independence National Historical Park.)

Top Left: James Madison in his forties. In midlife he had married and planned to retire from public life at his Montpelier plantation, but the Adams administration's unpopular Alien and Sedition Acts brought him back to the public stage, where he would remain. Painting by James Sharples Sr., 1796–1797. (From Independence National Historical Park.)

Top Right: Madison and longtime friend James Monroe split when Monroe ran against him for president, but Thomas Jefferson brought the pair back together. Monroe was Madison's secretary of state and succeeded him in the White House. Painting attributed to Felix Sharples, ca. 1807–1811. (From Independence National Historical Park.)

Left: Thomas Jefferson and Madison were longtime friends; Jefferson made Madison secretary of state. Madison succeeded Jefferson as president, and the two remained close all of their lives. Painting by Charles Willson Peale, 1791–1792. (From Independence National Historical Park.)

The Madisons frequently visited Richmond, Virginia, seen here in an 1808 painting completed just before Madison's inauguration, and they often stayed there for weeks. Watercolor on paper by J. L. Bouqueta de Woiseri, 1882. (From Virginia Historical Society [1953.2].)

This map, drawn shortly after the American Revolution ended, shows the United States during Madison's lifetime. Map by John Wallis, 1783. (From the Colonial Williamsburg Foundation. Museum Purchase.)

Independence Hall, in Philadelphia, was the setting for the signing of the Declaration of Independence and the US Constitution. Photograph by Carol M. Highsmith, ca. 1980–2006. (From the Library of Congress.)

James Madison was the driving force at the US Constitutional Convention. Painting by Thomas Pritchard Rossiter, 1872. (From Independence National Historical Park.)

It was not the canal that Madison saw as the great change in America, though. It was the highway.

Madison, like everybody else in the United States, was tired of traveling on narrow dirt highways, some just eight or nine feet wide. They flooded in rainstorms and became vast dustbowls in the hot summer months. The ruts in some were so deep that horse-pulled carriages were overturned when their wheels rolled into them. Everyone who traveled to Mount Vernon to see George Washington was delighted to see him and his wife but complained bitterly that to get to his country estate they had to ride down one of the worst dirt roads in the nation.

One incident in 1808 illustrates Madison's fury at the conditions of his beloved highways. He and his wife were returning to Montpelier from Washington following a fierce rainstorm. Roads were flooded. Madison wrote Jefferson that he nearly didn't make it home. "I got home Friday night by taking my carriage to pieces and making three trips ... over Porter's mill pond, in something like a boat, swimming my horses," he wrote in anger.[11]

Dolley dreaded traveling. Once, prior to a trip from Washington to Montpelier, she wrote that "my limbs yet tremble with the terrors and fatigue our journey." One of her friends wrote her in 1811 that his carriage hit a bump in the road and overturned. He was thrown from the carriage, another man fell out of the side door, the driver fell to the road, the rigging separated from the car, and the horses bolted off with it. The men found two of the horses and rode home on them.[12]

Everyone complained of being victims to the roads and weather. "We had a dreadful journey home. I was thankful that my bones were not broke," complained Dolley Cole Beckwith in 1804.[13] James Madison told the story of Governor William Cabell, who left his home to ride to the University of Virginia in 1826 and did so "traveling the whole way with this snow & hail in his face."[14]

Roads were poor everywhere, not just in Virginia. "The roads all along this way are very bad, encumbered with rocks and mountainous passages, which were very disagreeable to my tired carcass," wrote a woman about Connecticut roads in 1704. All travel was slow. The stagecoaches that traveled on highways between Jersey City, New Jersey, and Philadelphia, Pennsylvania, dubbed the "flying machines" for their speed, took two entire days to travel the ninety miles. When George Washington took command of the Continental Army at the start of the American Revolution, he rode from Philadelphia to Boston and the trip took him twelve days.[15]

Many roads carved out of forests, such as the "Wilderness Road" in the Allegheny Mountains and the "Natchez Trace" near New Orleans, followed old, narrow Indian trails that tended to lead travelers to other waterways and small villages. There were even toll roads, such as the sixty-two-mile Lancaster Pike, from Philadelphia to Lancaster, Pennsylvania, ordered by the state of Pennsylvania. Local residents besieged Madison with plans to build additional roads. One Louisiana group, championed by Madison, asked for federal help to build a second road from New Orleans to Ohio that would cut two hundred miles off the present journey. Their petition was one of many; they had a friend in Madison.[16] In 1796, the first highway atlas, by Abraham Bradley Jr., was published.

Madison wanted to build a national highway that would begin in Maine and run all the way down the eastern seaboard to Georgia, with numerous bridges, cutting through every large city in every state on the journey south. He believed that new, wider, smoother roads with crushed stone and not dirt, plus a multitude of long, wide, sturdy bridges, would make transportation easier and cheaper for businesses and, importantly, citizens trying to migrate to new homes in different areas of America.

Madison had no trouble convincing Jefferson, who always complained about roadways between Monticello and Washington. During his first term, on several occasions, the President Jefferson asked Congress to use surplus tax money to build new roadways and canals. Jefferson, like Madison, understood that highways would unite the regions. "New channels of communication will be opened between the states . . . the lines of separation will disappear, their interests will be identified and their union cemented by new and indissoluble ties," he said.[17]

Madison had plenty of help. Numerous congressmen, especially those who lived in districts with rivers and highways, wanted the federal government to help states pay for the roadways and bridges. Newspapers supported the idea, too. "It is the practice of wise nations to improve the navigation of rivers and to extend water communication into the interior of the country for the advantage of the agricultural interest. Will the Congress of the United States reverse the maxims of the civilized world?" asked the editor of the *Washington Federalist* in 1805, adding in his column that money had to be appropriated for bridges on the Potomac and other rivers, too as part of the bill.[18]

The arguments worked. At the suggestion of Madison and Jefferson, Congress agreed to appropriate $30,000 to survey the first national highway, the "Cumberland Road," designed to stretch from Cumberland, Maryland, to Ohio. The highway would be a wide roadway made of crushed stone and designed and maintained by the Army Corps of Engineers. Roadwork began in the spring of 1806. The planning of the road was a bit chaotic because different towns and counties in each state wanted the road to go through their territory. Politicians even insisted that it had to go through certain towns, or counties, because they had been loyal to the Republican Party in recent elections.[19] By the time most of it was completed as far as Wheeling, West Virginia, in 1818, the cost had risen to $6.8 million. It would go on to the middle of the country, Vandalia, Illinois, after several more million dollars and another five years.[20] The highway would bring about the opening of dozens of stables, inns, taverns, and general stores in its first few years and then entire communities. "As soon as the road is finished, a complete change will take place in the carrying trade between the Atlantic and the western waters," stated one editor.[21]

Most of all, the highway served as the nation's first gateway to the west. "In the early and balmy days of the road there came a class of hardy pioneers that paved the way for an expanding civilization," wrote chronicler Jeremiah Young.[22]

Stagecoach companies immediately began running tours over the National Road, promising travelers that on their stages they would see sights they had only dreamed about before. One advertised views of the old road General Washington traveled and the ruins of army forts. Others hailed sights such as valleys the revolutionary army had trudged through, towns connected to the Whiskey Rebellion and the homes of Revolutionary War heroes.[23]

Travelers saw all of those things and enjoyed them. "The whole of the scenery was very romantic, and beautiful, especially from the top of the heights to which we ascended. The view was fine, alternate hill and dale, often enlivened by clear meandering streams and by large cleared and fertile tracts of land or sometimes by neat little villages," wrote William Owen, who traveled the road by stagecoach in 1824.[24]

Stages stopped at towns where travelers could sleep over at hotels or at highway taverns. The popular taverns featured sleeping rooms or dormitories upstairs, well-stocked bars, and reasonably good dining halls for breakfast, lunch, and dinner. Many named themselves after British taverns, such as the Black Horse and the Wild Swan. They grew in number and size as traffic on the road grew.[25]

When the road was completed as far as Wheeling, a local farmer who had marveled at how many laborers had worked on the highway looked at it, turned to a friend, and said that it was "a roadway good enough for an emperor to travel over."[26]

⊱⚬⚬⚭

American transportation was not just land based, however. There was a movement to use oceangoing vessels on rivers. How to do that, though? The answer was steam power. John Fitch built the first steam-driven ship and on

August 22, 1787, in a very successful publicity stunt, sailed his forty-five-foot boat down the Delaware River, using a crude paddlewheel driven by an engine, in front of a large gathering of delegates to the Constitutional Convention in Philadelphia. Standing with them, eyes wide open in admiration, was James Madison. Fitch was granted a patent for steamships in 1791 and so was another inventor, James Rumsey. Another company, Briggs and Longstreet, was given a patent earlier, in 1788.

Fitch was replaced as a steamship pioneer by Robert Fulton, who had designed a submarine in France. Fulton, a Pennsylvanian who had moved to England for his health, had worked on canal designs in Great Britain and became interested in steam engines (the British were experimenting with steamships at the same time as the Americans). Fulton built a large steamship, the *Clermont*, and on August 7, 1807, while Madison was still secretary of state, stunned the country by sailing from New York City upriver, against the current, to Albany at an average speed of what was then a sensational five miles per hour.

Fulton and his partner, Robert Livingston, then plunged into the steamship business, targeting routes between large ports. They built the *New Orleans* in Pittsburgh in 1811 and soon put it into service on the Mississippi River between Natchez, Mississippi, and New Orleans. They soon had several boats on that route and others, and all of them maintained speeds of nearly ten miles per hour downriver. They carried freight and passengers in record times and at much cheaper rates than wagons. By 1817, a steamship ran east and west along the Potomac River. There were three steamboat lines between New York and Philadelphia and a line that connected New York to seaports in Connecticut. Three ships, the *Paragon*, the *Car of Neptune*, and the *North River*, sailed back and forth between New York and Albany on the Hudson River. By 1834, just before Madison's death, there were more than 1,200 steamships on the Mississippi and hundreds more on the East Coast. Thanks to the steamship, southern planters were able to double and triple their output of cotton and other products. East Coast vessels carried agricultural products and industrial supplies. The steamships helped to make New York an even larger seaport. In just two decades, the steamships changed American life. No longer would it take weeks to travel great distances and no longer would travelers have to suffer the indignities of badly constructed and poorly maintained highways. They could simply book passage on the thousands of new steamships in an ever-changing America.[27]

Toward the end of his second term, President Madison greeted DeWitt Clinton, the young mayor of New York City who ran against him for president in 1812, and Gouverneur Morris, whom he knew from the 1787 Constitutional Convention, at his office at the White House. They wanted to build a canal from the Hudson River to the Great Lakes. It would transverse over three hundred miles of land, forests, hills, meadows, and swamps, and would connect dozens of towns from the western banks of the Hudson River to the shores of Lake Erie. Narrow, flatbed boats would use it to carry cargo from the Ohio region to Albany, then to New York City, where it would be sent by ship to eastern seaports or Europe. Clinton told the president he had the enthusiastic support of New York's governor and so did the state legislature. The ever-ambitious Clinton told Madison that he supported it and added that it would mean thousands of jobs in New York State, both in the construction of the canal and in the many new posts and small towns they expected to grow alongside its banks. Madison, his hazel eyes glowing at the thought of a canal that could make history, agreed to back it through the federal government.

Members of Congress were not as visionary as the president, though, and, despite all of his lobbying, turned down the request. They suggested that if New York stood to profit so much from a canal, if New York would gain all of these thousands of new jobs, and if New York would win enormous publicity from the canal, then New York should pay for it. Why should Maryland pay for it? Or Pennsylvania?

New York did; a bill in the state legislature in 1817 funded early canal construction, in combination with a very successful state-wide lottery to raise money for the project. Work then began on what would become the world's longest canal to that date, 300-plus miles in length with eighteen aqueducts and eighty-three locks that would raise and lower ships nearly two hundred yards.[28]

In the end, the Erie Canal, which Madison was so enthusiastic about, was called the engineering miracle of the world, along with Egypt's pyramids. It not only connected cities such as Buffalo, Rochester, and Syracuse but also made them boom towns. They flourished with business from canal builders during construction and then canal users for years afterward.[29]

The canal was a success right away. It made back its $7 million cost in just twelve years. It earned millions of dollars each year for decades. The canal caused freight to drop from $32 a ton by wagon for one hundred miles to just $1 a ton for that same distance on canal boats.

The early success of the Erie Canal spurred the building of dozens of others. Most were designed to move goods a great distance to an economic market for sale, in the hopes that the canal would increase jobs of all kinds and create thriving towns along its route.

The Delaware Canal carried goods from Easton, Pennsylvania, down to Philadelphia, and then to the ocean on a path that hugged the Delaware River. The Lehigh Canal, an east–west waterway that opened in 1829, carried goods from inland factories and coal mines to Philadelphia. It changed the face of heating and manufacturing in the city. In the 1840s and 1850s, the canal carried over 1.2 million tons of coal per year, an unheard-of total at the time.[30]

∾∿∾

The president listened to many people on canals and highways, and one of them was Dolley. One thing everybody noticed about President Madison was the way that he listened to his wife on everything she had to say, and how he listened in conversations with other women. Most men in the colonial era saw women as second-class citizens, fit for child rearing, housekeeping, and little else. James Madison did not. His years of marriage to his wife had changed his mind about women. He wrote an educator that "the capacity of the female mind for studies of the highest order cannot be doubted; having been sufficiently illustrated by its works of genius, of erudition and of science."[31]

By the start of his second term, the Washington community, social and political, had become used to Madison the man and the differences between him and his predecessor, Jefferson. When his second term commenced, he had been in the White House for four long years, out of Jefferson's shadow, and the differences between the two were obvious. "Force and point and rapid analysis are the characteristics of the style of Jefferson; full, clear and deliberate disquisition carefully wrought out, as if the writer regarded himself rather as the representative of truth than the exponent of the doctrines of party or even a nation, is the praise of Madison," wrote Hugh Grigsby, who knew both men when they were older.[32]

In his second term, Madison continued to feud with Congress. Full of Republicans, Congress had voted down some of his important bills and, he thought, acted as their own branch of government, rather than one of three. He never lost his basic faith in Congress that he had outlined long ago, though. He had written that "the general legislature will do every mischief they possibly can and that they will omit to do everything good which they are authorized to do," but added that despite that, the democratic system ensures that the people will elect men of virtue who will be devoted to the public good. "If there be not, we are in a wretched situation," he added. Sometimes, though, he had to wonder.[33]

Madison urged Congress to do all that it could to promote education at all levels. In 1810, in his annual message to the legislature, he urged funding for a national university. "Such an institution . . . would be universal in its beneficial effects. By enlightening the opinions, by expanding the patriotism and by assimilating the principles, the sentiments and the manners of those who might resort to this Temple of Science, to be redistributed, in due time, through every part of the community, sources of jealousy and prejudice would be diminished, the features of national character would be multiplied," he said.[34]

Even though President Madison was assaulted on many sides by political enemies and foreign schemers, he still had his wife, the dauntless and invincible public-relations machine who worked overtime to make him look good. "Amid this cruel warfare of conflicting parties, so calculated to excite angry feelings, Mrs. Madison . . . met these political assailants with a mildness which disarmed their hostility of its individual rancor and sometimes even converted political enemies into personal friends . . . she succeeded at neutralizing the bitterness of opposition," said a friend.[35]

15

WAR LOOMS EVERYWHERE OVER AMERICA

*W*ar with England had been a hot issue since Jefferson's first term, when Great Britain began to intercept American shipping. For years, Jefferson and Madison had begged Congress to hold off on hostilities while diplomatic efforts were made to halt British aggression on the high seas. Everybody agreed to let them proceed. "It has been constantly contended by the republicans that they have the means in their possession, short of hostility, to coerce their antagonists into a sense of propriety; and they have always inculcated the prompts and courageous use of these valuable means, for the prevention of war and the assertion of our national privileges," wrote the editor of the *Washington Federalist* in the early days of 1808.[1]

The government had used subtle means to drive home its unhappiness with the British impressment of American sailors by the British. As early as 1808, James Madison had issued lengthy lists of names of impressed seaman to American newspapers that ran them in special stories. Later, he and others authorized the release of navy and army ship- and troop-strength lists to newspapers for publications to show the British the United States was ready for war.[2]

In Congress, some members were mild in their criticism of Great Britain and some were bold. Virginia senator William Giles stood up as tall as he could and read a long list of travesties from the British, from impressment of seamen to seizing of ships, to blockading ports. He fumed that it was nothing short of "British insolence."[3]

There were pro-British factions, just as there were British sympathizers in the American Revolution. "Such a faction has been nurtured among us since the peace of 1783, have been derived from various sources and have not failed to make a deep impression upon the minds of all who wished to preserve the independence of their country unimpaired," wrote the editor of the *Albany Register* in the spring of 1809. Diplomat William Pinkney told Madison the same thing a few months later when he wrote that "the British government has acted for some time upon an opinion that its partisans in America were too numerous and strong to admit of our persevering in any system of repulsion to British injustice."[4]

Throughout the years 1809, 1810, and 1811, a long parade of state legislatures passed resolutions backing any quasi-warlike decisions Madison chose to make. They all reflected the angry legislature of Georgia, whose resolution decried the "outrages of the British cabinet."[5] Madison thanked them all. "The full strength of every nation requires a union of its citizens. To a government like ours, this truth is peculiarly applicable ... [we need] more universal support of the constituted authorities in the measures for maintaining the national honor and rights," he told the Vermont legislature.[6]

There was a new Congress in 1809, though, swept into office with Madison, and it was an angry and resentful Congress. There were two new, young, persuasive leaders who took charge of Congress immediately—Senator John C. Calhoun of South Carolina and Representative Henry Clay of Kentucky. Clay, a dynamic individual, was elected Speaker of the House on the very first day he took office. He and Calhoun were both fed up with the embargo, saw no point in the Non-Intercourse Act, and tirelessly lobbied for war with Great Britain. They were the leaders of a strong prowar faction called the War Hawks. Clay would run for president three times and Calhoun would be vice president. Later, Calhoun, with his chiseled face, would let his hair grow long, which gave him a haunting look. Their view was that diplomatic means to halt England and France from stopping US ships and seizing American sailors had failed, the embargo had failed, and all media crusades and political crusades to convince the two belligerent nations to cease and desist had failed. All that was left was war. "If war came, it would be backed by 'the combined energies of a free people' ... wreaking a noble and manful vengeance upon a foreign foe," Clay thundered, and he added that if America did not fight Britain, it would "forfeit the respect of the world" and, worse, he added, "ourselves."[7]

Clay and Calhoun led a very large population of opinion, except for many residents of New England, who seemed to want to keep things the way they were and accepted the impressment of New England sailors as a small price to pay for continued profitable business with Europe.

Some powerful men felt that all nonwar means had been exhausted. Some suggested, too, that, financially, a war would cost less than the continued shipping crisis, which had cost American merchants, it was estimated, over $50 million per year. Even Jefferson was swinging toward war. He wrote the minister to France, John Armstrong, that the embargo had been discontinued "because losing $50,000,000 of exports annually . . . it costs more than war . . . war therefore must follow if the edicts are not repealed before the next meeting of Congress."[8]

Madison's time was repeatedly taken up with the crisis involving England and France. The conversation at all of Dolly's parties was consumed by it. Madison sometimes had to leave Montpelier in summer and return to the White House just to find out what returning US vessels' captains had to say about their trip across the Atlantic from Europe had been like. He came back to find out what passengers on British ships had to say. He always went back to the capital alone, leaving Dolly at Montpelier. He wrote her often from Washington. Once he wrote, "My dearest . . . the period, thou may be sure, will be shortened as much as possible. Everything around and within reminds me that you are absent and makes me anxious to quit the solitude. . . . God bless you, and be assured of my constant affection."[9]

The difficulties with England brought on hard times for his wife, too. In the winter of 1811, she thanks her sister for a letter "that raised my spirits which have been rather low in these troublous times."[10]

At the same time that Madison was traveling back and forth from Montpelier to Washington to address the crisis, Britain replaced its minister to America with Francis John Jackson, a tough-as-nails diplomat who looked down on American leaders as little more than snippy colonists. He had several cantankerous meetings with President Madison, whose angry demeanor caused Jackson to write home that Madison was as "tough as a mule." The new minister did not care for the Madisons at all. He wrote home to England that Madison was "a plain and rather mean looking little man, of great simplicity of manners and an inveterate enemy of form and ceremony." His regard for the president was laudatory compared to his views of the First Lady. He wrote that Dolley was "fat and forty but not fair." Jackson's wife annoyed Americans, too. She wrote that Washington food was "detestable, gross, no claret, champagne and Madeira indifferent." Jackson, playing politics, then traveled to New England, an antiadministration region, and met with the editors of Federalist newspapers, who took up his cause in denouncing the president.[11]

The more that Jackson denounced Madison, though, the more public opinion rose up in favor of the president. "[How] can a nation [England] expect to retain the respect of Mankind whose government descends to so ignoble a career?" Madison said, referring to Jackson.[12]

The country was glad that he never backed down against the British or French and that he was as tough as their ministers were. Around this time, too, the French minister told Madison that he had to stop merely calling Napoleon "Great and Good Friend" and call him "Emperor." Madison flatly refused. His popularity surged after that. "I think that James Madison's administration is now as strongly entrenched in the public confidence as Thomas Jefferson's ever was at its fullest tide," wrote Representative Ezekiel Bacon, then. And, too, voters backed up their verbal support of the president in November 1809 by electing another large majority of Republicans to the House and Senate. The Republicans kept majorities where they existed and gained them in many other districts. Both houses of the New Jersey legislature went Republican; and the Republicans picked up two more congressional seats in New York. Strident Federalist leader Thomas Pickering of Massachusetts was forced out of office, and the Republicans gained congressional and state legislative seats throughout traditionally Federalist New England.[13] Jefferson, watching the 1810 elections carefully, was pleased. He wrote a friend that "our difficulties are indeed great, but when viewed in comparison to those of Europe, they are the joys of paradise."[14]

Throughout 1809, 1810 and 1811, Dolley Madison took good care of her husband. Fully realizing the pressure he was under, and well aware of his many physical weaknesses, she did all she could to relieve his stress. She sat with him for an hour each day before dinner to talk about the presidency, the family, Montpelier, and anything else he wanted to discuss. She carefully arranged receptions and balls in such a way so that it was easy for Madison to leave early and get a good night's sleep as Dolley took his place as the social leader of all occasions. She changed the seating at dinners so that her husband sat in the middle of the table and she at the head so that she, and not he, could lead conversations, giving him much-needed rest. In Washington and at home in Montpelier, she took up more and more of the responsibility of running the households, supervising all personnel, arranging transportation, and making certain that friends often visited to take Madison's mind off the growing hostilities with England and France. She made certain that she and her husband visited Thomas Jefferson as often as possible, and hosted him frequently at Montpelier. She spent extra time with Jefferson's grandchildren at Monticello, playing with them and helping them make children's clothing. She invited many more families to Montpelier so that dozens of children were always around to help relieve the pressure on her husband.

In Washington, she bent easily to the political winds that blew stronger. At first, many Federalists now refused to attend her dinners, receptions, balls, and parties because they were angry at the president. Their boycott, the Federalists felt, was a well-designed show of force. Dolley shrugged her shoulders. She simply invited more Republicans and friends from around town. The parties rolled on, and the Federalists were not missed. Then they were back. "They have changed," Dolley wrote, "such a rallying of our party has alarmed them. They came in a large body last night . . . young and old together."[15]

Dolley was even more of a whirlwind when Madison was president than in her previous years in Washington. The number of her dinners and parties grew, and so did the number of people attending them. The party guest list was now around two hundred or more people per soiree. There were dinners just about every evening and a party, ball, or reception at the White House nearly every night. Madison's secretary, Edward Coles, complained that out of every fourteen nights he went to eleven dinner parties at the White House. He was sent to parties just about every night, so many, in fact, that he tired of them. He wrote in 1810 that "I am sick, yes heartily sick, with the number of our parties."[16]

Dolley cautioned her husband that the British had looked down their noses at the Americans for decades, so he should not worry about new slights or new, dim versions of American resolve. During these years, British diplomats in Washington continually wrote back to their prime minster that America would never fight a war. The administration and the people did not have the weapons or troops to do so and, more important, did not have the emotional resolve.

Dolley also insisted that Madison accompany her to numerous plays that were being produced in Washington. The pair loved the theater. One night, at the height of the worry over a prospective war with England, when the pressure was the greatest on Madison, they attended a production of *King Lear*. On the way home, their frightened horse bolted, flew out of his harness, and ran away. The driver, the president, and the First Lady were stranded. It was just after midnight, and the streets of Washington were empty. Horseless and with no one in sight to assist them, the three simply walked home. All the way, on that quiet night, Dolley chatted with both men in a conversation laden with small talk. The pair were all alone, arm in arm, walking quietly to the White House, the only sound in the air the sounds of their voices.[17]

By 1812, Dolley had become a master politician. Anything that the president did was praised or criticized as a political move, but the First Lady received none of that criticism. Everyone understood that the things Dolley did were always done to help her husband politically, but it was always one step removed. This freedom gave her enormous room to maneuver in the political work, but always in a subtle way. Congressmen who were mad at her husband were invited to White House parties and, if not turned into friends there, were at least made neutral by Dolley. Men who got into arguments at White House affairs were soon interrupted by a waiter, sent by Dolley, who offered them cakes and drinks. The argument cooled off. Certain people were seated next to other certain people at dinners so they could resolve their differences in a social way. The wives of leading political figures were all immediately befriended by Dolley and invited to all White House functions. If people liked her, they would like the president, too.

Dolley went out of her way to remember the faces and names of all the people who visited the White House, whether they were foreign diplomats, politicians, merchants, artists, or friends. There is no evidence that she wrote down lists of names, sat people at particular tables, or spent hours trying to put names with faces. She just had a good memory and put it to use. Dolley also remembered where people were from and always tried to establish some connection with her life and theirs. She remembered people's favorite plays, concerts, and books; she knew the favorite taverns of people, knew where they liked to sit and stand at horse races, and often recalled the names of their children. The president was not good at this; she was.

By the spring of 1812, Dolley had accrued, in twelve years in Washington, all the skills of a master politician. She had also picked up the greatest political skill there is—to make people believe you are not a politician at all.

Some of the politicking that went on in Washington disgusted her, though. In the spring of 1812, Vice President Clinton became very sick. Politicians, sure he would die, began circling his office like vultures, trying to get Madison to give them the job. "The Vice President lies dangerously ill, and electioneering for this office goes on beyond description—the world seems to be running mad," Dolley wrote.[18]

As the war approached, and people's anger against England and France increased, Dolley attracted more enemies. Residents of New England, especially, who were so opposed to the war, targeted Dolley as well as her husband. She was too regal, too royal, too rich, too elegant. Her defenders said she had a wonderful personality? Her critics then brayed that she talked too much. She was criticized by women for her daring display of cleavage, which seemed to go lower and lower as the years went by, and for the emeralds on her turban (too European). She was seen by critics as Madison's protector and, behind closed doors, his political director.

Dolley did not care.

"She is the greatest blessing of my life," the president wrote during those years.[19]

More and more senators and congressmen began to feel that only a war could end Britain's harsh sea policy toward America. Senator Samuel Smith of

Maryland denounced all critics of the embargo and all who did not think a war would be necessary. He scolded Massachusetts senator Thomas Pickering in a speech and then said, referring to President Madison, "Great God! Mr. President, can that man [Pickering] feel for American seamen who can say and write that the impressment of five thousand of our seamen by Great Britain is no cause for pretext only?"[20]

The American political parties hurled insults at each other and tried, month after month, to show that the other was guilty not only of libel, slander, and bad form, but of treason, too. The Philadelphia *Aurora*, the Republican paper, wrote in 1809 about the recently repealed embargo that "we are informed by the debates in the English parliament, that their friends, the Federalists, in America assured them that their party would be brought into power at the next general election and that . . . if they held out a little longer, the embargo would be taken off."[21]

American newspapers had sneered at the British reasons for impressing seamen and searching ships for years. Three years before the war began, the *Aurora* editor wrote "whilst Great Britain is fighting for the liberties of the world by enslaving our seamen, and making it a forfeiture of ship and cargo (and worse than death) . . ." Other papers, such as the *Baltimore American*, advocated a lengthy campaign to seize British ships and their sailors when found in American waters.[22]

Various congressmen had urged the raising of a new and much larger army to start a war against Great Britain. Some of the new army proposals were so comprehensive that they even included monthly pay schedules. Madison raised his eyebrows every time he read a story like that because he knew, they all knew, that the navy's gunboats were rotting, the army was quite small, and Congress had not appropriated funds to expand it. Hundreds of soldiers were also sick and not getting better. Fight a war? With what?[23]

Many newspapers had eagerly reprinted copies of letters sent from James Monroe and William Pinkney to Madison in the winter of 1806 assuring him that they had a deal with England, but history soon showed that they did not. Madison now cringed at the publication of the letters.[24]

One indirect consequence of the constant debates between citizens and legislators over the continuing crisis with England, in its third year when Madison took office, was that so much time was spent arguing about Great Britain and its sea policy that little time was left to discuss other foreign and all domestic matters. The government slowed down and then ground to a near halt by the end of 1809 as the British crisis mounted.

That crisis had grown in intensity throughout 1810. At the end of that year, his fury growing, Madison blasted Britain in his Annual Message to Congress.

He called for more funds for the army, more ships, and the revival of the Non-Intercourse Act against England, and he announced that America might soon occupy West Florida, a piece of land that it thought had come with the Louisiana Purchase but that Spain declared still belonged to her. The president also leaked secret letters from foreign ministers that insulted him and the American government. Madison was getting tough; the people liked that. Somebody, nobody knew who, continually planted stories in American newspapers about the enormous sums of money Napoleon was sending to Betsy Patterson Bonaparte, the wife of his brother. Why? Was Napoleon thinking of raising an heir in America? A prince? To take over America? [25]

When 1811 dawned, Madison found himself in a political dilemma. Spain continued to insist that it owned West Florida, but thousands of Americans lived there. Madison consulted many cabinet members and congressmen and finally made up his mind on what to do—nothing. He would wait to see what happened, knowing, of course, that something would. By early 1811, disputes arose between Americans and Spaniards in that area, and local, irregular militia forces began to seize Spanish properties. Madison then declared that he had to move American troops into Florida in order to protect American national merchant interests and the lives of Americans living there. It was a clever use of executive power, power he could wield without approval from Congress and power he could wield in 1811 because of the politics of the era. He knew that and did so. West Florida soon seemed secure and Madison then announced that he might as well do the same thing with the rest of Florida, too. He said he might seize Spanish-held Cuba as well and told one of his ministers that these steps were necessary to prevent Great Britain from doing the same thing. He needed to protect American interests and, in so doing, was acting legitimately as the national leader. It was a huge stretch of presidential powers, but nobody objected. [26]

In the fall of 1810, Madison received numerous signals from French and American ministers that Napoleon was agreeable to stopping French searches and seizures of American ships, but the agreement lay somewhere in the middle of many lengthy and convoluted documents. Madison ignored his ministers' insistence that Napoleon was really doing nothing and made a public announcement that the two nations had an agreement and applauded Napoleon for his understanding. Then Madison swung around and invoked the Non-Intercourse Act (no trade with England), taking war with France out of the equation. He wrote Jefferson, "We hope from the step the advantage at least of having but one contest [England] on our hands at one time." [27]

The threat against just England in the fall of 1810 started a chain of political events that led House leader Henry Clay to say in the summer of 1811 that war with England was "inevitable." Clay's views were important because he led what came to be known as the War Hawk Congress, a body full of members bent on war if Britain's shipping policy did not change. In addition to those members, there were many more who were simply tired of the country's vacillating position on war and wanted to "draw the sword," as one member put it. They all recognized that in Clay, too, they had a powerful Speaker and somebody who did not take abuse from anyone. One of Clay's first orders when he took over leadership of the House was to tell John Randolph to take his dogs out of the house chamber and never bring them back. Everyone applauded that order and a chastened Randolph kept his dogs at home.[28]

Clay, and other War Hawks such as Calhoun, wanted a conflict and an end to America's six years of submitting to British bullying. Clay was such a forceful leader and adept politician that he managed to get lopsided votes, such as 117 to 11, for prowar bills submitted by Madison. Ironically, one very important bill, to increase the strength of the navy with construction of a dozen ships and building a stockpile of lumber in navy yards for further construction, was defeated by congressmen who were landlocked and congressmen who hated the New Englanders, who made huge profits off sea businesses that would be helped by a large navy. The defeat of the navy bill left President Madison with a tiny navy to go up against England's, the greatest navy in the world, with more than six times as many vessels as the United States in North American waters alone.

Madison remained furious over Britain's sea policy for months and was certain that war lay ahead. He told William Reynolds of Rhode Island that "the violent and unprovoked conduct of the principal belligerents towards the United States justifies the feelings which it has excited in all good citizens. The readiness to maintain the honor and essential interests of the nation, of which you have communicated an example, is as seasonable as it is laudable."[29]

The president told Ambassador Pinkney, as he had told Jackson earlier, in heated language, what little faith he had in Britain. "It appears that the British govt. continues to be equally ignorant of our character and of what it owes to its own. . . . How can a nation expect to retain the respect of mankind whose govt. descends to so ignoble a career?"[30]

State after state and politician after politician complained to Madison about British sea policy and demanded that something be done to stop them from continuing it. By 1811, the British had impressed or jailed nearly five thousand American sailors. An example of national outrage can be found in a lengthy letter sent to the president by the Vermont General Assembly at the end of 1809; in it, the assembly claimed that "our territorial jurisdiction has been violated, the hospitality of our ports and harbors abused, our citizens murdered whilst in the peaceable spirit of domestic concerns, our national flag insulted, the blood of our seamen wantonly shed and the perpetrators of these horrible acts have been protected."[31]

Criticism of Britain came from everywhere, even Monticello, where Jefferson fumed about the growing crisis. "The infatuation of the British government & nation is beyond everything imaginable. A thousand circumstances announced that they are on the point of being blown up & yet they still proceed with the same madness & increased wickedness," he wrote Madison in early winter of 1809.[32]

What to do now, though? William Duane, the editor of the *Aurora* in Philadelphia, was, like all Americans, frustrated and angry. "That course which is best adapted to the interests and policy of the United States, tho it cannot be very well mistaken by men of sober minds, is not so easily pursued directly as it would be were the attacks upon the nation open instead of insidious," he lamented in a long letter to the president.[33]

The crisis with England had built to a crescendo by the end of November 1809, when Madison sent his annual message to Congress. In it, he blasted the British. "In the state which has been presented of our affairs with the great parties to a disastrous and protracted war, carried on in a mode equally injurious and unjust to the U.S. as a neutral nation, the wisdom of the National Legislature, will be again summoned to the important decision on the alternatives before them. That these will be met in a spirit, worthy the councils of a nation, conscious both of its rectitude and of its rights and careful as well of its honor, as of its peace, I have an entire confidence," he told Congress.[34]

By then, the president realized that Americans were so interested in the conflict between England and France that they did not really understand that a war between America and England was possible. "Public attention would be more animated if the situation in which we are kept by the war . . . and incidents growing out of it among ourselves did not divert the public feelings and resources," he told a diplomat.[35]

Others felt differently. Henry Clay was certain, by 1812, that America had to declare war on England. He told a friend he expected hostilities to begin shortly "whether against one or both belligerents the only point on which I find any diversity of opinion."[36]

Everyone seemed to worry about Madison's resolve for no good reason. He had been a strident opponent of the sea policies of both England and France for years, had been tough with ambassadors, and had never backed down from his beliefs. He had even fired Robert Smith, his inefficient secretary of state, and replaced him with Monroe in 1811. He acted, and he acted quickly. The president was his own man, too. He wrote Jefferson constantly, seeking advice but often ignoring his counsel. The firing of Smith was a good example. Jefferson had lobbied for the return of Monroe to Washington for over a year but was surprised that Madison dismissed Smith to make Monroe secretary of state. He told Madison that Smith's friends in Washington would now conspire to give Madison trouble because of the secretary's ouster. Madison paid no attention to Jefferson's feelings.

16

THE FIRST DAYS
OF THE WAR OF 1812

y the middle of June 1812, state legislatures, local politicians, and newspaper editors were certain that war would be declared. In Virginia, Thomas Jefferson wrote that "everybody in this quarter expects the declaration of war as soon as the season will permit the entrance of militia into Canada." During the second week of June, the state legislature of Maryland went into special session and appointed a committee to study the quick raising of a state militia. Newspapers reported that "within a few days" the "final question" of war would be decided in Congress.[1] All were nervous. Members of Congress remained at their posts, waiting for the war message, and would not leave the capital until they received it. "Congress will not adjourn . . . from the idea that it will make a bad impression," wrote Mrs. Madison.[2]

News came quickly.

Congress received a very strong message from President Madison declaring war on Great Britain on June 1. "The conduct of their government presents a series of acts hostile to the U.S. as an independent and neutral nation," he wrote, adding that "not content with these occasional expedients for laying waste our neutral trade, the cabinet of Great Britain resorted at length to the sweeping system of blockades, under the name of Order in Council, which has been molded and managed as might best suit its political views, its commercial jealousies or the avidity of British cruisers," he said.[3]

Several months later, in his first war message to Congress, Madison, in tough language, told the people not only that was war necessary but also that to avoid one at that point would be unthinkable and indefensible. America had been pushed too far. "To have shrunk from it . . . would have struck us from the high rank where the virtuous struggles of our fathers had placed us, and have betrayed the magnificent legacy which we hold in trust for future generations . . . would have acknowledged that the American people were not an independent people, but colonists and vassals."[4]

On June 4, the House of Representatives approved of the war, and the Senate followed on June 17. The House's Council on Foreign Relations issued a long, detailed report backing Madison on his war at the same time. Congress decreed that "the President of the United States is hereby authorized to use the whole land and naval force of the United States to carry the same into effect."[5]

Nobody realized more than President Madison that this war with England was an uphill conflict. The American army had but a few thousand men and very few of them had ever been in battle. There were few men left who had been officers in the American Revolution. Congress still insisted on its right to appoint generals, overriding the president, and would pick them based on politics and not on military experience. Congress, even after listening to Madison plead for more money for the army for years, had not appropriated anywhere near enough funding to fight a war. The navy was tiny compared to the vast British fleet. Even though Britain was heavily engaged in its war with Napoleon, it would have no trouble dispatching tens of thousands of troops to fight against the United States. Even that auxiliary army was much larger, and far better trained, than American forces.

Some of the War Hawks themselves, so eager for a battle with the British, shook their heads at the prospect of Madison becoming America's first-ever president to also serve as commander in chief. He lacked military experience and he had not shown the administrative experience necessary to lead a large army and fight a war against the globe's premier military power. John Calhoun wrote that "our President, although a man of amiable manners and great talents, has not I fear those commanding talents which are necessary to control those about him. He permits division in his cabinet . . . there is a great want of military knowledge and the whole of our system has to be commenced and organized."[6]

But Madison had enjoyed strong support for a war from a number of reputable sources, such as veterans of the American Revolution. One of them, John Keemle of Pennsylvania wrote him of soldiers who fought with Washington that "in '76 they risked their lives & fortunes for the independence of their country & though now less able to do it, still you will perceive by the expression of their sentiments . . . that they are again determined to make any remaining sacrifices on the same later & many of them have sons who would glory in joining their fathers in the offering." In the attached address, he said the men "will rally round the standard of the government as we did in the time that tried men's souls, determined to die as freemen, rather than live as slaves, under some imperious tyrant, whose will is law."[7]

The veterans of the revolution told Madison that they hated the British as much now as they had during the armed conflict of the 1770s. Former soldier John Stark wrote him that "I found them treacherous and ungenerous as friends and dishonorable as enemies."[8]

Summing up all of the veterans' letters was a note from George Washington's grandson, George Washington Parke Custis. He wrote him that he was proud of what his grandfather and his troops had accomplished in making a new nation and now worried about what would happen to it. He said the United States was "an empire of reason, proudly arisen amid the oppressions of a suffering world. May the last of the republics long be preserved in the pure & benevolent spirit of her Constitution & laws; great within herself, may she stand as a monument of virtue amid the storms of conflicting empires & present to future ages the ines- timable blessings of rational liberty." He did not want to see that empire perish.[9]

College students were ready to put down their books and pick up muskets, too. The president's nephew Alfred Madison wrote him from the campus of the College of William and Mary that "at this critical juncture of our affairs it is thought by many that war, or measures leading to a war, will probably be the result of the deliberations of Congress. Consequently, there are many young men in my acquaintance ready to become applicants for commission in the army," and he said he thought his friend William Pendleton would apply (Pendleton did enlist and fought in the war until its very end in 1816).[10]

An angry family friend, John Tyler, a state legislator from Virginia, wrote from Richmond that he not only supported Madison's get-tough policies but also wished they were even stronger. "I would seize British goods found on land, lock up every store [owner] and hold them responsible for consequences . . . I would imprison every British soldier in the states. By God in heaven, if we go on this way [no action], our nation will sink into disgrace and slavery."[11]

Madison's attorney general, Caesar Rodney (a nephew of Caesar Rodney, signer of the Declaration of Independence, who had also served as Jefferson's attorney general) kept asking Madison what he was waiting for. As early as 1810, the attorney general told the president that "from both [England and France] we have received sufficient cause for commencing hostilities. We have thus far avoided them, with either, by the pacific line of conduct adopted. Can we stand on this course any longer with safety?" Rodney added that a war would not be just for victory but "those rights which God & nature have given an independent nation."[12]

Madison had been receiving so many hundreds of letters of support, and calling for war, that he asked the public, through the *National Intelligencer* news- papers, to please stop writing him. He could hardly get through half of those mailed in from all over America.[13]

States and cities joined the war chorus, too. In New York, Commodore John Rodgers was ordered to take charge of five naval ships and prepare to sail. Over one hundred men in a local militia company were ordered to man a fort on the shore in New York City. Hundreds of militiamen in Boston did the same. Various legislatures announced plans to raise local militias to dramatically increase the size of the American army and navy. Newspapers supported the war and suggested that each state should build and donate one frigate to the navy and join together to raise dozens of large militia companies. States and cities printed lists of the cannon, muskets, and ammunition they had available. Municipalities called large general meetings to discuss the conflict and what they could do to help the federal government. One newspaper referred to the British disdainfully as "the unprincipled wretches."[14]

Most of the newspapers in the nation printed a letter from President Madison that urged all citizens to help. "I do, moreover, exhort all the good people in the United States as they love their country, as they value the precious heritage derived from the virtue and valor of their fathers . . . exert themselves in preserving order in promoting concord, in maintaining the authority and the efficacy of the laws and in supporting and invigorating all the measures . . . for obtaining a speedy, a just and an honorable peace," he wrote.[15]

The papers printed letters such as one from a group of Marylanders to President Madison back in 1810 that claimed that there was nothing like a war to bring the feuding parties in American politics together. The men from Maryland told the president that "one desirable result [of war] will follow; it will unite the friends of our republican form of government by whatever names they may be distinguished."[16]

The nation's newspapers began covering the war right away. One New York newspaper even announced that it was printing a special weekly paper each Saturday called *War* that would cover nothing except the conflict ($2 per year subscription). Hundreds of amateur poets, using their own names or pseudonyms, such as the "Patriot Muse" for a New York paper, began writing poems about Great Britain, which were published in journals throughout the country. Booksellers began running lengthy advertisements selling nothing but military books. Amateur musical composers penned songs to be sung for the conflict, such as "War Song," published in the Philadelphia *Aurora*, which reminded singers in one of its verses that "for soldier foes we have steel and lead, for traitors we have hanging."[17]

Newspapers continued to publish news of seized and searched ships and the names of American seamen captured by the British Navy. Writers contributed letters and columns to newspapers denouncing the British. Some were political and some were religious; the religious reminded readers that God was clearly on the American side of the dispute. Statements by President Madison and others in the American government were printed, along with editorials supporting whatever they said. Copies of letters leaked to the press, such as a heated one from Secretary of State James Monroe to the British ambassador, were reproduced word for word. Earlier, President Madison, using his friendship with Samuel Smith, the editor of the *National Intelligencer*, leaked confidential letters to him from high-ranking British and French diplomats to help generate and sustain public anger.[18]

Local artillerists opened up schools and held classes for amateurs to learn how to load and fire heavy cannon and muskets and how to use new artillery machinery. Men who fancied themselves military experts mailed plans for large new forts to President Madison and state governors. One man in New York built a detailed wood model of a new fort he wanted the city to construct in the battery, at the southern tip of New York City, so American artillery could pound any British ships in sight in the bay. He reminded readers that his new fort came complete with outdoor protection for artillerists so that they could fire away in rain and snowstorms.[19]

Newspaper editors used colorful language in hundreds of editorials supporting the war. "By the blessing of divine Providence, our country will yet emerge with renovated glory from the clouds and tempests that rage in her horizons and obscure her destiny," wrote one excited editor.[20]

All applauded Madison's declaration of August 20 as a national day of prayer, and his decision was lauded by the leaders of the different churches in America. Most of the states, such as Massachusetts, also declared their own day of prayer (Massachusetts governor Caleb Strong, however, asked that the almighty work hard not to bring victory to America, but to bring both sides to the peace table, and quickly).[21]

Newspapers ran letters from any American who had just returned from England or had sailed past England or recently met an Englishman, so that their readers could be current with news of the vile enemy.

Americans, now at war with England, began to applaud the French, the British enemy whom they had been denouncing for high-seas atrocities for years. The French navy, which had been sinking and capturing American ships all spring and summer, was suddenly and repeatedly thanked for turning over American seamen they had taken off British ships and put on board American vessels bound for home. States frantically disbursed arms for their militias. New York announced one week after war was declared that it had already shipped five thousand stands of arms to its western district to army troops there who might be involved in an invasion of Canada (ironically, the British rescinded their 1756 Orders of Council, which permitted their sea policy toward America, a victory for Madison and his Non-Intercourse Act, on the very day that the United States declared war, making the scuttling of the orders a moot point).[22]

Every tiny village in the country seemed ready for war. The town of Lynn, in Massachusetts, appropriated a $7 per week salary for any local resident who joined the army in addition to his regular federal army pay. Another Massachusetts town bragged that its local militia now numbered 1,200 men and was growing daily. Banks in Newport, Rhode Island, ordered British companies to withdraw their money. Several towns and counties urged an immediate draft to raise a huge army. Maryland began to raise militia units with a goal of six thousand men and prepared to pay them out of state funds.[23]

Rumors flew. One man reported that, without question, the British had six frigates lying in harbors in Bermuda ready to attack American seaports.[24]

Not all Americans favored an armored clash with Britain, though. Many New Englanders were against it. In a column in the Federalist *Palladium*, a paper that Madison hated, a writer argued that England had a huge army and the United States only had one thousand men. England had a mammoth navy and the American navy consisted of just a handful of ships sailing under inexperienced captains. The war could cost as much as $25 million, perhaps even more, he argued, and Congress had appropriated little money for the army in 1812. It was not a winnable war, and, he added, it was a war that would not be popular with the people.[25]

Another writer argued that President Madison had overstepped his boundaries as commander in chief in declaring the war. He said that Massachusetts had been at the forefront in the revolution because America needed to separate from Britain and form a new, democratic government. Now, he argued, fears that the new, powerful government would run amok were all coming true.[26]

As early as 1810, New Englanders, including Madison's friends, were arguing that most of the sailors impressed by the British were English deserters anyway, so why go to war over that? Weren't the English right? "What right has the United States to protect a deserter from the service of a foreign nation, whilst in the practice of punishing its own citizens guilty of a similar offense . . . a war with Britain at once unites us as an ally to Bonaparte and will dissolve the union," wrote one friend, Dr. George Logan.[27]

Many Americans were afraid that the United States would not only lose the war but be humiliated, too. Even Mrs. William Gale, the wife of the editor of the *National Intelligencer*, Madison's friend, was afraid of that. She wrote her mother that the British had a plan, that she was certain would succeed, under which the capital would be captured by their troops and the president, vice president and the entire cabinet arrested. It would "render this nation a laughing stock to every other in the world," she said.[28]

In a special session of the Massachusetts legislature, many members stood and spoke openly against the war. One legislator scoffed at Madison's reasons for the conflict. "This cursory view of the alleged causes of hostility, compared with your own observations, and recollection of the course of events, will enable you to judge not only of the sincerity of the administration, but of the solidity of their motives," he said.[29]

And it was in Massachusetts where the phrase "Mr. Madison's War," which would stick throughout the conflict and all of history, was coined by veteran essayist John Lowell, who made that the title of one of his 1812 political pamphlets. Another man who used the popular phrase about the struggle said he did so because "nobody else would father it" and then proceeded to blast the president for running it. He called it "a war of paradoxes" and added that "future historians will be extremely puzzled to know the hidden springs, the secret cause, of so paradoxical and extraordinary measure." The writer joked that Madison's war policy must come from the secret files of the Paris police department."[30] That writer argued that since New England dominated American shipping, it was New England that would suffer the most from a war. New Englanders urged the administration to work out some peaceful solution to the navigation problems American vessels had with Britain.

A New Englander wrote a friend from Washington that anti-British riots in Baltimore the previous week were an unwelcomed opening to the conflict. "The intention is to overawe all opposition by means of mobs, and the 'reign of terror' by our mad-caps is approved. May heaven protect our betrayed country."[31]

Some newspaper editors attacked Madison with his own words. They dug up copies of the Federalist papers and reprinted Madison's essays stating that states' rights were just as important as federal rights and that America could not let the federal government overwhelm the states. They said that was exactly what Madison was doing now, as president.[32]

The *Palladium* attacked the war against England with venom. "The cruel and unnatural war, into which the folly and wickedness of our rulers, entangled in the wiles of Bonaparte, has plunged our ill-fated country leads to speculation and inquiries in which we meet with much doubt and uncertainty. What is to be the fate of our country?" its editor asked.[33]

Officials of several New England towns and counties jointly protested the war in a long letter to President Madison printed in numerous New England newspapers. They called the war "an injustice" and "morally wrong" and said that the federal government was now treating residents of New England as enemies of the country, and not as friends. They were friends, too, they added with great pride, that had helped win the revolution.[34]

Two weeks after the conflict was declared, nearly seventy New England town officials called a special convention in Ipswich, Massachusetts, to see what the New England states should do about what a local newspaper called "the ruinous war." Two weeks later, in a lengthy statement, the convention came out against the conflict. "It is impossible to submit in silence," the chair wrote, "[when] a great people find themselves oppressed by their government, their rights neglected, their interests overlooked." Citizens of Plymouth and other towns did the same thing, and most of them voted to oppose the war.[35]

Nearly two thousand citizens of Rockingham County, in New Hampshire, met at a convention to denounce it. "We have witnessed, with sincere and deep regret, a system of policy pursued by the general government, from the embargo of 1807 to the present time, tending most obviously, in our view, to the destruction of the commerce of the states," the convention's official statement read.[36]

One man sneered, "I give you joy. I give you joy, friends from the bottom, the very bottom of my heart. A war with England! Thanks be to Mr. Jefferson. Thanks be to Mr. Madison. Thanks be to their illustrious fellow laborers, the very exact thing I wished!"[37]

One critic from Virginia, Madison's home state, expressed fears that everybody's taxes would be raised by the war. He said that the eleven million dollars the nation had to borrow to start the conflict would increase as the years of combat passed, and he assured friends that new taxes would be levied in each state to pay off the loans.[38]

The president ignored all of his critics. He found himself working alone more and more; he got things done. And the American president was in complete control of the war at all times. "Mr. Madison governs by himself," wrote the French minister.[39]

The war caused newspaper editors throughout the country to weigh in on the 1812 presidential election, just a half a year away, in which Madison would surely seek a second term. Some supported him, some denounced him, and some wondered if he decided until the summer to start a war to garner timely patriotic support for his re-election bid. Would he suspend the election because of the war?

To some Federalists editors, it did not matter. They just hated him. "We allude to the deficiencies of the present administration with affectionate regret, and solely with a view to their amelioration. The ministers of the President are responsible to him and he is responsible to the people for their adequacy in the duties of office. And our duty to our country will not suffer us to witness in silence the growing complaints of the insufficiency of [Madison]."[40]

It did not matter whom the Federalists nominated; they were behind him. That opposition candidate was a question mark for months, though, and wound up as a surprise. In the spring, New York Republicans, sour on Madison because of the embargo and transfixed by charismatic New York mayor DeWitt Clinton, sailed out of the Republican mainstream and nominated Clinton at their own convention. The Federalists, with no candidate, decided to back Clinton, too, in a "fusion" movement.

Most Republican newspapers supported Madison, but some supported Clinton. "The time when this nomination is urged demands its warmest support and forbids the admission of the faintest idea of postponing it. The administration must be stimulated to their best exertions, or the reputation of prosperity of the country sink into the most alarming jeopardy," wrote one Clinton supporter.[41]

The *Palladium* wrote that the election of anyone but Madison "would bind the union, which seems now ready to be dissolved by the distracted doings of Madison and Co." The editor noted that 91 of the 215 electoral votes were from New England and added that another few dozen anti-Madison votes could be round up in the Middle Atlantic States.[42]

Madison's opponents made fun of his height throughout the campaign, constantly referring to him as "the little man," "the little president" and "the little man in the palace."[43]

The highly personable DeWitt Clinton, eager to be president, decided to be all things to all voters. He was prowar, antiwar, and maybe-war. He was a nationalist and a states' rights champion, all in the same speech. He and his supporters were certain this big-tent approach would work.

Clinton's strategy failed miserably. Madison won the election, garnering 128 electoral votes to just 89 for Clinton. Observers attributed most of his success to the patriotism and support caused by the war (he was the first president to be re-elected in wartime. No president running for re-election in wartime has ever lost).

None of this criticism bothered James Madison. He moved on with dramatic steps. The president leaked the complete strength of the United States Army, with a list of officers and men, to the *National Intelligencer*, which immediately published the information. All the leading newspapers in the country reprinted the lists.[44]

Americans were not afraid of the British.

Mrs. Madison was a radical patriot throughout the war, never giving an inch of compromise in her support of her husband. One night, her friend

Mrs. William Thornton stood within earshot of Dolley and Secretary of State
Monroe. The pair were standing in front of a window, watching a small regiment of army troops march down the street. "I wish we had ten thousand of
them," said the First Lady, and an angry Monroe answered that "they [the
English] are all damned Rascals from the highest to the lowest."

"I wish we could sink them all to the bottomless pit," Dolley answered.

"She was absolutely violent against the English," wrote Thornton later.[45]

Nobody explained the success of the war better than Madison contempo-
rary Daniel Barnard after the president's death. Barnard said that the war was
waged "to compel the enemy to forego his injurious practices, not for the price
of forcing him to a formal recognition of our doctrines, or to a formal promise
of good behavior in the future, but to teach him that we understood our rights
if he did not; that, hold what opinions he would, the actual violation of these
rights would no longer be tolerated and that the practices of which we complained must cease now and cease forever; and that henceforward our security
should be found not in any concessions on his part if he chose to withhold them,
but in the promptness with which the good right arm of a brave and gallant
nation should be bared to do battle for justice and the right, in the name and by
the strength of the God of armies."[46]

17

THE WAR YEARS

Dolley

uring the War of 1812, all remained the same at the White House. The First Lady went out of her way keep the social life of the capital running at full speed, uninterrupted by the conflict, a war that, after all, was very far away. She continued the pace of hosting dinners, parties, receptions, and balls; living with relatives; shopping with friends; attending concerts; receiving visitors daily at the White House; serving as her husband's public relations director; and, as always, being the best-dressed woman in America. Dolley said good-bye to two young women from Virginia who had stayed with her that winter and reminded both that the parties never stopped at the White House, war or no war. They left, she bragged to a friend, "after having their heads turned with gaiety beau. Last night we were all at the Russian Minister's party which was brilliant, and pleasant."

She ended the letter with a note that a good friend of hers would visit her on his return to her city. The "good friend"? It was Judge Story, who as a congressman just a few years before had been critical of Dolley. Now he, like all who started out critical of the First Lady, was in her complete confidence.[1]

Dolley maintained two worlds in Washington, one with the war and the other without it. She insisted that the social life of the White House and the city continue unabated, and then, on her own, in the daytime, spent time on war matters with her friends and husband. The nonstop parties at the White House and embassies assured all that the United States was not hurt at all by the conflict with England, that it would soon emerge from it victorious.

Dolley prided herself on increasing the number of attractive women at White House parties. "Miss Hay is to be in the city soon, as well as Madame Bonaparte

& a multitude of beauties," she wrote her friend Phoebe Morris with pride. She conducted polls with young women she knew to determine whom everybody thought was the best looking woman at parties. She evaluated two women for a friend and then decided that they were both winners in the unofficial beauty contest. "You thought Miss Mayo less beautiful than Miss Caton. I think she has rather the advantage in this, but Miss C. excels in grace," Dolley decided.[2]

Dolley even wrote friends in Paris to buy expensive hats and dresses for her. "As you have everything and we have nothing, I will ask the favor of you to send me by a safe vessel large headdresses, a few flowers, feathers, gloves and stockings, black and white, and any other pretty things . . . draw upon my husband for the amount," she wrote Mrs. Joel Barlow, who lived in Paris with her diplomat husband.[3]

Mrs. Barlow complied, poking her head into all the high-end women's clothing shops in Paris and putting together a collection so vast and expensive that the shipping costs alone were over $2,000. She sent Dolley dresses, shoes, hats, and plenty of turbans. The First Lady did not know it, but she had an entire wartime ensemble. One of those dresses she wore at the 1815 White House New Year's Day party, just before word of the peace treaty and the victory at New Orleans arrived. She dazzled the crowd. She wore a robe of rose-colored satin, trimmed with ermine; with gold chains and clasps around her waist and arms; and with a white, satin turban upon her head, with a tiara of white ostrich plumes. "The towering feathers and excessive throng distinctly pointed her station wherever she moved," said Mrs. Seaton. Just two weeks earlier, she appeared at a ball, dressed in a sky-blue, striped, velvet dress, with a white turban adorned with emeralds and gold-and-white feathers. Two weeks prior to that, she hosted a reception at which she wore a white, cambric gown, buttoned up to the neck and ruffled around the bottom. She wore a peach-colored silk scarf over her shoulders, and the whole ensemble was topped off by a peach-colored turban.[4]

She bought all the elegant dresses she could find and encouraged everyone she knew in Washington to throw more parties. She told friends how much she anticipated the start of the racing season at the end of October 1812 and all of its social functions, and she wrote with delight to a friend that the Hamiltons had given an elegant ball at the Navy Yard. "They danced til morning," she wrote to a friend. She was pleased, too, she told all, that the French minister was not letting the war bother him. He was paving the road to his embassy. "[He] intends to frolick continually," she said.[5]

Why did she spend so lavishly and entertain so heartily while the country was at war? Public appearance. Dolley wanted all of Washington, all of America, to know that the president had no fear of England. Life would roll along as usual, parties and visits, as it always had. The war would be won by America. Nothing had changed. Nothing would. Everybody in America might have been nervous about the conflict, but not the First Lady nor the president.

Those who met her in those years were impressed and surprised at her appearance. One woman later wrote of her in those tension-filled years, "I can see her now. As we entered [the room], she was crossing the crowded vestibule, conducted by two fair girls, one on each side. She surrendered herself to their sprightly guidance with her benign sweetness. Her hair hung in ringlets on each side of her face, surrounded by the snowy folds of her unvarying turban, ornamented on one side by a few heads of green wheat. She may have worn jewels, but if she did they were so eclipsed by her inherent charms as to be unnoticed."[6]

Her husband worked harder than ever when the year 1813 began. He was consumed by the war and madder at Great Britain as each day, and each battle, went by. He told Congress that England's sea policies were "a system which, at once, [were] violating the rights of other nations and resting on a mass of forgery and perjury unknown to other times" and that it was "distinguished by the deformity of its features and the depravity of its character."[7]

Later that winter, Madison, seeing the war clearly as always, offered a succinct analysis of the fighting to friend John Nicholas. He told him that the United States should have entered the war with a large army and a powerful navy, but had not. Then they had lost early battles of Canada when General William Hull surrendered his army. "The decisive importance of this [a strong army] has always been well understood, but until the first prospect ceased, other means of attaining it were repressed by certain difficulties in carrying them into effect," he said, and he added that as commander in chief he had to veto several radical measures to assault Canada again. In his letter to Nicholas, and in letters to others, Madison exhibited a keen sense of what could be done and what could not.[8]

He paid equal attention to his regular army and militia units and, to do so, was in touch with people all over the country, not just in Washington. He was half commander in chief, half cheerleader. For example, in the late summer of 1813, he wrote a Kentucky man, "If any doubt had ever existed of the patriotism or bravery of the citizens of Kentucky, it would have been turned into an admiration of both by the tests to which the war has put them. Nor could any who are acquainted with your history and character wish the military services of your fellow citizens to be under better direction than yours."[9]

By the end of 1813, Madison had accrued as much military knowledge as his generals and secretary of war. He sent careful and detailed analyses of the war and the movements of both sides to all and understood why each side was operating the way it was. He could have been a general himself by that time.[10]

He had disappointing messages from his commanders all spring. General Henry Dearborn wrote him that his army was at a standstill because little of its equipment had arrived from the quartermaster's corps. Who was in charge of the quartermaster corps, the section of the army that issued supplies? It was Dearborn himself. He not only shrugged off his failures but also said he could not even do the job. "It is beyond my power," he told Madison.[11]

The president was happy to have Russia mediate the conflict but did not see much hope. He told William Plumer, a former Federalist senator from New Hampshire who had switched parties and was now the Republican governor of New Hampshire in April 1813, that only England could end the war. "Whether or not we are to have peace this year depends upon the enemy; our disposition & terms being known to everybody." He added that there would be no cease-fire "unless the B. govt. should entertain views & hopes with respect to this country."[12]

It seemed like every day someone in Congress or an important person in the government sent him lengthy letters full of diplomatic and military advice. They were all well-intentioned, but, requiring responses, did little more than take up the valuable time of the president.[13]

President Madison worked tirelessly on the war, staying at the office seven days a week and often each night, too. The stress on him rose dramatically by the middle of June 1813. The army and navy had suffered significant losses, and press criticism of the war had grown. Congress balked at the administration's plea for more money for the war and demanded a lengthy explanation of its supervision by the president. His frail body could not take the burden of the work and pressure, and he became very ill, wracked with a high fever, along with the return of the general weakness that had annoyed him all of his life. His doctors, not knowing what to do, merely prescribed quinine and plenty of rest. Dolley was not satisfied. She put the president to bed, monitored his care, gave him his quinine, washed him, dressed him, and nursed him twenty-four hours a day. She was terrified that he was going to die. The First Lady did not tell anyone of her fears, though, in order to prevent panic. A president dying at the height of a war? How would power be transferred to the vice president for the first time in history? Would the enemy step up the offensive to take advantage of a shaken country?

Others broadcast the bad news, though. One of the first to discover how sick Madison had become was new congressman Noah Webster of Massachusetts. He had visited the White House to give Madison paperwork from Congress and thought the president was very sick. "I did not like his looks any better than his

Administration," he said. Later, Webster was back again, and Madison looked worse. This time he was in bed, under the covers, drenched in sweat, Dolley at his side. Webster came back a few days later and reported that "Madison still sick ... I went ... to the Palace to present the resolutions. The President was in his bed sick of a fever his night cap on his head, his wife attending him." On June 19, Webster was back a third time and was surprised that Madison had taken a bad turn. "He is worse today," he wrote.[14]

The president's close friend, Monroe, asked politicians to stay away from the White House until Madison was better and told friends that he seemed stricken with a fever that would not go away. He knew how ill the president had often felt and that the chief executive had not been away from the White House for more than two weeks in two entire years because of the war. He was physically and emotionally battered and very vulnerable to illness.

The deathwatch began. Various resolutions of near-condolence were offered in the House and Senate. The *National Intelligencer* started to print daily health reports on the president. Republican newspapers wrote about him as if he were dead already. Former president John Adams, in Massachusetts, told friends that he heard Madison had just four months to live. "His death, in the circumstances in which the Republic is placed, would be a veritable national calamity," said French minister M. Serrurier.

The Federalist newspapers were sure Madison was going to die and lamented that his vice president, Elbridge Gerry, would make a poor replacement. Some speculated that the aging Gerry would die, too, and that Henry Clay would somehow wind up in charge. Some called for an immediate change in the Constitution to produce a better successor.[15]

At this point, in the middle of June, in an extraordinary move and angry with everybody, the First Lady shut the bedroom door and cancelled all White House functions. She did not permit anybody, not even the vice president or cabinet members, to see Madison while he recovered. He remained bedridden for three entire weeks; not even close friend Monroe could get in to see him. Numerous friends wrote her, begging for information about the president, but she refused to answer any of those letters, keeping her husband's condition very secretive. He was under the care of his wife and only his wife. The rumors now escalated. Had the president died? Was he incapacitated? If so, who was acting as president? Who was in charge? Was Dolley running the war? The country?[16]

It was the high-water mark of Madison's life. He had feared an illness just like this since he was a young man, certain that it would kill him. If he did not die, he would surely be incapacitated. He would have to stop work, whatever that work was, and permanently retire to Montpelier. This was doomsday.

But it was not. Madison fought his illness, with his wife's assistance. He did not die, did not permit himself to become incapacitated, and never, as far as can be ascertained, thought about resigning as president. What decisions Dolley made, or did not make, for him in those dark weeks remained a mystery. Madison recovered and went back to work in early July. He did not work full-time, and he did not look well, but he worked. His health was not completely recovered until the middle of July. Those weeks were as hard on Mrs. Madison as they were on him. "Now that I see him get well I feel as if I might die myself from fatigue," she said.[17]

The president's illness came just a year after Dolley's sister Anna went through a health crisis herself. In the spring of 1812, Anna was suffering from depression of some sort. She wrote her sister that she was miserable and felt alienated from her husband and family. Dolley, alarmed as always when it came to the well-being of her sisters, wrote a very sympathetic note to her. She said her sickness "causes me more grief than I can speak" and told her that "your constant indisposition, your low spirits, everything that disturbs you never fails to vibrate through all my heart. I flatter myself that you were healthy & happy. Without health, we enjoy nothing. Your estimable husband, lovely children fail to yield you that sweet peace which we ought only to seek for in this world."[18] Then Dolley asked Anna to come and visit her at the White House. There, she knew, she could cheer her up.

In the weeks after Madison's emergence from his bedroom, letters arrived at the White House from well-wishers all over America. Jefferson released a sigh of relief. "If the prayers of millions have been of avail, they have been poured forth with the deepest anxiety," he wrote. Jonathan Dayton of New Jersey was one of many who wrote that Madison had become such a skilled commander in chief that his death would have caused the collapse of the army. "I almost tremble, sir, when I think of the contentions, division & disasters to which your sudden removal at the critical period must have exposed us and have frequently thanked heaven for yet longer sparing your life to us."[19]

The nation's first presidential crisis had been averted, not by luck but by the desire of Madison to beat his sickness and by his wife's determination to keep him alive.

Throughout his sickness, and the conflict with England, Dolley worried constantly about national affairs. "[We are] in the mist of business & anxiety, anxious for the fate of the war," she wrote in the fall of 1812.[20]

At that same time, the Madisons lost their private secretary, Edward Coles. He had become ill, and they sent him to their physician, Dr. Physick, in Philadelphia, for treatment. Coles spent the fall and winter of 1812–1813 in Philadelphia, recovering. Dolley told him that she and the president missed him. "You will soon be well in spite of yourself. We indulge this pleasing hope in addition to that of your remaining with us to the last . . . there are none who feel a more affectionate interest in you than Mr. Madison and myself . . . your leaving us [would be] a misfortune."[21]

She wrote friends that Madison's illness made her sick, but there were many other times as First Lady that Dolley fell ill. For instance, she wrote Edward Coles in the summer of 1811 that "I have been extremely ill. I am just now recovering from three weeks' confinement during which I was most carefully nursed." In June 1811, she was confined to bed (with a "dangerous and severe illness") and was nursed back to health by Hannah Gallatin and a cousin. In the summer of 1812, she fell ill yet again, writing a friend that "for the last 10 days I have been very sick, so much so that I could not write or do anything. I am yet in my chamber."[22]

Dolley labored through her husband's crisis, and the war, with her own political and emotional grit, but she also had the love and support of her friends, who constantly picked up her spirits when they saw her or wrote letters of encouragement. Phoebe Morris was one. She wrote Dolley in the year leading up to the war that "I can love no other person as I now love you. In the moment of my separation from you tears were my only language. My affection for you is a sensation new to my heart; it differs from that love I feel for many of my young friends; it is more pure, it is more refined." Dolley wrote her back and told her that "I have wept over your charming letter" and added that she and the president cherished their friendship with her and her family.[23]

Dolley spent much of her time receiving and answering letters from men who wanted officers' appointments to the army as the fear of a war heated up and then began; they thought she could use her sway over the president to their favor. She received pleas from the wives, mothers, and girlfriends of soldiers who had been tossed into military brigs, asking for leniency. Other women begged her to use her influence with the president to gain pardons for their husbands, charged with desertion from the army. One woman, Deborah Stabler, asked her to get her son released from jail, where he had been put when he refused to serve in the army, telling recruiters he was a conscientious objector.[24]

She also had to keep track of the letters of introduction she received from all over America, telling her that the subject of the letter would soon by dropping by to see her and that she should meet them. These came from close friends, such as Molly Randolph, and total strangers.[25]

Throughout the war, she found herself spending large amounts of time helping political and military figures get over snubs from congressmen. She also found herself writing dozens of letters to sick friends and relatives, wishing them well and in some cases suggesting homegrown medical cures for their ailments.[26]

Dolley was surprised at the number of times she was misquoted or misrepresented by people and how that angered others. In the fall of 1809, someone told White House interior decorator Benjamin Latrobe that Mrs. Madison was very unhappy with his work, which was not true. She immediately wrote Latrobe that what he had been told was false; that she had nothing but admiration for his work, as did everybody else; and that she and the president had the highest regard not only for Latrobe but for his wife, too. She would investigate the matter, find out who the culprit was, and punish him or her. She did that frequently, and right away, and it easily repaired the damage by gossips.[27]

Dolley helped her husband as president whenever she could. Madison, like all presidents, was quickly consumed by all the work that faced him, especially with the added burden of the tattered relationship with Great Britain. Dolley told friends that the president did not get a good night's sleep and often awoke in the middle of the night to write down notes. She kept a candle on all night and left quills, ink, and paper nearby for his work. She told people that the stress wore out not only the president but her, too.

Those who saw Dolley in the prewar and war years all commented on how the stress of the war, her husband's labors, and the increased work of being in charge of an ever-growing social scene at the White House had affected her. One congressman who saw Mrs. Madison, dressed plainly, on a Washington street one morning at the start of the 1811 winter was stunned by her appearance. "Her eyes [were] dark and neither large nor brilliant—her cheeks I think were painted. The whole contour of her features was dull and un-interesting, her habit is too full to be graceful. She must be considered in ruins," he said.[28]

Dolley had reasons to be worn out in the early days of that winter. The fortunes of her brother, John, a clerk to the minister of Tunis, a job the president got him, had turned bad. The Payne sisters all felt that the new climate in Africa would help John cure his drinking; it did not.

He had been in Tunis since 1806. Over the years, Dolley had written him dozens of letters, most of which he ignored. In 1809, she wrote him that she wished he could come home and live in the White House with her and other members of the family. She filled him in on the death of their mother and sister. Then, fearful that his drunken stupors had made him unaware of news in America, she told him, incredibly, that her husband was now the president of the United States. She begged him to come home, where she and her sisters could take care of him. She did not want anything "to stay you one moment from my arms & heart, that are open to receive you" and added that she would arrange a life for him in America in which he would be completely independent.[29]

Dolley then used her influence with her husband to have John promoted to the number two post in Paris, where her friends Joel Barlow, the consul, and his wife could look after him. All was well at last, she hoped. Dolley was wrong. Her brother never showed up in Paris. The Barlows waited months in Washington, hoping he would arrive there instead to join them in the voyage to France, but he never did. They finally sailed for France, more than four months behind schedule, angering French officials and President Madison, too. Months later, in June 1811, John Payne finally arrived in America, with no explanation for where he had been. He was spotted in New York by a cousin, who told Dolley her brother had to sell everything he had to pay his bills.

He soon turned up at the White House, where he promptly borrowed $150 from Dolley. She told his sister Anna that "he has returned in greater difficulties than he went, being obliged as he thought to borrow money." She told her sisters that she had been wrong to send him to Tripoli, and blamed his drinking and dissipation there on people in the embassy in Tunis. She wondered, in letters to her sisters, what had gone wrong. They, like her, blamed everybody but their brother. The three agreed to take turns taking care of him, and John bounced around from mansion to mansion, disappearing for days at a time on the journeys. Dolley finally decided that she could persuade him to live a sober life. "He has taken up a good deal by my persuasion," she wrote. "I have dressed him and forced him to change bad for good society." And she had to keep in touch with her sisters to find out where he was, if they knew. Back in America, he continued to drink and wander, running up large bills that he could not pay.[30]

Dolley's overseeing did not work. John continued to drink. Like all alcoholics, he spent much of his life as a talkative and charming man, but then he slid into alcoholism. Dolley sent him to one of his sisters after a period of time and blamed the entire city of Washington for his problems, writing that she had sent way from "this den of thieves."[31]

John Payne was also a shadowy figure. He would disappear and remain absent for weeks, months, at a time and then, without warning, arrive at the front door of the White House, startling everyone. In the summer of 1811, Mrs. Madison wrote Edward Coles that "it seems that my dear brother was landed at Cape Henry. From thence, we suppose that he went to Norfolk. I am watching every carriage with impatience to see him arrive."[32]

When her brother was at the White House, Dolley took him everywhere. She showcased him at White House parties and brought him with her, or sent him with someone, to balls at foreign embassies. She then bragged to friends at how accepted John was and how much people enjoyed being around him. She had the same attitude toward her son, Payne, constantly fearing for his safety and his health when he traveled abroad to countries such as Russia. All the while, Dolley was up nights with her brother, sorting out his debts and talking to him about his problems. John was deeply in debt. He explained to her on one visit that he had to borrow money at Malta, an island in the Mediterranean, in order to enter France without being arrested. Then he ran out of money completely and returned to America. "He stays to sell his lands, arrange his debts *of all sort* here & then he intends to go into some business, heaven only knows what," she complained to her sister. "I have paid $100 for him since he got home & advanced $50 for his current expenses alas!"[33]

In April of 1812, as pressure was growing on Madison from all sides to declare war on England, Dolley again found herself saddled with her brother, John, and his problems. She sent him off to Harewood to stay with relatives and seemed glad to be rid of him. "It's not worthwhile to tell you the particulars of his last frolick, or the sum he spent on it. I re-fixed him with my all, even my credit, & sent him off in a hack with his friend Green, whose expenses I also paid, in order to secure his retreat [from here]."[34]

The president, frustrated by his brother-in-law, continually shook his head about John's problems and the inability of his wife to see that at this point there was really nothing anybody could do for him. At the same time, though, he told friends that his admiration for his wife was growing daily. She had stood beside him in every crisis of his administration and had not only chided his opponents but also howled at them. One example was the Gideon Granger affair in the winter and spring of 1812. Granger, Jefferson's old postmaster general, stayed on when Madison was inaugurated and caused nothing but trouble. He appointed local postmasters Madison did not approve of, was staunchly opposed to any war with Britain, and threatened to make public sexual digressions of Dolley and Anna Cutts (that he had invented). Madison fired him. A furious Dolley blasted him to all. In a letter to her sister, she called Granger "a fiend" and told her "you know what G. had been, and what he has done, years ago. I should tell you nothing new when I repeated his conduct & his communications to Davis. It is all beneath our notice though. G. is not below our contempt & hatred."[35]

The presidency, family troubles, war, and lengthy and severe domestic political scuffles, however, drew the Madisons closer. James Madison never referred to her anymore as "Mrs. Madison" at parties, balls, and state dinners, but just "Dolley." And he depended on her more and more to run the social calendar of the White House and, as his wife, to ease the worries he had from the office. Her buoyancy helped him considerably.

She also helped him navigate tricky political waters. The president often found himself helping businessmen with official clearances and permissions. It was perfectly legal, and they were very grateful for his assistance and wanted to thank him with gifts. Madison did not know how to handle businessmen, but Dolley did. She would write them, on his behalf, and, in vague notes, suggest they visit the White House and talk to him about their successful ventures. "Come then, as soon as possible, to my husband who will not call, though he wishes for you, every day," she wrote in 1810 to John Astor, whose trade with China had benefitted enormously from Madison's assistance in permitting Astor's fleets of ships to use US ports. Two years later, when the American treasury was practically bankrupt, Astor stepped in, and, through his own savings and that of friends, raised $12 million in government bonds for Madison to fight the war of 1812.[36]

Dolley was involved with intrigue often. She also spent much time during the war lobbying for her husband with recalcitrant senators and congressmen of his own party. Her charm went much further than her husband's political threats. At one point, Henry Clay told her "everybody loves Mrs. Madison." She smiled and said, "And that's because Mrs. Madison loves everybody."[37]

Mason Weems, an elderly man who spent a considerable amount of time with public officials over the years, insisted that Dolley's smoothly-running social world gave the president not only a place to escape the pressures of office but also an easy atmosphere in which to conduct unofficial business and get things done. "The crowds that attend your levees give you an influence which no other lady can pretend to have," Weems told Mrs. Madison.[38]

The First Lady's levity held up well in the short spring of 1812, the last calm days before the war. Washington was, as always, full of foreign ministers, old and new. There were tired old congressmen and energetic new ones, rich old merchants and hardworking new ones, lots of writers, and a few painters. There were foreigners who were spotted as frauds, duplicitous men disguising themselves just to be a part of Dolley's social world. There were inventors, such as Robert Fulton of steamship fame, bankers, and actors.

Dolley's sister Lucy was married again that winter, to Supreme Court Justice Thomas Todd, aged forty-seven, "a man of the most estimable character," according to Dolley in a ceremony attended by hundreds. Her sister was happy about being married but "in deep distress" at leaving Dolley and the White House. Dolley made her sister promise to live with her at the White House each autumn and winter when the judge returned to sit with the Supreme Court.[39]

Dolley did not really have to look out for Lucy; her sister was a realist who did not travel through life with mistaken apprehensions about anyone. In one letter to Dolley, she blurted out that she just hated Kentucky, where her new husband had taken her. "The solitude we live in here is almost killing. I have been out twice since we came home." She added, too, that Dolley must be "mortified" at some of the people she had to meet and told her to "bear it like a Christian." Dolley gossiped wildly with her sisters, sizing up male suitors for girlfriends and then quickly cutting them down. She said of someone she knew that "Miss Hay will play him false. I'm pretty certain she does not love him, but it won't hurt him much to be jilted." She wrote of one man, whom she herself had recently dropped, that no one liked him and that "everybody hooted at him for a fool," and she peppered her letters with snide remarks about dozens of men and women they both knew. Lucy had nowhere near the skill that Dolley had in keeping her mouth shut and her pen dry.[40]

The First Lady was happy Judge Todd had won her sister's heart, and happier still that young Lucy listened to her and did not marry beneath herself. She told all of her friends "how wise Lucy was to choose him in preference to the gay flirts who courted her. Yes, my regrets are all selfish, not for her, but myself."[41]

She lived in a world of rumors. Several people hinted that her sister Lucy was pregnant and had to get married. A rumor spread that Lucy had engaged in a feud with the wife of another Supreme Court justice. And, according to yet other rumors, several women close to Dolley feuded with each other. The wives of new ministers to Washington wondered what their role, if any, would be in a Washington social world completely dominated by Mrs. Madison. And John Payne continued to drink no matter where the family hauled him to dry out.

Dolley's parties helped to push away the blues for her, but they were not always as enjoyable as they might have been. She wrote in the dead of winter 1813, when there were few soirees, that "the city is more dissipated than I ever knew it; the week is too short for parties." To overcome that dissipation, of course, she threw more parties, regardless of plunging temperatures and snow that January. In March, she could write back to Phoebe Morris that she would have written her "if I had been blessed with one hour's leisure or quiet."[42]

It was a time for fending off rumors of war, too. She told James Taylor in the spring of 1811 that "vessels are expected hourly & the state of our relations in Europe will decide whether an extra session [of Congress] will be necessary—some very wicked & silly doings at home." Later, in the spring of 1813, after the war began, she said that "if I could, I would describe the feats & alarms that circulate around me. For the last week all the city & Georgetown have expected a visit from the enemy and were not lacking in their expressions of terror."[43]

The winters of 1810, 1811, and 1812 were bad ones for President Madison, too. Tensions had been building. One of his casual aides, Isaac Coles, the older brother of Madison's secretary, Edward Coles, even got into a fistfight with a man in the Senate chamber. His country had been submitting to British dep-' redations on the high seas for years, doing nothing about it, and he had been bullied by British ministers and politicians. Just before Christmas 1811, the London newspaper *Courier* insulted him in yet another of its seemingly endless anti-American editorials. "America fluctuates between her inclinations and her apprehensions," wrote its editor. "She seems always to stand TREMBLING and HESITATING on the slippery verge of war; and to be incessantly tossed about at the mercy of every event; a condition which, of all others, most directly tends to palsy the spirit, and to destroy the confidence of a nation."[44]

Young William Preston, who would later be a senator from South Carolina, wrote that Madison "appeared in society daily, with an unmoved and abstracted air, not relaxing, except towards the end of a protracted dinner, with confidential friends."[45]

At those dinners, with friends and political allies, the president, Dolley at his side, exploded. There in the dining room of the White House, behind closed doors, he was tough and strident and a different man than the wispy leader the public knew. Richard Rush, the new attorney general, who attended many of those dinners, wrote, ". . . the President, little as he is in bulk, unquestionably, [is] above [cabinet and Congress] in spirit and tone. While they are mere mutes . . . he on every occasion and to everybody, talks freely . . . says the time is ripe, and the nation, too, for resistance."[46]

At this point, with the country so close to war, the Madisons swatted away anyone opposed to the government's war policy, now in the planning stages. Dolley fumed at critics more than her husband. "John Randolph has been firing away at the House this morning against the declaration of war, but we think it will have little effect," she sneered in a letter to her sister. She told everyone she knew, as she had told people since his first inauguration, that her husband was working very hard. "I know . . . by the intense study of Mr. M and his constant devotion to the cabinet, that affairs are troublesome & difficult. You see, the English are stubborn yet but we anticipate their yielding before long."[47]

In the spring of 1812, the diplomatic picture was further clouded. Napoleon continued to resist all American efforts to achieve an agreement for freedom of the seas. In England, new parliamentary leaders were harsher than their predecessors on Americans and the war against American shipping became much worse, with no end to British oppression in sight. British prime minister Spencer Perceval was assassinated by a madman, but his death did not soften policy toward America at all.

Under enormous pressure, one night James Madison attended one of his wife's White House parties. Dolley kept watching him. He was stressed out from politics, the war, the weak military state of the United States, and pressure from nonwar politicians and newspaper editors, particularly in New England.

He looked terrible. A Federalist at the party that night was shocked by his appearance. "[Madison] has a serious look, devoid of penetration; his face is crooked and wrinkled; and his countenance does not exhibit the least trait of sincerity or candor. He is a little, dried up politician. He does not know how to behave in company; instead of going about among his guests and setting them at ease by saying something to each, he stands in the middle of the room and expects his visitors to approach him if they want to be favored by his conversation."[48]

The president's wife took extra care of him, always worried that his various ailments would return under the stress of the job and what appeared to be the upcoming war. "My dear husband is overpowered with business, but is in good health," she wrote confidently to her sister that week.[49]

One thing that strengthened Dolley's morale was the stream of visitors who came to the White House to support her and her husband in the upcoming war, which now appeared certain to start. She also had letters from friends all over the world, cheering her up. One lengthy letter from Sally McKean d'Yrugo, who was now the American wife of the Spanish minister, was a particular joy. Sally told her how much she had missed her on her recent trip to Brazil and how much Americans in Brazil admired Dolley. She signed off by writing "believe me, my dear Mrs. Madison, you are an old and affectionate friend."[50]

One thing that annoyed the Madisons was the endless swirl of rumors about the British. Rumors filed the newspapers and Dolley's parties. Everybody had some information, from an irrefutable source, that such and such was happening. An example was the spring of 1813, just before the first anniversary of the conflict. Ceaseless rumors caused Dolley to worry that the British would soon be on her doorstep. "Fears and alarms circulate around me," she wrote. "For the last week, all the city and Georgetown . . . have expected a visit from the enemy and were not lacking in their expression of terror and reproach."[51]

She did take solace from her husband's efforts to protect Washington. He had ordered the repair of a fort on the outskirts of town and sent five hundred regular soldiers and five hundred militia volunteers to camp on a large meadow in town, near a windmill, to protect the city and its residents if a British attack did come. It pleased her. "The twenty tents already look well in my eyes," she said.[52]

Madison's insistence on protection for the capital paid off because from time to time there were reports that a British army was marching toward Washington or sailing toward it on the Potomac. In 1813, a Thursday, for example, there was a rumor that several British warships were sailing up the river and were only fifty miles from Washington. As planned by the president, alarm guns were fired, church bells were rung, and every person in town was scurried toward an assignment. "Soldiers in every direction were mustering and in a few hours 3,000 or 4,000 troops were on their march to the fort fourteen miles distant. They were followed by carts loaded with ammunition, provisions an bagged of all kinds," wrote Elbridge Gerry Jr., the son of Vice President Gerry, caught in the middle of it.[53] Like many, Gerry Jr. wrote his name down on a list for volunteer guards to defend the town and waited for the call up, which did not come on that day.

Throughout the war, everyone acknowledged the hard work and effervescent spirit of the First Lady. Early in the war, in November 1812, Dolley was at a ball at Tomlinson's Hotel in Washington to honor some recent US war heroes. Suddenly, Lieutenant Hamilton, the son of naval secretary Paul Hamilton, arrived, fresh from the battle of a ship he served on, captained by Stephen Decatur, which had defeated the British ship, the *Macedonian.* Dozens of Hamilton's friends rushed around him, music was played, and the story of the battle was told. Without warning, Hamilton walked across the room and laid the flag of the captured *Macedonian* at the feet of Mrs. Madison, giving the battle flag to her, something that had never been done before. Dolley did not know what to do. A friend said her face changed colors because she was so astonished. Finally, praising Hamilton and all the sailors in the war, she accepted it to great applause.[54]

Mrs. Madison's influence in the war grew in the spring of 1813, after Edward Coles, Madison's personal secretary, became ill. Dolley, who was at the White House all day anyway, took over his responsibilities. This meant that she now arranged the president's appointments, decided who whom he would write letters to, met with visiting congressmen, and, most important, became privy to the all the top secrets of the war, as well as the president's private opinions of the country's military leaders. In a way, for a spring and summer she served as the assistant president.

All of the letters she wrote during the war were out-and-out propaganda. For instance, she wrote her son in the summer of 1814 that "the British on our shore are stealing & destroying private property, rarely coming to battle, but when they do are always beaten. . . . If the war should last six months longer the United States will conquer her enemies."[55]

She also helped the president to aid Albert Gallatin, his highly trusted secretary of the treasury, whom many members of Congress never grew to like. Madison wanted to put Gallatin on a peace commission to end the war, but

Congress insisted that he could not be on the peace commission and continue as secretary of treasury at the same time. Dolley wrote Gallatin's wife, "Nothing has borne so hard as the conduct of the Senate in regard to Mr. Gallatin. Mr. Astor will tell you many particulars that I ought not to write, of the desertion of some whose support we had a right to expect and of the manoeuvring of others always hostile to superior merit. We console ourselves with the hope of its terminating both in public good and Mr. Gallatin's honorable triumph."[56]

In the end, the Senate did approve Gallatin as a peace commissioner, but only after he resigned from the Madison cabinet.

Throughout 1813 and 1814, Dolley complained to friends that the reluctance of Congress to appropriate funds for enlarging the army and navy, which Madison begged for, was going to turn tragic. She felt even worse in the spring of 1814, that after the first defeat of Napoleon in Europe the British could now turn all of their sail and cannon firepower on America in one great lunge to win the War of 1812. From the spring of 1814 into the late summer, Mrs. Madison, and others, worried about an attack at either Baltimore or Washington. Dolley and her husband dismissed "official" predictions that the British would ignore Washington and assault Baltimore in a prodigious land-and-sea operation involving several dozen warships and ten thousand troops.

One thing Dolley refused to do was abandon her friends because of the war and politics. The premier example of this was the saucy Elizabeth "Betsy" Patterson Bonaparte, the young wife of Napoleon's twenty-year-old brother. Betsy, an American, had fallen for Jerome Bonaparte at a dance and married him shortly afterward. The two became a sensation on the Washington party circuit because Jerome was the brother of perhaps the most famous, and certainly the most feared, man in the world and Betsy showed much cleavage in her gowns when in public. Dolley had taken Betsy under her wing and befriended her when everybody else sneered at the girl.

In 1814, as the war raged, Betsy's fortunes collapsed. Napoleon refused to recognize the marriage of his brother to Betsy, would not meet her, and, in fact, refused to permit her to enter France. He ordered his brother to leave Betsy and return home to France, where the emperor promptly married him off to an acceptable French woman. Betsy was left alone with a hefty $50,000 per year alimony support.

Betsy fretted that the loss of all her social luster would mean an immediate ouster from the White House and Washington social circles that were run by Mrs. Madison. She had nothing to fear. Dolley, in fact, felt sorry for her. Betsy, like so many millions of others, was a victim of Napoleon's wrath. Dolley continued to invite her to all the White House dinners, receptions, and parties.

Because Dolley acknowledged her, so did everyone else. It made Betsy feel better. To keep Betsy in the White House social world without her husband must have angered Napoleon, so it made Dolley feel better, too.

Dolley kept up correspondence with old friends, too. She wrote Thomas Jefferson's daughter Martha for years after her father left the White House, and, when James Madison died, Martha was one of the first women to send condolences to Dolley.

The war caused Dolley to become even more personal to all than she had been during her husband's first few years as president. Sarah Gales Seaton said that at wartime parties Dolley would welcome guests and then, as an extra personal touch, sit down between two or three or four of them and talk for quite a while before returning to her general duties as hostess. She persuaded musically talented people at parties to sing or play the harp or piano in one of her drawing rooms to entertain the crowd. She also took to wearing the fashionable new flat caps at formal dinners, in addition to her turbans, shocking everyone.

A woman at a wartime dinner, without realizing it, captured Dolley's popularity in an instant. Dolley was a queen, she said, but never displayed the personality of one, always remaining a common woman.[57]

Later, when the war ended, the president asked his wife to throw one of her famous receptions to welcome the new British minister, the rather-illustrious Sir Charles Bagot, descended from Lord Henry Bolingbroke. His wife, said to be rather beautiful, was the niece of the duke of Wellington, the same duke who had just crushed Napoleon at Waterloo.

Their star power did not daunt Mrs. Madison. At her party, she not only invited every important politician in America but also added Chief Justice Marshall and all the members of the Supreme Court, as well as some of the peace commissioners, a bevy of senators and congressmen and several US Army generals. And, of course, on top of them all, like the voluptuous icing on the cake, there was Dolley. She dazzled everybody. Mrs. Madison wore a rose-colored satin and white felt gown whose train swept the floor behind her for several yards. She was adorned in a gold necklace and bracelets. Finally, the First Lady wore a huge turban of white velvet, trimmed with white ostrich tips and a gold, embroidered crown.

Sir Charles Bagethot was stunned. "She looked every inch a queen," he said.[58]

18

THE EARLY YEARS OF THE WAR

The commander in chief hung maps of Canada, the Great Lakes, New England, and the Atlantic seaboard up on the walls of his office in the White House; wrote letters; signed orders; kept files; met with political figures; brought in newspaper editors; and held meetings. The War of 1812 was the very first conflict in United States history in which the civilian president donned the robes of the military leader, the commander in chief of all armed forces.

Everything that Madison did as commander in chief set precedent. As military leader in wartime, he had to raise a large army, recruit militia units, expand the navy, get ammunition, name generals, and create a battle plan for the war. He had to assemble a war council in the White House, deal with a belligerent Federalist Party and equally disdainful Federalist newspaper editors, maintain the support of his Republican Party, gain support from the nation's clergymen, and, at the same time, pass bills, collect taxes, and run the nonmilitary side of the country. It was a daunting task.

At the start of the war, Napoleon Bonaparte did not let up in his own campaign to search American merchant vessels and impress sailors, as he had been doing for months. Madison could not fight one war with the British and another with the French. He also could not give in and join forces with the French against the British. He wrote a fiery letter, aimed at Napoleon, and had it printed in the *National Intelligencer*. In it, he said that "our government will not, under any circumstances that may occur, form a political connection with France. . . . It is not desirable to enter the lists with the two great belligerents at once, but if England acts with wisdom, and France perseveres in her career of injustice and folly, we should not be surprised to see the attitude of the United States change toward those powers." He sent copies of the letter to his minister in France, Joel Barlow, and told him to be ready for an American war with France if England ended its war and the French continued their hostilities toward the United States.[1]

The president quickly found himself the well of all responsibility for the war. It was not a good place to be in, but Madison did not flinch. He plunged into the work of the conflict each morning and kept at it all day. Attorney General Richard Rush was surprised and impressed that Madison worked so hard. He was also pleased that Madison never gave in to British demands. He was, Rush said, "obstinate" against the British. Rush also wrote that "we have great good in him."[2]

The president also had to deal with the leaders of the Native American tribes in the Northwest Territories. They all complained bitterly about mistreatment by the American government and the local settlers in the Ohio region. Madison knew that they were right, and he also knew that if he did not resolve their problems they would side with the British in the war. He could not have the armed resistance of a half dozen tribes, with hundreds of warriors, allied against him. He also had to work with the War Hawk congressmen, led by Henry Clay, who saw the war as an opportunity to annex all of Canada in a sweeping victory. Americans had thirsted after the vast terrain of Canada for decades. They had invaded the country with the British in the French and Indian War and, on their own in the American Revolution, each time without success, but they might achieve victory in the War of 1812. It was an unintended consequence that might bring huge rewards in the future. Jefferson had doubled the size of the United States with the Louisiana Purchase, and the annexation of Canada would double it again. For years, Madison had believed that Canada would become part of the United States simply because it was next door. "When the pear is ripe, it will fall of itself," he said. Newspapers thirsted after Canada. When the war was just a year old, the editor of the *Boston Chronicle* wrote that "the Canadas ought in no event be surrendered . . . much valuable blood has already been shed and too much treasure been expended, to permit us to indulge for a moment the idea of resigning this country." Madison also believed, as did most Americans, that the Canadians would rather be Americans than remain British. Even British commander Isaac Brock thought that might be true. "[They] were either indifferent to what was passing or so completely American as to rejoice in the prospects of change of governments," he said. Yet President Madison could not publicly say he wanted to grab all of Canada. After all, this was supposed to be a defensive war against England, not a glaring attack on Canada.[3]

The president did not want to dampen the enthusiasm for the war anywhere, but he soon found that he had to do exactly that in the most unlikely of places: the White House. There, his energetic, highly ambitious secretary of state, James Monroe, caught war fever and asked for a battlefield command as a general. Monroe not only was the secretary of state and former governor of Virginia but also had been an officer in the American Revolution. He had enough military experience and administrative experience to act as a general. Madison did not want that, though. Monroe might make a decent general, but he was an even better secretary of state. The president did not want to lose his diplomatic skills in the crucial months ahead just so that Monroe could race off and win some battles. He also needed Monroe because the Virginian was part of his White House brain trust for economic and political matters, as well as for the war. Besides, the departure of Monroe, some in the cabinet said, would open the door to bring Thomas Jefferson back to Washington to replace him as secretary of state. What a splendid idea, his aides said. Jefferson had not only been a great president but was, they reminded Madison, a secretary of state once before, for President Washington. Much as Madison loved Jefferson, he did not believe that the third president, knee deep in his farming at Monticello, would come back. Although he would never say it, he also did not need a former president around, offering advice. The country had one president already; it did not need two. Monroe would stay in Washington and Jefferson would remain at Monticello.

Madison had wars to fight wherever he turned, even in his own cabinet. Dr. William Eustis had been a weak secretary of war who elicited no confidence in Congress, and Madison wanted to replace him. To do so, he had to plunge into a nightmare world of intrigue and political infighting. Everybody in Washington was loathe to take the secretary of war job. It involved an enormous amount of work and the secretary seemed to be criticized from all corners of Washington. And what if America lost the conflict? What would happen to the secretary of war, who lost the war?

Madison personally hated to see Dr. Eustis go, but he was pressured by many in the government to fire him, especially Gallatin, whom he trusted. Gallatin did not like Eustis and told the president that Eustis simply did not have the skills for the job. Madison needed a secretary of war whose "knowledge and talents would save millions and the necessary business would be better done," said Gallatin.[4]

Eustis had no military experience and scant administrative skills. He spent most of his time reading maps and corresponding with arms merchants and ignored the war. He supported his older generals and refused to acknowledge criticism of them by younger generals, such as Winfield Scott. He corresponded with generals in the field but never passed along their letters to Madison; he often instructed generals to write him and not the commander in chief. One congressman called Eustis "a dead weight," and Paul Jennings, Madison's slave, said he was a "rather rough, blustering man."[5]

Madison wanted to replace Eustis with Senator William Crawford of Georgia, whom he admired, or General Henry Dearborn, but they both turned him down. Then he wanted to move Monroe from State to War but feared a congressional uprising if he did so. Then he thought about his friend Gallatin but knew that Congress despised Gallatin and would never approve him. Finally, Madison settled on John Armstrong, a former minister to France, whom nobody liked. Monroe told the president that Armstrong not only could not do the job but also was personally offensive to all who met him. Gallatin said he did not have the disposition for the job, did not have any loyalty to the administration, and might undermine the president. Madison, with no one else to turn to, went with Armstrong anyway. It would turn out to be one of the biggest mistakes he ever made.

The president then turned to the Navy Department, where Paul Hamilton had run things inefficiently for several years. Hamilton was a friendly and loyal secretary, but he did a terrible job running the navy in peacetime and now was doing a worse job in wartime. He had been a drunk for years and, it was rumored, never stayed at the office past noon. The president and others had tried to help Hamilton but failed. "Mr. Madison and his friends tried by every means to cure him, but it was useless," said French Minister Serrurier. Madison talked Hamilton into resigning and replaced him with William Jones, a staunch Republican whom he had tried to get to take the navy job for eleven years. Jones, a Philadelphia merchant, was not only a good administrator but, as a former sea captain, also understood the needs of the sailors in the navy. The hardworking Jones turned out to be one of Madison's best wartime appointments. The president said of him later that he was "the fittest minister who had ever been charged with the Navy Department." Rush was relieved as much as he was pleased by the appointments. He said that is was "delightful . . . to all those who for months past have been agonized at the imbecility of the two departments, to think that now probably the two most able men the nation has in it . . . are the two men appointed."[6]

Madison's shuffling of the cabinet pleased Congress. So did an extraordinarily tough annual message, delivered in the winter of 1812. Rush told Madison that he was no longer a peace president but a war president. He needed to send Congress a hard, strident message from a wartime chief that told each member, and the nation and the world, that the United States would never back down and would win its war. He told the president what was needed in the message was "a blast of war against England" and a message that would "thwack . . . these gentlemen patriots among us who are perpetually aiding and abetting the enemy." Madison put together a furious message, one from the heart, one so full of Armageddon language, though, that it startled Rush. He helped Madison tone down the message, against the president's better instincts.[7]

The message called for more recruitment, a larger navy, and higher pay for soldiers. It also included a note that the country could do this because a recent $6 million loan had balanced the budget, knowing full well, from Gallatin, that the coming year would probably show a substantial deficit, not a balance.

The president solved the problem of getting men to volunteer for the general army or militia by increasing the pay of privates from $5 a month to $8 and added substantial bounty fees to make the army a satisfying occupation.

The very first War Hawk Congress promptly approved President Madison's wide-ranging budget requests. Soldier pay was increased by 60 percent, "imprisonment for debt" army recruits released from confinement and signed up, recruiting budgets increased, and funds provided for a doubling of the size of the navy, something that had never been done before in American history. Later, Congress gave Madison the power to appoint officers for twenty new regiments, created twelve new generalships, and gave the president the right to name them (some of his choices were poor, but others, such as Zebulon Pike, Lewis Cass, George Izard and Duncan MacArthur, were quite good), and completely overhauled the quartermaster corps.

Back in Washington, Madison took it upon himself to make regular calls on the different men who worked in the War Department, just to show his interest. He listened to their complaints that they were overworked and needed help and asked Congress for two more assistant secretaries of war to handle the work (he was at first turned down).

Then the United States received a totally unexpected victory in the war. The frigate *Constitution* had defeated the much larger and faster British warship *Guerriere*, burned it, and sunk it to the bottom of the Atlantic. The Americans had ravaged one of the star warships of the huge British Navy and its nearly one thousand ships and made it look easy. Militarily, it was a small victory, just one single ship, but from a public-relations standpoint, it was a mammoth accomplishment. The triumph was reported enthusiastically in most of America's newspapers and started a firestorm of pride in the people. It was one of several public-relations victories in the war that, in the end, meant more than military success itself.

There was other joy in the White House, too; Payne Todd moved back in. The gadfly, the irresponsible son, still spending far more money than he had and traveling the world as if he was a roving ambassador of goodwill, returned to his family in the spring of 1812, just as the war was starting, and remained for six months. Dolley was thrilled. She was glad to have him home where she could keep an eye on him and where, she thought, he would be so pleased with the White House social world that he would stay. She suggested that he help her work as the president's private secretary and he agreed. She invited him to all the parties and he went. She introduced him to all of her friends and many young, unattached women and he was pleasant to them all. She crossed her fingers and hoped that he would marry one of them and she would help him settle down. She felt a new chapter in his life, in her life, had started.

There was joy of another kind too. By the end of 1812, Napoleon had become so involved in his lengthy campaign to invade and defeat Russia that he had practically forgotten about the United States. French searching of ships and seizing of seamen had dropped off considerably over the last year; the French minister was quiet; and the president was relieved. He knew that he could not fight two wars at once.

And there was help from the private sector. The old Congress was getting ready to go home and the new Congress would not be sworn in until March 1813. Madison had told Congress he had enough money to fight the war, but he did not. He was $16 million short. Antiwar New England bankers ridiculed his early efforts to borrow money from them, but three other bankers, people who believed in Madison and some who owed him favors, stepped in to help. The irony was that the three bankers were not patriotic, homegrown Americans whose families went back to the seventeenth century but three foreign-born bankers who had made America their new home—David Parish and John Jacob Astor, from Germany, and Stephen Girard, from France. Astor was happy to help the president because, with Dolley's intervention, Madison had permitted Astor's ships access and egress from any American port they visited, saving Astor an enormous amount of money. Now he had repaid the favor. The men knew the American government was in serious financial trouble and had nowhere else to turn, but they did not raise their interest rates to make an easy profit. They kept them about the same and a relieved government borrowed $16 million. Secretary of the Treasury Gallatin knew where to spend every penny of the loan, too, and assured Madison that they could now pay their military bills through the end of 1813.[8]

And, too, in that winter, there was an offer from the czar in Russia to negotiate an end to the war. His forces had just beaten back Napoleon, which enhanced his stature in world politics, and he thought that having a role in an end to the conflict between Great Britain and America would make him a world leader. Madison sent John Quincy Adams, already in Russia, Senator William Crawford, and Gallatin to Moscow. His selection of Gallatin surprised all. Gallatin insisted on the position. He was tired of political opposition to him, was fed up with press criticism, and yearned for another post. Now, he thought, he might help win the war. Madison wished him well but knew he would miss him. One thing Gallatin did, though, was to leave a treasury with lots of money, skilled middle-level administrators, efficient and easy-to-follow books, and a department on very good relations with the military. Gallatin also agreed to take Madison's stepson, Payne, with him to give the boy a chance to travel and broaden his horizons. Dolley was happy at this chance for her son. Britain refused to attend any talks in Russia, so the peace conference was moved to Belgium.[9]

Madison, ever the loyal friend and political ally, kept Thomas Jefferson appraised of his actions throughout the War of 1812. For example, after he shook up his cabinet by firing William Eustis as secretary of war and Paul Hamilton as secretary of the navy, he wrote the third president that "I have not time to explain the late changes in the Executive Department, if I were disposed to trouble you with them." Jefferson just wrote back that "I think you could not have made better appointments."[10]

Madison was always thankful for Jefferson's ideas and suggestions, but he knew, too, that his predecessor had never been the commander in chief in wartime, had limited military command in the Barbary War, three thousand miles away, and had a detestable love of out-of-date ideas. One of the biggest was war by gunboat. Jefferson had authorized the building of gunboats during his presidency. He loved them. He wrote Madison that the answer to all his problems with the British Navy was the gunboat. The trusty gunboat, small but deadly, could slip in and out of inlets and coves on the East Coast and sink enemy shipping. No one in the navy agreed with him. Madison wrote him back and gently told him that it was a wonderful idea, but the navy said it would be difficult to put the gunboat into the war just now.

The one comfort of the letters from Jefferson was his unshakable faith in Madison. Jefferson told his successor again and again that he had to dismiss losses, military disasters, and press criticism; stick to his plans; and forge on. In the end, he would win. Jefferson wrote him in the winter of 1813, "the public mind [is] not discouraged, and it does not associate its government with these unfortunate agents [Generals]. These experiments will at least have the good effect of bringing forward those whom nature has qualified for military trust; and whenever we have good commanders, we shall have good soldiers and good successes. God bless you and give you that success which wisdom and integrity ought to ensure to you."[11]

The Madison White House was overcrowded throughout the war, and that was fine with the president. He loved having relatives from his family and his wife's clan living around him. It not only gave him a full social life that he never had in all of his long years of living alone as a bachelor but also helped to relieve the stress of the presidency and the war. He could not walk down a hallway without bumping into a houseguest or relative. It was a much different home than when Jefferson lived in it, often with just himself and an aide as the sole tenants. Madison's relatives on both sides often sought help from the president, from short-term to long-term loans, jobs, introductions, and connections. He never turned them down. He saw it as his responsibility as a member of two families and as a way in which he could help people and spread some joy within the family. Sometimes this turned out to be a good idea, and sometimes it did not. Throughout his second term, Madison came under considerable criticism for nepotism, with critics charging that one had to be related to the president to get a federal job. The first guests to move in after the war started were, naturally, Dolley's sister Anna and her husband, Richard Cutts. Anna was and always would be Dolley's closest relation. Cutts was well liked by the president. In 1812, the Massachusetts congressman was defeated for re-election in an area of the country where most Republicans lost in the antiwar vote tide. Cutts was finishing out his term in the White House. In order to keep him there, Madison appointed him as superintendent of military supplies. Eight Madison relatives would work for the federal government throughout the war. The Cutts family, with four children, lived in the White House for nearly two years. They became as visible as the First Family itself.

Joining the Cutts family was young Edward Coles Dolley's cousin and the president's personal secretary since 1810. The well-educated Coles (College of William and Mary) was from a wealthy Virginia family from a large plantation near Monticello. He was a good letter writer and an efficient administrator. He worked for the president and, whenever Madison was out of town or ill, he worked with Dolley to help run the White House. He was a permanent fixture on the White House and Washington social scene, even though he annoyed many capital residents with his strong antislavery views. He frequently badgered the president about slavery too, and repeatedly asked him to free his nearly one hundred slaves at Montpelier. Coles socialized frequently with Payne Todd, who was twenty-one years old when the war started and was back at the White House for six months.

Coles and Payne were joined as residents of the White House by another young man, nineteen-year-old Robert Madison, the president's nephew. He had been sent to the White House to prepare for college under the wisdom and tutelage of the president. Madison provided instruction for him under a local Episcopal minister, the Reverend James Laurie, and then sent him off to Dickinson College, in Carlisle, Pennsylvania in 1813. Young Robert sent dozens of letters to Madison while he was at Dickinson, complaining about just about everything. A year later, he quit school and joined a local militia company that fought the British after they invaded the area.

Finally, there were two vivacious young women from Richmond, Dolley's cousin Betsy Coles and her friend Maria Mayo. Dolley thought the two helped to enliven the social scene at the White House. Residence there also gave both a break from their much quieter existence in Richmond. The pair was quite popular in Washington.

As the war droned on, New Englanders continued to balk, relations with foreign powers tottered, press criticism increased, and congressional displeasure grew. President Madison would need the support of every single person in the White House, and elsewhere, and need it soon.

∽◯◯∾

The war began badly and became worse.

General William Hull was in charge of United States troops in the Midwest and planned an invasion of Canada to begin the war. Madison had met Hull several months earlier when he arrived in Washington with Dearborn. Hull had not impressed him. In the summer, Madison ordered Hull to move into Canada opposite Detroit, defeat the British at Fort Malden, defeat any hostile Native American tribes, and then get ready to march through the country.

The invasion was a debacle. Hull waited two weeks to attack Fort Malden and then became fearful that he himself would be attacked by Native Americans after the fall of an American fort at Mackinac, in the upper part of Michigan. He did not attack Malden, then he turned around and marched back to the American fort at Detroit. He was surrounded there by an army led by British general Isaac Brock, who demanded that he surrender. Hull, to the surprise of all, did. Brock made prisoners of his two thousand men. Madison had not only lost the first battle of Canada but lost his entire army, too. Worse news followed. Brock marched his army, with his prisoners, to Niagara, where he set up camp and taunted the Americans nearby that he had taken their entire army at Detroit.

Hull was roundly criticized in Washington. Mrs. Madison asked a friend, "do you not tremble with resentment at this treacherous act?" Richard Rush called him "a gasconading booby" and "horrid coward." Rush, incredibly skilled at reading political barometers, reminded Madison that Hull's debacle was not just a military loss but a public-relations setback as well. He said that Americans were now "exposed to the sneers of Federalists, the exultations of Tories, the contempt, the deserved contempt, of the British here and in Europe, of the very Indians! It is sorrow indeed."[12]

Madison was now intent on storming into Canada. He dismissed Hull's failure and sent another army, with eight thousand men, to Detroit to prepare for a second assault.

At the same time that Hull failed in his efforts to invade Canada, General Dearborn, senior leader of all American forces, arrived at Albany, New York, to discover he only had 1,200 men, most of them untrained militia. He was not about to attack Ontario, Canada, across from Niagara, with such a small force. He had also made no arrangements with Hull or anybody else for a coordinated attack on Canada in a move to split in half British defensive forces there. He even wrote Madison to ask whether he or Hull was in charge of the army.

The fearful Dearborn sat in Albany when he received a note from the British offering an armistice. Dearborn was now relieved and, without consulting the president, agreed. Madison ignored the armistice and ordered Dearborn to attack Canada three months late.

In addition to the defeats and reluctance to attack, the Americans failed to rally any Canadian citizens to their cause. They fumed, too, that many Canadians even acted as spies for the British. Albert Gallatin said of Canada that "the series of misfortunes exceeds anticipations made even by those who had least confidence in our inexperienced officers and undisciplined men."[13]

Madison swiftly changed his overall strategy. Britain now controlled Canada and the Great Lakes, especially Erie and Ontario, with its navy. The president decided to dramatically build up the American navy in order to defeat the British on the Great Lakes. Control of the Great Lakes would enable the Americans to attack Canada again, unimpeded by warships and the troops they carried. He told his cabinet that a larger navy should have been built in 1783, when the revolution ended, or in 1789, when the new government took over. He appointed tall, lean Commodore Isaac Chauncey naval commander of the Great Lakes and ordered the building of new ships. He was so angry at the meeting, Richard Rush said, that he told the cabinet that if the British had thirty ships, the Americans had to build forty. Former president John Adams, often his critic, slowly turning, as were others, to Madison's side, praised him.[14]

There were many differences between the War of 1812 and the last American conflict against the British in the revolution. First, in the revolution the Americans had a superb commander in chief in George Washington, who had significant military previous experience in the French and Indian War.

Madison had no military experience. Second, Washington lived with his army and made his decisions in camp; Madison lived a thousand miles away from his army and made decisions in the White House. Third, Washington developed a system of spies that let him know what the British troops, and his own, were doing within twenty-four hours. Madison worked with a pathetic communications system in which news took days to travel; his spies learned little. Fourth, after his 1776 crossing of the Delaware, Washington had the support of almost all Americans and the press in the war; Madison did not. Fifth, Washington had the complete support of the Continental Congress, but Madison had both the Federalists and many of his own Republicans against him.

The president always had to worry about political opposition to the war, especially in New England. "The Federalists in Congress are to put all the strength of their talents into a protest against the war and that the party at large are to be brought out in all their force," Madison wrote Jefferson. Richard Rush added more bluntly that "Massachusetts and half New England I fear is rotten."[15]

Madison's one great weakness as a president at the start of the war was that he did not possess the political skills to hold his own party together with him and to blunt opposition from the Federalists. He had a two-to-one majority in Congress and yet everything he tried to pass in Congress became a chore. If he had the numbers in delegates and was, he believed, in the right in his thinking and planning, why could he not win people over?

The answer, as Rush pointed out, was that he just did not have those unique leadership skills needed for the job—at the moment. Rush told a friend when the war was about to begin that "Mr. Madison is not a Mr. Jefferson or a General Washington, either of whom, from their vast ascendancy over Congress and the public . . . might be gratified in any little executive freak dear to their heart."[16]

The president received much help in that area from his wife. It was in the early months of the war that Dolley Madison struck up a deep friendship with Congressman Henry Clay. She liked Clay as much as she liked any other public figure in the country. He was intelligent, witty, full of good stories, and a social lion. He was also one of the few politicians in Washington who enjoyed snuff, as did Dolley. She offered him pinches of her snuff all the time at receptions and parties and he thanked her for it. She saw in Clay a man of roughly her own age who could, with a little push from her, help her husband's programs in the House. She talked to Clay frequently about politics, reminding him, as she reminded everybody, that she knew *nothing* about politics at all. What her husband was trying to do, but needed help in doing, was promote the states' rights policies of his Republican Party but, at the same time, use his powers as president to increase the national powers of the entire federal government.

Madison did not see a clash between states' and federal rights, but a union. He understood, though, and Dolley understood, that they had to be very careful in talking about the issue because most people saw it as a sharp conflict. If Madison could succeed at melding the local and federal interests in his own party, he would create a very strong nation with people as certain of their state and local rights as their federal protections. Dolley saw Clay as a man who could help her husband succeed and, in the future, lead that drive himself.

Clay saw a friendship with Dolley as a way to become a close ally of the president and get him to help Clay push his economic goals for the government, which he called the "American System." A strong Madison could do that but a weak president could not. Clay needed to make Madison a stronger president and, through his powerful position as Speaker of the House, could do that. Clay and Dolley, both rambunctious pubic personalities, were united by more than snuff boxes.[17]

Her friendship with Clay was an example of the increased social politics that Dolley advanced when the war began. She used numerous backdoor channels to find out information. For instance, she would talk to dozens of Washington wives about politics in an effort to sort out where their husbands stood on particular issues. She would send friends to talk to people to find out who was spreading rumors about the Madisons, or their friends, and then befriend the villains to end their campaign. She listened to gossip to pick up rumors that were actually true in order to help her husband. She jumped into the middle of arguments between politicians to calm the waters and bring them back together again. These were things she could do and her husband could not because she was the First Lady and he was the president. He was one of the most powerful men in the world, but his office reined him in. Dolley was under no restraints at all and conducted all of her missions with a smile and a public good word for everybody. Her social politics aided her husband tremendously as the war started.

As the news of Hull's surrender and the fall of both Detroit and Fort Mackinac became public, James Madison needed all the friends his wife could find.

19

WAR

Land and Sea

*H*ull's surrender to British commander Isaac Brock began an 1812 chain of setbacks that could lead to nothing but defeat. Madison was in charge of a relatively new army that was beefed up by emergency call-ups and new, untrained militias. For hundreds of years Britain had a large standing, well-trained army, and there was its mammoth navy. Madison wrung his hands in frustration.

All the news that arrived at the White House from the war front was bad. British general Brock's encampment at Niagara, with Hull's entire army with him as prisoners, unnerved American commanders, and most of these commanders had no wartime experience. Stephen Van Rensselaer, a rich landowner from New York, was one of them. He panicked at Brock's arrival. "Alarm pervades the country and distrust among the troops," he wrote New York governor Daniel Tompkins, "While we are growing weaker our enemy is growing stronger." Hearing of his panic, General Dearborn further deflated Van Rensselaer by telling him that it was possible that he and his army could be captured, too.[1]

A short time later, American general Alexander Smyth arrived at Niagara to join forces with Van Rensselaer in a joint attack on Canada. Smyth refused to serve under Van Rensselaer, though, and then a miffed Van Rensselaer attacked Canada on his own, minus Smyth's army. He was defeated at Queenston Heights and most of his army taken. It was both a military and public-relations disaster. Shortly afterward, Van Rensselaer retired from military life. Smyth took over his army and bragged about what he was going to do to the British army in Canada, but staged only one half-hearted attack, on Fort Erie, could not take it, and withdrew his men. His army was soon dispersed. Later, Dearborn, with six thousand men, attempted to attack Montreal, which was defended by just five hundred British soldiers. He made several feints at the city and then withdrew, defeated yet again. British newspapers made fun of him. One said that he "advances backwards."[2] Dearborn then resigned, too.

Back near Detroit, General William Henry Harrison and General James Winchester argued over who was in command of the army. Harrison wrote the president that his plans to take Detroit and move into Canada were impracticable. The roads were too muddy for an advance on Detroit, he did not have enough men, his troops were untrained, and his civilian agents were bunglers, he complained. Madison shook his head in disbelief at the incompetents who ran his army.

In 1813, Madison ordered attacks on Kingston, York (Toronto), and the Niagara frontier in Canada, but only the attack on York succeeded. Following that victory, there was a deep split between American commanders in the region that further delayed any progress.

At the same time that Madison's army was stalled in the northwest, the British set up a naval blockade from New York City down the Atlantic coast to impede American trade (they did not blockade New England ports in hopes that those states would force the national government to give up the war). Crusty British admiral Cockburn burned numerous vessels he found near Norfolk, Virginia, and burned Fredericktown, Georgetown, and Havre de Grace on the northeast Maryland shore. His actions shook America. It seemed that the British could strike wherever and whenever they chose.

The elections in the United States had brought good news (the defeat of John Randolph by Thomas Jefferson's son-in-law) and bad news (the return of the strident Federalist Thomas Pickering from Massachusetts to Congress). Madison had a majority in the House but was uncertain how votes would go in the relatively evenly divided Senate, full of cantankerous critics, many from his own party. The Senate's intransigence continued to cripple him as chief executive.

The news from the navy was grim. The American ship *Chesapeake* was sunk in a battle with the British fleet off the coast of New England, following a fierce battle (which was made memorable by dying American commander James Lawrence's plea, "Don't give up the ship!"). The British press memorialized the battle as symbolic of British sea superiority.

And then an odd thing happened. The loss, and Lawrence's death, was not seen as a defeat in America. It was hailed as a victory and Lawrence became an instant martyr. Poems and songs were written about him, newspapers hailed him in editorials, congressmen delivered eulogies about him, and Oliver Perry renamed one of his ships the *Lawrence*. His last words, "Don't give up the ship!" became the new motto of the navy.[3]

What happened to Lawrence was yet again an example of what often happened during the war. The people and the press took a defeat and spun it into a victory. The Americans did not have many victories in the war, and those they had were small, but the people and the press built them up into historic triumphs, continually building the story that America was winning the war.

One thing President Madison did not have to worry about was his tiny navy. The United States had only seventeen ships in the summer of 1812, including seven large frigates. Four of them carried forty-four cannon and the rest carried thirty-six. They had all been built longer than the average frigates. The frigates, and all the other ships, not only were seaworthy but also had been maintained meticulously by the navy. Although the army had few officers that had ever seen combat, the navy was full of combat veterans. Its commanders and seamen had been active in the Quasi War with France in the late 1790s and in the Tripoli wars in the early 1800s. They had been trained as young men and had been with the navy for years. The seamen were excellent sailors and gunners. One problem the United States did have in the early months of the war was in attracting new sailors. Madison solved that the same way he solved the problem of increasing the size of his army. He simply spent millions on signing bonuses, advance pay, and higher salaries. It worked.

The navy also benefitted from War Department confusion. It was decided to separate the navy into two squadrons, but the decision was not made for weeks. In the interim, Captain John Rodgers took it upon himself to set sail for England and sink as many ships as he could. He did not find any on that voyage, but his cruise terrified the British, who feared he would bombard their seaports. Rodgers's early departure had the unintended consequence of making Britain believe the Americans had a complex plan for victory at sea and many more ships than they actually did.

The British Navy was mammoth. In the war against Napoleon, the British Navy won two hundred battles and lost just five. The British ships were deployed all over the world, though, and many stuck in the Mediterranean to fight Napoleon's navy. Consequently, they sent few ships to America, giving the United States time to gain a foothold in the Atlantic and on the Great Lakes.

Brilliant American commanders gained notoriety, and impressive victories, throughout the war, beginning in 1812 when Captain Isaac Hull, the nephew of the disgraced General Hull, found himself trapped in the Atlantic on his ship, the *Constitution*, by a squadron of five British ships. He fled but could not find a wind to help him escape. He then put his sailors into longboats and had them pull the boat. That did not work either, so he sent men far ahead of the ship to drop its anchor. Then they pulled the boat, using the anchor as a foothold on the ocean floor. The British could not capture him. He gained more and more ground and eventually sailed safely into the Boston harbor. The long, dramatic chase was the talk of both England and America, and all saluted the resourceful Hull.

Hull refitted the ship, took on supplies and more men, and set sail again, gunning for British warships. He found them. On August 19, he encountered on of the best, the *Guerriere*, whose captain had been challenging American captains to fights in newspapers. The *Guerriere* fired first, but its shells fell short. It turned and fired again, but the volley was too high. Meanwhile, Hull, in the navy since he was fourteen and a veteran of the Tripoli wars, got in front of a northwest wind and, adjusting his sails constantly, rushed the *Guerriere* but held fire until he was just fifty yards away. Then he fired his cannon and tore up the *Guerriere*. In the hot fire between the two vessels, a cannonball from the Guerriere bounced harmlessly off the side of the *Constitution*. A seaman yelled that the ship must have sides of iron and the nickname "Old Ironsides" was born.

Hull was not alone in beating the British on the high seas. Young Stephen Decatur sailed his huge, fifty-six-gun ship *United States* close to the Canary Islands, off the coast of Africa, where he found the British ship *Macedonian*, with forty-nine guns. The *United States* maneuvered quickly to gain an advantage over the *Macedonian*. Decatur got off seventy broadsides to the enemy's thirty and captured her easily, later turning her into an American ship. President Madison instructed Congress to pay a $200,000 prize to the very grateful officers and crew of the *United States*. A short time later, the *Constitution*, now under the command of William Bainbridge, sunk the *Java* off the coast of Brazil. The *Essex*, with forty-six guns, captured the British ship *Alert*, and also captured a British troop transport carrying 160 soldiers on their way from the island of Barbados to the United States. In the winter of 1812 and spring of 1813, American vessels recorded victories over dozens of much larger British ships, capturing most and sinking some.

No one caused more of a sensation than Captain David Porter. He was ordered to captain the *Essex* and join the *Hornet* and *Constitution* in the southern Atlantic, but he missed them. Then, on his own, he decided to sail south down the coast of South America, around Cape Horn and out into the Pacific Ocean. He decided that if he could sink or capture a number of British whaling ships, he could hurt the overall British economy and, at the same time, establish United States' mastery of the Pacific. He brought along his thirteen-year-old foster son, David Farragut, who would later be a naval hero in the Civil War.

His voyage was a triumph. Porter and the men on his *Essex*, a frigate with thirty-two guns, captured or sunk dozens of small British whalers and captured nearly two hundred sailors. Porter, giddy with success, then sailed westward to the Marquesas Islands in the south Pacific, anchored and spent the winter there, his men repairing their ships in the morning and frolicking with native girls in the afternoon. Porter wrote in his journal that "the valuable whale shipping there is entirely destroyed and the actual injury we have done them may be estimated at $2.5 million, independent of the expenses of vessels sent in search of me."

Porter and his one-ship navy sailed back to Chile, where they were attacked by two British ships sent halfway around the world with the sole goal of capturing him. In a fierce fight, the British captured the *Essex*, killed fifty-eight sailors and wounded sixty-six (thirty-one drowned). Porter had been badly defeated and lost his ship, but he had become so famous that when he returned home, he was given a boisterous welcome and became a national hero.[4]

At the same time, Madison authorized the establishment of "privateers," private merchant ships that were outfitted for war with dozens of cannon. The United States had great success with the privateers in the revolution and would have it again in the War of 1812. Madison authorized about five hundred privateers, most smaller ships that carried about 100–150 sailors and dozens of cannon. As in the revolution, President Madison authorized the privateers to sell or auction off all the goods they seized on captured ships. A small percentage of the money went to the federal government, but the overwhelming majority went to the privateers themselves. In addition to that booty and their regular pay, the privateers were given $25 bounty per prisoner of war they brought to shore. Sometimes they seized ships with two hundred men on them, so the bounty was profitable.[5] It was enough. That winter and spring, the privateers sunk or captured 450 British ships. The ships were taken not in any one ocean but all over. Hundreds were captured in the warm waters of the Caribbean, and hundreds off the chilly coast of Canada. American commanders sunk British ships off the coasts of Portugal, Spain, and France. Some privateers were based in France and sunk dozens of ships cruising in the English Channel. They captured larger British merchant ships carrying valuable cargo, troop transports with hundreds of men, and, in one famous instance, a ship carrying 150 horses for the British army in Canada.[6] The victories of both the privateers and the United States Navy were not just numbers, either. The loss of so many ships forced the British government to build dozens of new ships at a high cost. Merchant ships insisted that convoys of British warships surrounded them on their way across the Atlantic, which cost more money and reduced the number of ships that could fight. In addition to all that, insurance premiums on all merchant ships were raised because they ran the risk of being sunk by the Americans. This created great fear in Parliament and in the British press. A Canadian editor wrote in a panic that "American privateers annoy this place to a degree astonishingly injurious; scarcely a day passes but crews are coming in that have had their vessels taken and sunk." The *London Times* wrote of the West Indies that "the American privateers are still enabled to range unmolested."[7]

The privateers captured or sunk 1,500 naval or merchant ships during the war. They brazenly attacked large British man-of-war convoys, well-protected merchant ships, and troop transports. Dozens of them routinely cruised around Great Britain, looking for local shipping to plunder. American captains had no fear, and the privateers and the navy struck terror into the hearts of British citizens.

There was some cheer for the president in September. Admiral Isaac Chauncey wanted to concentrate his attention on Lake Ontario and was looking for someone to replace him in Lake Erie. He heard of a twenty-seven-year-old captain who was tired of running gunboat squadrons and eager for larger battles. His name was Oliver Perry. When he arrived at the Great Lakes, Chauncey decided that he was exactly the kind of captain he was looking for and put him charge of the navy on Lake Erie; Perry soon made history. He oversaw the completion of four vessels on Lake Erie and then transferred five more from the Niagara River. He had small, inexperienced crews, though, and had to beg commanders in the army and navy for help. William Henry Harrison sent him one hundred Kentucky riflemen and several dozen former sailors in his army. Perry recruited locals, even though they had no naval experience. Also with him were black freedmen and teenaged boys. He took his small flotilla and ragtag crew out on to the lake and engaged British commander Robert Barclay and his squadron. Perry surprised all by spreading sand over the decks of his ships so that his men would have traction if waves washed over the decks. He arranged to attack with the wind to his back, giving him an advantage. Perry sailed directly into the middle of the British fleet and became entangled with their two largest ships. His ship, the *Lawrence*, along with an enemy ship, was badly disabled. Perry escaped by leaping into a longboat and rowing to the *Niagara* to continue the battle amid a hail of musket balls. He then sailed the *Niagara* directly at the British ships, cannon blazing. He disabled several, and the rest surrendered. Perry scribbled a note to Chauncey that made the young sea captain famous forever: "We have met the enemy and they are ours."[8]

It was a huge victory for the Americans, and Perry became an instant national hero. Madison approved $260,000 in prize money, plus three months' additional pay to Perry and his men.

The American press cheered their navy, but the British press blasted the English navy. The *London Times* charged that the British government bought out "the impatient 'dogs of war' muzzled and clogged."[9]

President Madison celebrated too soon. Six weeks later, he learned that Generals James Wilkinson (whom Winfield Scott labeled an "unprincipled imbecile"[10]) and Wade Hampton, in command of two armies supposed to attack Montreal, had fallen into bickering. There was no attack and, in fact, the armies wound up fleeing from Canada, harassed by a British force. Shortly after that, the English retook York and, in a series of short battles, chased the remaining American forces away from the Niagara River region. The British fleet at the northern end of Lake Champlain, in New York, repeatedly defeated American vessels on its waters.

At the end of the year, Madison's confidante, Attorney General Rush, was in despair. In a letter to John Adams, he said that the nation "seems to fight for nothing but disaster and defeat and, I dread to add, disgrace ... the prospect looks black. It is awful."[11]

Adams, who was slowly becoming an ally of former foe Madison, wrote a calm letter back to Rush and told him that all the nation needed was, he said in a metaphor, to winnow the wheat from the chaff—to streamline the army and navy, find new commanders, and find more troops. All would be well, Adams assured him. Rush showed Madison the letter and the president smiled; "Opinions from such a quarter had the smack of rich and old wine," he told Rush.[12]

There had been severe setbacks and humiliations in 1813. Perhaps the most disgraceful was the massacre of American troops near Frenchtown (now Monroe, Michigan), near the Raisin River in the Detroit region. President Madison's great fear had always been that the Native Americans fighting with the British would become unruly and that the British would not be able to manage them. In a skirmish near Frenchtown on January 20, 1813, the British defeated the Americans after hundreds of their Native American allies attacked the American rear, slaughtering over one hundred soldiers and scalping them. The Americans left about one hundred wounded prisoners behind in Frenchtown, under the care of local residents, but the Native Americans came back and butchered all of them. The incident soon became known as the Raisin River Massacre.

In Virginia, two thousand troops under British admiral George Cockburn defeated a badly organized militia force of 450 men and seized Hampton. The soldiers ran amok, led by the Chasseurs Britannique, French prisoners of war who had joined the Redcoats to avoid imprisonment. Frenchmen beat up numerous residents of Hampton, burned several buildings, and, worse, raped a number of local women. Their crimes were all written down by British officers. Americans were outraged. The British were, too, and the Frenchmen were promptly sent to Canada, where they spent the remainder of the war.[13]

As 1813 ended, President Madison was privately glum but publicly buoyant. In December, he sent the new Congress his fifth annual message. In it, he praised the increase of business and shipping in the country, said the war had brought about unity between the people of the different regions of the nation, and insisted, as always, that America would win the conflict. In a line that was to have immense meaning for him and the country just a short time later, he said, "The war, with all its vicissitudes, is illustrating the capacity and the destiny of the United States to be a great, a flourishing, and a powerful nation, worthy of the friendship which it is disposed to cultivate with all others."[14]

⌘

The year 1814 began on a chilly January day in the White House when Secretary of War Armstrong met with President Madison to promote new generals. To complete the list, Madison added the name of Andrew Jackson, who had just successfully defeated an army of Creek Native Americans in Florida. He told Jackson to March toward New Orleans, in the far-off Louisiana Territory, just on the off chance that the British might think of attacking the critical port city.

Madison also knew that in the spring of 1814 his armies in some areas of the nation were much better. They had been together for a year or longer and had learned how to be soldiers. Their aim with muskets and pistols was better; they drilled each day; they marched and maneuvered better; and, for no identifiable reason, they had more spirit, more national pride. The president helped the army function by revamping the high command. He created the General Staff. This was a team of generals that oversaw different aspects of the army. It ran the army, but did not run its military operations. He also created a board of navy commissioners to do the same thing.

The British were ready to put an end to the tedious war across the Atlantic in the summer of 1814. They had finished with Napoleon and could turn all of their attention to the pesky Americans. Their plan was simple. They would send a large army to Canada to attack the New England states, forcing them to petition the Washington government for peace. At the same time, the British Navy would tighten its blockade of American seaports, and its fleet would destroy the American navy and the massive flotilla of privateers. A special army/navy team would attack the southern city of New Orleans, seize it, and bottle up the Mississippi. The war would be over. Right on schedule, the British sent ten thousand more troops to Canada, plus a large fleet of warships, in the early spring of 1814, to reinforce the armies there.

There were holes in the British plan. The head of their armies in Canada, George Prevost, was a capable governor but an inexperienced military leader who could not command men. The British fleet had been completely unable to stop the privateers in two years, so why could they be throttled now? British ships had not done a good job of sealing up seaports. An attack by a massive army out of Canada would have to cover hundreds of miles, with soldiers marching over a terrain of lakes, rivers, mountains, meadows, and swamps. The Americans found it impossible to go north to Canada in the revolution, so why would it be easy for the British to do it going south?

Britain's supreme military strategist, the duke of Wellington, who had just defeated Napoleon, scoffed at the entire operation and told friends that America was too large to conquer and, even if you did, was too big to occupy. Revolution would follow revolution. Still, the British persisted.[15]

Madison sent his new generals and larger army to engage them. This time, under new, young leadership, the Americans fought well. They defeated the British at Chippewa and Lundy's Lane, near Buffalo, New York, and established themselves as a force north of the border.

At the same time, though, the British Navy arrived off the coast of Eastport, Maine, and threatened it. Other ships appeared up and down the East Coast as a general panic ensued. Where would they strike? What seaports would they shell? How many Americans would they kill?

Madison was tentative in this latest crisis. He did not know what to do. Neither did anyone in his cabinet. At the same time, Gallatin's message from Europe arrived, informing Madison not only that the British were intent on winning the war but that the British people, still stung from the revolution forty years earlier, wanted revenge and were completely behind the country's army and navy. They were not going to give up, and there was not going to be a compromise.

Madison warned America to get ready for an attack somewhere on the Atlantic seaboard. He wanted to "be prepared as well as we can to meet the augmented force which may invade us," he said. What could he do? If he called up all the militia in all the states to be prepared for an assault, he would meet the British with thin and untrained forces. He could not send his armies to specific seaports because he did not know where the British would strike. His intelligence, unlike Washington's in the revolution, was thin. He knew nothing and just waited to see what would happen.

Foreign diplomats in Washington immediately saw what was happening. "The cabinet is frightened," wrote French Minister Serrurier. "It continues, however, to keep a good face externally, but the fact is that it has a consciousness of its weakness and of the full strength of the enemy."[16]

Madison learned in the middle of the summer of 1814 that his secretary of war, Armstrong, had been insubordinate; he had lied to him, deceived him, and usurped his power. Armstrong had written numerous letters to General Harrison that caused him to resign. He had ordered all of his commanders in the Canadian region to correspond only with him and to ignore the president, the commander in chief. He had reorganized army regiments, which was normally authorized by the president. Finally, he had led Andrew Jackson to believe that Madison had tried to block his promotion, which was not true; Madison had the highest regard for Jackson.

Unfortunately, Madison did not fire Armstrong on the spot, as he should have. He was so worried about the impending British invasion along the Chesapeake that he felt he needed Armstrong to defend the city. He also did not criticize General William Winder, an ineffective commander who had told ten thousand militiamen in the Washington area to be prepared for a British invasion, but provided them with no plans for a defense of the city and spent his time riding about the countryside and not directing his troops. The president felt that he needed the two men, as deficient as they were, because there was no time to put other men in their place with the British army and navy so close.

Madison was wrong, but, months later, he would acknowledge the mistake and take swift steps to correct it. In August 1814, none of that was his concern, though. The Redcoats not only defeated a collection of American militia but also went on to burn the Capitol, the White House, and several other government buildings.

Shortly after that, the British set their sights on nearby Baltimore, a bustling seaport and one of America's largest cities. In mid-September, Admiral Cockburn sailed into the Baltimore harbor with the intent of leveling Fort McHenry. The British army sent a force to take the fort by land, but they were repulsed by a hard-fighting local militia company working with the regular army. Pushed back, Cockburn then opened fire on the fort with the guns from his fleet on September 13. The Americans in the fort fired their guns, but their range was too short. Cockburn, in possession of guns with longer range, continued his fire all night. It seemed that the British would completely level Fort McHenry and sweep their way into Baltimore.

Watching the bombardment that night from the deck of one of the British ships in the harbor was Washington lawyer Francis Scott Key, a friend of Dolley Madison's. He was there to arrange for the discharge of a prisoner, Dr. William Beams. The doctor was certain that the fort would be gone by morning. The British fired 1,800 shells at the fort over a twenty-five-hour period. Forty Americans were killed in the bombardment. The bursting of the shells in the air throughout the night made the scene appear to be a summer carnival, but the bombs bursting in the air did not stop. Thousands of people in Baltimore watched the carnage all night, depressed. Few could sleep from the noise of the shells as they exploded upon impact with the walls of the fort.

In the morning, below deck, Dr. Beams asked Key what had happened to Fort McHenry. He asked him if the American flag was still there. Key went up to the deck, and, to his amazement, the American flag was still flying high over the battered walls of the fort. It had not been lowered; the Americans had withstood the horrific bombardment. Key scribbled a short poem as he looked at the flag over the fort and, later, expanded it. He called it "The Star-Spangled Banner," and later it became America's national anthem.

By the end of 1814, the British and the Americans had problems that did not seem to be solvable. The British constantly had trouble supplying their troops and never could harness their sea power into a formidable force. They did hold Canada for most of the war but could never invade the New England states successfully. For every victory the British achieved, they later suffered huge defeats. By the summer of 1814, the Redcoats had seemed to establish their mastery of the battlefield, but then, in just a few months, they were defeated at Chippewa, Lundy's Lane, and Fort Erie. By the end of 1814, too, the war, added to the price of the Napoleonic Wars, was becoming costly—with little result.

In America, throughout the war, thousands of merchants and farmers illegally traded with the British. Smuggling had become a sport. One Massachusetts customs official said local merchants did so much illicit trade with the British that "his inspectors dare not now attempt to search stores or houses there, for smuggled goods, as the mass of the population are interested in their concealment and so far from giving assistance, threaten such oppositions as renders the attempt . . . futile."[17]

Selling goods to the British was kept secret in most places, but in some, such as Provincetown, Massachusetts, it was quite open. Nearly sixty ships were engaged in carrying American goods out to British ships, where they were purchased by the Crown. "The fact is notorious," wrote the editor of the *Lexington Reporter* in the summer of 1813, "that the very squadrons of the enemy now annoying our coast . . . derive their supplies form the very country which is the theater of their atrocities."[18]

The president tried to stop the illegal sales of goods to England and open trade with the British with a new embargo that forbid American ships from leaving ports for worldwide trade and with a series of restrictive measures, such as closing all American ports to foreign ships unless three quarters of its crew were from that nation, forbidding the importation of most British goods, and putting an end to the ransoming of captured ships. There were other, harsher, restrictions, but Congress would not pass them.

Both sides were harsh in the treatment of prisoners in 1813 and 1814. The British tossed some American prisoners into dank British prisons back in England, such as the notorious Dartmoor, which housed 6,500 Americans, most from New England, all of whom were treated badly. In one dispute, six American prisoners were shot dead by their guards. Letters home from Dartmoor outlined the terrible conditions there. "The return of our people from British prisons have filled the newspapers with tales of horror," wrote the editor of *Niles Register*.[19]

President Madison threatened to execute British prisoners. The American press protested the confinement of Americans in England, and the British press screamed about threatened executions by Madison. "If Mr. Madison dare to retaliate by taking away the life of one English prisoner America puts herself out of the protection of the law of nations and must be treated as an outlaw," complained the *London Courier*.[20]

By the end of 1814, both armies and navies had ground to a stalemate. America was simply too big to defeat, and Britain was too powerful to lose the war. Almost no progress was being made, and when it was, setbacks somewhere else in the war counterbalanced them. All was gloomy.

20

THE MONTPELIER OF THE PRESIDENT

The Summer White House

*E*veryone who visited Montpelier was amazed at the way the road, the very bumpy road, out of Orange Court House wound gracefully past streams and forests westward to the sprawling plantation. Carriages, wagons, and horses carried travelers to the 5,000-acre farm through forests of poplar trees, weeping willows, and stands of oak trees. They arrived from the west side, below the hill where the gracious mansion sat gently on top of a long ridge. If they arrived early in the morning, the sun crept over the tops of the forests and shone down on them. Just after he became president, in 1809, Madison added two spacious wings, one on the north side and one on the south, and finished his basement into a long set of additional spaces, with oversized rooms throughout the home to accommodate all of the guests who visited the president and his wife, many of whom stayed for days. When completed, Montpelier consisted of thirty-three rooms and 12,500 square feet.

Madison added the new wings to give the home a presidential look, although it was nowhere near as big as the White House. The north wing was turned into a large bedroom for the Madisons, plus another room, and the south wing added more living space for James Madison's aging mother, who previously lived in two rooms. It looked regal, like a palace awash in kings and queens in some far-off European country.

The front of the house impressed visitors. "You now pass through a gate into a large field & just before you is the house of Mr. Madison. It stands in a long slope of land, the country about it being somewhat diversified, a slat fence painted black with white posts surround the house at quite a respectable distance, curving in front," wrote visitor George Shattuck.[1]

Charles Ingersoll, who visited later, after Madison had left office, said the house and its grounds resembled "something like a park" lined with white-thorn and red-bud trees. It was "a well looking house about half a mile off, the whole cleared and improved with trees in clumps and other signs of ornamental agriculture," he wrote. In summer, the pillars of the front portico were encircled by roses and strands of jasmine that climbed up to the second-floor terrace.[2]

Harriet Martineau, who visited around the same time as Ingersoll, enjoyed Montpelier but said the surrounding area was dismal. "For the greater part of the way, all looked very desolate; the few dwellings were dingy. The trees were bare, the soil one dull red, the fences shabby," she wrote.[3]

The lawn behind the home was filled with trellises overwhelmed with plants climbing their way up them. The forests of the Blue Ridge Mountains were about fifty yards behind the house. A tin cup that was used to measure rainfall hung near the front gate. A mill and several farm buildings sat about one hundred yards from the house, near a creek that connected to the Rapidan River.

A small village of slave homes stretched away from the home to the south, along with farm sheds, a building for the outdoor kitchen, smokehouses, and fruit orchards. To the southeast was a formal garden, designed by Frenchman Monsieur Charles Bizet, where the Madisons and visitors often strolled. The garden was started just after Madison's first inauguration and was completed shortly afterward.

Inside, visitors found numerous changes to the home from before Madison's elevation to the highest office in the land. In his first-floor parlor, where guests were greeted once they entered the mansion through an interior lobby, the president had installed a number of white, marble busts of famous people and had hung large portraits of Napoleon and other people, which were purchased by Payne Todd in 1816 on a trip to Europe. More large portraits hung in a second parlor behind the main parlor that was often turned into a bedroom for guests. The floors of the hallways were continually washed and waxed by servants. Visitors were surprised at Madison's collection of busts and portraits. The walls of one entire first-floor hallway were lined with portraits of famous people. Anna Thornton thanked him for "displaying a taste for the arts which is rarely to be found in such retired and remote situations."[4]

Several new fireplaces had been built in the home to provide more heat for the expanded structure. The new, wooden dining-room table was large enough for a dozen people to sit around it, and more tables were set up in the room and in the hall when more guests were there. There were splashes of red included in the color scheme to reflect Dolley's favorite hue.[5]

Upstairs, Madison turned the flat rooftops of each of his two new wings into outdoor terraces. Jefferson designed the Chinese railings, painted white, that stood on the perimeters of the terraces. Both rooftop terraces were used for parties in spring and summer, and guests were urged to spend time there. Anyone standing or sitting on the terrace had a view of the tobacco fields and the mountains in the distance.

The south terrace also overlooked a second street of new slaves homes, built around the time that Madison was first inaugurated. The large, rectangular houses were designed by Madison as duplexes, with living space upstairs and downstairs. All of the twenty-three domestic slaves who worked with Dolley in the house lived there because it was close by. Madison had architectural suggestions from Thomas Jefferson in the renovations of the main house in both 1797 and 1808–1809. He used some of his ideas and discarded others because he wanted a presidential home, but not a second Monticello. Madison employed two design and construction chiefs, James Dinsmore and John Nielson, to complete the renovations in 1808 and 1809; and he paid for them both with his $25,000 salary as president and out of his own funds.

The home was the centerpiece of his farm. Montpelier sat in the Piedmont area of western Virginia and was on Davidson soil, special, rich, natural dirt that was considered to be among the best in America for raising crops.

Getting to Montpelier had always been a chore. It was a tiring and tedious three-day trip from Washington by wagon, carriage, or horseback. All of that ended when Madison was elected president, though. Many families in Virginia invited the Madisons to stay at their houses on the way to Montpelier, and there were festivals for them from the capital all the way to Orange Court House. In the summer of 1811, for example, the First Couple left Washington, accompanied by militia troops, to the bridge that led to Alexandria. Virginia troops met them and escorted them over the bridge in a parade attended by hundreds of well-wishers. That night there was a dinner and a ball in Alexandria to honor them. Then, on the way to Montpelier, they stayed two nights at the homes of a wealthy friend and were lavishly entertained on both evenings. The Madisons always traveled in style; it was good to be the president.[6]

Visitors to Montpelier found the president and his wife far more relaxed there than in Washington. "It was five o'clock when we arrived and met at the door by Mr. M who led us into the dining room where some gentlemen were still smoking cigars and drinking wine. The [stress of each day was] dispelled by the cheering smile of Mr. Madison. Then Mrs. Madison entered the moment afterwards and after embracing took my hand," wrote Margaret Bayard Smith.

Later, Mrs. Madison took Smith to her room upstairs. She sat on the sofa.

Dolley pulled her up by her hands and placed her on the wide, comfortable bed, then jumped up in the air and landed on the bed next to her, laughing heartily. "Wine, ice, punch and delightful pineapples were immediately brought [to us]. No restraint, no ceremony. Hospitality is the presiding genius of this house and Mrs. M is kindness personified," Smith added.[7]

Friends could not wait to get there. Anna Thornton thought that on all her visits to Montpelier. "We shall turn our backs on this dull tho' great city [Washington] and greet with joy our beloved friends beyond the mountains," she wrote.[8]

Montpelier was always filled to capacity with relatives and visitors. The average number of people staying in the home when the Madisons were in residence ranged from twenty to twenty-six, and sometimes more. Madison was one of seven remaining children, and each of them had large families. Most of the children were old enough to travel by the time he was president, and Madison welcomed them whenever they arrived. James Madison's nieces and nephews stayed with him for days and weeks on end. He supported many of them with gifts of horses and clothing, gave them loans, and even paid for the college tuitions of some. One was nephew Robert Madison. The president paid his way through Dickinson College, in Pennsylvania. Madison's favorite was niece Nelly Conway Willis, who continued to live at her plantation just a few miles from Montpelier after her husband died. She had fifteen slaves whom her father gave her in his will and brought some of them to Montpelier when she visited. She was often at the Madison estate, and the president rode to her home frequently. Neighbors nicknamed a large tree in front of her home "the president's tree" because Madison always tied his horse up there when he visited. Also, his sister Sarah gave birth to nine children and visited Montpelier frequently, bringing all of them with her.

Dolley had three sisters and three brothers. The two older brothers drifted away from her, but her three sisters and John Payne remained close. Anna, her husband, and their children visited often, and so did Lucy after her husband, Judge Todd, died in 1826. The Madison and Todd relatives always brought their children to Montpelier; there were often more than a dozen kids in the house at any one time. Madison's marriage gave him a stepson, Payne, and a fourteen-year-old sister-in-law, Anna, who had lived with them until her wedding. Dolley's other sisters lived with them at Montpelier for long periods of time, too. In addition to this, they all lived in his private home in Washington, and in the White House, for years, bringing their own children back with them to stay for weeks and months at a time. When those children became adults, they then brought their own kids to the Madisons' homes. The president also had the company of the children of his friends and relatives in Orange County.

Dolley loved the children and never complained of the noise they made. "I should not have known that they were here," she said to a friend. "At this moment, we have only [twenty-three] in the house. We have house rooms aplenty." She always encouraged friends and relatives to bring their children with them on visits.[9]

As a child, President Madison had been part of a very large family with twelve children. Montpelier was a small home then, with only a few bedrooms. They were quite crowded with the twelve noisy children. The dozen siblings played together, rode horses together, and visited friends and relatives with their family. It was a large and happy family.[10] He had always wanted a family like that when he became an adult. Madison was a man who, until the age of forty-three, had no prospects of a family, and then a limited one due to his apparent sterility. But through circumstance, and to his joy, he wound up with one of the largest and most boisterous families in the country. The president's Montpelier was a home teeming with loud and energetic children racing through the halls and across the lawns. They loved their uncle, who, with his wife, did everything he could for them. The ones who gave him grief, such as Payne and brother-in-law John, the president put up with and assisted whenever he could, never complaining about them to outsiders.

Dolley's brother John, who remained an alcoholic all of his life, lived a few miles away with his eight children on a farm that Madison helped him purchase. His meager income from farming was augmented by a salary the president paid him to help with paperwork. Even though he lived nearby, John was often late in arriving at Montpelier and often disappeared for weeks, as he had done over the years. In the late summer of 1811, Dolley complained to her sister that "John was to follow us directly but three weeks gone by & he has not come. You may guess at my anxiety. He set out from Washington several days ago for Orange but he lingers, I know not where."[11]

After John died, three of his children moved to Montpelier permanently, and the other five lived there much of the year. They were all at Montpelier often during Madison's presidency. Dolley's youngest sister, Mary, married John Jackson, a Republican congressman. She died in 1808, and her daughter, Mary, began to spend a lot of time at Montpelier. She practically lived there permanently after 1825. Sister Anna and her children were usually at Montpelier each summer, as her husband, Richard Cutts, struggled through one financial crisis after another throughout the war and afterward. He lost his investments in a shipping company in the war, along with $5,000 Madison had loaned him. He owed a significant amount of money, went bankrupt, and even spent time in debtors' prison. He nearly lost his home in Washington, but the Madisons, with a loan, saved it for him.

The Madisons were constantly visited at Montpelier by senators, congressmen, governors, and other officials while he was president. That's why he expanded the house. Ironically, during some years as president, he spent only a week on Montpelier because presidential business was so pressing. When he did travel to his plantation, he used it as the "summer White House," working from his office, his bedroom, the front porch, the backyard, or the library, which grew even larger with books that visitors gave him as gifts. Dolley hosted parties for all, whether relatives, friends, or politicians. The most important people in the country dined side by side with her nieces and nephews and friends from Orange Court House. One summer, she had ninety guests for dinner; extra tables were set up in different rooms of the home. In another summer, the Madisons had nearly fifty unexpected visitors one night and had to feed and entertain them. Sometimes at large barbecues or parties the president and his wife had so many guests, and so few cots in the house, that they set up tents in the fields in front of the mansion, where the guests stayed overnight.

"At these feasts, the woods were alive with carriages, horses, servants and children—all went—often more than one hundred guests . . . happy at the prospect of . . . pleasure and hilarity; the laugh with hearty good will, the jest after the crops, farm topics and politics. . . . If not too late, these meetings were terminated by a dance," wrote one guest.[12]

People did not enjoy visiting Montpelier just because of all the people there whom they would meet. They liked to go because Montpelier was one of the most opulently decorated homes in America. Madison's father had seen to that. Colonel Madison was convinced that a person's station in life was determined not only by business success but also by how he lived. He purchased expensive dishes and glasses for his home, laid imported Turkish rugs down on the floors, and hung expensive paintings on the walls. The house that President Madison grew up in was a well-appointed home already. When his father died and Dolley took over the interior decoration of Montpelier, it became an even classier abode. Madison left the interior work to his wife and concentrated on the physical renovations and expansion of the building. He did such a good job that friend James Monroe and other Virginians asked him for architectural advice in the construction of their own homes.[13]

Renovating the home, whether in the 1790s or in 1809, took up a considerable portion of Madison's time. In 1798, he wrote James Monroe that he was "in the vortex of house building in its most hurried stage" and that "I have met with some mortifying delays in finishing off the last shaft of the chimneys and in setting about the plastering job. The prospect is at present flattering, and I shall have no time in letting you know that we are ready to welcome Mrs. M and yourself to our habitation."[14]

The house was always full of people and loud with noise. The Madisons did not have enough bedrooms for everybody, so, like many Virginians, they put cotlike beds and bunk beds in the main hallways upstairs and downstairs, and in many other rooms, so guests could sleep. On oppressively hot nights, they kept all the doors and windows open to allow fresh air to drift through the mansion. Servants would remove the beds, quickly, in the morning when everyone rose for the day, and the house would return to its normal look.

The relatives and guests kept Dolley busy. "The house is now full of family," she wrote in the summer of 1811. "William Madison, his wife and children & [others]. I have scarcely a moment to breath [*sic*]. They are here for some days. . . . We have Mr. & Mrs. Bassett two days, expect Mr. & Mrs. Eustis, Mrs. Page & family every day & all those people, with Miss Hornerzill of Richmond, are here but Mitchell is with us. We have four additional chambers. My head is turned."[15]

During Madison's presidency, Montpelier was the place to be, socially, when the Madisons were in residence there, and everybody who visited the Madisons told friends back in Washington what they discussed and did for activities. Madison's friends in the capital all knew what was going on at Montpelier and how busy it was. Mrs. Anna Thornton wrote Dolley in the summer of 1809, for instance, that "I understand that you are overwhelmed with company."[16]

Dolley received all of the Washington news from guests who visited her, and she sent out dozens of letters each summer to relatives and friends apprising them on the events of her life. She let friends in one state know what their mutual friends in another were doing, who was courting and marrying whom, and, from 1812 to 1815, how hard her husband was working on the problems of the war.

Their social life at Montpelier was less elegant than it was in Washington, but the parties were just as frequent and the dinners just as crowded. The isolation of Montpelier did not bother James and Dolley; they visited Jefferson at Monticello, spent time in Richmond, and visited friends in Orange Court House and other villages.[17] One thing they insisted on was the continuation of their impressive dinner parties. Dinner at Montpelier was more casual than at the White House, but servants brought endless trays of food that included cakes, bread, cold meat, and pastries. After dinner, the men smoked cigars on the porch and the women chatted in the parlor. Servants carrying lamps through the hallways took guests to their rooms around nine or ten in the evening, and the house quieted down. Servants and maids acted as quasi hosts for the Madisons when guests were there, taking them to their bedrooms, waking them in the morning, and bringing them downstairs for a lavish breakfast.[18]

During their summers at Montpelier, the Madisons caught up on local news that they did not get during the ten months they spent in Washington and discussed mutual topics, such as oppressive heat and snow-filled winters. In the summer of 1812, the Madisons exchanged stories with friends in Orange County about the series of earthquakes that had rolled through Washington, DC, and central Virginia the previous winter and shook houses and scared residents.[19]

By the time Madison's second term ended, the home, with its gorgeous new wings, was as complete as it would ever be. Now, by 1816, it was a finished estate with many stables, slave quarters, outbuildings, gardens, and lawns. When Anna Thornton visited in 1802, she wrote in her diary that "the grounds are susceptible to great improvements and when those he contemplated are executed, it will be a handsome place and approach very much in similarity to some of the elegant seats in England."[20]

By 1816, it was.

The Montpelier that Madison returned to during his two terms as president had grown into one of the most successful plantations in Virginia, and all of that success was due to Madison's skills as a farmer. By the early 1790s, he had taken over the administration of the farm from his father, who was then in his eighties. Madison read all the books on farming he could and solicited advice from Jefferson. Throughout the 1790s, Montpelier bloomed as a plantation. Madison, who oversaw an average of forty to fifty slaves a year then, had his "hands" (as he called the men and women in bondage) plow long, straight rows for planting and brought in water from nearby creeks that was run into and out of his field with small dams. Slaves built new outbuildings, tobacco warehouses, corn houses, and stables. Each year or two, they worked with Madison in opening up new fields for cultivation. He grew fruit orchards wherever he could. With the help of his overseers, Madison studied the different parcels of land and knew which were in the "Davidson soil" tract and which were not. The president knew how to irrigate the fields from streams that ran down from the mountains around his farms. And he had maps on which he wrote where underground limestone deposits were located. Showing all the skills of an accomplished farmer, Madison wrote Jefferson with satisfaction in the 1790s, "On one of two little farms I own, which I have just surveyed, the crop is not sensibly injured by either the rot or the rust and will yield 30 or 40 per cent more than would be a good crop in ordinary years."[21]

He not only kept accurate notes on farm business and plantings while at Montpelier but also remembered everything when he was away in Philadelphia as a congressman. For example, he and his father had planned an orchard they would start with some nuts Jefferson had brought to Montpelier on one of his visits. "It does not seem necessary to decide now on the spot for the Pecan trees.

... They can be easily removed at any time. I have not fixed on any particular no. of apple trees. I would choose a pretty large orchard if to be had and of the sort you think best. If a sufficient number cannot be got for Black Meadow [a farm] and Sawney's [another farm], I would be glad to have them divided."[22]

He had, like Washington, Jefferson, and others, mastered the art of tilling his soil and rotating his crops to keep it fertile. Like Washington, he was one of the few farmers in Virginia to realize that Europe needed more and more wheat from America as the years passed, in addition to the regular amounts of tobacco. He reorganized his lands to grow more wheat and make more of a profit off it. He received good notices on his wheat and tobacco from intermediary distributors in Richmond and in London, too.[23]

The president was justifiably proud of his farm.

21

INTO THE WAR'S STRETCH

The year 1815 started with the same sad dreariness in which 1814 had ended. No peace treaty had been delivered to America from Ghent, Belgium, where diplomats had been meeting in an effort to end the conflict; British troops were rumored to be preparing a land and sea assault on New Orleans; and the Federalist press throughout the country continued to criticize President Madison for his war policies.

Added on to all of that trouble was the Hartford, Connecticut, secession convention, called by delegates from three states in New England who were intent on taking their states out of the United States in order to resume their shipping business with England and other European countries. The secession movement in New England had been growing since July 1813, when Madison almost died, when longtime Massachusetts politician Thomas Pickering wrote, "I believe an immediate separation would be a blessing to the 'good old thirteen states.'" To spite Madison, the proponents of secession continually quoted his own persuasive essays in *The Federalist* that argued colonies could break away from the motherland if they had good reasons to do so. The secession movement, endorsed by many Federalist newspapers in New England, picked up steam. At Hartford the delegates voted to oppose federal orders concerning the war and said that state taxes could only go to state expenses and not to pay for the war, that the federal government could not draft New Englanders for its army, and that New England would be responsible for its own defense. They also voted to eliminate the three-fifths slave-voting clause in the Constitution and added several more inflammatory, anti-South, amendments to it. The members of the convention, held in the middle of the chilly 1814 December, sent a delegation to Washington to apprise Madison and Congress of their decision.

Madison was worried sick over the convention. He feared that if the three New England states fled the Union, so would others. He also thought the New

Englanders were traitors. "You are not mistaken in viewing the conduct of the eastern states as the source of our greatest difficulties in carrying on the war; it is the greatest if not the sole inducement to the enemy to persevere in it," he wrote.[1]

His secretary, Edward Coles, told him that the delegates were meeting "to hatch treason, if New England will support them in it" and that they wanted to do everything possible to cripple the country. Monroe was even angrier. He told Madison to dispatch a company of troops to Hartford and arrest everyone there for sedition. Madison, ever the moderate, decided to wait and see what the outcome of the convention turned out to be.[2]

Madison may have fretted over his troubles in Hartford, but he had reasons to celebrate, too. The British believed that the army attacks along the East Coast, the bombardment of Fort McHenry outside of Baltimore, and the torching of Washington, DC, would destroy American morale and end its will to fight, but they had just the opposite effect. Americans rallied around the cause, their troops, and the president in a complex blend of patriotism. First, they were furious that the British had the nerve to burn down the Capitol and the White House, which they considered a violation of all military tradition. Second, they steeled their resolve to win the war. Third, although the people at first blamed Madison for the losses in the war and especially the torching of the capital, they now reversed their opinion and saw him as a heroic figure for commanding the troops in the field and for risking his life by returning to Washington to start an immediate drive to revive the war. He refused to admit defeat and never took a step backward. Madison was not unnerved by the torching of Washington, either. He refused to flee town. He was a little man who was standing tall, and all Americans applauded him for that. Even DeWitt Clinton, who ran against him for president, stopped blaming him.

There was an extra, special, dimension to the public's view of the burning of Washington—Dolley Madison. The First Lady's saving of George Washington's portrait was seen as a heroic act because she risked being captured by the British. But there was something else. The people, like Dolley, connected the portrait of first president with the American cause in the war. The public agreed with Dolley that if the British could have destroyed that picture, they could have destroyed the United States. So she risked her life to save it, and did. That act, combined with her husband's front-lines leadership of the army in the heat of the battle-field, and his tough stance when he returned to Washington, impressed everyone. There would be no turning back now. America would not be defeated.

The Madisons had an immediate problem that was just as important as reorganizing the armed forces. The loss of the Capitol and the White House meant that the country had no housing for its government. The president tried to get the government running again as he returned to the charred corpse of the White House, now just a hulking set of walls. He had no home and no office. Senators and congressional committees had to meet in small rooms in boardinghouses, in the living rooms of private homes, or in taverns. When Congress met in full session, it had to cram itself into one of the large public rooms at Blodgett's Hotel.

Across the river in Alexandria, the British had looted a series of warehouses, carting off thousands of dollars' worth of food and supplies. Residents of that town were terrified that the English would be back again, and soon, to attack their warehouses once more. People were depressed throughout the region. "I do not suppose the government will ever return to Washington. All those whose property was invested in that place will be reduced to poverty . . . the consternation about us is general, the despondency still greater," said Margaret Bayard Smith.[3]

People who met the president in the days following the burning of the city found him deflated. William Wirt wrote his wife that Madison was "visibly shattered and woebegone. In short, he looks heartbroken."[4] He said Madison was furious at New Englanders who still opposed the war and had held a secession convention. Wirt said that the president felt they were "full of sedition."

Mrs. Madison was angry, too, when she returned to tour the smoking ruins of her home and the other buildings on a warm June day. Her friend Margaret Bayard Smith said she was very perturbed and found it difficult to speak without tears forming in her eyes. Later, Dolley told Mary Latrobe , the wife of interior decorator Benjamin Latrobe, of the day the White House was torched, "I confess that I was so unfeminine as to be free from fear, and willing to remain in the Castle! If I could have had a cannon through every window; but alas! Those who should have placed them there fled before me and my whole heart mourned for my country."[5]

The president also had to deal with the seemingly endless parade of refugees returning to the city on horseback or in wagons, heads down and just as depressed as him at what they saw. Their beautiful government buildings, including the Treasury and War Departments, destroyed, burned to the ground. The city's leading newspaper, the *National Intelligencer*, had been shuttered by the British and its presses wrecked. All of the books of the Library of Congress were destroyed. The roofs of both wings of the Capitol were in ashes, with charred pieces of timber sticking up out of them. The Navy Yard and the arsenal grounds were large piles of rubble. The stale smell of smoke still drifted in the hot summer air. People displayed blocks of stone with accusatory graffiti against General Winder and Secretary Armstrong strewn throughout lots.

There were charcoal-etched signs everywhere critical of the government and the army. One read, "James Madison is a rascal, a coward and a fool."[6]

Madison could not have found an unhappier band of people than his neighbors. At least they had housing to return to, though; he did not.

A Virginian who rode through town just after the attack wrote, "The appearance of our public buildings is enough to make one cut his throat, if that were a remedy. The dissolution of the Union is the theme of almost every private conversation."[7]

Madison's friend William Thornton met him and James Monroe on horseback and told the president that he represented a large group of citizens who wanted Madison to dispatch a delegation to the British and surrender. The president fumed. "It would be dishonorable to send any deputation, and . . . we [will] defend the city to the very last," he shouted at him, his voice full of fury.

Thornton told the president that he had no army to defend the city. Then, even angrier than Madison, James Monroe snapped at Thornton, "It the deputation moves toward the enemy, it will be repelled by the bayonet."

A shaken Thornton turned and rode away.[8]

In addition to the attack, there was the fear all over the United States that Britain could now turn all of her ships, guns, and men on the country because the war against Napoleon had ended. A writer in the London press wrote that the British "talk with delight of the sending of Lord Wellington's army to the United States; they revel in the idea of burning the cities and towns, the mills and manufactories of that country; at the very least they talk of forcing Mr. Madison from his seat and new-modeling the government."[9]

Around then, at his lowest point in the war, the president received an unexpected, rousing letter of support from Thomas Jefferson. "Had [General] Washington himself been now at the head of our affairs, the same event would probably have happened," he wrote; he congratulated him on his tough stand, his leadership of the army, and his recent victories. It bolstered Madison's spirits.[10]

The one thing that surprised Washingtonians, and all Americans at that point, was the overall toughness and resolute, evenhanded, and calm leadership of the commander in chief. Lieutenant James Edwards said that "[Mr. M] was tranquil as usual and tho' much distressed by the dreadful event . . . not dispirited," [11]

Officials of the cities of Philadelphia and New York invited the beleaguered government back. Georgetown offered to lend the government its seminary building for a fee of a mere $10 a week. Local hotels wanted to become home to the government for $16 a week. One man snorted that efforts would be made by southerners to move it to Baton Rouge, Louisiana.[12]

The Madisons saw the efforts to move the government back to Philadelphia, and they were considerable, as not only a bad idea but also as an effort that would show Britain, and the world, that England had won its battle with Washington. That could not happen. The Madisons were intent on remaining in Washington to carry on the war, taking up residence somewhere in town. Leaving would be a sign of weakness, of defeat. It could not be done. Friends of Dolley's said she told them outside the ruins of the White House, "we shall rebuild; the enemy cannot defeat a free people."[13]

Washingtonians sprang into action and came to the rescue of the president and Congress. John Tayloe, the wealthiest man in town, invited Madison and his wife to live at his home, the luxurious Octagon House, one of the biggest homes in America, until they could move back into the White House. Octagon House was a huge, elegantly decorated, three-story house at the corner of New York Avenue and Eighteenth Street that was large enough for the Madisons' residence, government offices, and drawing rooms for receptions. They moved in right away. Madison set up an office, moved aides into the building, and resumed running both the government and the army.

Local men, led by bankers Thomas Law, John Van Ness, Daniel Carroll, and Richard Lee, met in one of Dolley's drawing rooms at Octagon House to conduct a drive to raise $500,000 to pay for new offices for Congress. A red-brick building was constructed in just six months on the site of the present-day Supreme Court to house both houses of Congress, and all offices and rooms were rented in a number of other buildings throughout town. Wealthy city residents began a building boom with the construction of new, large homes, a signal to the nation that they were sticking with the government and that the government was staying in Washington.

At that same time, Dolley was asked to become an official at the City Orphan Asylum. She brought friends along to serve on the board and went to work raising money and running the asylum. She saw it not only as a good deed but also, given the timing, as a way to let the rest of the nation know that she and her influential friends were staying in Washington; that the capital would bounce back; that the British had merely burned down buildings, not a city; and that Americans could stick together, no matter what, and fight on.

The president went right back to running the government and the army. Secretary of War John Armstrong was forced to resign; Madison appointed James Monroe to take his place as the temporary secretary of war. The army was quickly reorganized by Monroe and was ready to fight again in just days.

There were calls from many politicians to move the nation's capital but others were against the idea.

The new city, just sixteen years old, already had hotels, taverns, and stores. Their owners would all go bankrupt if the federal government departed. The value of homes, large and small, would plunge; farms started up outside the capital would go out of business. The villages of Alexandria and Georgetown, which thrived as suburbs of Washington, would shrink and be ignored.

Madison would not leave Washington. He had been a congressman who, with many others, had decided years ago with President Washington that the government needed to be in its own location, in its own city, midway down the East Coast so it was central to all Americans, not just those in the northeast. The capital was going to stay on the banks of the Potomac, he told friends. His wife agreed. She did not want to leave the town where she had spent sixteen years creating a social world for the American government and made so many friends. Quietly, Dolley and her friends went to work lobbying congressmen to keep the capital in the District of Columbia.

The *National Intelligencer* resumed printing at the end of August with borrowed type. The editor joined the chorus of supporters for keeping the capital in Washington. The journalist wrote that it would be a "treacherous breach of faith" with citizens who had "laid out fortunes in the purchase of property in and about the city." He said the very thought of the government's departure filled Washingtonians with "abhorrence and astonishment." In a patriotic burst, he added that leaving would be "kissing the rod an enemy has wielded."[14]

Dolley went to work rebuilding the vast social world that she ran in Washington prior to the attack. She believed that the re-creation of that world, with all of its parties—and all of its invitees, regardless of political party, wealth, or station in life—not only would help residents of the city get back on their feet but also would show the Brits and the world that nothing had changed in the capital and that nobody in it, drinking champagne, laughing at humorous stories, eating the best beef, or dancing to the music of large orchestras, had much time to worry about the British army and or its crude generals and ill-mannered soldiers. Dolley could not produce the social extravaganzas that became commonplace at the White House, but she could still throw a party to remember. She made up her mind to re-create the White House social world at Octagon House, with just as many events, although on a smaller scale because of the smaller size of the building. That started on September 14, less than three months after the burning of the White House. Hundreds of people wearing their finest clothes arrived in elegant carriages or on horseback, making the party, and the new start of Dolley's social season, a smashing success. All of the nighttime parties and the huge crowds they attracted spurred people to start calling Octagon House "the house of a thousand candles." One month later, in its final vote, Congress approved a bill to keep the nation's capital in Washington.

Dolley was back, the capital was back, and so was the United States.

❧

The peace negotiations in Ghent dragged on through the winter months and the holiday season of 1814 . The Madisons were despondent. There was no news from Belgium, the Hartford Secession Convention was underway, and the Federalist press continued to be critical. "Madison, this man, if he deserves the name," ranted the editor of the *Federal Republican*, had brought "dishonor, disappointment and disaster" to the country.[15]

In addition to all of that, the Washington, DC, area had been hit with a flu epidemic and many residents were ill.

Negotiations dragged in Belgium. The Americans did not trust the British ministers at Ghent. They dawdled and delayed while at the same time a British naval and army force sailed to New Orleans to take the city, and with it the Mississippi valley, crippling all American transportation and business in the area. Were the peace talks just a foil to cover increased British warmongering? Dolley Madison complained bitterly to a friend that "the prospect of peace appears to get darker and darker. . . . [Britain] will not make peace unless they are obliged to, and it is their policy [she had learned from John Quincy Adams] to protract the negotiations as long as they can."[16]

Extremely worried about an attack on the Mississippi valley, Madison dispatched Andrew Jackson to defend New Orleans and sent him as much ammunition and supplies as he could. Jackson brought his regular army with him but, when in New Orleans, Madison sent him additional men from Kentucky and Tennessee. When General Jackson arrived, he heard rumors that a force of twenty-five thousand infantrymen was with the British fleet of ships that were getting closer to Louisiana. Afraid that he did still not have enough men, Jackson declared martial law, put the entire city under his personal control, and then asked for volunteers for new militia units. He took anybody who walked in the door. He even recruited the pirates of fabled buccaneer Jean LaFitte, whose men knew every inch of the bayous the British would have to march through, to help him. Added to the pirates were local merchants, citizens, teenaged boys, Frenchmen from Haiti, visiting salesmen, and freed blacks. Altogether, Jackson put together a force of just over five thousand men. He borrowed all of the cannon he could find in the area and set up a ragged mile-long line of defense near the Mississippi River between the watery swamp and the city.

The British fleet finally reached New Orleans. They attacked on December 28 with a 6,000-man army, but were beaten back. On January 1, 1815, they began an artillery barrage of the American position but were driven back again by American cannonading that destroyed a dozen of their guns. Then, on January 8, just after dawn, the British began their main assault. In true British tradition, they began to march slowly through the bayou, long red lines of men sloshing their way through the waist-high reeds and grass in the swamp. Their army endured a long series of miscues that morning. Needed long, wooden ladders had been left behind; maps were found unworthy; a dam the Redcoats built to help them transport wagons collapsed. Their leaders knew nothing of the territory they had to move through. Their one advantage was the weather. An early-morning fog covered their movements as they slowly advanced. Then, suddenly, around 8 a.m., the fog lifted. The British army was within range, the Americans had coordinates from the pirates, and Jackson's cannon exploded, cutting them down. The pirates, black freedmen, and townspeople opened up with their muskets, firing at will as quickly as they could reload. Thick clouds of smoke rose from all of the discharges of muskets, pistols, and cannon. British troops, so used to fighting on sunlit, flat, open meadows, bumbled and stumbled through the thick terrain and were confused. The barrage from the American line, with soldiers encouraged by Jackson riding his horse back and forth and shouting orders, was thunderous and nonstop. When one part of the line of cannon ended its fire, a second part of the line opened up. It was an incredibly professional performance by a mostly amateur army. The carnage was terrible. One seasoned British soldier, a veteran of the European wars, said the Americans unleashed on them "the most murderous [fire he] ever beheld."[17]

The British had over seven hundred killed and a total of two thousand dead, wounded, and missing—a full one third of their army. It was one of the biggest and most embarrassing defeats in British history. The Redcoats were wiped out quickly and lost most of their top generals and officers, leaving the infantry all alone without leadership and direction. The cannon fire increased. The Redcoats fled at 8:30 a.m. and were fired upon until they were out of range. Jackson had not only defended and saved New Orleans but also scored a great historic triumph over the British, last seen running for their lives through the swamp in a shameful retreat. "[Fire] from our guns and our musquetry opened on them with such irresistible effect . . . leaving the ground strewn with dead and dying . . . a spectacle of carnage," wrote New Orleans postmaster Thomas Johnson, who was there, in a letter to Dolley. And, Johnson added, "the British have evacuated the country. The city is in a ferment of delight. The country is saved, the enemy vanquished . . . general joy."[18]

It was a victory that was lauded from one end of the United States to the other, whose importance resonated throughout the world, and, later, resonated throughout history via newspapers articles, poems, books, movies, plays, and television shows.

Prior to the battle of New Orleans, ministers of Great Britain and the United States were locked in talks to end the war. The Americans had had enough of a war they only entered into in order to end British impressment of sailors and searches of ships. England, finished with its wars against the now-exiled Napoleon, did not want to continue the struggle, especially since witnessing the resiliency of Madison and his government after the burning of Washington. President Madison had made it clear, in quickly reorganizing his government and making plans to rebuild the capital, that he was tougher than people believed. Under Madison, the Americans would never quit, and the British would never win. The ministers finally reached a peace agreement.

Madison, friends said, looked anxious and worried. Dolley, though, a friend wrote, held up the public-relations front at the Octagon House quite well. A friend wrote that "Mrs. Madison [was] as blooming as a country lass."[19]

A copy of the peace treaty arrived and was taken by courier to Washington on February 14, 1815, and crowds gathered as the rider carrying the finalized treaty made his way to the president's office at Octagon House. Hundreds of people waited outside. Acting out of sheer instinct, Dolley flung open the doors to her home and invited all in as her husband and the cabinet went over the treaty line by line in their makeshift cabinet room. Congressmen and senators arrived soon after the initial crowd was let into the home, followed by members of the Supreme Court and various government offices and newspaper people. As the hours went by, the crowd grew. Drinks flowed, music was played, and Dolley moved throughout the party like a professional organizer, like the Dolley of her White House days, talking to everyone and helping all to get ready to celebrate the new treaty.

The treaty did not cede to the United States any part of Canada, award reparations for the burned capital, or provide monetary awards of any kind. The 1756 British Orders of Council, a thorny issue for years, had been abandoned when the war began and was no longer an issue. The document did not end impressment, although the ministers, and Madison, agreed that it had to end since the Napoleonic Wars were now finished. What Madison was left with, really, was a draw, but he, his wife, and others, did not see it that way. They saw it as a huge public-relations victory. Guests at the party waited and waited, and then Dolley's cousin Sarah "Sally" Coles, who had been standing outside the cabinet-room door all night, walked into the main ballroom, a smile spreading on her face, and, all eyes on her, shouted "Peace! Peace!" Servant/slave Paul Jennings picked up a violin and struck up "The President's March," more drinks were brought around, and everyone who had crammed into the home cheered lustily.[20]

Dolley was elated. "The most conspicuous person in the room . . . was Mrs. Madison herself, then in the meridian of life and queenly beauty. No one could doubt who beheld the radiance of joy which lighted up her countenance and diffused its beam all around that all uncertainly was at an end and the government of the country had in very truth passed from gloom to glory. With a grace all her own, to her visitors she reciprocated heartfelt congratulations upon the glorious and happy change in the aspects or public affairs," wrote one man who was there.[21]

The president and his cabinet then appeared at the party, dignified and somber. Paul Jennings, who had been with them in the cabinet room earlier, wrote, though, that "Mr. Madison and all his cabinet were as pleased as any, but did not show their joy in this manner."[22]

The entire country celebrated along with the Madisons and their friends in Washington. Americans combined Jackson's victory at New Orleans with news of the peace treaty into a huge psychological and public-relations victory. The United States had defeated the British Navy several times on the Great Lakes and in the Atlantic, crushed its army at New Orleans, held up against a ferocious naval bombardment at Fort McHenry in Baltimore, and survived the attack on Washington. Its men, shaky at first, had become veteran soldiers and won the war. The president, learning military skills as he went along, had become a hands-on commander in chief, a tough leader.

Everyone remembered, too, that throughout the conflict Madison had remained firm and was never shaken by any of the many defeats in the war or the tide of public opinion against him, even the betrayal of friends such as William Thornton. He was a rock. Pennsylvania senator Jonathan Roberts visited him the night before the peace treaty arrived, at a time when everyone was certain the war was over, and found him alone in the Octagon House. Madison greeted him warmly. "The self-command, and greatness of mind, I witnessed on this occasion was in entire accordance with what I have before stated of the President, when to me things looked so dark," he said.[23]

In a few weeks, it became apparent, too, that the impressment of American sailors at sea had stopped. Madison told everyone, again and again, that America had gone to war to stop impressment. That impressment had ended. America, therefore, achieved its single goal in the war. It had won.

All of this had its effect on Congress. The legislature took an early vote on whether or not to move the government to Philadelphia. It lost. Congressmen voted 79 to 37 to keep the capital in Washington. They would vote again, and the final vote margin would be nine votes. In the end, it was decided to resurrect the White House and the Capitol and keep the national government in Washington. The Senate soon appropriated large funds to rebuild all of the structures that had been burned in the city. By the end of 1816, some of the Capitol had been rebuilt (it would be reoccupied in 1819), along with all of the Treasury and War offices and the Navy Yard. In September 1817, the White House was finished and President Monroe and his wife moved in.

As construction began on government buildings, Thomas Jefferson sold most of the books in his huge collection at Monticello to Congress to restart the Library of Congress. President Madison created the post of Librarian of Congress and appointed writer George Watterston the first librarian. In 1816, a group of men headed up by John Quincy Adams founded the Columbian Institute to promote the arts and sciences in the town. In 1816, more single-family homes were built in Washington than in the previous five years. Two new, large churches opened their doors, and dozens of shops opened on Pennsylvania Avenue. The population of the city grew and would double within the next few years.[24]

There was prosperity across the nation. The New England shipping business profits bounced back immediately as their vessels sailed the seas unimpeded by searches by the English and French. The industry's jailed sailors were released and sent home. The price of tobacco nearly tripled, and the price of cotton quadrupled. The total amount of exports from the United States jumped from $45 million in 1815 to over $68 million in 1817 and climbed higher the next year. In the two years after the war, unemployment dropped and so did the national debt. The total cost of running the federal government dropped to just $22 million a year.

Public opinion on Madison soared. He had gone from being the derided "little man in the palace" to a national hero. America had won the war, had disgraced the British at New Orleans, and once again enjoyed freedom of the seas. England would never war on the United States again. The New England secession movement died, business was better, farming was more prosperous, and Americans were happy. "Their first war with England made them independent; their second made them formidable," wrote an editor of the *London Times* about the United States.[25]

The Madisons, James and Dolley, were the two most popular people in the country during the president's last two years in office.

There was one more piece of business, the ever-annoying Barbary pirates off the coast of North Africa. Madison had helped Jefferson defeat the pirates of the Barbary States in 1805, but during the War of 1812, the bandits were back on the high seas in the Mediterranean, stopping US merchant ships and once again seizing American sailors. Madison paid little attention to the renewed war because he had to defeat the British. That war was finished. Now it was off to Tripoli to tangle with the Mediterranean pirates once more. The president sent two squadrons of warships, one under Commodore William Bainbridge in Boston and one under Commodore Stephen Decatur, a hero in both the first Barbary War and the War of 1812. Decatur's fleet was composed of the frigate USS *Guerriere*, with forty-four guns; the *Constellation*, with thirty-six guns; and the *Macedonia*, with thirty-eight guns; plus six sloops with between twelve and sixteen guns each. They encountered the pirate fleet near Gibraltar and captured two of its largest vessels. Decatur then sailed on to Algiers and threatened to attack it. The dey agreed to negotiations. Decatur returned the two ships he had captured to the dey and the dey, surprised and fearful of the large and powerful American fleet, completely capitulated. He vowed never to harass American shipping again and to release all captured US sailors plus several dozen Europeans who had been taken. The dey agreed to pay $10,000 in reparations, never to demand tribute again, and never to harass American shipping. He agreed to pretty much the same deal with British negotiators six months later. The second, and final, Barbary War was over in triumph for America, and Madison.

The world saw Madison's actions as swift and decisive, the work of the leader of a world power. The old tentativeness of America in its relationship with the Barbary States under both Jefferson and Madison was gone. There was no more threatening or diplomatic sword rattling. President Madison made up his mind to end the war and subdue the pirates and did so. He showed a fierce determination that he had never shown in his life. He was a new man.[26]

His view of government had changed dramatically. He was no longer firmly in the corner of the states' rights champions who feared a big and powerful federal government. Now, as his presidency wound down, James Madison had become an extraordinarily powerful and confident national leader. He had no trouble getting Congress to establish a national bank to back up American money in times of trouble. In his budget messages and State of the Union addresses, he moved further and further toward a powerful presidency, certain that the national government could do things that states could not. Only the national government could have fought the War of 1812, and only the national government had the money for national transportation, education, defense, and banking. He needed more taxes and more spending and pressed Congress for authorization on those issues. He had found that a special tax just to fight the war had worked, and it would work for presidents for hundreds of years to come.

Madison was applauded by all. Jefferson wrote him just after the war ended to tell him that he had not only transformed the American character but also shown all of Europe, and all of the world, that the American country and people had changed forever. Historian Henry Adams, whose nine-volume work on the War of 1812 is still considered the premier account of the conflict, wrote that "in 1815, for the first time, Americans ceased to debate the path they were to follow. Not only was the unity of the nation established, but its probable divergence from older societies was also well defined. . . . The American, in his political character, was a new variety of man."[27]

Everything had changed in America during Madison's two terms and his eight years as the secretary of state. The nation's population boomed. The total number of people living in America in 1817, when Madison retired, was about four times as great as when he wrote the Constitution. The three western states of Ohio, Kentucky, and Tennessee had developed rapidly, and the 1820 census would show their growth from 370,000 in 1800 to 1.7 million in 1820. The country's churches had flourished and were now found all over the land, and not just in the large cities. When the revolution ended, there were forty-four newspapers in America; in the 1820s, there were more than five hundred. The one-party system that began with George Washington had folded, and there were two strong parties. Then the Federalists died and were to be replaced by the Whigs. Men's and women's fashions had changed, again and again, during his eight years in Washington and would change yet again in his retirement.

James Madison had had, in the twilight of his presidency, established a happy balance between a powerful federal government over a collection of vibrant state governments. He had moved a long way from the Madison of the mid-1790s, and so had the nation.

The president was "the *great* little Madison" at last.

22

HOME TO MONTPELIER

Retirement

*A*s the steamship carrying the Madisons out of the nation's capital slowly slipped its moorings and began to churn along the wide Potomac, the former First Couple passed a scene they had never anticipated when they arrived in Washington sixteen long years before. Then, the brand-new capital was less than a year old. There were just three thousand or so residents and a few large, mostly uncompleted, government buildings. The center of the city was covered with wide, vacant, uneven, dirt-filled lots; rolling meadows; and soggy wetlands. Some of the streets, such as Pennsylvania Avenue, stopped somewhere out in a wet swamp. There were a few parties at the homes of the comfortably well off, some taverns, a boardinghouse or two, and long horseback or carriage rides to Georgetown and Alexandria over the Potomac.

Upon arriving at the new capital, President Jefferson had written Madison, "we shall have an agreeable society here, and not too much of it." He was right then but wrong now. In the spring of 1817, as the Madisons stood at the rail of the ship and waved good-bye to friends, Washington was a very different place.[1]

Several dozen large, finished government buildings anchored both the business and residential centers of town. The Capitol and White House, burned in the war, were under reconstruction and were nearly finished. Dozens of noisy taverns filled with residents and visitors dotted the terrain. The population of the town had tripled, to nearly ten thousand people, and the city, without a newspaper in the summer of 1800, now had four. The populations of Georgetown and Alexandria had also tripled in those seventeen years.

The size of the city was much larger and far more diverse. Thousands of people moved to town to take the increasing number of federal jobs and jobs with companies that did business with the government. Independent stores and factories hired many more workers. There were now more than a dozen busy boardinghouses and several elegant, spacious hotels lining the streets. The city's social life had exploded, with theaters and music halls now open full-time and regular troupes of entertainers performing in them. Bookstores attracted hundreds of people, several schools had been built, and national science and philosophical centers had been established.

Margaret Bayard Smith, looking back on her years at the capital, which were the same years as the Madisons', wrote:

> When I first came to the city [1800], I found myself almost as much a stranger as I did twelve years ago, and when I recalled to mind the society which had so often circled round our fireside and beheld them scattered over the world, separated by the waves of the Atlantic, some by the ocean of eternity, sadness and sorrow mingled with the pleasures of recollection. Washington [now] possesses a peculiar interest and to an active, reflective and ambitious mind has more attractions than any other place in America. This interest is daily increasing and with the importance and expansion of our nation, this is the theater on which its most interesting ideas are discussed, by its ablest sons, in which the greatest characters are called to act. It is, every year, more and more the resort of strangers from every part of the union, and all foreigners of distinction who visit these states and visit this city.

She added that residents of the new city, official and unofficial, unlike residents of European capitals, turned the very formal assets of the town into very informal places to make friends. Men and women spent time at the capital meeting new people each time they visited. She said that the key to the city's development into a village of friends and not just residents were the drawing-room socials hosted by Dolley Madison and others. It was there, she said, that the wide-open guest lists, with foreign ministers arriving after local merchants and duchesses after college students, made the city whole. Smith said that when she first arrived in town, just ahead of the Madisons, the socials and drawing-room parties drew only a few dozen residents. Now, a typical party attracted some three hundred guests, and far more clamored to be added to the invitations list.[2]

The city had been bulging in size for years, but the number of new residents really spiked when Madison's first term began in 1809. "The city is thronged with strangers," a local resident wrote that winter. "Yesterday we saw four or five carriages-and-four come in and already two have passed this morning. I don't know how many [women] have come from Baltimore. There are parties every night and the galleries are crowded in the morning," she wrote.[3]

All of those who visited Washington had to travel down narrow, dirt road-ways on slow-moving horses or in carriages and buggies whose wheels caught every bump in the road. It took three days to travel ninety miles. The country around the capital that visitors drove through, though, was beautiful, well worth the rocky ride. On mornings, it was often covered with a thick, milky fog. As the sun rose, the fog was broken and the tops of hills and the forests beneath them became visible, all dotted with streams and depressions and jutting rock ledges.

The departure of Madison in 1817 brought on the presidency of James Monroe, the third consecutive Republican president and third consecutive Virginian. He, like Madison, presided over a House and Senate where Republicans enjoyed a comfortable majority in seats. Madison never felt that the Republicans had gained power and held it simply because of their policies. He always told people the reason was also the failure of the Federalists. Many agreed with him. "[People] overlook the overbearing and vindictive spirit, the apocryphal doctrines and rash projects, which stamped on federalism its dis-tinctive character; and which are so much in contrast with the unassuming and unvarying spirit which has marked the Republican Ascendancy," wrote Dr. William Eustis, looking back in 1823.[4]

Madison had left the growing and powerful government in the hands of the man who had served him so well when he was president, just as Jefferson had left him in charge when he went back to Monticello. Madison was confident that the federal government, strengthened by the War of 1812, was a good one.

One of the biggest changes in America during Madison's years in office was the tidal wave of European immigrants arriving daily at American sea-ports. Many Americans were concerned that the new arrivals, hundreds of thousands of them, would take American jobs and reshape American character. Madison was not one of them. He welcomed the new arrivals and saw them as a way to build American spirit. In 1794, he had introduced a bill to allow immigrants to move to America with a wait of only five years before they could become citizens (they had to pledge loyalty to the Constitution). Ever since then, throughout the battles over the Alien and Sedition Acts, he had champi-oned the immigrants.[5]

The political world of the United States and its immigrants had changed substantially from the day Madison first went to the Continental Congress in 1780 as a young man. Now there were two major political parties, a self-imposed two-term limit on the presidency, a large Congress with two houses, a functioning Supreme Court, and a new national capital. This ever-changing political landscape was heralded by Madison. He had predicted this altered scenery back in 1787. "The [people] have not suffered a blind veneration for antiquity, for custom, or for names, to overrule the suggestions of their own good sense, the knowledge of their own situation and the lessons of their own experience. Posterity will be indebted for the possession and the world for the example of the numerous innovations displayed on the American theater."[6]

The steamship trip out of Washington was a pleasant one. The boat was jammed with well-wishers. Madison and his wife were eager to get back to Montpelier. James Paulding, who accompanied him on the trip, was astonished at the buoyancy of the chief executive as he headed into retirement. Paulding said he "was as playful as a child, talked and jested with everybody on board . . . [like] a school boy on a long vacation."[7]

As they sailed down the Potomac, they saw small villages on each side of the river rising up over the slopes of meadows and out of forests, indicative of the tremendous population explosion the country had experienced during Madison's sixteen years as secretary of state and president. When James Madison went to Congress for the first time in 1779, America had just over two million people. The population of the country had increased dramatically, and by the time he left office the country had over eight million residents, quadruple the number that lived within its borders when the revolution began. New York, which had just over ten thousand residents during the revolution, had nearly one hundred thousand when Madison left office, edging past Philadelphia (92,000) to become the nation's most crowded city (Baltimore was third and Boston was fourth).[8]

President Madison was so popular, and so politically acclaimed, that when he left office, John Quincy Adams, soon to be president himself, told Madison that he could have won a third term easily and won it with huge support from the Federalists. He wrote that "such is the state of minds here, that had Mr. Madison been a candidate, he would probably have had the votes of Massachusetts and consequently of all New England."[9]

The Madisons had been packing for weeks and had sent off a long train of wagons containing their possessions to Montpelier before they boarded the boat. After they left the ship, they traveled southwest to Orange Court House by carriage, cheered on by all of the people they met on the way. When the Madisons arrived home at Montpelier, riding up that long, gorgeous entry road from the highway, Dolly found a letter from her friend Eliza Collins Lee. In it, Lee congratulated her and welcomed her to retirement among the trees and fields of her beloved Montpelier. "On this day eight years ago, I wrote to congratulate you on the joyful event that placed you in the highest station our country can bestow. I then enjoyed the proudest feelings, that my friend of my youth, who never had forsaken me, should be thus distinguished, and so peculiarly fitted for it . . . talents such as yours were never intended to remain inactive," she wrote, reminding Dolley of her great success as First Lady. "You will retire from the tumult and fatigue of public life to your favorite retreat in Orange County and will carry with you principles and manners not to be put off with the robe of state." A Supreme Court Justice, William Johnson Jr., wrote Dolley, "[You] carry with you to your retirement the blessings of all who ever knew you . . . you may long enjoy every blessing that heaven bestows to the meritorious."[10]

It was a warm welcome-home present and she cherished it. There were many letters from friends in Washington wishing her well in retirement and thanking her profusely for her friendship. One was from Lucia Kantzow, a diplomat's wife, who wrote that "the kindness I received, and the happiness I found, in making your acquaintance with the respect & gratitude I feel towards you, and your husband, is impossible [to describe]."[11]

She put all such letters in her desk drawers and then, with her husband, plunged into the work of running the house and the four farms that made up their plantation.

Each morning, after breakfast with Dolley and whoever was visiting, Madison walked to the stables, had a servant saddle up a horse, and then began a long ride through his plantations, the soft breezes in his face, riding partially for exercise, partially for the fun of it, and mostly to check with slaves and overseers on work projects and crop harvests. His rides were usually pleasant, but sometimes they were not. James Paulding went riding with him one day in 1818. "We rode to a distant part of the estate bordering on the Rapidan River . . . a ferocious stream, and subject to occasional inundations. There had been a very heavy shower the day before; the river had overflowed its banks and covered two or three acres of fine meadow with gravel some inches deep, so that it was completely spoiled," said Paulding.[12]

Madison visited his aging mother Nelly each midafternoon and spent an hour or so talking to her. Nelly, who was rarely sick, lived to be ninety-seven years old. Her son added the north wing of the house to provide her with extra living space. Nelly kept to herself and had her own slave staff to care for her.

Nelly Madison kept busy all of her life. She knitted constantly and spent long hours reading books. "My eyes, thanks be to God, have not failed me yet, and I read most part of the day. But in other respects I am feeble and helpless," she told one visitor when she was in her nineties.[13]

She always told guests at Montpelier how much she was grateful to the care that her son and daughter-in-law gave her. "I owe everything to her," she said to

Margaret Bayard Smith, pointing to Dolley, who was sitting nearby in her room "She is *my* mother now, and tenderly cares for all my wants."[14]

Back home at Montpelier in the summers of the 1830s, Dolley made light of the recession, her sagging plantation business, and her son. She was chipper when she wrote lifelong friend Anthony Morris one summer, "We are all in high health, and looking on promising crops, flocks and herds as well as on the world of fashion around us. My great nephew & niece with a pair of neighbors being pleased to get married since our return has brought about more than our usual gaiety. I gave them in unison a large party of two or three days continuance, before and after which Anna and Payne went the rounds as bridesmaid and Best Man."[15]

The Madisons joined guests for dinner around 4 p.m. each day. Dinner usually lasted until 6 p.m. or so, depending on how many visitors were at the table. Visitors loved dinners because Madison, far more cheerful among friends and relatives than strangers, regaled everyone with stories from his life, which, of course, featured the most famous and important men and women in the world. Margaret Bayard Smith said that at these dinners, guests listened to "living history" and added that she had been with Madison at other times, with strangers, when the president was cold and repulsive.

A visitor to Montpelier, H. D. Gilpin, who visited him in retirement, said that Madison looked good. "[He] is quite a short, thin man, with his head bald except on the back, where his hair hangs down to his collar and over his ears, nicely powdered, old as he is . . . and seems very hale and hearty. The expression of his face is full of good humor. He was dressed in black, with breeches and old-fashioned top boots . . . looked very nice." Then Dolley arrived with panache, as she always did. Gilpin wrote that she was "quite stylish in a turban and fine gown. She has a great deal of dignity blended with good humor and knowledge of the world."[16]

After dinner was over, guests would join the Madisons in the parlor during wintertime, or on the front porch or in the flower-filled back gardens during the spring and summer months. They would spend two hours or more talking about the events of the day, friends, and family.

Madison spent much of the time talking to guests about his own career, the War of 1812, and current politics. It was then, when darkness began to slowly fall over the Blue Ridge Mountains, that the real James Madison emerged, the colorful and funny raconteur who loved to tell stories and listen to a good joke. It was at these after dinner discussions that Madison let down what little hair he had left. The talks were especially engaging when he had old friends from his political days at his side, a glass of wine in their hands. People like Jefferson,

Monroe, and Henry Clay, relaxing in large, comfortable chairs, joined Madison in stories of presidents and wars and Congress and arrogant diplomats. They sat for hours, engaging all with the stories of the United States they had made. Their tales soared with drama and shook with humor. It was there, with the sun setting on the hills and with close friends and old political allies around him, that James Madison shone.

The president also loved to talk just after breakfast, before the sun drenched the fields in front of his home. Paulding sat with him many mornings that first summer of retirement. "I seat myself on the western portico, looking towards the Blue Ridge, while Mr. Madison would commence a conversation sometimes on public affairs, in connection with his previous public life, in which he spoke without reserve & from which I gathered lessons of wise practical experience, sometimes in literary and philosophical subject and not infrequently, for he was a capital story teller, he would relate anecdotes highly amusing as well as interesting. He was a man of wit, relished wit in others & his small bright blue eyes would twinkle most wickedly when lighted up by some whimsical conception or exposition."[17]

Dolley had always enjoyed gardening at Montpelier and in retirement had plenty of time for it. She worked as hard in her fruit-filled gardens, which were next to the house, as Madison did in the fields. She wrote one of her nieces, "our garden promises grapes and figs in abundance but I shall not enjoy them unless your mamma comes and brings you to help us with them," she wrote, adding that a frost had killed most of her green peas.[18]

Work outdoors did not diminish Dolley's beauty. Many thought the gardening, and the hours on her knees and hands caked in dirt made her even more attractive. Margaret Bayard Smith saw her in the gardens in 1827. "Time seems to favor her as much as fortune. She looks young and she says she feels so. I can believe her, not do I think she will ever look or feel like an old woman," she wrote.[19]

The president also spent a considerable amount of time discussing farming with guests. All considered him one of the best farmers in Virginia and listened intently to his advice. He told visitors to carefully irrigate and rotate their crops, maintain large forests for firewood, and keep a careful eye on what produce England and European countries needed. That was how he had become so successful. For example, the European need for wheat had dropped throughout the recent war, so Madison shifted over and grew tobacco.

He also experimented with seeds to grow new crops, such as those Jefferson brought him from Monticello. He grew strains of new wheat and corn from seeds sent to him from friends in South America. He produced his own special ears of corn and then sent boxes of them to Monroe and other friends so that they could use them for their own experimentation.[20]

The former president went into detailed discussions of farming equipment—how much of it he had and how he had always tinkered with it in order to make farm machines more suitable for Virginia soil than for soil they had been tried out upon in New England and the Middle Atlantic States. One example was a plow invented by George Logan in Philadelphia in 1793. Madison and workers fused together the two parts of the plow, making it one machine. He wrote Jefferson that "the detached form may answer best in old, clean ground but will not stand the shocks of our rough & rooty land, especially in the hands of our ploughmen." In another note, he wrote that "I have tried the patent plow amended by fixing the colter in the usual way. It succeeds perfectly and I think forms the plow best suited to its object."[21]

As a farmer, Madison often experimented with his livestock to create new breeds. He tried to breed ordinary sheep with imported Merino sheep that were rams. The president was one of several farmers in Virginia who did that. George Washington had inbred types of buffalo.

At postdinner discussions with friends about agriculture, Madison said that he also believed that farmers led better lives and lived longer. He said the exposure to plants and trees, and just walking about in fresh air all day, was healthy. The president told his friends and relatives that hard farming made men stronger psychologically as well as physically. Farm work was good for the body and the soul. He reminded all, too, that he had farms in other areas of Virginia and in Kentucky. He and Dolley owned a home in Washington as well as Montpelier and, he said quietly, they had nearly one hundred slaves. He thought that depressions and recessions would not hurt the Madisons because they had large assets. He was wrong on that. A depression in farming in the 1820s and early 1830s, plus several bad harvests highlighted by lengthy frosts and a lack of rain, plus general crop failure, plus an economic downturn, did cause him severe financial problems—as did his practice of paying for relatives' college tuitions and covering the bills of his brother-in-law John and stepson, Payne. The reason that he survived the depression was that he had so much land that he could sell off 100-acre patches of it for several thousand dollars each and use that money to pay bills, retire the debts of family members, cover college tuitions, and simply hand out money to friends and relatives—even though there were many who asked for it. Jefferson and Monroe barely broke even on their farms each year, even with an unpaid workforce of slaves. Others, who went bankrupt, left the county and moved somewhere else in Virginia or to another state.[22]

When the postmeal talks ended, around nine or so in the evening, everyone was escorted upstairs to bed by the servants. If there was a large crowd of overnight guests, the servants would bring out beds and set them up in rooms or in the hallways. In hot weather, doors and windows were flung open for ventilation, much like they had in the times of Madison's presidency.

Madison loved to sit on his front porch and look out over his land in the morning; so did Dolley. Sometimes his wife reminisced about their days in Washington with friends and said she would like to move back there. She missed the parties and the politics. She told her niece Dolley that she was happy in her "quiet retreat," but missed the "maneuverings and gossip of the old days" at White House socials. She missed Richmond, too. Except for Washington, Richmond was the social capital of the South. Socialite Abigail Mayo wrote in 1804 that in Richmond she attended a ball, dozens of dinner parties, and several theater parties in a month. Everyone there was eager to see Dolley. Mayo wrote her, "I have had many inquiries about you from your friends here, who would delight to see you again in this capital and if you will but make me a visit I am sure you will have reason to believe they are sincere in their professions of admiration and esteem." Dolley remembered all of the good times there and constantly reminded friends of them. "I told you how delighted I had been with the society of Richmond," she wrote one in 1800.[23]

The First Lady, like everyone, did the best she could to protect her husband and family when medical epidemics struck Virginia. Sometimes her exertions did little good, such as in 1831, when cholera took the lives of George and Sam Washington, her sister Lucy's two sons, who were in their early twenties.

In his late seventies, Madison began to show some signs of physical deterioration. His eyesight was not as sharp as it used to be and his hearing was impaired. He walked slower than he had previously. Yet those who met him then thought he was doing far better than they expected in an era when three quarters of men died before the age of fifty. A man who met him in 1829 remarked that he "was in tolerably good health, thin of flesh, rather under the common size and dressed in his customary black, old fashioned clothes. His form [was] erect, his step firm but somewhat slow, [he] walks without a staff, his visage pale and abounding in small wrinkles, his features well-proportioned but not striking, his head bald . . . his forehead of common size, his brow grey, heavy and projecting, his eyes small and faded, his nose of ordinary size and straight, his mouth rather small."[24]

His wife hardly ever left his side, whether to help him with his books, arrange his schedule, care for him when he was sick, or just have an early-morning conversation with him. He told all who visited how much he loved her.[25]

In retirement, Madison was urged to join the Agricultural Society of Albemarle (County) and soon became its very respected president. He became absorbed in the work of the society and its farmers and even wrote a lengthy pamphlet on farming that was widely read and frequently discussed.

He worked hard on his farm, consulted with anyone interested in his opinion, took care of a very large extended family, visited friends and relatives throughout Virginia, wrote speeches, answered hundreds of letters, cared for his wife, oversaw work crews in the fields at Montpelier, and paid his son's debts. He was always annoyed by people who accused him of relaxing in retirement. The president wrote one man that "it is an error very naturally prevailing that the retirement from public service, of which my case is an example, is a leisure for whatever pursuit might be most inviting. The truth, however, is that I have rarely, during the period of my public life, found my time less at my disposal than since I took my leave of it; nor have I the consolation of finding that as my powers of application necessarily decline, the demands on them proportionately decrease."[26]

Throughout his retirement, Madison's advice was constantly sought by newspaper editors and public officials, at both the state and federal levels. He always stood by the Constitution, no matter how many political schemes were hatched. One idea that infuriated him was Jefferson's suggestion that conventions be called to settle disputes between state and federal court systems. Madison castigated Jefferson for his plan and reminded him that the cornerstone of the Constitution was the ability of the US Supreme Court to overrule state courts.

The president quickly became a revered elder statesman. He kept up with all the international and national news by reading newspapers, which he had on subscription, plus magazines and, as always, a torrent of books on history and politics. Friend Richard Rush, now minister to England, sent him copies of all his diplomatic correspondence, as did President Monroe. Madison consulted with both and was deeply involved in decisions to make treaties and choose allies in diplomatic squabbles (he was instrumental in the planning of the Monroe Doctrine).

Madison quickly forgave England for the War of 1812 and urged all to make peace with the British. He became one of history's first proponents of an organization that would serve a purpose akin to the later United Nations, writing in 1820, "were it possible in human contrivance to accelerate the intercourse between every part of the globe that all its inhabitants could be united under the superintending authority of an ecumenical council, how great a portion of human evils would be avoided. Wars, famines, with pestilence as far as the fruit of either, could not exist; taxes to pay for wars, or to provide against them would be needless and the expense and perplexities of local fetters on interchange beneficial to all would no longer oppress the social state."[27]

His wife helped in his work as an elder statesman. She constantly wrote the wives of diplomats around the world and invited all to visit them at Montpelier on any trip they took to America. Many did.

Madison avoided politics but complained bitterly about the rise of his former general, Andrew Jackson. He was disgusted with Jackson's uncouth manners and egomaniacal personality, and the crude, rude followers who surrounded him day and night. He was all in favor of the westerners becoming part of the political process, just not *those* westerners. His wife was aghast when she learned that some of her magnificent red drapes had been ruined at the riotous postinaugural party Jackson threw at the White House.

One of the most rewarding aspects of President Madison's retirement was his appointment to the board of governors of the brand-new University of Virginia, founded by Thomas Jefferson and others and built to challenge northern schools such as Harvard, Yale, and Princeton as a top institution of higher learning. Madison and Jefferson attended a meeting with nineteen other members of the board and voted to merge the proposed state university with tiny Central College, already in Charlottesville. Jefferson, with Madison's assistance, would be in charge of the design. Madison was happy to be on the board because as president he had tried to get a national university built and had always loved higher education. He was also happy to leave Montpelier and spend several days with Jefferson and other old friends.

Planning for the university, and the construction of the first buildings, went well, but the official opening of the new school was delayed due to the late arrival of professors from Europe by ship. Finally, on March 7, 1819, the opening took place with eight professors and sixty-eight students. Jefferson was elected rector, or board chairman. After Jefferson's death, Madison took over as rector. Throughout his years on the board, Madison kept busy planning the expansion of the university, bringing in new professors, and obtaining funding for it. When he died, he left the school money and his entire 4,000-book library, which became the cornerstone of one of the largest libraries in America.

The other public enjoyment Madison had was an invitation to a convention in Richmond in 1829 called to create a new state constitution. It was the first time James and Dolley Madison had left the Orange Court House/Montpelier area in over twelve years, and it was a shock to the president. While his fame was still intact, his political power was not. He arrived as an Orange County delegate and controlled no votes except his own. His views of slavery and its role in the new constitution were jeered at by many. Virginia had changed and so had the country, and Madison knew it.

The Madisons spent three months at the home of cousin Sarah "Sally" Coles Stevenson in Richmond for the duration of the convention. He and Dolley went to luncheons, parties, balls, and receptions and had a marvelous time. The Richmond nightlife was in fine contrast to the contentious days the ex-president spent at the convention, where the proslavery feelings grew hotter and hotter as each day passed. Madison chaired a committee to determine how slaves would be counted in the voting process because the state was in two very separate sections. The westerners, with far fewer slaves than the easterners, wanted a white-only vote clause, but the easterners insisted on a total population, black-and-white, count for the vote. Madison suggested a white-only vote for delegates in the lower house and a full population vote for the upper house. He was castigated by many and was shocked when even accused of treason. He fell back and compromised, offering the traditional three-fifths vote for each slave. That was voted down, and the easterners, through heavy-handed politics, grabbed power and rammed through a proslave population vote so they could control both houses of the legislature.

Madison realized that while he was venerated, he was not followed anymore. He knew, too, that his efforts at age-old compromise, which had always worked, now failed. And finally, he knew that slavery had catapulted forward in the social conscience as an issue. It was becoming a runaway train.

He had the admiration of all in Richmond, though. At one point, dozens of men gathered around the seventy-eight-year-old former president just to introduce themselves and shake his hand. All told him how they had looked up to him over the years. He and his wife were at the center of every party they attended and Dolley, as always, was the star. The president smiled broadly at all the receptions, but on their way home, Madison told his wife that the political world of Virginia, and the United States, was changing fast. He was not optimistic about the wild change, either, and he saw dark days ahead.

23

A NEW LIFE AMID THE FORESTS

*B*etween 1809, when James Madison took office, and 1817, when he retired, Montpelier took on a new and much grander look than in previous years. Madison had spent much time adding the two wings to give the house expanded size and a very European look. The guest list of presidents, vice president, senators, congressmen, and judges gave the house a history and elegance, an importance, that no other home in America enjoyed, except for Monticello and Mount Vernon. The interior of the home was special. Madison had collected portraits, busts, and sculptures from all over the world and put them on display in the back parlor, main parlor, and dining room. Less important, but still impressive, portraits adorned the walls of other rooms in the home. Foreign visitors, who scoffed at all American mansions as poor copies of European palaces, agreed that the artwork inside the home gave it a veneer few residences in America possessed.

Some foreign visitors turned out to be not so welcome, though, such as the marquis de Lafayette. The fabled Frenchman, an important figure in the American Revolution, decided to make a grand tour of the United States in 1825. His trip was heralded by the press. "Nothing is spoken of in the North but the Marquis; he has even for a while made the people forget the four Presidents," wrote Phoebe Morris.[1]

He first went to Monticello to be feted by Jefferson and then to Montpelier to be a guest of the Madisons. They staged a parade for him in Orange Court House, and he was the guest of honor at dinners at their home. His traveling companion was Miss Frances Wright, a feminist and abolitionist. Madison gave Jefferson, Lafayette, and Wright a tour of his plantation, and it was on that tour that Lafayette and Wright scolded Madison over his ownership of slaves. He told Madison that it was not only wrong for anyone to have slaves but a shame to have nearly a hundred, as Madison did. Was not the revolution fought to end Americans' enslavement to England? How then could Americans still have slaves?

Madison was stung by the rebuke. As always, Dolley said nothing about the Frenchman's criticism. She wrote her brother-in-law that "I never witnessed so much enthusiasm as his appearance occasioned here and at our court house, where hundreds of both sexes collected together to hail & welcome him. He has promised to spend some time with us again, before he leaves the country," blithely ignoring the dispute over slavery. Later, Wright wrote an appreciative note for the Madisons' hospitality and included a copy of her abolitionist prospectus, which she said Madison's support would help. "[Although] from the fear of alarming the minds of those who hearing of the plan without understanding its spirit & object must meet it with opposition, it is necessary to proceed with caution," she said. Madison ignored it.[2]

Dolley did not lose her good looks over the years, although she had gained twenty pounds or so as First Lady and some said that she looked heavier ("portly," sneered one woman). The First Lady aged well. Everyone she used to know in Washington was surprised at how young she looked when she turned sixty. Her hair was not yet gray, her step was lively, her smile was wide, her yen for a good party was unmitigated, and her lust for life was unquenchable. She drifted about the house and grounds like a faint breeze, beautiful still. People who met her in her sixties and had not known her before were shocked at her grace and beauty, which had not dimmed a bit with age. And she had the energy and agility of a young schoolgirl. She walked ramrod straight, with her head held high, and she was always the object of much admiration. At parties in Richmond, held in conjunction with the Virginia State Convention, she was greeted as an icon. She wore her traditional turban to parties and dances. Anne Royall, a journalist who met her there, said that she was "tall, young, active and elegant" and possessed "warm affability." Another remarked that she did not look like Mr. Madison's wife, but like his daughter. Others said she was "as active on her feet as a girl."[3]

The former president and his wife seemed to have adjusted well to retirement back at Montpelier. One visitor wrote that they "looked like Adam and Eve in paradise."[4]

⚭∽∾

Dolley spent many days of her retirement acting as a matchmaker for friends and family. She constantly tried to pair up her cousin Edward Coles, who served as Madison's secretary for several years, and a young woman in Virginia. Coles had spent an extraordinary amount of time trying to meet women and then even more time thinking about their suitability—too much time. Dolley wrote him in the autumn of 1819, "I am afraid, dear cousin, that while you and I deliberate who to choose for a wife, we shall lose some of the finest girls now grown." She ran off a list of lovely, well-connected young women who did not have the time to wait for Coles and married or became engaged to someone else. "Still I have hopes for you," Dolley finished optimistically, "that your future one may become manifest to reward your merits and long search."[5]

Her efforts did not cease with Coles. She tried to marry off her son, Payne, for years, attempting to match him up with young women in Washington and then, when she retired with Madison, throughout Orange County—with no success. She took the two daughters of her sister Anna under her wing after Anna died in 1832. She tried to instruct the girls, through letters and in person when they traveled to Montpelier, on how to meet men and how to determine which were the best men to meet. She did not believe in luck or happenstance. "We have all a great hand in the formation of our own destiny. We must press on that intricate path leading to perfection and happiness by doing all that is good and handsome, but before we can be taken under the silver wing of our rewarding angel," she wrote her niece Mary.[6]

She suggested eligible bachelors as if they were targets. Russia's minister Baron Paul Von Krudener was one. "You set your cap or curls at him. . . . I see no objection to your becoming Baroness de Krudener," she told Mary Cutts.[7]

And she warned her girls, loudly, of young men she did not deem suitable. She called one, W. Willis of Orange County, "a good hearted ignoramus."[8]

And if all of that was not enough, Dolley wrote their father, Richard Cutts, and encouraged him to get them out of the house to meet as many young men as they could.[9]

Very few of her "dream" couplings ever succeeded. Worse, Dolley's constant barrage of suggestions and streams of letters with romantic advice angered the young people she was trying to help. She apologized to Mary Cutts. "I asked too many questions in my last, did I not? Yes, but you are very good & amiable my dear to write me as much as you do & I value you accordingly though I may complain a little now and then."[10]

Madison met thousands of people in retirement at Montpelier, Richmond, Orange Court House, Monticello, and other places. He regaled them with stories.

"I have always considered Mr. Madison, emphatically, as the sage of his time," said James Paulding, who first met him in retirement and came to know him well.

He had not perhaps so much genius as Mr. Jefferson, but in my opinion his mind was more consummate and his faculties more nicely balanced than those of his predecessor; who though justly called the Great Apostle of Democracy. I think sometimes [Jefferson] carried his doctrines to the verge of political fanaticism. Mr. Madison had the power of condensing in his speeches & his writing in great perfection, though he did not always exercise it, for such is the appetite of the people of this country for long speeches, and discussions, that they don't like to swallow the truth in an incontrovertible axiom but prefer it strongly diluted with verbiage.[11]

And Paulding, like all the other visitors, was witness to the magnificent round of parties, balls, and barbecues hosted by the former president and First Lady at Montpelier. The whole countryside was alive with activity when they threw open the doors of Montpelier for frolics that lasted for days. "At these feasts the woods were alive with carriages, horses, servants and children—all went—often more than 100 guests . . . happy at the prospect of . . . pleasure and hilarity, the laugh with hearty good will, the jest after the crops, farm topics and politics," wrote Mary Cutts. They all attended barbecues hosted by others in town or nearby and enjoyed them.[12]

Few realized the drain on the Madisons that their whirlwind social life caused. The president, who enjoyed fragile health to begin with, was often tired after parties. Dolley was laid low by the social life, too, complaining in the summer of 1833 that "I have been more indisposed than usual this morning. I could not go to breakfast with a party of eight, two ladies among them, on account of illness."[13]

In addition to the physical effects of their social life, there was a large drain on the Madisons' assets throughout his retirement, which was because of the steep debts from family members. The president had routinely loaned money to relatives in his family and Dolley's for years. Sometimes loans were paid back, and sometimes they were not. The president had real problems in the mid-1820s, after the crop depression. He had turned down his brother-in-law Richard Cutts, a land speculator, for a large, $10,000 loan because he did not trust his judgment. Then his son, Payne, had offered to loan Cutts $4,000 if his stepfather put up the remaining $6,000. He did, reluctantly. Cutts lost all the money. Dolley wrote him a sharp letter demanding the money back.

"It is with understandable grief, my dear brother, that I understand the threatening situation of your affairs. I will not insult your sensibility by descanting on the devoted friendship and affection for you and yours ever felt by Mr. Madison and myself because you know it. . . . I entreat you to secure to

me the amount of all the money lent you in a house, lots or some other property, in case you have at this unlucky moment to part with what you possess in
Washington. It is only in such a case, where other creditors may take all, that I
would ever remind you of the debt. Yes it is more for your sake than mine that
I now write to ask you for God's sake, to do this just thing that you and your
children may profit from it. . . . You must preserve the confidence of a ready and
efficient friend by acting as I suggest," she wrote Cutts in a near panic in 1824.
Madison also lost investments in two companies that built roads, the Swift Run
Turnpike Company and the James Madison Company. He had tried to get a
$6,000 loan from the Bank of the United States, which he had brought back to
life as president; he was turned down.[14]

Cutts nearly lost his house in Washington, DC, to creditors. James and
Dolley stepped in at the very last minute to pay off his creditors and gain ownership of the home. They allowed the Cutts family to stay there for years. Five
years later, though, in 1829, Cutts had still not paid back any of the $6,000 to
Madison or the $4,000 to Payne on the old loan. "It almost breaks my heart to
think of it. Mr. Cutts owed him more than this [Payne's debt] of the money.
Payne entrusted to him to place [it] in the bank; still that is not the purpose
. . . my pride, my sensibility, my every feeling of my soul is wounded," she
lamented to her sister about Cutts.[15]

Less farm revenue came in at the same time that Madison was stuck paying
off family debts. The recession affected everyone. Thomas Jefferson complained to Madison that he was broke. Jefferson, a far less diligent manager
of his farms and spending than Madison, had very high monthly bills for the
upkeep of his mansion and slaves and owed thousands of dollars in debts he
had assumed for relatives. At the same time, the recession had caused his crop
prices to plunge. He had no realistic way to raise more money and floundered.
Madison's friend James Monroe was practically penniless, too. Monroe had
lived lavishly while a foreign minister in Paris, spent a considerable amount of
money building his mansion, and used additional funds entertaining hundreds
of people at his private home and in Washington for years. He was never able
to pay off his debts, which totaled over $75,000 when he left the White House
in 1825.

Madison wrote Jefferson in 1826, "Since my retirement to private life such
have been he unkind seasons, and the ravages of insects, that I have made but
one tolerable crop of tobacco, and but one of wheat; the proceeds of both of
which were greatly curtailed by mishaps in the sale of them. And having no
resources but in the earth I cultivate, I have been living very much throughout
on borrowed means."[16]

The Madisons were just getting over their anger with Cutts in 1832 when Anna, his wife and Dolley's sister, died suddenly of dropsy to the heart. Dolley was crushed. She wrote a mournful letter of condolence to Richard Cutts and then added a postscript. "She would have parted from her heart's best blood for the happiness of her offspring. One who from the height of worldly prosperity ... was reduced ... to a small income, and while [her husband] gazed on, his energies paralyzed ... this good mother devoted herself to ... her children. She brought them up in a fear of the lord, she implanted pure principles ... she taught them to listen to the still small voice within. ... Her daughters she ... taught ... a taste for poetry, the classics her own love of the beautiful and true," she wrote.[17]

The death of Anna was just one of the many deaths of family members and friends of the Madisons in those years. As the pair aged, their friends began to pass away. Madison's mother, aged ninety-seven, died in 1829. Catlett Conway, whose father was Nelly Madison's brother, died in 1827. Catlett and James Madison were childhood playmates. Madison's sister Frances "Fanny" Rose died in 1823. His nephew Robert Madison died young in 1828, and his three children lived with Madison much of the year in the years after that. Many of the children of his brother William died in the 1820s; William's wife died in 1832. Dolley's brother-in-law Supreme Court Justice Thomas Todd died in 1826. Two of her nephews died in1831. Her brother-in-law John C. Jackson passed away in 1825. Several grandchildren and nieces and nephews died in the 1820s and in the early 1830s. The Madisons outlived them all.

Thomas Jefferson died on the Fourth of July in 1826, the fiftieth anniversary of the signing of his Declaration of Independence. He corresponded regularly with Madison until his death. Toward the end, sensing he was going to pass on, Jefferson wrote his friend a poignant letter. "The friendship which has subsisted between us now half a century and the harmony of our political principles and pursuits ... [have been] sources of happiness to me through that long period," Jefferson said. He told Madison that if ever there was a good government for a democratic people, "one which, protect by truth, can never know reproach it is that to which our lives have been devoted." He asked Madison to take care of him when he was dead, and told him "I leave with you my last affections."[18]

Madison wrote back, "You cannot look back to the long period of our private friendship and political harmony with more affecting recollections than I do. If they are sources of pleasure to you, what ought they not be to me? We cannot be deprived of the happy consciousness of the pure devotion to the public good with which we discharged the trusts committed to us." Then he added, "I offer to you the fullest return of affectionate assurances."[19]

Later, after Jefferson's passing, Madison wrote tenderly about him, "It may be on the whole truly said of him, that he was greatly eminent for the comprehensiveness and fertility of his genius; the vast extent and rich variety of his acquirements, and particularly distinguished by the philosophic impress left on every subject which he touched. Nor was he less distinguished for an early and uniform devotion to the cause of liberty . . . and to the equal rights of man."[20] Dolley wrote her son, "Mr. Jefferson died on the 4th, about 12 or 1 o'clock. Mr. M feels his departure deeply, as no doubt his family must."[21]

His friend James Monroe, who resumed his close friendship with Madison after he left the White House, died in 1831.[22]

As he aged into his eighties, Madison talked more and more of how he had become the very last of the Founding Fathers. They had all died. Now he, James Madison, who was sickly, feeble, and bald, was the last.

Madison spent much time putting together his official papers, which included letters he had written over the course of fifty years, speeches, and notes. He took his copious notes to the Constitutional Convention, long secret and stored away, and edited them with the idea of publishing them as a book to ease his financial burdens. He had thousands of pages of papers, and he recruited Dolley and his brother-in-law, John Payne, to help him. The trio worked every day for nearly a year, planters turned librarians, to put the papers into an order. They edited them, changing some of the language and adding notes to make the president more likable to history (Dolley's comments indicated changes, but we don't know what all of the changes were).

At first, Dolley was annoyed by the project because it became very time-consuming and kept her and the president virtual prisoners at Montpelier until the work as finished. After year three of the letters project had concluded in 1824, with the end nowhere in sight, Dolley complained that "this is the third winter in which he has been engaged in the arrangement of papers and the [business] appears to accumulate as he proceeds, so that I calculate its outlasting my patience and yet I cannot press him to forsake a duty so important or find it in my heart to leave him during its fulfillment." She came to enjoy the project, though, and it was concluded primarily due to her hard work on it.[23]

The winter work and worries once again renewed Dolley's hopes to take some trips away from Montpelier, where she often found herself a prisoner, far from the parties, dinners, and glitz of Washington and Richmond. She wanted "to make [her husband] much more [healthy] so when the season advances, for exercise abroad [for neither] he nor I could ever be quite well again if we remained stationary, as we have been for many years past."[24] She always appreciated the beauty and grandeur of Montpelier but regretted that she had been so close to family and friends for sixteen years in Washington and now was far away from everybody. "The spring advances, the flowers are blooming, the trees changing to green & yet my heart is solitary," she lamented in a letter to her sister Anna in 1818. "My eyes overflow with tears as I look around on the beauties of nature & reflect that my sisters are far from me."[25] For that reason, she encouraged all of her relatives and friends to visit her at Montpelier, and most of them made the trip from Washington; she had company just about every week in decent weather.[26]

Some criticized her for losing touch with them because she had moved far from Washington. "I have anticipated with great delight the pleasure of hearing from you since your residence in the country. You remember my dear friend that you promised me at Washington that you would certainly write, but I have waited with the most anxious solicitude in vain, not one line have I received," complained Dolley's friend Jackie Blount in 1817.[27]

Dolley had many letters from friends in Washington and in other capitals describing the high life that she not only was once part of but ran. "Dinner parties are always going on. We dined in company yesterday with Lord Erskine, who really kept the table in an uproar with his witty anecdotes. He is full of animation and uses very decided language at all subjects," wrote Kitty Rush, an old friend who had just moved to London; then she filled an entire page with a description of her social life, a life that Dolley craved.[28]

Some begged her to get away from Montpelier and visit them; one was Maria Scott, who did it, she said, because of "the happiness you create for friends around you." Everybody missed her. "We have thought a great deal about you since you left us," wrote Ellen Coolidge in 1820. Dolley, in quiet, isolated Montpelier, wrote one woman back that she was so bored, "I must therefore write a dull letter." In another, she wrote that "our amusements in this region are confined to books and rural occupations." She wrote her friend Caroline Eustis in Washington that she was living in "the midst of enlightened and amiable people," and she added, "would to heaven we could join you there."[29]

She missed the flashy gossip of Washington. She must have been wide-eyed when she received a note from Ellen Coolidge that James Madison's life-long enemy, John Randolph, had apparently lost his mind. He had roared in the middle of a bank that he had forgotten his name and made an X on a paper for identification. Then he swore he would not return home without a wife and insisted a Miss Wickham, who did not even like him, marry him. Ellen Coolidge chortled, "He is considered perfectly insane!"[30]

Dolley complained to all, "not a mile can I go from home."[31] And she started to tire of people telling her how lovely Montpelier was: "The beauty of the scenery . . ." oohed one woman after a visit there.[32]

Dolley felt herself smothered. She was happy to spend her days caring for her husband, but she was frustrated that her caretaking kept her away from the active and busy life she loved. She wrote that she was "anxious and confined" and received all of her political news from visitors or Washington newspapers. Everything was a step removed for her and the president. They lived just ninety miles from the capital, yet felt a million miles away.

Friends in Washington, knowing of how she missed the world of parties that she had created, kept her abreast of all the social news. Women such as Judith Walker Rives and Phoebe Morris filled her in on all the slight, trivial personal details that Dolley devoured and then passed on to her husband. The Madisons thirsted after all the political news and gossip they could find. Dolley wrote her niece in the spring of 1830, "I confess I do not admire the contention of parties, political or civil, though in my quiet retreat I am anxious to know of all the maneuverings of both, the one and the other, so, be not timid in laying their claims before me, no one shall see statements by myself."[33]

She was just as interested in scandals, such as the Peggy Eaton uproar in the Andrew Jackson administration. Jackson's secretary of state had married Peggy, and she had become the hostess for President Jackson because he was a widower. She fulfilled Dolley's old role. Peggy, though, had been married to another man when she began her affair with Eaton, causing a gossip nightmare for the entire administration. People took sides and did, or did not, attend parties because of their feelings on the scarlet-tinted Peggy. Jackson ordered cabinet officers to visit her and be seen with her at parties; many refused. Dolley loved it and could never get enough of it. She told friends that the inability of Peggy to function as hostess, and her insistence on doing so, would cause trouble. "The conduct of the P[resident] & his cabinet is indeed astonishing & exhibits a melancholy perspective, as well as re-trospect to our country, but I doubt not of, impeachments, by & by, if they go on in this lawless & unfeeling manner."[34]

Eventually, Jackson became so enraged by the entire affair that he fired his cabinet and appointed a new one, causing huge political ruptures in Washington's political, as well as social, life. The news saddened the former First Lady and president. "I'm afraid the license people take with the tongues & pens will blast the good of the country & display all sorts of evil traits of character that can mark a selfish & savage race," Dolley told her sister.[35]

As the years went by, the Madisons' friends visited less and less often. When they did arrive, the Madisons were thrilled to see them. An example was a visit from Sam and Margaret Smith, whom they had not seen in nineteen years, when they last stopped at Montpelier, in 1828. The Smiths did not know what to expect from the president, now seventy-seven, or from Dolley, who had just turned sixty. They immediately caught up on each other's lives. "How we did talk," wrote Margaret Bayard Smith. "We went over the last twenty years and talked of scenes long past and of persons far away or dead. These reminiscences were delightful . . . time seems to favor her as much as fortune. She looks young and says she feels so. I can believe her, nor do I think she will ever look or feel like an old woman."[36]

Their gloom was brightened by two events. First, Madison suddenly felt better after the New Year of 1835. Second, acclaimed British writer Harriet Martineau arrived for a three-day visit to interview Madison. She was writing a multivolume book about the United States. Martineau had already interviewed dozens of national leaders and toured most of the eastern seaboard. She wanted to meet Madison, though, because she believed that everything that was American, and different from the rest of the world, was due to the Constitution that he wrote. She arrived at Montpelier at the end of February, right when Madison was feeling much better and was able to engage people in lengthy conversations.

Martineau had a bumpy carriage ride from Orange Court House to Montpelier on the highway about which Madison always complained bitterly. She found Madison, then eighty-three, very alert and sitting up in a soft chair in his large apartment on the first floor of the mansion. He was propped up on a large pillow and wore a black silk gown, a grey-and-white cap, and gloves to protect his arthritic hands. He was deaf in one ear but heard well in the other, spoke with elegance, had twinkling eyes, and had a well-shaped face for his age. The English writer said that he looked just like the popular engravings of him. He had an "uncommonly pleasant countenance," Martineau said.[37]

Martineau was worried that Madison would not be able to talk for long at each interview session she wanted to conduct, but it was Martineau, not the president, who became exhausted. She had to be taken to a couch to recline every few hours. The eighty-three-year-old president would then get up and pull his chair next to the couch and keep talking.

She was surprised and impressed by the fact that the overriding theme of all Madison's talks was his unshakeable belief in the democratic system and the American people. He had "an inexhaustible faith, faith that a well-founded commonwealth may, as our motto declares, be immortal; not only because the people, its constituency, never die, but because the principles of justice in which such a commonwealth originates never die out of the people's heart and mind."[38]

Martineau was impressed with Dolley, too, whom she found in good spirits. At that point, she had interviewed many public figures who knew the Madisons, and they gave her their own evaluations of Dolley's skills as a First Lady and, behind closed doors, the president's political confidant and adviser. "She is a strong-minded woman, fully capable of entering into her husband's occupations and cares; and there is little doubt that he owed much to her intellectual companionship, as well as her ability in sustaining the outward dignity of his office," Martineau wrote.[39]

Martineau was always surprised at what Madison had to say. The aging president dazzled Martineau with his knowledge of European history and English writers. He talked at great lengths about the history of farming in ancient Rome and how it progressed over the centuries. He stunned Martineau with his beliefs that women should be treated the same as men throughout America and throughout the world.

Early the next morning, the president was up just after sunrise and in the dining room when Martineau and Dolley came downstairs. He was spry and friendly. "The active old man, who declared himself crippled with rheumatism, had breakfasted, risen, and was dressed before we sat down to breakfast," she said in surprise.[40]

Their next two hours were filled with his reminiscences of fifty years of US presidents and government. He knew everybody in every state and analyzed them for Martineau. His letters and newspapers then arrived (he devoured his newspapers every day), but "he threw them aside saying he could read the newspapers every day and must make the most of his time with us. He asked me, smiling, if I thought it too vast and anti-republican a privilege for the ex-presidents to have their letters and newspapers free, considering that they were the only earthy benefit that they carried away from their office," she said.[41]

The next day, Madison told her that he supported the separation of church and state and added that he thought more religious freedom was allowed in America than anywhere else. That day, feeling even better, he gave her a tour of the house, showed her his paintings and busts of famous people, and took her out to the front lawns and back lawns of the home. When the morning newspapers arrived, Martineau noted many stories about politics and France, and Madison went off on a lengthy analysis of France and its ties to the United States. He talked about the governments of England and Russia at length and, again and again, came back to why the United States had been so successful with its new democratic system. He had told her that "in a small republic there is much more noise from the fury of parties while in a spreading but simple working republic, like that of the Union, the silent influence of the federal head keeps down more than ever appear." She then added that he had supreme confidence, still, that a large country with many political views does not bring chaos but organized progress and more freedom, not less.

When she left Montpelier, saying good-bye after three long days of inter-views and conversation, Martineau wrote that "Madison reposed cheerfully, gayly, to the last, on his faith in the people's power of wise self-government."[42]

Madison had been fading. As he passed eighty, he finally began to slow down. He caught the flu just before Christmas in 1827 and took a long time to recover from it. The next summer he was so sick, and for so long, from the bilious indis-position that had bothered him all of his life that he even missed the annual meeting of the University of Virginia board of governors. One year later, he fell victim to another of his numerous bouts with rheumatoid arthritis and found it hard to move his fingers. In the winter of 1832, his arthritis became worse and his hands became useless. That winter, Dolley wrapped his legs in oiled silk and gave him salt baths, but they did not offer much help. He cancelled the annual family trip to Warm Springs in the mountains. "I am still confined to my bed with my malady, my debility and my age, in triple alliance against me. Any convalescence, therefore, must be tedious, not to add imperfect," he wrote that summer.[43]

Everyone who visited him at Montpelier admired Dolley's work as his amateur nurse. She waited on him from sunrise to sunset. "Her devotion to Mr. Madison is incessant and he needs all her constant attention," noted Martineau.[44]

His condition became progressively worse as the year 1835 rolled on. A despairing Dolley said in the early winter of 1835 that "my days are devoted to nursing and comforting my patient, who walks only from the bed in which he breakfasts to the one in the little chamber. . . . Anna [Dolley's niece] who is a sterling girl, stays much at home with me and sleeps beside my bed ever since the illness of Mr. Madison in April. . . . He is better now but not yet well enough to walk across the two rooms."

Madison wrote his cousin, Hubbard Taylor, of "the infirmities belonging to [advanced age] . . . to which are added inroads on my health, which among other effects have . . . crippled my fingers." Throughout 1835 and 1836, unable to move his fingers he dictated most of his letters to Dolley or brother in law John Payne, still battling alcoholism, and signed them in his own hand.[45]

It was a winter in which Dolley became sick, too. She had trouble with her eyes, was constantly fatigued, and, in general, was worn out form taking care of her bedridden husband.[46]

In the balmy spring of 1836, to his surprise, Madison was visited by Charles Ingersoll, an old political friend whom he had not talked to in over twenty years. Ingersoll was traveling through Virginia that spring and slept overnight at an inn at Orange Court House in mid-May. He decided to ride over to Montpelier in the morning for a brief visit to pay his respects to the president and ended up staying for three days.

"He is very infirm, 85 years old last March, never was strong, and is now extremely emaciated and feeble. . . . He cannot sit up, except a little while now and then to rest from reclining on a sofa; and at first, when I saw him, he wore gloves, which were laid aside, however, as the weather became warm. We found him more unwell than usual and with a difficulty of breathing, which affects his speech, so that Mrs. Madison told me I [should] just talk and let him listen. But as I wanted to listen and he appeared to grow better every day; our conversation [was] animated without fatiguing him."[47]

When he was well enough to speak, Madison regaled Ingersoll with stories of George Washington, Thomas Jefferson, Alexander Hamilton, and others. The president talked for a long time on the American system of government. "Mr. Madison's temper is perfectly amiable and the best word I now [use] to describe his love of the country is to call it beautiful or lovely patriotism, such natural profound and pure republicanism," Ingersoll said.[48]

Ingersoll was James Madison's final public visitor.

For Dolley, life became very busy when Madison was in his eighties. She spent most of the day caring for him and the rest of the day worrying about him. She would carry on engaging conversations with visitors in a room of the mansion and then, like a machine that feels tremors miles away, she would blurt out "I must go to Madison," rose and left. He had to be kept warm in winter and be tended to constantly. The former First Lady was her own drug store, inventing different medications for her husband and herself when her eyes became inflamed ("milk and water or cream and sometimes with fresh butter"). She never complained about her new, full-time job as nurse, but she did mutter that visitors never understood how sick he was. "He receives letters & visitors as if he was made of iron, to his great disadvantage & mine," she said.[49]

But all that medical worry was nothing compared to the suffering the Madisons endured in their retirement because of their relationship with their son, Payne.

Dolley was so used to paying Payne's bills in different cities and states that she even established a phrase for the process. She did it to keep him out of jail, she told friends, and said that the debt range of $200 to $300 was "prison bounds."[50]

People always fawned over Payne, but it was in very indirect ways. They wrote her about how handsome he was, how people loved being around him, and what fond memories they had of him as a small boy. The memories and descriptions always rang hollow, as if they were covering up some dark secret. For example, in June 1812, just before the war began, Sally McKean d'Yrugo, the American wife of the Spanish minister, wrote that "your son Payne has been twice to see me, but unfortunately I was out both times; the Marquis saw him and says he is a fine young man, grown so tall and handsome. I shall make an effort to find him today and intend to ask him if he remembers that when a little fellow he pulled off General Van Courtland's wig at the very moment he was making me a flourishing compliment." It was like so many letters sent to her about Payne. They said much, and yet they said little.[51]

People who knew Payne when he was in his early twenties always complimented Dolley about him and rarely complained of his outlandish behavior. Dolley wrote everyone about what wonderful things people had to say about Payne. She told her sister in the summer of 1812, for instance, that "Payne is in Baltimore yet and as much admired and respected as you could wish, he writes me that Mrs. Patterson and Mrs. Bonaparte are very attentive to him and he is invited to all the great houses there. We intend to send him in a few months to Princeton."[52]

Dolley treasured all of the compliments about Payne and the deep feelings of love for him that they stirred within her. But her visions and dreams of her son were far more pleasant than the reality of him. Over the next few years, Payne's troubles would multiply and threaten to bring Montpelier and everything the Madisons owned and cherished toppling to the ground.

24

PAYNE TODD

"The Serpent in the Garden of Eden"

*P*ayne Todd, the tall, thin, handsome, dark-haired, troublesome son of Dolley and James Madison, the life of the party wherever the party was being held, had returned home in the 1820s to Montpelier to be with his parents in retirement. Dolly was certain that if her beloved Payne lived with them at the plantation, she could save him. The former First Lady was a loving mom and a hopeless enabler who gave her son everything he asked for and things he never asked for, or even fantasized about, all in an effort to somehow turn him into the contented young man she dreamed of. He would be married, with children, happily strolling the grounds of Montpelier, smelling the flowers, with a wide smile on his face—someone all could admire. She never realized that his personal problems, which were considerable and did not diminish with time or place, would always prevent that and always leave the former First Lady frustrated and heartbroken.

Payne was impulsive; was a victim to roller-coaster highs and lows; was unable to complete simple tasks; had no regard for money; imposed on his parents and their friends endlessly; failed in all his romances; could not work for anyone else; had no direction in his life; paid no attention to schedules or deadlines; and, everyone said, did not seem to have any genuine feelings of emotion toward people, not even toward his parents. Yet, at the same time, he was very good looking, bright, and charming; and was a marvelous conversationalist, a good dancer, and a dazzling young man full of ambition. He drifted through life, though, with no wife, no family, no job, no money, lots of debts, and no goals. The Madisons were distraught.

He was so irresponsible that the president or Dolley constantly had to write him and tell him to pay his bills. In 1823, for example, Dolley wrote him that his father was angry with him because his debtors kept bothering him for the money. "Your papa tells me to remind you of the debt for papers to Mr. Walsh & the Franklin Gazette."[1]

Payne, who was twenty-six years old when Madison retired, had been like that since he was a small child in Philadelphia. The president had sent him to St. Mary's Seminary, in Baltimore, which was an expensive and refined prep school for the children of the wealthy. He was sent there for eight years so that he could grow both intellectually and as a man, but his time at the school did not change him. The former president had given Payne jobs, important ones, such as a clerk for his diplomatic team sent to Europe to help end the War of 1812, and he had failed at all of them.

There was always veiled anger about Payne in conversations and letters from friends and colleagues. John Quincy Adams, for instance, wrote in his diary that on one morning in Europe he was awakened at daybreak by the noisy end of an all-night card game in the room of Henry Clay, an inveterate gambler. Playing cards with Clay until dawn was young Payne Todd. Adams wrote in his diary, "Just before rising, I heard Mr. Clay's company retiring from his chamber. I had left him with Mr. Russell, Mr. Beutzon and Mr. Todd at cards." Another day, Adams wrote of Payne that "it is surprising he has sufficient talent to succeed in anything he undertakes."[2]

When the commissioners all returned to America, Todd was not with them. Madison's son, who had been in Russia and Europe for two years, did not return home with William Crawford and James Bayard, but went to London with Henry Clay and Albert Gallatin instead. He sent his baggage and artwork he had purchased for the president along to America, in Crawford's care. Back in London, Todd was spending his nights gambling and being with women. The Madisons did not hear from him. When he finally returned to Montpelier, in September, an entire summer late, he revealed that he had run up bills of $6,500 buying art and other items and that he also owed Richard Cutts $1,500 for unknown expenses that Madison assumed were tied to drinking, woman- izing, and gambling. The president had to pay all of Payne's bills and, as always, a small smile on his face, apologize for him to the other commissioners, who, naturally, smiled back and assured him that all had gone well.[3]

The Madisons could not keep track of where their son was going or where he had been. He, like Dolley's brother John, often disappeared for weeks and months on end and did not write to them. Payne ran up incredible bills in a variety of stores and boardinghouses and sent them all to Madison. Even when Madison approved of his spending money, such as for paintings in Paris, Payne spent three and four times what he was allocated and never blinked an eye.

No one understood Payne. If he was Dolley's son, why wasn't he more like Dolley? If Madison had raised him from childhood, why wasn't he more like the president? The Madisons did not understand their son either and told close friends that he had simply, like other young men, fallen victim to the temptations of the world, which was easier for him to do because he was the son of the president.

Given the accounts of him in letters and archives, Payne Todd was probably a sociopath, a person who does whatever he wants to do regardless of the consequences, and regardless of whom he hurts. He, like most sociopaths, was a very good liar and someone who could always talk people into lending him money to pay his bills. All he needed, as sociopaths constantly contend, was a helping hand and a new start. He continually told his parents that maturity would end his problems. He may have added that as the son of a famous man, it was hard for him to succeed in the world because people expected too much. He never worried about anything, was certain someone would get him out of trouble anywhere he found it, and led an aimless life, with no regard for anyone, always knowing that things would work out. And it they did not work out, he did not care.

And he was, like many sociopaths, utterly charming. All of his letters to his parents were written clearly and contained much lucid thinking and emotion. He reported news of the world, and of his life, just like any other son. He let his mother know how her friends, whom he had visited in different cities, were doing. He wrote from Russia, for example, about how appalled he was that the British burned Washington and destroyed the White House, his home. "This act of the enemy meets with universal excoriation and has induced for the first time the Paris journals to publish what was supposed contrary to the inclination of the British Government. I must also regret my absence, for if I could have been serviceable in no other way I might have been perhaps useful to my mother," he wrote in the summer of 1814.[4]

He made friends easily and was considered a sociable young man. Everybody who knew him at first liked him. Eliza Collins Lee took him to a steamship wharf and waved good-bye to him as the boat drifted down river. "[The ship's] smoke reminds me of his departure," she wrote. Dolley's niece, Fanny Madison, praised Payne to her aunt and told her "give my best wishes & thanks to your kind son and tell him his goodness has not been bestowed on ungrateful minds."[5]

But, after a while, the troubled side of Payne wore them all out.

His relationships with women were worse than they were with men. He partied all over America and Europe and dated dozens of women. Some of the relationships lasted for months but, as always, the women simply tired of his boorish behavior and broke off the romance. If he was this way as a boyfriend, what would he be like as a husband?

Payne exhibited odd habits. He complained of pains in his teeth, legs, and arms, and of a lifelong rheumatism. He smoked too much and drank too much. Sometimes he woke up early and sometimes late. When he arose, he would often wrap himself in a blanket and lay in front of the fireplace for hours. He kept records of what he ate, when he drank, and when he abstained. He never signed his letters to his mother. He kept a secret diary in ciphers and was proud of it. He was forty-four when Madison died, but he had the mentality of a teenager. He was intent on running the plantation, just as his father had, but he was incapable of doing that. A manager, William Dixon, ran it, but complained to Dolley, who was in Washington, that Payne was often not around to be consulted or had fled for several weeks, often taking the keys to buildings with him. With Payne gone, there was no formal supervision of the slaves, and they often starved. No work was done.[6]

Payne fell prey to temptation often because he was handsome and had a gregarious personality, and because he was the son of America's chief executive. He was a bona fide celebrity. Everybody wanted him at their parties. All the men wanted to drink with him and all the girls wanted to dance with him. People circled around him at parties, gave him their cards for future contact, and introduced him to their closest friends and family. People cut him in on business deals, went to the races with him, took him to lunch. Men gladly took him to gambling casinos, taverns, and brothels, happy to be of service to him, to enjoy the high life with him. It was a glittery world in which any normal person could tumble into trouble easily, but for a sociopath with money like Payne, it was a world in which one disaster followed another.

His days in Russia were a good example. He and the other American commissioners were invited to the czar's parties at his elegant palaces, with their wide ballrooms and high ceilings, and never-ending flow of liquor, but only royals were permitted to dance with the czar's sister. Payne was allowed to dance with her, though, because he was a president's son. He was invited everywhere, went everywhere, was admitted to every party, and was lauded by all there—because he was "Mr. Madison, the President's son."[7]

The Madisons just wished he could remain at Montpelier, get into a local business of some kind, have an office in Orange Court House, and settle down. He often talked about marriage, family, and helping his stepdad at Montpelier, but nothing ever came of it.

Then, to the surprise of all, in the summer after the Madisons retired to

Montpelier, Payne asked his stepfather to help him buy a 104-acre tract of land near Montpelier so that he could live there and start a silkworm farm that he thought he could turn into a profitable industry. He had met men in Paris who had made small fortunes through the silk business. His parents were thrilled. He could live and work on his business and be nearby. Running the farm and business would give him responsibility and help to turn around his life. Dolley's brother John had moved back to the Orange County area and he was doing better, so why wouldn't the same happen to Payne? They settled on a piece of land a few miles away on the road to Gordonsville. The land was cut in half by a stream and had some rock ledges and a small home that Payne could live in while he started his business. Payne immediately named it Toddsberth.

Now, as a landowner, Payne could vote, hold office, become a respectable citizen, and, Dolley daydreamed, carry on the Madison name in national politics. Toward the end of 1818, Dolley paid $540 for the farm and handed it over to her son. Payne started to remove leaves from mulberry trees at his father's home as food for his silkworms. He hired a silkworm expert from France and brought him over to help with production. At first, he set up his shed, with trays for eggs, near Madison's house, but he later moved it to Toddsberth. Now he needed to keep larvae clean and heat the shed properly, year round, to induce the growth of silk and spin it into sheets. Payne was intrigued by the silkworm industry, and Madison was delighted that his stepson finally seemed to have something to do that made sense. They both waited for the silkworm business to grow.[8]

In April 1820, Payne said that he'd like to visit Dolley's old friend, the very single Phoebe Morris, at her home, Bolton Farms, in Pennsylvania. Dolley's heart leaped. He needed a wife. Then he could have children and she could have grandchildren. She had tried to match Payne up with eligible young women of every persuasion throughout Virginia, and Washington, for years, with no success. She immediately wrote Phoebe and asked if Payne could visit her to renew their friendship. Phoebe, as interested as Dolley in a marriage to Payne, and in a renewal of her own relationship with Dolley, whom she loved, agreed and invited Payne to her farm. She and her family cleaned up the farm, tidied up the interior of the house, ordered special foods and drinks, and awaited his arrival with great anticipation.

Payne left Montpelier in early April and promptly disappeared. No one ever found out where he went. New York? Philadelphia? Baltimore? Europe? Nearly four months later, he finally turned up at the Morris farm, startling Phoebe, who had given up all hope of seeing him again. "[He] has made the most favorable impression in all of our hearts," Phoebe's uncle immediately wrote Dolley. "Indeed, my excellent friend, I can't convey to you the pleasure his company afforded to us all."[9]

And then, as always, Payne tired of Phoebe and left Bolton Farms after just four days. She and her uncle tried to talk him into remaining for at least a few more days, but he refused. Phoebe told Dolley that Payne was probably bored by the slow life at Bolton, far from the exciting nightlife of Philadelphia. She might have put him off, too. "I dare say he has been sufficiently wearied of my questions, for I was so glad to see him and know everything about you, how you looked, what you did and what you put on, etc. all the minute details which I thought my long absence would make reasonable," Phoebe wrote Dolley.[10]

And, too, although it was never expressed, it's possible that Payne was tired of talking to people who talked about nothing but how much they loved his parents.

There was never a good explanation for Payne's departure from the Morris home. He just could not remain there for long. His impulses drove him to move on, and he never considered how his sudden departure would hurt Phoebe. He never understood how his odd activities hurt any of his friends or his parents, and he really did not care.

Phoebe's letter concerning Payne's lack of interest in her was one of the many letters Dolley had received from prospective daughters-in-law and friends who had hosted Payne, whether he was fourteen or twenty-four. Everyone loved him very much and had a very good time with him and wished him all the best of luck. No one ever told Dolley what a problem Payne had been, and would always be, because they did not want to break her heart. These letters and conversations only built up the delusional world in which Dolley Madison resided. "[A friend] wrote me yesterday that you were popular in the city. I should like to be with you to witness it, as the respect and love shown my son would be the highest gratification the world could bestow upon me," she wrote to Payne (this from a woman whose husband was the president of the United States).[11]

Back at Montpelier, an undaunted Dolley forgot about Phoebe Morris and began new schemes with new young women to lure her son into marriage, writing letter after letter to their mothers or friends in an effort to set a meeting and start a romance. After all, she thought, her son was a good-looking young man and was quite enticing. Added on to that, the woman who married him would be a close relation to the president of the United States and would live at Montpelier, which they could expand to an even larger home if need be for Payne and his family. What on earth was wrong?

Their son never abandoned them. He would spend long periods of time, eighteen months to two years, at Montpelier and then go off to another city for months at a time. He would always return to Virginia. Payne did not simply drift aimlessly at Montpelier when he was there. He worked on his silkworm business and spent much time improving and expanding Toddsberth, his new home, eventually finishing the house at five comfortable rooms. He ran errands for his parents, helped to refurbish their house, bought things for them when he traveled, and was of considerable help in emergencies. Although he remained behind in one typhus epidemic, he helped to get both Madisons packed and sent them off to safety from the disease in Baltimore.

Dolley originally told Payne that the epidemic was ebbing. "I had a wish to travel a distance from home on account of the typhus fever, but that fear has been dissipated for the present by the children in the house getting well and the Negroes also. I trust therefore that you will not leave your business unfinished on my account, though I cannot express my anxiety to see you," she wrote.[12]

Paying no attention to her instructions to remain far away, Payne rushed to Montpelier and arranged transportation for his parents to Baltimore, where residents were safe from the fever. An enormously thankful Dolley, telling everyone how her son risked his life to save hers, wrote Payne from there that "I cannot express my desire to see you." She had good reason to thank him, too. The fever and other diseases were the scourge of the country. Edward Coles wrote from New York later that "the influenza, scarlet fever & measles have been very prevalent and by afflicting many persons, and placing many families in mourning, have kept out of society many of its greatest ornaments. Many of the families here that I know, and like best . . . had their houses closed either by sickness or its effects."[13]

But when they returned to Montpelier from Baltimore, the old Payne was waiting for them. He left his silkworm business in the hands of his French worker (the climate in Virginia turned out to be not suitable for silkworms and the business failed) and departed from Toddsberth and Montpelier for various eastern cities. Dolley, in denial, as always, reasoned that travel was good for a young man. And perhaps, somewhere, he would find a wife and she would reshape his life. That was Dolley's never-ending fantasy. Her husband loved Payne but saw right through him. He kept bad news about Payne away from her, told her to stop worrying about him, always expressed that he saw a bright future for him in conversations with her, and extolled his virtues to her. In private, he fumed about his irresponsible, reckless stepson. He also continually paid Payne's bills, each one larger than the next. Altogether, Madison estimated he paid over $60,000 (about $1 million in today's money) to cover Payne's unpaid tabs over the years. He often did not tell his wife about the bill payments because he worried that it might hurt her.

There were times when an irate Madison refused to pay Payne's debts and they mounted. He did not communicate with his son for months one year and refused to send money that Payne requested in his letters. The result was that Payne wound up in debtors' prison, yet again, and Madison, once more, had to bail him out.

If he could not get funds from his father, he borrowed money from his uncle, Richard Cutts, always explaining that there was simply no other way to obtain money.

The Madisons had so little faith in their son's ability to take care of himself that they asked their friends in different cities where he wandered to keep an eye on him, and they did. For example, Sophie Bache and her husband looked out for Payne in Philadelphia and told Dolley that he had been sick but recovered from "the fever." She told Dolley that not only were she and her husband looking after Payne but also that she had friend George Dallas look in on him, too.[14]

The Madisons had to do that because Payne rarely wrote to them or responded to their letters. Dolley often wrote him just to beg him to write back, often reminding him that her letters to him were waiting at the local post office for him to read them. He rarely did.[15]

Dolley received numerous letters from friends in different cities who sent some news of her son. He had been rumored to be engaged to Anne Coles of Williamsburg, but nothing every came of it. There was a woman he met in the Virginia mountains in the summer of 1820, but that relationship went nowhere, too. In 1816, he was said to be ready to marry a young woman who was smitten with him. "She said she had never seen anybody like Mr. Todd," wrote the friend. That relationship, for which Dolley had so much hope, and yet such suspicion died, too. Sarah "Sally" Coles Stevenson, always on the lookout for prospective wives for Payne, wrote Dolley at Christmas 1820, "Tell cousin Payne he will find his old flame disengaged and quite as pretty as ever."[16]

By 1817, when her husband's second term was coming to a close and Payne was twenty-six years old, Dolley confided to a cousin that she was convinced Payne would never marry and that he would "become a rover."[17]

There were other young women in other cities, but those relationships went nowhere. Then there was a surprise letter from Payne in Philadelphia. He was enjoying the city and was involved with a woman, and had been for some time, but it did not seem to be leading anywhere. At about the same time she had received his letter, Henry Clay had asked about Payne. So had many others. They all told the Madisons that perhaps the best way for Payne to mature was for him to live at home with them, so they could keep an eye on him. On the loose, he would always get into trouble.

His mother wrote Payne a sharp letter. "I am ashamed to tell [people] when asked, how long my only child has been absent from the home of his mother! Your Papa and myself entreat you to come to us; to arrange your business with those concerned to return to them when necessary and let us see you here as soon as possible. Your Papa thinks as I do that it would be best for your reputation and happiness, as well as ours, that you should have the appearance of consulting your parents on subjects of deep account to you and that you should find it so on returning to Philadelphia," she said.[18]

Payne told her he was coming home, but he needed $20 to get him there. Dolley, naturally, sent him $30. At other times, she mailed Payne expensive pieces of her jewelry, without telling her husband, and told him to sell the jewelry and use the money to pay his debts or to sustain his high-flying social life. She would casually mention in her notes that she had recently paid off local debts for him, such as $200 he had owed a Mr. Holloway for over two years.[19]

His mother literally pined for him. She told him in 1827 when he was sick in Philadelphia that "I felt so full of fear that you might relapse that I hastened to pack a few clothes & give orders for the carriage to be ready [to see you]."[20]

They did not hear from Payne again and then, just before Christmas, he arrived. There he was, handsome and delightful as ever, as well dressed as any of the dandies in Paris or London. He resumed work in the silkworm shed, joined them for many dinners in the mansion, and greeted all of their old friends during the Christmas holidays. He renewed friendships with cousins he had spent years with as a child and he had hosted on trips to Washington and Richmond. Everyone met him and everyone was enamored by him.

Payne had no real feeling for his mother. He never repaid her loans or money forwarded to him by the president, and he often took advantage of her. The most blatant example of that took place in 1838. Payne talked his mother into giving him fifty acres of Montpelier land, on which stood a gristmill. It was a gift that made Dolley feel good, naturally. What she did not know was that Payne planned to sell the land and pocket the money. He did that four months later. Payne sold forty-one acres to James Newman for $571. Dolley then had no land and no money. It was typical of Payne's relationship to his parents.[21]

In 1824 and 1825, Payne plunged into debt, yet again, and his mother sent him money through the mail to cover his bills. He could not pay his rent, either, and the president paid for that as well. Bills arrived from all over, even a $500 bill from a lottery parlor in Washington, which Madison paid. Madison wrote his son, then thirty-three, "What shall I say to you? Weeks have passed without even a line ... soothing the anxieties of the tenderest of mothers, wound up to the highest pitch by your long and mysterious absence ... as ample remittances were furnished for all known purposes, your continuance where you are under such strange appearances necessarily produces distressing apprehension. Whatever the causes of [your long absence and debts] you owe it to yourself as well as to us to withhold them no longer. Let the worst be known, that the best may be made of it. . . . You cannot be too quick in affording relief to [your other] present feelings."[22]

Payne disappeared again in 1826, and this time events took a dark turn. The Madisons had no word from him but several letters from his creditors. He had piled up bills in Philadelphia and still owed his rent money. Friends paid some of his bills, and Madison thanked them and told them to never do that again. He wrote Payne's landlord that he would cover his bills, but that he would need time to get the money. The landlord threatened to have Payne tossed into debtors' prison, again, if the bill was not paid. Madison then heard from his old political crony in Philadelphia, Postmaster Richard Bache, who said he had cashed Payne's check for $300, but the boy then vanished. He told the president that if Payne did not give him the $300, he would have gone to jail. The president immediately mortgaged 361 acres of land for $2,000 to cover his son's latest debts.

The president's emotions were in a tailspin over Payne, his debts, and his prison terms. "Can it be that though released from detention by one creditor, you have entangled yourself with another? . . . Lose not a moment in making known your real situation that what can be done for it may be done," he said in the dead of winter that year.[23]

Madison wrote his son a sad letter. In it, he told him that he had not told his mother of the most recent of his many unpaid bills that his stepfather had to pay. He asked Payne to come home and stay home so he could keep out of trouble. "Come then, I entreat and conjure you, to the bosom of your parents who are anxious to do everything to save you from tendencies and past errors and provide for comfort and happiness," he said.[24]

That effort did little good. Payne later moved to New York and spent several months there. His arrival home was, as usual, further delayed. In New York he spent time with women, gambled (gambling was legal in New York then and the city was home to numerous gambling dens), and drank. The Madisons had no idea where he was getting his money from or how much he had spent, or owed. Dolley continually covered for him in letters to relatives and friends. She wrote her niece that "[Payne] writes in fine health and spirits and says he will yet be detained two or three weeks longer in that city. I flatter myself with the hope of seeing him soon. No, it's impossible for him to prefer Virginia . . . to the North," she said. It was one of many letters that told us how well Payne was doing and how much everybody liked him and how his travels were making him a real Renaissance man.[25]

Of course, Payne was not a Renaissance man at all, just a man who spent more money than he had. He went back to Philadelphia to spend more money and, in the spring of 1829, again wound up in debtors' prison. Madison, getting ready to attend the Virginia convention that year to write a new state constitution, once again bailed him out. One year later, he had to bail him out of another debtors' prison in Washington. Paying Payne's bills was a routine for Madison, something he was used to doing. In the winter of 1822, Dolley showed James a heartfelt plea from Payne for money so that he could return to Montpelier. "My good M. came in & I consulted him about sending money to P. He directly drew an order & told me to enclose it to you, that I must beg you to send to him directly if you can, hire a messenger, do so," she wrote Anna Cutts.[26]

The Madisons were in so much of a hurry to pay Payne's bills directly or through intermediaries that they even gave the intermediaries tips ranging up to $20 for a few minutes' work and paid the intermediaries' expenses for any travel they incurred in a visit to Payne.

Payne would have gone to jail in New York, too, but John Jacob Astor loaned him $600 to pay off his bills. He gave him another $1,600 to cover his debts on similar binges in Philadelphia and Germantown. Payne took money that Astor gave him for those debts and lost it in a gambling casino. Creditors kept following him for the $1,600 he owed, and Madison had to get one of his tobacco agents in Virginia to pay the bill. Madison then mortgaged more of his land to raise money to cover the debt. His former secretary Edward Coles, who knew Payne well, once loaned Madison $2,000 to pay Payne's debts.

Dolley begged her son to return home in order to stay away from the dens of temptation that she felt were ruining his life. Friends told Payne that his mother was getting sick over his absences. His uncle wrote him that his return would have a "beneficial effect in tranquilizing her nervous agitation. . . . She has been lying down since this morning complaining of great chilliness and shivering."[27]

Despite his mistreatment of her, Dolley never deserted her son. She constantly wrote him loving letters that, between the lines, begged him to calm down and simply be normal. She told him of their retirement and of news in the lives of his cousins. She wrote in one letter that she had no real reason to write but that she just enjoyed "the pleasure of repeating how much I love you and to hear of your happiness." She would often close her letters to him with "May Heaven bless thee."[28]

By this time, 1830, the Madisons were at their low point in their relationship with their son. Dolley, ever the enabler, was upset that he could not mature as she wanted him to and was forever spending money, money she did not have. In 1809, Dolley had sold the Madisons' properties in Philadelphia (at much lower prices than she expected) to pay Payne's debts that, by that time, were running about $3,000 per year (about $51,000 today). His bills were even higher in the 1830s.[29]

Their son was also a victim of the debtors' prison phenomena of the late 1830s. The recession caused by the Panic of 1837 had caused such financial strife that debtors were thrown into prison in order to get their friends or families to pay off what they owed in order to free them. Payne wound up in debtors' jails several times.

The president, who had put up with Payne all of his life, wrote Coles a melancholy note that reflected his feelings about his wayward child. "His career must soon be fatal to everything dear to him in life … with all the concealments and alleviations I have been able to effect, his mother has known enough to make her wretched the whole time of his strange absence and mysterious silence."[30]

By the mid-1830s, Payne was settled in his spendthrift and irresponsible ways, and the Madisons knew it. The president continually wrung his hands over his son, but Dolley was resolved to keep sending him money. Now, she rationed, the funds were not to help him live his profligate life but to keep him out of prison in whatever city he wandered into. His mother had simply given up on him. Finally.

She wrote him in 1835, "I was glad to hear [my letter] with the enclosure [money] reached you. You did not tell me whether you had been successful in your collections. If not, you will want supplies proportioned to your detention; I am anxious that you should have them, and you know the little I have in my power is at your command, though but a 'drop in the bucket.'"[31]

And she always warned him to keep out of whatever towns where he had found trouble. "You will finish your business 'ere you leave a place which you may not find it convenient to return to directly," she said once of his stay in Washington, where he always borrowed money that he could not pay back.[32]

The more the Madisons helped their son, the more they hurt themselves. The farm business was failing in the 1820s and 1830s. When it did improve, the shortage of laborers at Montpelier, due to sales of slaves to raise money to pay Payne's debts, left a small workforce that could not accomplish much, anyway.

Everybody sympathized with the Madisons and their struggles with their son. Edward Coles, who knew the Madisons and Payne, probably summed it up best in describing Payne's life at Montpelier: "[He is] the serpent in the Garden of Eden."[33]

But the worst was yet to come as Payne's irresponsibility grew and he turned his claws on his parents.

25

THE MADISONS

Slavery and Stormy Years

*W*hen James Madison was a little boy, he played on his Virginia farms with young slave children whom his father owned. He went to the College of New Jersey for higher education and brought along a slave, Sawney, to act as his valet. When he traveled to the Continental Congress during the American Revolution, he was accompanied by a slave. When he married Dolley, their house was full of Madison's slaves. More slaves worked for him on his plantation and in Washington when he was secretary of state and when he was president. He retired to Montpelier, which was worked by nearly one hundred slaves, and spent much of his time each day working with and talking to his slaves. All of his meals were cooked and served by his slaves. When he looked out the window of his bedroom on the second story of the Montpelier mansion in the morning, he stared at his slaves' dozens of wooden cabins one hundred yards down the slope in front of the home or thirty yards east of it; when he went to sleep at night, he peered out at the slave cabins again. Madison lived in a world of unending slavery.

Madison's life was like that of many slave-owning planters in Virginia. Slaves worked large farms that produced profits for their owners. Some planters, such as George Washington and Robert Carter, had more than three hundred. Most slave owners had only a handful, often just two or three. And these slave owners did not even represent the majority of Virginians; three quarters of Virginians did not own any slaves at all. The large plantation owners, wealthy men like Madison, controlled the state and county governments and helped to run the Federalist and Republican Parties. They used their influence, political clout, and extensive network of friends to perpetuate slavery. It had thrived in

Virginia since shortly after the establishment of the disease-ridden Jamestown plantation in the early 1600s. By 1817, when Madison retired, slaves made up nearly half of the population of Virginia and, thanks to slavery, the plantation-ridden state was one of the most prosperous in America.

Madison hated slavery. He had spoken out and written against it all of his life. He was blunt about it, too. When the Constitution was being argued in 1787, southerners insisted that their slaves be counted as three-fifths of a white man to help them in population counts that would earn them congressional seats and give them power in the new government. Madison said the issue was strictly over "having and not having slaves." He had argued at the convention, too, that pushing back the stoppage of the slave trade from Africa from the proposed year of 1800 to 1808 would not make any difference in what he said was an evil practice. He also sneered that the clever insertion of the word *migration* into official government documents to describe the movement of people from Europe to America also included the movement of slaves from Africa to the United States and from one slave state to another, which he opposed.[1]

In 1789, as the new government was taking office, Madison wrote a long memo calling for the creation of a colony in West Africa where freed blacks and freed slaves could be sent from the United States to end slavery here and return tens of thousands of blacks back to their homeland.

He also urged establishing some western colony in America, in the new and unsettled frontier on the Great Plains, where transported slaves could establish new lives for themselves as free men and free women. Madison told everybody he knew that he was opposed to slavery. Visitors to Montpelier recalled his recoiling from the practice in conversations and horseback-riding trips around the plantation. One woman wrote that Dolley always blurted out in conversations that no slaves were whipped at Montpelier and that everything that could be done to make their lives more tolerable was done by the Madisons. The couple had to talk about it continually, though, because as the years went by, the issue became more and more controversial in Virginia and in the nation. The Madisons rarely brought up the subject of slavery; slaves appear in very few of their letters and public speeches, and when they are mentioned they are usually referred to as "the hands" and not "the slaves."

Back in the mid-1780s, just after the end of the Revolutionary War, Madison wrote Edmund Randolph that he wanted "to depend as little as possible on the labor of slaves." In 1785, he spoke up in the state assembly to support a bill introduced by Thomas Jefferson to bring about the gradual emancipation of slaves in Virginia (it was defeated). He and Jefferson were applauded for their efforts by the heads of antislavery organizations in both the North and the South.[2]

And yet later, when he had power, whenever he had the chance as a congressman or as president to actually introduce or support legislation to end slavery, Madison always backed off. During Madison's first term in the Continental Congress, Benjamin Franklin tried to get him to champion a bill to end slavery and he refused. Madison said the reason was that it would annoy slaveholding congressmen. "The number of vessels employed in the trade to Africa is much greater than I should have conjectured. It hope it will daily diminish and soon cease altogether ... should the evil still go on, it continues to be my opinion that the interposition of the general government ought to be applied as far as may be constitutional. ... At present I not only flatter myself that the necessity may not exist but apprehend that a revival of the subject in Congress would be equally unseasonable and unsuccessful."[3]

No matter how loudly or how often the Madisons wailed against slavery, though, they would not divest themselves of their slaves. Neither did Jefferson or the others. The South's prosperous planters complained about slavery, excoriated it, pitied their slaves, and vowed to get rid of them, but when they all died, they still had their slaves. Patrick Henry, another slaveholder in that era and a long-time political foe of Madison, explained their feelings best when he said of slaves that "I am drawn along by the general inconvenience of living without them; I will not, I cannot, justify it." Then Henry added that he had to keep them. "If we cannot reduce this wished for reformation to practice, let us treat the unhappy victims with lenity, it is the furthest advance we can make towards justice. It is a debt we owe to the purity of our religion to show that it is at variance with that law which warrants slavery." Many of them believed future calamities would occur because of slavery. "Indeed I tremble for my country when I reflect that God is just; that his justice cannot sleep forever," said Jefferson.[4]

The Madisons and their friends were not only lenient toward their slaves, but, gingerly, brought them into their activities, always there against the walls at Christmas, out in the yard in summer, with them, smiling, at barbecues, taking care of the kids and enjoying the family travels. They saw the slaves as friends without any official acknowledgment and believed that the slaves saw them that same way. Older slaves were lovingly referred to as "uncles." The Madisons would refer to their help as part of the extended family, such as Dolley's note to her niece in which she wrote lovingly that "even the old negroes and young ones want to see you."[5]

Dolley's cousin, Sarah "Sally" Coles Stevenson, joked about bumpy roads and slaves that "unless indeed Uncle Sam was on the box, a very respectable old gentleman everywhere, but with the reins in his hands I shall never forget the fright he gave me."[6]

Madison's best friend, Jefferson, was one of the most strident voices against slavery in the country. He had even tried to write a clause into the Declaration of Independence that denounced it. He told people all of his life how much he hated slavery. Yet Jefferson did not free his slaves, despite severe criticism of his behavior by many, north and south. In his lifetime, Jefferson owned approximately six hundred slaves; he freed a total of just seven. He even allegedly carried on a long-term love affair with one, Sally Hemings, and had six children with her. His own solution was taking good care of his slaves. He believed that in providing them with shelter, clothing, and food, and extensive freedom within the plantation, he was behaving in a Christian way. He told others that slave owners had a moral obligation to care for their slaves, their "people." To free them, they said, would be to turn them loose in a country where they would be unable to function. Slave owners would care for them; others would not. Slaves were better off in bondage, Jefferson contended, provided for by loving owners such as himself. Nobody followed that mantra for a longer time, and more fervently, than James Madison.

Thomas Jefferson was challenged, and harshly, by antislavery advocates. One of the fiercest was Edward Coles, James Madison's secretary, who also badgered Madison on the issue of slavery. Coles wrote Jefferson in 1814 that he should lead the movement to free the slaves "from your known philosophical and enlarged view of subjects and from the principles you have professed and practiced through a long and useful life." He added that "I hope the fear of failing, at this time, will have no influence in preventing you from employing your pen to eradicate this degrading feature of British Colonial policy, which is still permitted to exist, notwithstanding its repugnance" as well to "the principles to our evolution as to our free institutions." Coles added that Jefferson's leadership of the antislavery cause, even more so than his presidency, would make him a great man.[7]

In his reply, Jefferson shrugged off his criticism and told him that most Virginians were not against slavery. He told all that he was too old to lead an antislavery movement anyway and that leaders from the next generation had to do that. Madison averted Coles's attack, too, telling him again and again that he agreed with him but could do little to end slavery.

Like all southern slave owners, Madison believed that without slaves his farms would go bankrupt. None of the slaveholders in Virginia embraced the idea that paid workers toiled harder for salary and bonuses and, in the end, made farms more profitable than slave-run farms. Farms in the northern states that did not have slaves in 1817 succeeded on that basis, and their owners suggested the concept to southerners for two hundred years. They were sneered at.

By the time Madison retired, there were numerous antislavery societies in Virginia, begun by the Abolition Society in Richmond, founded by Robert Pleasants in 1790, and the Society of Friends, the Quakers, which had a Virginia Meeting organization thriving in the state at the same time. They even hired agents from Virginia to travel through other southern states looking for runaway slaves to rescue. In 1785, the General Committee of the Virginia Baptists criticized slavery as "contrary to the word of God." In 1790 they condemned it as "a violent deprivation of the rights of man and inconsistent with a republican government" and urged Baptists to do everything legally possible to eliminate it.[8]

Madison, Jefferson, and others saw the emancipation of slaves by sympathetic and well-intentioned owners as misguided idealism that had to be cut off before it could spread throughout Virginia and the South. As long as owners took care of their slaves, they assured everyone, all would be well.

Leading planters in the state became officials of some of the antislavery societies. The organizations gained many followers but could never get legislation outlawing slavery passed. Leading political figures always talked them out of it. George Washington tried to get a bill introduced in the House of Burgesses to eliminate slavery in the late 1760s and was persuaded by other legislators to withdraw it. In 1774, he and George Mason published the Fairfax Resolves in numerous newspapers that called for the elimination of slavery.[9]

James Madison was deeply conflicted by slavery. He opposed it everywhere he could and in any public gathering that would listen to him, but, in fact, he was one of the slaveholding public officials who, although championing the prohibition of slavery, worked hard to make sure no laws were passed to eliminate it. In 1791, Pleasants wanted to introduce a bill to end slavery in the Virginia legislature. Madison dissuaded him, rather bluntly, telling him that "those from whom I derive my public station are known by me to be greatly interested in that special of property, and to view the latter in that light."[10]

Madison's views of slavery had been further upended by stern criticism of the institution by George Washington. During the American Revolution, Washington warned Americans that they should stop arguing that they needed to be free because they had become slaves to England. He fumed that none could make that charge because many Americans owned slaves themselves. New Jersey minister Samuel Allinson wrote that it would be the "lasting disgrace" of Congress to argue that America was enslaved and not to free the real slaves here "if they should spend so much time to secure their own liberties and leave no vestige of their regard to those of their fellow men in bondage to themselves." Foreigners agreed. A British philosopher, Thomas Day, wrote in 1776 that "if there be an object truly ridiculous in nature, it is an American patriot, signing resolutions of independence with the one hand and with the other brandishing a whip over his affrighted slaves." Writers were in agreement with Day; Thomas Paine, whose inspirational pamphlets helped to fuel the early days of revolution, added, "If they could carry off and enslave some thousands of us, would we think it just?"[11]

Madison knew what the arguments in favor of slavery were, and they were repeated to him all of his life by friends and relatives. They were succinctly stated by a man who adopted the pseudonym Eliobo in a continuing series of letters depicting the pros and cons of slavery in the *New Jersey Journal* newspaper in the winter of 1780–1781. Madison, in Congress in Philadelphia at that time, read every newspaper he could find and must have perused this one.

Eliobo's arguments for slavery were (1) owners provide for slaves' basic needs in life, such as food and shelter; (2) blacks were lazy and could not function in society; (3) slaves were happy; (4) freed blacks will rape white women; (5) freed slaves will obtain firearms and get what they want by force; and (6) freed slaves would join forces with American Indians and attack white villages. In some form, all slaveholders agreed with the arguments of the letter. Those against the arguments, such as Madison, knew that many of their neighbors embraced them.

Charles Cotesworth Pinckney of South Carolina had told friends that many opposed the Bill of Rights to Madison's Constitution because such legislation usually said that "all men are by nature born free" yet "a large part of our property consists in men who are actually born slaves."[12]

Many of Madison's friends were members of antislavery societies. Tench Coxe, one of his friends from the revolution, belonged to the Pennsylvania Abolition Society and kept him abreast of their work. He even told Madison at one point that the group had been trying to get Benjamin Franklin to introduce an antislavery measure at the Constitutional Convention, but that did not happen.

Many Virginians considered slavery a curse on their state. When Kentucky separated from Virginia and its officials met to discuss their new constitution, David Rice, who had moved there from Virginia, told them that "holding men in slavery is the national vice of Virginia."[13]

When Madison was president, several leaders of large abolitionist organizations met with him in an effort to engage his official support of their antislavery crusade. In the winter of 1813, as he was consumed in work over the war with England, he met with a representative of the Pennsylvania Abolitionist Society. Afterward, they released a statement that blasted slave owners. "That notwithstanding the laws which Congress have enacted inhibiting the slave trade, as well as for the punishment of citizens who may be concerned in the infraction of them, the inhuman, and unjust commerce in African subjects, continues in defiance of those laws and in violation of every honorable and benevolent principal to be pursued by some American merchants." The document went on to state that its members had proof that seventy thousand men and women were kidnapped from Africa in 1810 and illegally taken to the United States as slaves. They were transported and delivered, the abolitionists charged, because foreign governments and the US government did nothing to stop the slave trade. Officials just looked the other way. They begged Madison to step in and curb it. He did not.[14]

Many antislavery leaders argued that if legislators would not end slavery, God would punish the entire country. One said that slavery was "a solemn mockery" and "insult to God" and that "the national sanction and encouragement [of slavery] ought to be considered as justly exposing us to the displeasure and vengeance of Him, who is equally Lord of all."[15]

The editor of the *Connecticut Courant* newspaper howled that "the existence of slavery may be viewed as one forcible cause of a final separation of the United States" and called slavery "extreme wickedness."[16]

Yet, at the same time, columns ran in newspapers, both in the North and in the South, stating that a study of slavery in ancient Rome and Greece showed that bondage did not make those nations weaker; it made them stronger. Southern congressmen extolled it in their speeches and, if they didn't directly applaud it, warned others that southerners believed in it. "I will tell the truth," said one southern lawmaker. "A large majority of the people in the southern states do not consider slavery as even an evil."[17]

When confronted directly with slavery, Madison often retreated from his position of a slave owner to that of a libertarian, or so he thought. When he went home to Virginia at the end of a term in the Continental Congress, in 1783, he sold his slave Billy, who had lived with him for several years. Under Pennsylvania law, Billy would then be free after seven years. Madison wrote his father that Billy had become "too thoroughly tainted to be a fit companion for fellow slaves in Virga.," and that he was "covering that liberty for which we have paid the price of so much blood, and had proclaimed so often to be right & worthy the pursuit, of every human being."[18]

He pushed his "back to Africa" theory from his early twenties until his death. None of his slaves wanted to go to Africa, though. They were Americans and wanted to remain here. British writer Harriet Martineau was surprised when Madison told her that the slaves were opposed to going to Africa. "He accounted for his selling his slaves by mentioning their horror of going to Liberia, a horror which he admitted to be prevalent among the blacks," she wrote.[19]

Those slaves who remained with him all of his life, such as Paul Jennings, liked him. Jennings wrote that he was close to Madison and never saw the president lose his temper toward any slave on the plantation or in the White House. But many of Madison's slaves, whom he thought loved him and his wife, were very happy to leave him when sold to someone else. He noted that in letters to friends. He sold several to a county neighbor to pay a debt in 1819. "I am persuaded [he] will do better by them than I can, and to whom they gladly consent to be transferred," he wrote Edward Coles.[20]

Madison's views on slavery were never seriously challenged. Life rolled on in both slave states and free states, speeches were made and speeches were ignored, tobacco sold and profits appreciated. Then, in 1820, came the storm over the Missouri Compromise. Following heated debates, as a solution to the entry of more states into the Union and as a way to quell a brewing social and political storm, Congress decided to admit Missouri as a slave state and, to balance the number of free and slave states, to admit Maine, which had broken free of Massachusetts, as a free state.

Madison agreed with those who wanted Missouri admitted as a slave state, but for an odd reason. He told friends that Missouri would not be invaded by a large number of slaveholders with hundreds of slaves, but probably by hundreds of families each with just a few slaves. Those slaves, he believed, would have better lives until the day, up ahead, when slavery was ended in the country. He stuck to his views against a tidal wave of antislavery invective against the Missouri Compromise by hordes of northerners who were growing increasingly unhappy about the power of slavery in the growth of America.[21] The arguments over the Missouri Compromise showed, too, that Virginia's slaveholders and political leaders, such as Madison, were not really in favor of eliminating slavery after all; they just wanted to delay it, hoping the antislavery movement would die. It would not.

Madison was always afraid, like many, of what Jefferson said in a wonderful metaphor about slavery: holding the wolf by the ears and being afraid to let him go.

Madison had written the marquis de Lafayette in 1820, five years before his arrival in America for a much-heralded tour, of the "dreadful fruitfulness of the original sin of the African trade" and fended off attacks by Lafayette when he toured Montpelier later. Madison continually told Lafayette that he wanted to free his slaves, but he kept turning his back on all opportunities to do so. Fanny Wright, Lafayette's feminist companion on his 1825 tour, later wrote Madison and said she wanted to set up a farming collective made up of freed slaves. The bondsmen and bondswomen would work for a certain amount of time to pay off the price of their freedom and, at the same time, be taught how to read and write and run a farm. After a certain point in time, they would be freed and given farmland. She was very confident the collective would work. Madison sneered at her. He told her discipline could not be maintained on such a farm and that "the prospect of emancipation at a future day will sufficiently overcome the natural and habitual repugnance to labor."[22]

Madison's alternative idea, hatched in 1819, was to institute a gradual system of emancipation so that plantations would not be left workerless when manumission was accomplished. He was not certain how to do it, but he told friends it was the best plan. Part of it was to get the federal and state governments to sell off millions of acres of public property and use the revenue to pay slaveholders for their slaves and to grant slaves their freedom. The slaveholders, with all that money, could then begin a new system of paid-labor farming and hire back tens of thousands of black and white paid laborers.

He estimated that all of the money needed to free the slaves, some $600 million, could be raised with the sale of 200 million acres, or just one third of total public lands, at a very reasonable $3 per acre. It seemed like a good solution for everybody. "And to what object so good, so great, so glorious could that peculiar fund of wealth be appropriated?" he asked.[23]

The president never seemed to think through his abolition plans. He insisted on gradual emancipation for blacks, who insisted with equal fervor on immediate freedom. He was convinced that his plan would work because the need for slaves had declined since farming, in general, had declined. He never injected the cotton industry, starting to boom in the late 1820s, into this equation; planters needed more, not fewer, slaves.

One thing he did do, though, and constantly bragged about, was to buy and sell slaves with contracts that called for their emancipation after a few years, usually five or seven. These agreements enabled him to free slaves on a delayed basis. In 1804, Madison purchased a slave named David for $400. "It being understood," his wife wrote, "that at the expiration of five years he is to become free & that in the meantime Mr. M. is to be his owner." Dolley did the same. In 1810, Francis Scott Key worked out an arrangement in which Dolley would loan her black freedman servant Joe $200 with which he could use as an advance to purchase the freedom of his wife from Key. The husband and wife would then work for a certain number of years as paid workers and pay off the rest of the price of the wife. Dolley agreed. The Madisons based these contract ideas on established British slavery views from earlier times, that slaves could be considered like indentured servants and bonded for a specific period of time. This way, in a few years, Madison could actually "free" his slaves, or so he argued.

To their credit, the Madisons also tried to hire freed blacks when they could, rather than buy more slaves. In 1808, friend John Tayloe found two coachmen in Richmond, both freed blacks, for the Madisons. One was hired. Three other freed blacks were hired to work in the gardens of Montpelier.[24]

Madison was named the president of the American Colonization Society in 1833, a few years before his death and, even though ill during most of his term as leader of the group, he helped them gain publicity and raise money. He lobbied for the group, via letters, with Congress. Visitors told him that his plan to have all northerners pay half the cost of transportation to Africa would never work. They didn't own slaves; why should they be burdened by the cost? He waved them all off. Since northern merchant ships had brought the slaves to America, northerners were responsible for paying the cost of sending them back, he insisted, completely blind to reality. The slaves had to go to Africa, he argued. They could not remain in America because they would be unable to intermingle with the whites, despite the fact that tens of thousands of them freed after the revolution in the north had done just that, and successfully, even though it was painful.

Madison paid no attention to charges that the colonization movement had made little progress under his presidency and during his membership. The slave movement in America was now huge and slavers threatened to take their bondsmen and bondswomen into the new territories and, in time, get those territories made into slave states. After all, over the last several decades, the thirteen original colonies had added eleven more states, with more states in the Louisiana Territory probable within the next ten or twenty years. There would soon be one million slaves in America and the "peculiar institution" was a hot issue in each state, yet all Madison worried about was putting a few hundred slaves on ships to send back to Africa.

He ignored any and all other solutions for the freedom of the slaves. One of the best sent to him was from his own former secretary, Edward Coles. The visionary Coles moved from Virginia to Illinois, a free territory, so that he could free his slaves and start his own life all over again in a state not crippled by slavery. Coles freed his slaves on the way to Illinois, gave them farmland, and showed them how to live on it as free men and how to cultivate it. He remained with them for several months, providing instructions so that they could make it on their own as freemen farmers. It worked.

Madison congratulated Coles, writing him, though, that his plan only succeeded because of his help. He said that "with the habits of the slave, and without the instruction, the property, or the employments of a freeman, the manumitted blacks, instead of deriving advantage from the partial benevolence of their masters, furnish arguments against the general efforts in their behalf."[25]

Coles had acted swiftly and successfully; Madison never did. He continued to complain about slavery and yet continued to do nothing to end it.

As the slavery issue grew in intensity through the 1830s, politicians in South Carolina began to suggest that their state, and perhaps other southern states, leave the Union and form their own government in order to protect slavery. This alarmed Madison. He did not believe the pro- and antislavery clashes could actually split the government of the country he had personally designed at the Constitutional Convention. He wrote Henry Clay, "What madness in the South to look for greater safety in disunion. It would be worse than jumping out of the frying pan into the fire; it would be jumping into the fire for fear of the frying pan."[26]

Madison seems to have trusted his slaves even though a slave, with assistance from two others, murdered his grandfather Ambrose Madison in 1732. One of the slaves was hanged for the slaying and the other two received twenty-nine lashes for conspiring with the killer.[27]

The most slaves Madison ever owned at once was 108 in 1802. He sold many off in the 1820s when the economy went bad. Madison did not rid himself of one or two, either, but sold them in large bunches. In October 1834, as the leaves added a magnificent hue to the surroundings at Montpelier, he sold sixteen more to W. H. Taylor. He sold entire families and couples, together. By 1834, his scant farming income had to be made up somewhere and the president found some salvation in unloading his slaves. He did not free them, but sold them, thinking that in letting them go somewhere else he had, in a sense, liberated them, but he only liberated them from Montpelier. He sold nearly two thirds of his slaves between 1802 and 1834, but his revenue from all of that traffic still left him near the bankruptcy line. He had profited from slavery, but now, with the value of slaves much lower due to the general farming recession in the South, Madison was actually losing money on his investment in slaves. The president continued to sell off hundreds of acres of land during that time to pay his bills and the debts of his son and others. Madison had no real investments from which to get cash and had no involvement in nonslave farming to earn money. He had become a victim of the slaver economy and did not have a solution to his problems, which continued to mount as he aged. The Madisons realized, too, that by selling their hardest-working slaves in order to obtain funds to pay off their son's debts, they were now left with those who were too young or too old to work very hard, and their farm business fell off considerably.

He insisted that churches had convinced slaveholders to treat their labor force with more leniencies and this made the lives of the South's hundreds of thousands of slaves better. Masters now made their slaves Christians and took them to church. Others often brought doctors and nurses to their plantations on regular visits to care for their slaves. Some spent extra money on clothing for slaves, let them sell crafts they made at city and village markets, gave them guns for hunting, and wrote passes so they could visit friends and family on other plantations.

Madison had told overseer Mordecai Collins always to make certain that there was an extra cow on hand which could be milked by the slaves for their tables. They also had to have extra food kept in special barrels to be eaten at their leisure. The overseer was advised "to treat the Negroes with all the humanity & kindness consistent with their necessary subordination and work."[28]

Madison often scolded slaves but never permitted overseers to whip them. He wrote his father once that a slave who had misbehaved on a trip with him to Fredericksburg was given some "serious reprehensions and threats from me, which have never lost their effect."[29]

His slaves appreciated his attitude. One, Paul Jennings, who was with him from 1810 until his death, said that "whenever any slaves were reported to him as stealing or 'cutting up' badly, he would send for them and admonish them privately, and never mortify them by doing it before others, they generally served him faithfully. He was temperate in his habits."[30]

But why didn't he free his slaves and start a new life as a farmer with paid labor? One answer might have come from Thomas Clarkson, the leading British abolitionist during Madison's retirement, whose efforts to end the slave trade in British-held territories had failed. Clarkson wrote that abolitionists believed that in England, as well as in America, the end of the African slave trade would mean better treatment for slaves on American plantations and eventual freedom, but that did not happen. "We did not sufficiently take into account the effect of unlimited power on the human mind. No man likes to part with power and the more unbounded it is, the less he likes to part with it."[31] Was that the view of Madison, not only a man of power on the plantation and in Orange County but also formerly the most powerful man in America?

His wife, who said she was as opposed to slavery as the president, continued to utilize her domestic slave staff to provide labor for her lavish parties, as she had done in Washington. She organized all of the female and male servants, gave them instructions before each soiree, and oversaw their work. She had them live in slave cabins within fifty yards of the mansion so they could be called upon whenever she needed them. Each morning, she met with a slave "manager" and went over the day's work in the mansion with her. Throughout the day, Dolley supervised the work of the slaves and gave them keys to buildings and cabinets that she kept on a large keychain tied around her waist. She told all of her visitors how much she deplored slavery and yet, like her husband, used her slaves to provide her with a comfortable life.

Dolley kept her relations with her domestics very quiet. She wrote no more than a few lines about her slaves in her hundreds of letters to friends and rarely talked about them, except to remind one and all that the Madisons' slaves were never whipped. Like her husband, she spent her adult life bemoaning slavery and yet did nothing to free the slaves or help the antislavery crusade. Privately, she complained bitterly about her slaves, especially in her retirement, when she thought slaves took advantage of her age and her husband's infirmity. In the summer of 1818, for instance, she complained to her sister Anna that her most trusted slave, Sukey, was annoying her constantly. "Sukey has made so many deprivations on everything, in every part of the house that I sent her to Black Meadow [one of their farms] last week but find it terribly inconvenienced to do with her & suppose I shall take her back again, as I feel too old to undertake to bring up another," she said, and then, heatedly, she added "so I must even let her steal from me to keep from labor myself, more than my strength will permit, I would buy a paid but good ones are rare & as high as $8 & $900s."[32]

She never looked at her slaves as real people. In 1822, she wrote her sister Anna about a business transaction involving a number of items and listed them as "furniture, the negro girl, cow," with no differentiation between the three. Whenever she referred to guests who brought slaves with them, she added them to the entourage, like horses. In 1806, she talked of "Mrs. Randolph and suite stayed until yesterday morning. I sent Kitt with their Negroes."[33]

Dolley had a dim view of slaves as workers and once described the hands who worked in her orchards as "lazy women." She wrote several people that her slaves simply would not work without an overseer pushing them to finish their chores each day. Yet, at the same time, she always insisted that the overseers who worked for her did not beat her slaves and treated them well. "As to over-seers, I'm glad you refused the first two, Burnly and Shackleford. No whipper of negroes should ever have our people or any others," she said.[34]

Payne Todd was callous toward his slaves and often used them as barter in business transactions or to settle a debt. He had dinner with a man in 1843 and tried to sell him two teenaged male slaves to help satisfy his mother's debts, something his mother did not know about. The man, who did not trust Todd, said the offer seemed "suspicious" and paid no attention to it.[35]

Dolley, like her husband, knew all about the various slave insurrections that had taken place in Virginia. Slave Gabriel Prosser led a revolt in 1800 in Richmond. The hundreds of insurgent slaves planned not only to capture or kill a number of white merchants and planters in the state capital but also to kidnap the Madisons' friend, Governor James Monroe. Friends in Richmond told them all about it. In 1811, five hundred slaves rebelled in Louisiana, and one hundred were killed in battles with whites. Later, in 1811, slave Denmark Vesey planned a large insurrection in Charleston, but it was scuttled and he was hanged. In 1831, there was an even larger slave rebellion, this one led by Nat Turner, in which fifty-one whites were murdered, many in Virginia. The whites throughout the state were badly shaken by it. There is no way to tell what Dolley really thought, but in the letters that do exist, she paid little serious attention to it. "I am quiet, knowing little about it and that I cannot help myself if I am in danger. I hope we will all be on our guard after this," she wrote a friend about Vesey's rebellion.[36]

Madison's dogged insistence on keeping slaves, despite his moral abhorrence of the practice, helped to bring about the tragic economic downfall of his family. He spent so much money on buying slaves and on slave upkeep that he had none left for farm equipment or even for the basic upkeep of his mansion and other buildings at Montpelier. When Charles Ingersoll visited him in 1836, he was astonished at how run-down the entire plantation seemed.

Madison, and his friends throughout Virginia, held onto slavery as the foundation of their economy, constantly ignoring paid-labor plans suggested by others, the pleas of northern congressmen, abolitionist leaders, civic organizers, and ministers. They would not let go. In the North, the Industrial Revolution began to flourish in the early 1830s with the success of the Erie Canal and others, the growth of the cities, and the explosion of manufacturing. Its non-slave society flourished. In the South, slavery was an albatross for all. It held them back from exploring manufacturing and shipping and the use of their extensive land holdings for anything other than slave-driven tobacco, sugar, and cotton production. Controversies over slavery divided neighbors and friends, and it was under attack from churches following the Great Awakening. The Madisons never let go of slavery, and, in the end, it brought about their ruin, and the ruin of many. Ellen Coolidge, a relative of Thomas Jefferson, whose slave plantation was bankrupt at his death, said that northerners were "at least a century in advance of us in all the arts and embellishments of life." She added that "the canker of slavery … eats into [Southern] hearts, and diseases the whole body by this ulcer at its core."[37]

Madison knew that. Near the end of his life he was visited by Charles Ingersoll and told him that his farms were no longer productive. "Mr. Madison told me that ever since his Presidency he has been obliged to live beyond his means selling off some of his capital continually, and that he is now in debt. He spoke often and anxiously of slave property as the worst possible for profit."

Ingersoll and Madison discussed southern versus northern farming. "When I mentioned Mr. [Richard] Rush's productive farm of ten acres, near Philadelphia, he said he had no doubt it was more profitable than his with two thousand."[38]

Slavery helped to bring about the near collapse of the plantation. So had the farming recession that set in during the 1820s (just after the national recession of 1819), his imbalance of too old and too young workers, and, as the years went by, his lack of travel, increased isolation, and distance from the commercial world.

Near the end of his life, Madison poured out his bitterness over slavery to Harriet Martineau at Montpelier amid hours of conversation. Slavery was a stain on both Virginia and America, he said. "He acknowledged without limitation of hesitation, all the evils with which it had ever been charged," she wrote. Madison told her slavery had debauched slave girls who became mothers as young teenagers with white or black fathers for their children. Blacks were treated terribly all over America, north as well as south. White women treated their domestics as children, he said. Slaves in the lands opened up by the Louisiana Purchase were treated as "beasts." The masters, who should have accumulated wealth from their free slave labor, instead "lived in a state of perpetual suspicion, fear and anger." He lamented, too that in eighteen years, the American Colonization Society had removed fewer than two thousand slaves while the overall slave population of the United States increased by more than sixty thousand and, in the 1830s, was growing ever more rapidly (it would reach four million by 1860).[39]

The success and profitability of slavery had given James Madison the freedom and time to write the Constitution, serve in Congress, and run the country as president, but in the end that same slavery brought about personal gloom and economic ruin for him and his entire family. In his last years, he knew that Montpelier was going bankrupt, that he had no cash reserves, and that, when he died, his wife would be left with a huge debt. She would be in ruin and slavery was the cause.

26

DOLLEY

Triumph, Tragedy, and History

*I*n June 1836, a fragile James Madison turned to his wife, Dolley, nearly always at his side, and told her that he was on the "descending" side of life and that his death was not too far in the future. He was right. Dolley, frantic that he had become so depressed and weak, had summoned a doctor from Baltimore to see her husband, but the physician told her there was nothing he could do for the president; he was simply slipping away. Madison knew he had little time left. "I have outlived myself," he wrote a friend.[1]

He had outlived an era of enormous change in America, some of it due to his work as secretary of state and president and the rest of it due to the progress of the private sector, unimpeded by presidential or congressional restrictions during the administrations of Jefferson or Madison. Their long-held belief in a national government that functioned without interfering with the general economy had brought about significant progress in the country. The war caused imports to drop and homegrown goods to increase in quantity and price. The war had not only brought about a huge American navy to patrol the seas, but a much larger, and successful, merchant class of shipping. Those ships now hunted not only fish in the Chesapeake Bay but whales in the far reaches of the Pacific Ocean. The spinning machine, cording machine, steam engine, automatic milling machinery, the lathe, interchangeable parts in machines, and the assembly line in factories had all created a quick shift from a farm economy, when Washington's first term began, to the Industrial Revolution, at full throttle when Madison died in 1836. For example, the boom drove the sales of factory-made woolens from $4 million in 1810 to nearly $20 million in 1815. The number of spindles in cotton miles in that era increased sixteen fold.

Madison, a farmer himself, acknowledged to all that manufacturing gains in America, particularly in the North, had been exceptional, and that the slave-driven plantation system was failing, even at Montpelier. It was possible, he said, and other Republican leaders agreed, that the old agricultural South and industrial North were going to merge, aided by national transportation gains, led by the brand-new railroads, which would bring about a whole new American society. America, in Madison's public life, had become a much larger nation, but that increase was due to the waves of immigrants that arrived daily. Madison, who was opposed to the Alien Act of 1798, had not only welcomed them with open arms, but, as secretary of state and president, and in retirement, applauded their arrival. Cities had risen dramatically in his lifetime. The population of Washington had quadrupled since he arrived, as had the population of Richmond; New York City had exploded from a mere ten thousand residents during the revolution to over three hundred thousand at the time his wife, Dolley, died in 1849.[2]

He was fading. In his last days, James Madison looked out from the second-floor terraces of Montpelier at a whole new America, a whole new world. It had been a time of whirlwind change and unparalleled drama, and he had steered the United States through it, and steered it well.

By the mid-1830s, the president had stopped talking about politics to visitors and correspondents. "The political agitations are only known to us through the newspapers. They exhibit a complexity and confusion in the state of parties and in the prospect before us, which are impenetrable to those, in retired situations, and not a little so, perhaps, to those on the principal theater," said Dolley, adding that her husband also did not want to express his views because of the "further developments" that would bring in the simmering state of national politics.[3]

Everything that Madison did now took far longer and drained his strength even more. The last actual piece of work he finished was to write a thank-you note to a man who had sent him his manuscript on a piece depicting the life of Jefferson. Madison took a very long time to write the short note, and his barely legible signature slipped off the side of the page.

He had been ill for several years by the summer of 1836. Dolley kept relatives and friends up-to-date with his ailments and her worries for him. In 1832, she told a friend that "he has not left the house. A painful and diffusive rheumatism has confined and reduced him very much and for some days past. He has been suffering . . . we trust [that] will yield to the medicine." In the spring of 1836, she wrote her sister Lucy that "my dear husband has been unusually sick for some days and is at present unable to write, or even to exert his thoughts without oppressive fatigue." Many times she would just tell people that "my husband has been often sick of late."[4]

The president told his visitors to pull their chairs very close to the couch on which he reclined so that he could hear them. He had been unable to get out of bed or off of his couch for the last six months. Visitors were told to speak loudly and carry most of the conversation because Madison was always so tired. Still, he impressed all. "His mind was bright and with his numerous visitors he talked with as much animation and strength of voice as I ever heard him in his best days," said slave Paul Jennings, who attended him daily in his final years.[5]

Dolley cared for and nursed him constantly. A few years earlier, she wrote a friend of her need to take care of the president in a note that showed her love. "I hope, with great care, to carry my husband through this trying season of chills to that which generally renovates him. He is in better health at this moment than he was a month ago, though still feeble and confined to his room, where my time is spent in the usual efforts to console and amuse him," she wrote.[6]

No one knew how long he would hang on in the early summer of 1836. Several friends had suggested that he take new medicines, stimulants, to stay alive so that he could die on the Fourth of July in 1826, the sixtieth anniversary of the signing of the Declaration of Independence, as Jefferson and Adams had died on the fiftieth anniversary. Madison scoffed and told them he would go when he went. Just a few weeks prior to his death, he left a short memorial to his country. The president wrote "the advice nearest to my heart and deepest in my convictions is that the Union of the States be cherished and perpetuated. Let the open enemy to it be regarded as a Pandora with her box opened; and the disguised one, as the Serpent creeping with his deadly wiles into paradise."[7]

On June 28, his slave Jennings shaved him and helped him dress. Slave Sukey, as old as the president, served him breakfast in a chair in his back bedroom on the first floor. He could see the sun rays washing the backyard of the house outside his window. Sukey said later that he had trouble swallowing and she had asked him why. "It's nothing more than a change of mind, my dear," he said, and then his head dropped to his chest, his breathing stopped, and he died.[8]

His death crushed his wife, who just two weeks before told a friend who asked about the president's life, "I can only feel that he was good and perfect in all these [areas] and that nothing short of true religion can make a man perfect. He was accomplished in literature and science as his writing manifest."[9]

While he was buried at Montpelier, and mourned by his relatives, his friends, and his slaves, there was an outpouring of condolences, and veneration, for the president across the United States and in Europe. "The last of the great lights of the revolution ... has sunk below the horizons ... [and]

left a radiance in the firmament," wrote an editor at the *National Intelligencer*. Politicians all over America offered thoughtful eulogies of him, John Quincy Adams spent two months working on a two-and-a-half-hour-long eulogy that was delivered in Boston. But perhaps Henry Clay, talking to a friend years earlier, described Madison best. When asked to compare him to Jefferson, Clay said that "Jefferson had the most genius," but that "Madison most judgment and common sense." He added that sometimes Jefferson's impulsive behavior led him to "rash and imprudent and impracticable measures, while Madison [was] cool, dispassionate, practical, safe." Then Clay added that Madison was, "after Washington, our greatest statesman."[10]

Perhaps his slave, Paul Jennings, who had been with him all of his life, put it best: "Mr. Madison, I think, was one of the best men that ever lived."[11]

The governor of Virginia ordered muskets fired all day long on July 1, 1836, to mourn Madison's death and commemorate his life. Throughout Virginia, and in other states, people pledged to wear black mourning bands around the sleeves of their shirts for thirty days. Dolley's friends all made plans to visit her as soon as they heard the tragic news. One of the first was Jefferson's daughter, Martha, who wrote her, "God bless and support you dear friend under your present affliction." Perhaps the most moving tribute came from a cousin's husband, Andrew Stevenson, who wrote that "his illustrious services & public career, consecrated by the gratitude & love of his countrymen, will hand him down to posterity as one of the first and best of men. Although you have lost one of the best husbands that ever woman had, you should derive comfort in the reflection that you were so long blessed with his society and shared his happiness and glory."[12]

Madison was buried in a field a few hundred yards from his home that was splashed with sunshine each day.

☙❧

With her husband gone, Dolley was the proprietor of Montpelier, in charge of the four farms, thirty-two slaves, and a run-down plantation. She was also the sole parent of Payne Todd, now forty-four, whose problems were increasing, instead of decreasing, as he aged.

Her grief consumed her and Dolley found it difficult to slip out of her malaise. She knew that Madison was fading for over a year, and she was prepared for his end. Her husband had laid out detailed plans for her to run the plantation after his death, three of Madison's clerks who worked on his papers agreed to stay on and help her and she convinced her niece Anna Payne, alcoholic brother John's daughter, to live with her permanently and serve as her secretary when her father sold his farm and moved to Illinois, another victim of bad times in Virginia (John said he also wanted to move to a free state and was bothered by Madison's slave policy[13]). Dolley went horseback riding every day for exercise and escape; she had letters of condolence from dozens of top federal and state officials, including President Jackson, that encouraged her; and she plunged into the work of selling Madison's papers to a book publisher to further cement his historical position and to make desperately needed money to pay bills. The former First Lady had much to do.

"She has at present and will have for some months so much important business to give her attention to that I hope when she has time to reflect on the past her distress will be so softened as in a measure to pass away," said her niece Anna.[14]

"The important trust sustained me under the heavy pressure of recent loss and formed an oasis in the desert it created in my feelings," Mrs. Madison wrote Henry Clay in 1837. A month after the president's demise, a sad Dolley wrote Eliza Collins Lee, "Indeed I have been as one in a troubled dream since my irreparable loss of him. ... I owe his wishes, that I should be calm, and strive to live long after him." A friend, Septima Meikleham, visited her after Madison's death and said that "the change was most sad. The house seemed utterly deserted. The great statesman, loving husband, kind master and attentive friend was gone. And we three seemed lost in the great desolate house." She added that Dolley, aged sixty-eight, was "broken hearted."[15]

Dolly kept busy running Montpelier and was certain that as long as she was occupied she would not miss her husband. She wrote a friend that she "was involved in a variety of businesses, reading, writing, and flying about the house, garden and grove, straining my eyes to the height of my spirits, until they became inflamed, and frightened into idleness and to quietly sitting in drawing room with my kind connections and neighbors, sometimes like the 'farmeress,' and often acting the character from my rocking chair."[16]

She decided, probably at the urging of her son, Payne, to revive Madison's tobacco business, which had been stagnant for years. Her problem was that she had only thirty-two laborers, down from a high of 108 in 1802, and they were too old or too young to work very hard. So Dolley, who always professed her hatred of slavery, began to buy slaves with what little money she had to create a larger and sturdier workforce. She did this over the next four years, raising the number of her slaves to 103. By 1840, her tobacco crops consumed most of her time, and she was deeply involved in the farming business. She did all of the contacts with tobacco agents in Virginia, writing one in 1840 that "we have now sent you the last hogshead of tobacco from the last crop with thanks for all your kind attention" and requested fifty pounds of bacon from him "for black people [by return car] to be paid for by the proceeds." She had advice on farming from neighbors and friends, and people sent her different strains of tobacco seeds from all over America.[17]

The revived tobacco business did not prosper, though, since in 1837 America entered one of her worst recessions, an economic downturn that affected the country for years. The Panic of 1837 was caused by land speculators in the west who borrowed enormous sums of money and could not pay it back, the instability of American banks, and the general failure of the wheat crop throughout the country. Grain prices were so high that mobs in New York attacked grain houses and looted them. A collapse in British banking that same year caused large banks in London to call in foreign loans to America and other countries to reestablish their credibility. And a recession in Europe caused a dramatic drop in the prices of American goods shipped there.

The panic hurt Montpelier, and each year Dolley had the additional costs of the clothing and the feeding of the seventy-one new slaves she had purchased before the economy wobbled. Her debts mounted. Her son's wild entrepreneurial dreams did not help, either. By 1840, Payne, who had failed at everything he had tried, opened up a marble quarry on his farm. The land contained some marble beneath it, and he planned to mine it and produce marble in the shape of steps and other configurations. Geology was one of Payne's hobbies, and he had read several dozen books on marble, making him, he told his mother, an expert. People purchased marble from Europe, so why not sell the marble cheaper at Montpelier? He needed help, though, and so his mother, yet again certain that her son had finally found a successful business, gave him a dozen of her slaves, and then added more to her farms.

Earlier, she had given him slaves to work and live at his farm, Toddsberth, and help him increase the size of his ramshackle home there. With this new labor, all paid on Dolley's books, Toddsberth grew. There was a main building and several cottages that surrounded it. Payne's outlandish architecture made Toddsberth the talk of Orange County. In addition to some small cottages, it had a large tower-shaped main house with a dining room and spacious ballroom for dancing and parties. He wanted his mother to move there into one of the cottages. He did not want her to have to walk around the building on her way from Montpelier to get into the cottage, though, so he made one of the first-floor windows a large window/doorway for her to enter through. It was the joke of the county. Dolley never did move there. She did give her son all the furniture he desired from the mansion, and he looted the rest of the home. He took two large feather beds, chairs, mirrors, half a dozen chairs, a dining-room table, a dozen paintings, dishes, glasses, shelves, and decanters. He planned to make Toddsberth larger and larger as his marble business boomed, but, like all of his other ventures, it eventually died.

No one liked Toddsberth. Mary Cutts told a friend that it was the residence of an eccentric and that she and members of her family thought the entire complex looked ridiculous. She frowned at Payne's contention that his mother would one day live there with him.

In the Civil War twenty years later, a soldier, H. H. Chamberlayne, who stumbled upon Toddsberth, wrote that "the marks of the poor spendthrift [Payne] are still to be seen, walks that he began, never to finish, an attempted ice house turned into a stately pleasure dome, like Kubla Khan's, quarries opened for marble which was not there."[18]

A few years later, Payne stunned his mother with an odd request. The federal government's consul to Liverpool, England, had resigned, and Payne wanted the job. He knew that his mother was a close friend of President John Tyler and asked her to get him the post. It was a well-paying job and he told Dolley he would give her $5,000 a year out of his salary, which would stabilize her always-unsteady financial situation. She went to Tyler, who said he would take it under advisement. He asked for a background check on Payne and then called Dolley back to the White House. Diplomatically, and very gently, he said that "Mr. Todd is not fitted for the office."[19]

He was, in fact, unsuited for any job, something that friends told Dolley throughout her retirement, in a soft way, but she never paid attention to them. When the president died, Payne returned to Montpelier and tried to help his mother sort out the terms of the will. He butted in, overriding lawyers, and wrote dozens of legal-like letters himself to various relatives to whom Madison had bequeathed something. It did not help his mother at all.[20]

Everyone in Dolley's family, neighbors, friends, and even strangers, knew how reckless and unfeeling Payne Todd was and denounced him in scathing terms when talking to each other about the Madisons' son. James Paulding, who knew Payne well, wrote Jared Sparks in 1836 that Dolley was going to let Payne sell the Madison papers to publishers. "If you are acquainted with him, you need not be told that he is the last man in the world to compass such a business," he wrote, and he offered to help Payne to prevent a debacle. What he did not know, though, was that Dolley had asked friend George Tucker to negotiate with publishers for her. Tucker met with executives at Harper Brothers and reached an agreement. A few days later, though, Tucker met Payne Todd on a New York street. Payne heard what he was in town to do and abruptly informed him that his mother had just sent him to New York to do the same thing. He told Tucker to cease talking to anyone and go home. "I thought that any further efforts on my part were unnecessary and my continued inquiries were consequently suspended," Tucker wrote Dolley. Friend William Rives always referred to Payne as "the prodigal son."[21]

Dolley's prime job after her husband's death was to sell his papers to a New York publisher. Unfortunately, she entrusted the task to her son, Payne, who told her he knew people in New York, whom he had visited often, and could get a good price for them. She could not have picked a worse agent. Payne did little, was a poor representative, and, after a few weeks of talks with publishers such as Harper Brothers, was back home without any money.

Dolley believed Payne's story about the lack of interest in her husband's papers, despite Tucker's success, and then decided to stop seeking a publisher and to sell them instead to the federal government, completely ignoring further attempts at New York publishers just because Payne said so. She wrote President Jackson and asked him to recommend that Congress buy the papers.

Congress was surprised at Dolley's insistence that they pay her $100,000 for the papers; the government had paid George Washington only $25,000 for his papers. Representatives told her brother that the fee was way too high; Dolley backed off and said she would accept $50,000, but that was rejected, too.[22] Congress did buy the papers, but for just $30,000. Dolley, who needed the money, accepted the offer. Congress also extended her free mailing privileges, as her husband had, to help keep her living costs down.[23]

It took Congress more than two years to buy the papers, though, and nearly four to publish them after politicians convinced President Martin Van Buren to pocket veto them for a congressional term. Dolley had to hold off her creditors and wait for Congress to act. Later, she decided to sell volume 4 of her husband's papers and this time went herself to see the editors at Harper Brothers, who had turned her down on the first three volumes. They again backed off on a deal because Dolley was unwilling to agree to their terms, which were pretty standard for authors. She never engaged anyone in the publishing industry, who knew what they were doing, to represent her as an agent or even just an adviser. She had no idea what she was doing and always turned to Payne for advice, and Payne had no idea what he was doing, either.

After she failed with the publishers on volume 4, she asked Payne, who had mishandled the first three volumes, to represent her again. He told her that the problem was not the publishers; it was her. "I am to confer with the Harpers as soon as I can see him about a different in balance in your favor and an advance on books and money. Your writing would not be understood, and might embarrass my obtaining any for you," he told his mother bluntly.[24]

Instead of rebuking him and finding someone else, Dolley did what he told her. This deal fell through, too, though. An author of a book about Harpers said that "the answer may be that Mrs. Madison would not accept their terms—presumably a half profits arrangement."[25]

The former First Lady then decided to sell volume 4 to Congress, too, since Payne had said it was impossible to sell the work to any commercial publisher. Having watched Payne fail miserably dealing with Harper Brothers, Dolley incredibly retained him again to represent her in the deal with Congress, too. She begged him to do it. "If you love me ... tell me when you will come to offer the papers to Congress and to do something with the 4th volume. . . . Oh, my son, I am too unhappy not to have you with me and not to have even your opinions and directions, what do I do myself or what individual to engage and at what time."[26]

Payne did not come to Washington but told his mother to keep him apprised of any talks with Congress through the mail. She soon had a meeting with two congressmen, both friends of hers who would do anything to help her, who told her they could get Congress to buy volume 4 for the $30,000 for which they had purchased the first three volumes. It was still short of Madison's suggested price of $50,000. Dolley did not accept the offer or even name her price when they asked her what it was. She told them they had to deal with her son, Payne, far away at Montpelier. "Now my dear Son, will you say at once what you think best to these particular questions. They seem to dwell on the $30,000 as if that were the proper sum, but I must speak now as they are impatient. Oh, that you, my beloved, were fixed in all things, to cooperate with me, I will not say to act solely for me, because I have become the object of interest, and less would be done without me. I want you to reply in a few days."[27]

The papers of her husband were special not only to her, but, she believed, to the whole country as well. They told the story of the Constitution, his life as secretary of state and two terms as president. They were, Dolly told President Jackson, "his legacy."[28]

And what did her beloved son do in this critical matter? Nothing. Dolley never heard from him and, on her own, agreed to Congress's $30,000. Then Congress adjourned without technically agreeing to the deal. Payne, furious, jumped into Dolley's business again and went to New York with an old note from his mother authorizing him to act on her behalf and tried to revive the deal with Harpers. This time he succeeded in selling the book, but only at a low price. Payne then decided to squeeze Congress to get more money out of them by telling them of his contract with Harpers. Congress did not care, but Harpers did. Their executives felt they had been manipulated by Payne and pulled out of the contract. This left Congress as the only buyer and, knowing all about the Harpers dispute, it made a deal with Dolley for the low, $30,000 amount. Payne had made a mess with not just one publisher, but two, and at the same time. And then, on top of all that, Congress did not act on the purchase for another year, leaving Mrs. Madison desperate to meet her bills. These, of course, included more loans, which were never repaid, to her son. The money Dolley sent to Payne constituted an endless river. In the fall of 1836, her niece said she sent him $100 one day, $100 the next day, and then another $100 two days later. "[She] wishes you to tell her how much more you want that she may endeavor to send it soon," he niece added.[29]

She turned to the rather useless Payne at a time when her debts had mounted considerably as the recession of 1837 droned on. She was borrowing money in Washington to pay her monthly bills and annual debts while waiting for the $30,000 from Congress that was continually delayed. She told her son that "we are without funds and those we owe are impatient" and that she needed to sell volume 4 and earn money so that she could maintain her "respectable standing before the world."[30]

In Washington, she asked Payne to bring all of Madison's papers to her so she could turn them over to Congress in order to be paid the $30,000. He did not. "I cannot understand, of course, without explanation, the refusal to accept & take charge of the original manuscripts. Money will not be paid without these being first delivered," she wrote him, exasperated.[31]

Her costs were high and some of her relatives did not help. Her brother-in-law William Madison, who lived nearby, sued her for $2,000 that he insisted the president owed him. She also found herself in court just because she could not easily reach all the dozens of people to whom her husband had bequeathed money in his will. Dolley had to get a lawyer to file a suit against all of them to get them to make their whereabouts known and then pursue them so she could give them the money. It was tedious, time-consuming, and expensive. She had to pay all the taxes on her business and assets, had little revenue coming in from the plantation due to the small workforce and stagnant farming business, and had practically no income from the financial holdings of the Madisons, which had been relentlessly depleted over the years by payments to cover their reckless son's debts. Following a $2,000 gift to the American Colonization Society, a $1,000 gift to Princeton University, a gift to the University of Virginia, and other gifts to relatives in her husband's will, the Montpelier estate and Madison finances were actually $9,000 in debt.

All was not over when Dolley finally received her $30,000 from Congress. Her friends in Washington were terrified that Payne Todd, who had her power of attorney, would abscond with the money and leave her penniless. "Her son Todd is here playing the fool in high style as far as I can hear. It will never do to let him get hold of this money, or to have anything to do with it. The man is deranged if he ever had any sense ... what orders she has given her son I know not, but if she has given him any to pay her debts with it [money] will certainly be squandered," John Campbell, the treasurer of the United States, wrote. Another public official, George Featherstonhaugh, was absolutely convinced that Payne Todd would loot Dolley's accounts. "It is, however, too well known that his intimates are the Blacklegs and Gamblers of Washington. Their gigs and flasks stand at his door and he appears to be in their hands. Mr. Todd's habits and facilities of temper will probably make him their victim and this money will in all likelihood be lost to Mrs. Madison," he said. To prevent that, Congress authorized payment of the $30,000 over several years.[32]

All of this stress often made Dolley sick. Her eye problems returned. Payne sent her books written by oculists and doctors applied leeches and blisters to the backs of her ears and even bled her several times. She bathed her eyes with milk and water plus sassafras tea. Dr. Physick, who treated her for her knee thirty years earlier, sent a lotion to be applied to her eyes. Local doctors visited her and gave her herbal medicines. All of this did little good. "My general health has suffered much," she said in the autumn of 1836.[33]

She looked and felt terrible. Her brother said that "the inflammation around the eyes is a little abated, but not so the soreness and rawness, and the discharge is unchanged in consistence, and perhaps increased in quantity, and the white balls are slightly inflamed; one more so than the other. The itching and burning sensations of the lids the same."[34]

Her illnesses often caused her to cancel visits to friends, such as one in the spring of 1838. "I feel too dull and dismal to appear before you this evening," she wrote her host.[35]

Her relatives advised her to sell all of Montpelier and move to Richard Cutts's home, a two-story brick house on Lafayette Square, in Washington, that she and her husband owned and lent to Cutts and his family and which was now occupied by the family of Senator William Preston. The Prestons could move elsewhere, and she would be independent and back in Washington with her lifelong collection of friends. The house was a handsome, two-story brick home with dormer windows on the third floor. It overlooked a square full of trees that was populated by birds. Washingtonians enjoyed walking there. In Washington, she would also be free of the burdens of running and paying for Montpelier.

Before he died, Dolley and her husband had been following events in Washington, particularly the social whirl, at a distance at Montpelier. Dolley could never completely detach herself from the social life of the capital. "I hope you will soon be at the parties and will give me a detail of what is going forward, amidst the various characters in Washington," she wrote her niece in 1831. A friend wrote Dolley breathlessly that 2,800 people were invited to a party President Adams gave at the White House for Andrew Jackson. "It was really a very brilliant party & admirably well arranged. The ladies climbed the chairs & benches to see General Jackson and Mrs. Adams with him, which gratified the general curiosity."[36]

Dolley's friend Judith Walker Rives went to a wedding in the capital and joined over one thousand other guests. "Everybody appeared in fine humor and finer dress, but, alas, such crushing of flowers, feathers, silks, satins, crape never was witnessed before. I am sure the rooms after the route was over must have resembled a [mess]." Rives added, a glint in her eye, that "the spirit of dissipation appears now to be reviving."[37]

It was not just the parties that the Madisons longed to hear about from friends but also the city itself, which had grown so quickly during their sixteen years there and continued to expand. Friend Judith Walker Rives wrote in 1829 of "the broad bosom of the Potomac, sparkling in the sun and covered with little vessels with their white sails swelling in the breeze. Beneath our feet as it were lies the whole city, sometimes blazing in the beams of the rising or setting sun and sometimes so completely enveloped in mist that the few stately looking buildings on the opposite heights appear like castles in the air."[38]

Edward Coles, Madison's former secretary, who was carving out a nice life for himself in Illinois, filled his letters with hot rumors he had heard out of Washington, such as one that a bank in London had forgiven James Monroe a large debt because of some secret services Monroe rendered to them to help in business with the French government. He told her of government officials in New York who were fired for taking city money and spending it on themselves, of boarding-school heads forced out of town by rising housing costs. He thrived on news of secret organizations, such as "The Club," a group of powerful Washingtonians who met at each other's homes every Friday night. The Madisons devoured the news and gossip while in retirement at Montpelier.

And, as always, Coles would slash people whom he did not like. In a letter to Dolley in 1832, he slammed the Gallatins, Hannah and Albert. "She has become very fleshy & he much changed in his appearance by wearing an ugly wig," he wrote.[39]

Mrs. Madison moved back to Washington on a part-time basis, in the fall and winter of 1837, the flowers in full bloom, forests deep green, and the creeks gurgling throughout Orange County. Dolley Madison had lived at Montpelier since she was a new bride in 1794, forty-two years earlier, and now she was leaving for half the year. It was a big step in her life.[40]

She had always enjoyed the house on Lafayette Square. Her son had the walls painted a soft color so that a loud color would not disturb her eyes. "I like it, of course," she said of the color. The house was large but not too large and centrally located for visiting friends and getting around in the ever-growing town. "My house in Washington will do very well, no doubt," she told all.[41]

Dolley's health was not good. Her eyes continued to bother her. They were either inflamed or did not enable her to read well, except when she wore glasses. She bathed them in different solutions and was often bedridden for days at a time. In 1836, to get some rest and to seek a cure for her eyes, she took the advice of friends and spent several weeks on vacation at White Sulphur Springs, Virginia, not far from her home and a favorite vacation spot for the elite in Virginia that featured special waters that all believed had medicinal benefits. She went there, she wrote a friend, with a "sad, impatient spirit" but enjoyed the visit. "[I was] drinking moderately at the waters and bathing my poor eyes a dozen times a day. The effect was excellent. My health was strengthened to its former standing and my eyes grew white again," she wrote Anthony Morris.[42]

By 1842, as the Industrial Revolution took hold in the North, the former First Lady realized that her enhanced farming business, co-run with her by Payne, had failed. Revenues were low and there were no profits. "Produce of every kind is down to the lowest ebb. . . . Crops are tolerably good yet the farmer realizes nothing from them," Dolley wrote her niece Lucy Todd that October. Bad crops and low prices were nothing new. The Madisons had dismal crops for years. In 1832, Dolley told her son that "the last tobacco both of Mr. Madison and John's was a failure." They had expected $17 per hogshead and received only $7.[43]

She had to juggle high costs for her extra slaves, loans to her son, and upkeep at the mansion. She, like all the other homeowners in the South in that era, were part of a "hosting system" in which travelers, many complete strangers, stayed at her house for days at a time, at her cost. She welcomed all and had hundreds of visitors each year. In addition to that, Dolley could never give up her crown as America's queen and continued to spend lavishly on parties for relatives and friends at Montpelier.

Everybody who knew her assumed that her husband had left her an extraordinary amount of money to pay for her plantation, enlarged workforce, and extravagant lifestyle. After all, he was the president, wasn't he? And the couple had lived lavishly in Washington and in Montpelier for nearly fifty years. They must be rich. Dolley never told anyone except her inner family that she was broke and could not continue at Montpelier. Her brother-in-law Richard Cutts wanted her to pay back a $1,500 loan, and she could not. She was considered a credit risk in Orange County and told Cutts that she could not borrow money from anyone, adding that she was now spending more than she had with no financial answer in sight. "I stay at home in waiting ... here is property in both land and Negroes but they cannot command one hundred [dollars] at this time, and I fear that I have not sufficient in the bank to pay my discount there." Family members were shocked.[44]

They were also surprised at her new attitude toward slavery. She had been against the practice all of her life and had vowed, with her husband, never to sell her slaves because the Madisons took good care of them and did not want to sell them to unscrupulous planters who might make their lives miserable. Her need for money changed her view. In 1836, she sold a number of her slaves to the slave buyers that wandered throughout Virginia, looking for good property at reasonable prices. Edward Coles was with her one day in November 1836, when she permitted slave buyers to examine her slaves for possible purchase. "The poor creatures would run to the house & protest against being sold & say their old master had said in his will that they were not to be sold but with their consent," said Coles.

He watched Dolley sell a woman and her two children to nephew Ambrose Madison, leaving the woman's husband at Montpelier. Coles said that Mrs. Madison did not want to sell the slaves, or break up families, "a most painful task," but felt she had to do so to earn money to pay her bills.[45]

Dolley was extremely worried, yet never let anyone outside the immediate family know about her problems. She continued to charm the world. Noted artist J. Eastman Johnson was one of those enamored of her when he painted her portrait. "She comes in every morning at 10 o'clock in full dress for the occasion, and, as she has much taste she looks quite imposing with her white satin turban, black velvet dress and a countenance full of benignity and gentleness. She talks a great deal and in such quick, beautiful tones. So polished and elegant are her manners that it is a pleasure to be in her company," he said.[46]

The only way she could stay solvent, friends and lawyers told her, was to sell Montpelier and live off the money in Washington. She found a buyer for the entire plantation in 1842, Henry Moncure, who bought it in increments over several years. Payne remained at his farm with a small staff of slaves. Moncure, who did not care for Payne, bought everything, including Mrs. Madison's slaves. She moved to Washington on a permanent basis, leaving behind Montpelier, but not Payne's problems and his never-ending requests for money.

What she also left behind was a dangerous, new life for her slaves. They were all to go with the property to Moncure, and she paid no further attention to them, even though, in the summer of 1844, they were still hers. She received a frantic letter from one of the slaves, Sarah, that stunned her. "The sheriff has taken all of us and said he will sell us at next court unless something is done before to prevent it. We are afraid we will be bought by what are called Negro buyers and sent away from our husbands and wives. If we are obliged to be sold perhaps you could get neighbors to buy us that have husbands and wives so as to save us some misery which will in a greater or less degree be sure to fall upon us at being separate from you as well as from one another. The sale is only a fortnight [away]."

Mrs. Madison was shaken. She did not know that William Madison, determined to get his $2,000, was working with the sheriff to seize the slaves and hold them as payment on Madison's debt. Dolley also did not know that a full month before the threatened seizure William Madison had gone to her son, Payne, and convinced him that what he wanted to do was proper. Payne went along with it and, worse, never told his mother about it. When Dolly did hear about it, she immediately signed all the papers to sell Montpelier to Moncure, so that the slaves all went to him and not to William Madison. "The beautiful place was sold and the colored population with it, far below value, to prevent separation from their homes," wrote Lucia Cutts.[47]

Dolly had always wanted Payne to inherit Montpelier, but now that was not possible. He remained at his shabby dwelling nearby at Toddsberth, with his eccentric habits and odd businesses, and Moncure moved into Montpelier.

An era ended.

In the end, it was Payne's recklessness and general incompetence that drove Dolley to sell her beloved Montpelier. She had trusted Payne to run it with her, hoping, as always, that he could succeed at something in his life. She was wrong, of course. Payne could not succeed at anything. She waved off attacks on Payne's catastrophic handling of the farms, but friends and relatives were cutting in their denunciation of Payne. Her niece Lucy wrote scathingly that Dolley's "extravagant, idle son" ran the farms so badly that his ineptitude "obliged her to sell the dearly loved Montpelier, together with the slaves, to Mr. Moncure." A friend, Septima Meikleham, said that Payne "had run through the fortune her husband left her, $100,000 and Montpelier."[48]

Whenever friends or relatives questioned Dolly about Payne and his strange ideas, Dolly always smiled and said "my poor boy, forgive his eccentricities—his heart is in the right place."[49]

Other family news was bad, too. James Todd, the son of her niece Lucy, had adopted many of Payne's habits. He owed money everywhere, and it brought his mother nothing but worry. "I did not know that you had ever borrowed any money from Joseph Crane until lately. What amount did you borrow and has it been paid? Let me know in your next letter. If it is too great an amount I can settle it," she wrote him of one bill. She inquired, too, what happened to money she had recently sent him to pay a second bill that had "vanished."[50]

Dolley's brother, John, had floundered in Kentucky. A friend there, George Washington Spotswood, said he "does not have an acre of land fenced. He has devoted most of his time to dissipation." He added that one of John's daughters married an alcoholic and the other married a man he considered "good for nothing." He smirked that "if they were my daughters, I would rather see them dead." Spotswood added that John was penniless, his farms were bankrupt, and his wife had left him.[51]

❧

Dolley was distraught, but she hid her horror and looked magnificent when she moved to Washington as a half-time resident in 1836. Everyone who knew her in her retirement at Montpelier marveled at how well Dolley appeared and how the years had not ravaged her. "She looks just as she did twenty years ago and dresses in the same manner, with her turban and cravat; rises early and is very active, but seldom leaves the house," said Charles Ingersoll, who spent several days with the Madisons just before the president's death in 1836.[52]

She was glad to be back in the capital. Dolley had always missed Washington and its active social life. Back in 1822, she had told her sister Anna about all the miles from her in the capital that "I am at such a distance & am so despairing at the difficulties & disappointments of seeing my sisters." In 1838, after Madison's death, she told Margaret Bayard Smith that "in truth, I am dissatisfied with the location of Montpelier, from which I can never separate myself entirely, when I think how happy I should be if it joined Washington, where I could see you always and my valued acquaintances also of that city." She lived the Washington life vicariously through her nieces who resided there. She wrote them often and begged them to give her all the details of their social lives. In one letter she told Mary Cutts that "I should have been delighted to see [niece] Dolley and yourself [with] those pretty and brilliant characters at Mrs. White's elegant ball."[53]

The First Lady's love of Washington over Montpelier was evident throughout her public life, when she wrote letters from Montpelier asking about Washington, even when she was due to return to the capital in a few weeks. In 1808, just a week before her planned arrival in the capital, she wrote Anna Thornton, "I am glad to find that you have gay parties now & then & hope they will continue as I hope to join in your bustle by & by. I should like to see a good play once more." A year earlier she asked her niece Lucy, "tell me how you amuse yourselves in Washington."[54]

When Dolley arrived back in Washington in 1837, twenty years after she had left it, she feared that most of her old friends had died or moved away. The diplomats she knew would have returned to their countries. The merchants who had attended her parties were now probably in their seventies, too, deceased, or retired. When she looked through the Washington directory, though, she was surprised to find that many people and families that she had known remained in town. Many were now older and had sons and daughters who lived and worked in town, too. Some of the politicians she knew so well, such as Henry Clay, were still in office and were more powerful than ever. Many of the socialites she knew in her forties were now in their sixties but were still hosting parties.

What surprised her the most was that so many Washingtonians remembered her, and fondly so. She had dozens of welcome letters upon her return, some from ministers from European countries, all wishing her well in what appeared to be the final chapters of her life. One of the very first people in town to visit her on Lafayette Square was former president John Quincy Adams, now serving as a congressman from Massachusetts. Adams had been a casual acquaintance of Dolley when her husband was president and had never visited Montpelier. He expected to find a decrepit old woman but was astonished at Mrs. Madison. "I had not seen her since 1809. The depredations of time are not so perceptible in her personal appearance as might be expected. She is a woman of placid appearance equable temperament and less susceptible of laceration of the scourges of the world abroad than most others," he wrote.[55]

A parade of well-wishers followed Adams. They all found Dolley, in her seventies, as delightful as ever and were all stunned that she had not aged much in appearance. And she looked just like the Dolley of old—elegant. Her grandniece wrote of one party that "Aunt Madison wore a purple velvet dress, with plain straight skirt amply gathered to a tight waist, cut low and filled in with soft tulle. Her pretty white throat was encircled by a lace cravat ... thrown lightly over her shoulders was a little lace shawl or cape, as in her portrait ... I thought her turban very wonderful, as I had never seen anyone else wear such a head-dress ... her eyes were blue and laughed when she smiled and greeted her friends who seemed so glad to see her."[56]

Mrs. Madison was also the lucky beneficiary of political history. She brought one of her grandnieces to a White House gala when Martin Van Buren was president, as she always brought her grandnieces along with her in order to introduce them to high society. The girl met Abraham Van Buren, the president's son, and fell in love with him. They were married shortly thereafter and Dolley immediately found herself on the guest list for every White House function. The fortuitous marriage returned her to her social glory.

Several years later, Van Buren lost his reelection bid to William Henry Harrison, who ran with Dolley's longtime friend and prominent Virginian John Tyler as his running mate. Harrison died a month later and Tyler became president. He was unmarried and made his daughter-in-law, Mrs. Robert Tyler, his "First Lady." She did not know what to do and turned to family friend Dolley, America's longest-serving First Lady, for advice. Dolley took her under her wing and happily trained the girl in Washington and White House social life. Mrs. Tyler also put Dolley on the permanent guest list and turned to her for advice at all the White House dinners and balls. Daniel Webster joked to Dolley that since she had been prominent in the administrations of Jefferson, Madison, Van Buren, and Tyler, she was "the only permanent power in Washington."[57]

Dolley was back on the social circuit again, and invitations poured in as she set her own calendar of parties at her home. Lists she kept showed that she made two hundred visits to friends in 180 days and attended an average of three parties a week, plus her own. In addition to parties, she was often invited to musical concerts, plays, and public ceremonies. In Washington, she was just as close to nieces and nephews as she had been to sisters twenty years earlier and spent much time at their homes. She was a welcome guest at weddings for the children of adults she had known once and now knew again. Many of her old friends, such as Eliza Collins Lee, Anna Thornton, Mrs. Tobias Lear, and Margaret Bayard Smith, were widows who lived in town and were thrilled to renew their friendships with her. It was the first time she had seen Mrs. Lear in years. The last time was the funeral of her husband, President Madison's close friend, who stunned Washington when he committed suicide in 1816 following a political smear campaign against him. At her own parties, Dolley entertained as elegantly as she had at the White House and as lavishly as any hostess in town. A New Yorker, Phillip Hone, wrote that "she is a young lady of fourscore years and upward, goes out to parties and receives company like the 'Queen' of this new world."[58]

Her niece Lucy wrote that "her return to Washington was hailed by all, those who formerly knew her and those who desired to know this First Lady of the land. Her home was filled morning and night with most distinguished of all parties. . . . It had been twenty years since she had left the city, the favorite of society, yet she came [back] without influence or power and the citizens welcomed her return. . . . She had infinite tact, and always saw the good and not the evil, which exists in all."[59]

One of her new friends was Congressman Daniel Webster of Massachusetts, who wanted to be president. He lived in Swann House, just a few blocks from Dolley, and oversaw a lavish social life at his home with his wife, who had befriended Dolley. Webster noticed how popular Dolley was and saw that many viewed her as a bridge back to the old pre-Jackson Washington, when life was calmer and more elegant. Webster invited Dolley to dozens of his parties and saw her frequently. He made an arrangement to purchase her slave, Paul Jennings, and give him his freedom after a few years. When Jennings started to work for him, he told him that whenever he returned to Swann House from the market, he should buy extra food and drop it off at Dolley's on the way home.

Not everybody was happy to have the charismatic former First Lady around, though. William Seward of New York, a rising Whig star who later served as Abraham Lincoln's secretary of state in the Civil War, saw her as a major nonpolitical star of the Democratic Party (the old Republicans had become the Democrats) and a threat. "All the world paid homage to her, saying that she was dignified and attractive. It is the fashion to say so. But, I confess, I thought more true dignity would have been displayed by her remaining in her widowhood, in the ancient country mansion of her illustrious husband."[60]

Mrs. Madison, like everyone else, was jolted by events in the ever-growing and ever-tempestuous Washington. In February 1838, a friend of hers, Mr. Graves, killed a man named Cilly in a duel that followed an argument. The city's population was shocked, and many demanded justice; lynch mobs were formed to punish the survivor, Graves. "[I] feel more horror at the wicked act than if I had never seen them. You can have little idea of the sensation it has created here . . . there was danger of a mob in the city," she wrote.[61]

Mrs. Madison traveled all over and by land and by sea. Dolly was a guest on board the *Princeton*, an elegant yacht, with President Tyler, most of his cabinet, and a number of senators , congressmen, and diplomats. After dinner, the guests went on deck to witness the firing of new, large cannon on board the ship. The top government officials were on the deck where the gun was bolted; Dolly and other women were finishing dinner in the dining room with President Tyler. Inexplicably, the gun suddenly blew up, causing an explosion that ripped open the ship and was seen and heard for miles. The secretary of state, the secretary of the navy, and numerous other officials were killed. Rumors flew that it was a plot to assassinate Tyler. All night, Lafayette Square was crowded with Dolley's friends, who believed she had been killed, too. They were relieved to see her alive. Mrs. Madison was so shaken by the explosion that she refused to talk about it for the rest of her life.

And she kept quiet about her son, Payne, too, whose eccentricities grew as the years flew by. Just before the sale of Montpelier, he spent time in his father's library, sitting down amid the more than four thousand books. He read the works of William Cowper, who was said to be insane, a sure sign of trouble, friends told his mother. He ruminated about his fortunes. Then he decided that as the son of a president he would claim his rightful place in the world and began to replicate his now-deceased father's personality, an effort that seemed comical to many. At forty-four, Payne had accomplished nothing. At forty-four, his father had been married, had run a successful plantation for years, had served numerous terms in Congress, and had written the United States Constitution.

And Payne was losing money every month at Montpelier. "I am now as low in finances as I well can be," he wrote in his diary.[62]

Mrs. Madison had hoped that life on quiet Montpelier in tranquil Orange County, far from the urban world of bars and casinos, would help him. The solitude had just the opposite effect. He drank even more in his odd housing at Toddsberth and, when sober, managed to single-handedly drive Montpelier into bankruptcy. His management of the plantation was so bad, and his treatment of the slaves was so haughty, that Dolley left the comfort of Washington and headed back to Montpelier for two entire years. There, back home, she tried to make the farms profitable, but failed.

During those final two years at Montpelier, Dolley rented out her Washington home to pay her bills, kept in touch with friends in the capital, and had assistance with everything to do with Washington from her old White House manager, Jean Pierre Sioussat, who had become a bank executive. He did everything possible to handle her business in Washington and tried to help her straighten out her hopelessly tangled financial affairs.

The summers of the 1830s were not only hot and oppressive but also dry. A terrible drought hit the area in the summer of 1838. Dolley, at Montpelier, suffered with everyone else. "The whole South has partaken deeply in this misfortune. . . . In the region of the White Sulphur [Springs] water to drink has been scarce . . . there was hope in the mountains that the millennium was near," she wrote.[63]

Back home at Montpelier in the summers of the 1830s, Dolley made light of the recession, her sagging plantation business, and her son's troubles. She was chipper when she wrote Anthony Morris one summer, "we are all in high health, and looking on promising crops, flocks and herds as well as on the world of fashion around us. My great nephew & niece with a pair of neighbors being pleased to get married since our return has brought about more than our usual gaiety. I gave them in unison a large party of two or three days continuance, before and after which Anna and Payne went the rounds as bridesmaid and Best Man."[64]

Dolley's parties in Washington were popular, as popular as those she hosted at Montpelier. In its annual New Year's Day party coverage, the *National Intelligencer* highlighted the reception at the White House hosted by President Van Buren, a party thrown by former president John Quincy Adams, and Mrs. Madison's soiree. A reporter at Dolley's house that day said that Mrs. Madison, now seventy years old, was "young in old age, cheerful, animated and happy in conversation, loving all and beloved by all . . . James Madison owed something of his greatness to his wife."[65]

Dolley was just as popular as a dinner guest. William Kemble met her at a dinner at the White House in 1839. "The old lady is a very hearty, good looking woman of about 75. Soon after we were seated, we became on the most friendly terms & I paid her the same attentions I should have done a girl of 15, which suited her fancy very well."[66]

And she met many people in her old age whom she had first met thirty or thirty-five years earlier. Senator William Preston was one. He first met her as a teenager when James Madison was secretary of state. He saw again her in 1839. "For my part I loved and venerated you from my earliest dawn off reason and those sentiments inculcated upon my infancy have been confirmed by the knowledge of [your] life and by the concurrent feelings of all who have a perception of the influence of benevolence, grace, worth and wisdom. I do hope that you may long live to enjoy the high consideration in which you are held," he gushed.[67]

There were those who wished her well upon her return to Washington because she had made it such a wonderful place to live when she was First Lady. "That a long and happy evening of life may be before you in Washington, and that you may ever find in its society those rational enjoyments and pleasures which you so long and singly dispensed to others there is, dear Madam, the sincere wish," said Richard Rush, who served in her husband's cabinet.[68]

Everybody in Washington wanted to meet her and be seen with her. Samuel Morse invited her as a guest when he sent the first Morse code message over the telegraph. When both Charles Dickens and Washington Irving visited Washington as the guests of President Tyler, each insisted on meeting Dolley at dinner parties. President James K. Polk invited her to his inauguration and she sat in his presidential box. In an unprecedented move, Congress authorized that a seat in the chamber of the House of Representatives be kept for her so she could sit in on congressional sessions whenever she pleased.

Her last years were not always easy. In 1845, Payne was once again broke and pleaded with his mother for $6,000 to pay his bills. She took some money she had from the sale of Montpelier and borrowed more and sent it to him.

The loan to Payne completely bankrupted her. Upon hearing of her plight, a congressional committee voted to give her $25,000 for the remaining trunk of James Madison's papers, not really sure what was in them. They made certain that she received $5,000 of it right away to pay her bills. Payne hastened to Washington when he heard about the extra money and argued with several members of the board that oversaw the payments that they should give him some of that money. They refused. Angry, he sued the board.

Dolley, approaching her eightieth birthday, finally snapped when she heard about the arguments and subsequent suit. Furious with Payne, she wrote him a heated letter. In it, she asked him to apologize to the trustees. She told him that "I am much *distressed* at the conversations you held and the *determination* you expressed on the subject of bringing suit against my trustees. . . . I say all of this for you because I do not believe even *yourself* if you declared such an intention [no apology] which would at once ruin your fair fame. Your mother would have no wish to live after her son issued such threats, which would deprive her of her friends."[69]

Payne's reaction? He read the letter at Toddsberth, shrugged, and never wrote back.[70]

He reappeared in Washington several months later, though, when he heard his mother was going to finally make out her will. He wanted to be sure that he received everything. He badgered Dolley, now eighty years old and with her health failing, to give him all that she had. Payne had written her husband's will for him, Payne reminded her, so it was natural for him to write hers. She did not resist. In it, she deeded everything to her son. He brought in friends of his to witness the signing. The reading of the will to verify what it said and the signature took only thirty minutes. Payne had, at long last, apparently gained everything the Madisons had.

When Dolly told her nephew Madison Cutts, he was outraged. He demanded that she write a new will that replaced Payne's, and she did. In the new will she gave Payne her Lafayette Square home and all of her possessions. She split what was left of the $20,000 trust fund between Payne and her niece Annie Payne Cutts, who had lived with her for fifteen years and taken care of her; Annie was thankful and Payne was furious.

Dolley signed the new will on her deathbed. She passed away on July 12, 1849, just a week after the Fourth of July. What followed was a historical marvel.

All of the leading newspapers in the country published eulogies of her, which hailed her long years of public work, her years as First Lady, her work for the City Orphan Asylum, and her assistance to so many people. They all remembered her as far more than one of the First Ladies, though. She was revered in death, as she had been revered in life: as an American icon, a singular sensation that the United States had never seen before and would never see again.

The *National Intelligencer* obituary reflected the thousands printed around America:

> She continued until with a few weeks [of death] to grace society with her presence and to lend to it those charms with which she adorned the circle of the highest, the wisest and best during the bright career of her illustrious husband. Whenever she appeared, everyone became conscious of the presence of the spirit of benignity and gentleness united to all the attributes of feminine loveliness ... all of her own country and thousands in other lands will need no language of eulogy to inspire a deep and sincere regret when they learn the demise of one who touched all hearts by her goodness and won the admiration of all by the charms of dignity and grace.[71]

Her funeral service was held at St. John's church, in Washington. From there, the funeral cortege traveled to the city's Congressional Cemetery, where she was laid to rest. The service was similar to that accorded American presidents. The processional line was led by Reverend Smith Payne, a family friend who conducted the service, then followed her doctors, the pallbearers, her family, and then, in a long line, President Polk and his wife, the members of the cabinet, hundreds of members of the diplomatic corps, nearly all the members of the Senate and the House of Representatives, judges of the Supreme Court and district courts, military officers from all branches of the service, the mayor and city officials, and representatives from all departments of the federal government. There was one last prayer session at her grave, and then she was buried in the middle of the city that she and her husband had loved so dearly. Her body would be moved to Montpelier nine years later, where it was buried next to the president's.

On January 17, 1852, Payne Todd, at sixty-one, died in Washington of typhoid fever. His body was taken by carriage to Congressional Cemetery; the carriage was followed by one, single, unknown mourner. During his last days, talking about his relationship to his parents, Payne Todd told a friend that throughout his life he had been his own worst enemy.

NOTES

CHAPTER 1. SAVING GEORGE WASHINGTON IN A CITY ON FIRE

1. *National Intelligencer*, August 20, 1814.

2. Dolley Madison to Edward Coles, May 12, 1813, in Dolley Madison Digital Edition, ed. Holly C. Shulman (Charlottesville: University of Virginia Press, Online Rotunda Edition, 2010–2013) (hereafter referred to as DMDE).

3. Ibid.

4. Dolley Madison to Edward Coles, May 18, 1813, in ibid.

5. Abigail Adams to her sister Elizabeth, in *Dolley Madison: Her Life and Times*, by Katherine Anthony (New York: Doubleday, 1949), p. 116; National Geographic Society, *The Capital of Our Country* (Washington, DC: National Geographic Society, 1923), p. 7.

6. Noble Cunningham Jr., ed., "The Frances Few Diary," *Journal of Southern History* 29, no. 3 (August 1963): 349.

7. Ibid., pp. 351–52.

8. Lucia Cutts, *Memoirs and Letters of Dolley Madison, Wife of James Madison, President of the United States* (1886; repr. Port Washington, NY: Kennikat Press, 1971), pp. 108–11.

9. Harry Ammon, *James Monroe: The Quest for National Identity* (New York: McGraw-Hill, 1971), pp. 323–24.

10. Irving Brant, *James Madison* (Indianapolis, IN: Bobbs-Merrill, 1941–1961), 1:294–95.

11. Ibid., p. 293.

12. Ibid., p. 295.

13. Ibid., p. 297.

14. Ammon, *James Monroe*, pp. 332–33.

15. C. Edward Skeen, *Citizen Soldiers in the War of 1812* (Lexington: University of Kentucky Press, 1977), p. 135.

16. *Baltimore Patriot*, August 31, 1814.

17. Cutts, *Memoirs and Letters of Dolley Madison*, pp. 108–11.

18. Anthony, *Dolley Madison*, p. 224.

19. Earl Pomeroy, ed., *Military Affairs Magazine* 12, no. 3 (Autumn 1948): 171.

20. Ibid., p. 110.

21. Thomas Jefferson to Thomas Flournoy, in Cutts, *Memoirs and Letters of Dolley Madison*, pp. 97–98.

22. Dolley Madison to Anna Cutts, August 23, 1814, in ibid., pp. 108–11.

23. Harold Eberlein and Cortlandt Van Dyke Hubbard, *Historic Houses of George-Town and Washington City* (Richmond, VA: Dietz Press, 1958), p. 202.

24. Anthony, *Dolley Madison*, p. 199.

25. Alan Lloyd, *The Scorching of Washington: The War of 1812* (Washington, DC: Robert B. Luce, 1974), p. 168.

26. Anthony Pitch, *The Burning of Washington: The British Invasion of 1814* (Annapolis, MD: Naval Institute Press, 1998), p. 87.

27. Charles Ingersoll, *History of the Second War between the United States of America and Great Britain Declared by Act of Congress, the 18th of June, 1812, and Concluded by Peace, the 15th of February, 1815* (Philadelphia, PA: Lea and Blanchard, 1845–1849), pp. 206–-207.

28. Paul Jennings, *A Colored Man's Reminiscences of James Madison* (Brooklyn, NY: George C. Beadle, 1865), p. 11; Lloyd, *Scorching of Washington*, p. 168.

29. Catherine Allgor, *A Perfect Union: Dolley Madison and the Creation of the American Nation* (New York: Henry Holt, 2006), p. 314.

30. Ibid.

31. Anthony, *Dolley Madison*, p. 230.

32. Anne Hollingsworth Wharton, *Social Life in the Early Republic* (Philadelphia, PA: J. B. Lippincott, 1903), pp. 166–67; Dolley Madison to Anna Cutts, August 23, 1814, in DMDE.

33. Lloyd, *Scorching of Washington*, p. 14.

34. Pitch, *Burning of Washington*, p. 66.

35. Louis Serrurier to Charles Talleyrand, August 27, 1814, in DMDE.

36. James Ewell, *The Planter's and Mariner's Medical Companion*, 3rd ed. (Philadelphia, PA: Anderson and Meehan, 1816), p. 633.

37. Pitch, *Burning of Washington*, p. 77.

38. Ibid., p. 91.

39. Ibid., p. 64.

40. The destruction of the Navy Yard was chronicled by Colonel Tom Tingey, who did so in a report to the secretary of the navy, *National Intelligencer*, September 8, 1814.

41. Sir Harry Smith, *Autobiography of Lieutenant-General Sir Harry Smith* (London: Murray, 1903), p. 200.

42. John Williams, *History of the Invasion and Capture of Washington, and Events Which Preceded and Followed* (New York: Harper and Brothers, 1857), pp. 254–55.

43. James McGregor, *Washington from the Ground Up* (Cambridge, MA: Belknap Press, 2007), pp. 46–47.

44. Mary Stockton Hunter to Susan Stockton Cuthbert, August 30, 1814, in Hunter Family Papers, New York Historical Society.

45. Margaret Bayard Smith, *The First Forty Years of Washington Society*, ed. Gaillard Hunt (New York: Charles Scribner's Sons, 1906), pp. 104–105.

46. William Thornton remembrance, *National Intelligencer*, September 8, 1814.

47. Ibid.; Williams, *History of the Invasion and Capture of Washington*, p. 266.

48. Williams, *History of the Invasion and Capture of Washington*, p. 173.

49. Pitch, *Burning of Washington*, p. 125.

50. Matilda Sayrs, "Reminiscences," Alexandria (Virginia) Library, special collections.

51. Ibid., p. 173.

CHAPTER 2. OPPOSITES ATTRACT

1. Catherine Allgor, *A Perfect Union: Dolley Madison and the Creation of the American Nation* (New York: Henry Holt, 2006), p. 24.

2. John Todd to Dolley Madison, July 30, 1793, in Dolley Madison Digital Edition, ed. Holly C. Shulman (Charlottesville: University of Virginia Press, Online Rotunda Edition, 2010–2013) (hereafter cited as DMDE).

3. Dolley Madison, *The Selected Letters of Dolley Payne Madison*, ed. David Mattern and Holley Schulman (Charlottesville: University Press of Virginia, 2003), pp. 14–15.

4. Dolley Madison to James Todd, October 28 and 31, 1794, and February 1784, in DMDE.

5. Nancy Isenberg, *Fallen Founder: The Life of Aaron Burr* (New York: Viking Press, 2007), p. 124.

6. Fawn Brodie, *Thomas Jefferson: An Intimate History* (New York: W. W. Norton, 1974), p. 301.

7. Catherine Allgor, *The Queen of America: Mary Cutts's Life of Dolley Madison* (Charlottesville: University of Virginia Press, 2012), p. 52; Lucia Cutts, *Memoirs and Letters of Dolley Madison, Wife of James Madison, President of the United States* (1886; repr., Port Washington, NY: Kennikat Press, 1971), 1:14.

8. Irving Brant, *James Madison* (Indianapolis, IN: Bobbs-Merrill, 1941–1946), 1:630.

9. Catherine Coles to Dolley Madison, June 1, 1794, in Madison, *Selected Letters of Dolley Payne Madison*, pp. 27–28.

10. Margaret Bayard Smith, *The First Forty Years of Washington Society*, ed. Gaillard Hunt (New York: Charles Scribner's Sons, 1906), p. 61.

11. Virginia Moore, *The Madisons: A Biography* (New York: McGraw-Hill, 1979), p. 15.

12. Thomas Jefferson, *Papers of Thomas Jefferson*, ed. Julian Boyd and Barbara Oberg (Princeton, NJ: Princeton University Press, 2007), 7:240; Brodie, *Thomas Jefferson*, p. 178.

13. William Wilkins to Dolley Madison, August 22, 1794, in Madison, *Selected Letters of Dolley Payne Madison*, pp. 29–30.

14. Cutts, *Memoirs and Letters of Dolley Madison*, 2:16.

15. James Madison to Dolley Madison, August 1794, in DMDE.

16. Ethel Arnett, *Mrs. James Madison: The Incomparable Dolley* (Greensboro, NC: Piedmont Press, 1972), p. 63.

17. Dolley Madison to Eliza Collins Lee, September 16, 1794, in DMDE.

CHAPTER 3. THE HAPPY GROOM RETIRES FROM PUBLIC LIFE

1. Ralph Ketcham, *James Madison: A Biography* (New York: Macmillan, 1971), p. 286.

2. George Washington to James Madison, May 5, 1789, in *The Writings of George Washington*, by George Washington, ed. John C. Fitzpatrick (Washington, DC: Government Printing Office, 1932), 30:311; Richard Smith, *Patriarch: George Washington and the New American Nation* (Boston: Houghton-Mifflin, 1993), p. 24.

3. Ketcham, *James Madison*, p. 314.

4. Alexander Hamilton to Edward Carrington, May 26, 1792, in *The Papers of Alexander Hamilton*, by Alexander Hamilton, ed. Harold Syrett, vol. 11 (New York: Columbia University Press, 1961–1987), pp. 425–45.

5. Dumas Malone, *Jefferson and His Time* (Charlottesville: University Press of Virginia, 2005), 2:324; Ketcham, *James Madison*, p. 333.

6. Stuart Leibiger, *Founding Friendship: George Washington, James Madison and the Creation of the American Republic* (Charlottesville: University Press of Virginia, 1999), p. 220.

7. Adrienne Koch, *Jefferson and Madison: The Great Collaboration* (Birmingham, AL: Palladium Press, 2005), p. 172.

8. Thomas Jefferson to James Madison, December 28, 1794, in Malone, *Jefferson and His Time*, 3:187.

9. Thomas Jefferson to James Madison, in *The Republic of Letters: The Correspondence between Thomas Jefferson and James Madison, 1776–1826*, ed. James Smith (New York: W. W. Norton, 1995), 2:854–55.

10. Thomas Jefferson to Edward Rutledge, November 30, 1795, in *The Writings of Thomas Jefferson*, by Thomas Jefferson, ed. Paul Ford (New York: 1892–1899), 7:39.

11. Thomas Jefferson to James Madison, December 28, 1794, in Malone, *Jefferson and His Time*, 3:187.

12. James Madison to Thomas Jefferson, in Smith, *Republic of Letters*, 2:855.

13. James Madison Jr. to James Madison Sr., March 12, 1797, in *The Papers of James Madison: Secretary of State Series, Presidential Series, Retirement Series, Personal Papers*, ed. Robert Brugger et al. (Charlottesville: University Press of Virginia, 1986) (hereafter cited as *PJM*), 16:500–501.

14. David Ramsey, "The View from Inside," in *The Ambiguity of the American Revolution*, ed. Jack Greene (New York: Harper and Row, 1968), pp. 33–34; Thomas Jefferson to James Madison, December 28, 1794, in Smith, *Republic of Letters*, 1:866–68.

15. John Adams to Abigail Adams, January 1797, in *PJM*, 17:xix.

16. Hubbard Taylor to James Madison, May 1, 1797, in ibid., 17:4–5.

CHAPTER 4. RETURN TO MONTPELIER, 1796

1. James Madison Jr. to James Madison Sr., February 23, 1795, in *The Writings of James Madison*, by James Madison and Gaillard Hunt (New York: Russell and Russell, 1968), 6:213.

2. Ralph Ketcham, *James Madison: A Biography* (New York: Macmillan, 1971), pp. 373–75.

3. Irving Brant, *James Madison* (Indianapolis, IN: Bobbs-Merrill, 1941–1946), 3:323–24.

4. Ketcham, *James Madison*, p. 387.

5. Anna Maria Brodeau Thornton, September 5, 1802, in Anna Thornton Diary, 1793–1804, Ann Maria Brodeau Thornton Papers, Library of Congress; Matthew Hyland, *Montpelier and the Madisons: House, Home and American Heritage* (Charleston, SC: History Press, 2007), pp. 60–62.

6. Mary Bagot, August 20, 1817, in *Exile in Yankeeland: The Journal of Mary Bagot, 1816–1819*, ed. David Hosford (Washington, DC: Historical Society of Washington, DC, 1984); Anna Thornton to Dolley Madison, August 21, 1809, in Dolley Madison Digital Edition, ed. Holly C. Shulman (Charlottesville: University of Virginia Press, Online Rotunda Edition, 2010–2013) (hereafter cited as DMDE).

7. Hyland, *Montpelier and the Madisons*, pp. 54–56; James Blair to James Madison, April 25, 1797, in *The Papers of James Madison: Secretary of State Series, Presidential Series, Retirement Series, Personal Papers*, ed. Robert Brugger et al. (Charlottesville: University Press of Virginia, 1986) (hereafter cited as *PJM*), 17:2.

8. James Monroe to James Madison, November 30, 1794, in *PJM*, 15:403.

9. Memorandum to Monroe from Madison, in ibid., 15:498; James Madison to James Monroe, January 15, 1796, in ibid., 16:202.

10. Hyland, *Montpelier and the Madisons*, p. 58.

11. Ibid., pp. 58–63.

12. Margaret Tinkcom, "Caviar along the Potomac: Sir Augustus John Foster's

'Notes on the United States,' 1804–1812," *William and Mary Quarterly*, 3rd ser., 8 (January 1951): 90, 98.

13. James Madison to Thomas Jefferson, January 21, 1798, in *Political Writings of Thomas Jefferson*, ed. Merrill Peterson (Charlottesville, VA: Thomas Jefferson Memorial Foundation, 1993), p. 121.

14. James Madison to Thomas Jefferson, December 29, 1799, in *PJM*, 2:151.

15. James Madison to James Monroe, February 5, 1798, in ibid., 17:73–75.

16. James Madison to Thomas Jefferson, May 13, 1798, in ibid., 17:131–33; Dolley Madison to Dolley Cutts, December 1831, in DMDE.

17. James Madison to Thomas Jefferson, December 25, 1797, in *PJM*, 17:63–64.

18. Thomas Jefferson to James Madison, June 1, 1797, in ibid., 17:10–11.

19. John Snowden and William McCorkle to James Madison, August 8, 1797, in ibid., 17:41.

20. Brant, *James Madison*, 1:467.

21. Thornton, September 13, 1802, in Anna Thornton Diary; Katherine Anthony, *Dolley Madison: Her Life and Times* (New York: Doubleday, 1949), p. 261.

22. Sally McKean d'Yrugo to Dolley Madison, August 3, 1797, in DMDE; Dolley Madison to Eliza Collins Lee, October of 1794, '95 or '96, in DMDE; Robert Honeyman to Dolley Madison, July 19, 1799, in DMDE; Dolley Madison to Eliza Collins Lee, January 12, 1800, in DMDE.

23. James Monroe to James Madison, December 10, 1797, in *PJM*, 17:60.

24. James Madison to Thomas Jefferson, February 1798, in Madison and Hunt, *Writings of James Madison*, 6:310.

25. James Madison to James Monroe, December 17, 1797, in ibid., 2:119–20.

26. James Madison to Thomas Jefferson, June 10, 1798, and December 29, 1798, in ibid., 2:148–49.

27. James Madison to Thomas Jefferson, March 12, 1798, in ibid., 2:130–31.

28. James Madison to Thomas Jefferson, April 2, 1798, in ibid., 2:131.

29. James Madison to Thomas Jefferson, April 15, 1798, in ibid., 2:136.

30. James Madison to Thomas Jefferson, May 20, 1798, in ibid., 6:121.

31. Thomas Jefferson to James Madison, April 6, 1798, and April 15, 1798, in *PJM*, 17:198, 113.

32. *Gazette of the United States*, April 24, 1798.

33. Samuel Chase to James McHenry, December 4, 1796, in *The Life and Correspondence of James McHenry, Secretary of War under Washington and Adams*, by Bernard Steiner (Cleveland: Burrows Brothers, 1907), p. 203.

34. In James Morton Smith, "Sedition in the Old Dominion: James T. Callender and 'The Prospect before Us,'" *Journal of Southern History* 20, no. 2 (May 1954): 339–40.

35. *Aurora*, May 15, 1799.

36. James Madison to James Monroe, May 23, 1800, in *PJM*, 17:389–90.

37. Noel Gerson, *The Velvet Glove: A Life of Dolley Madison* (Nashville: Thomas and Nelson, 1975), p. 104.

38. Ketcham, *James Madison*, pp. 400–402.

39. James Madison to Thomas Jefferson, April 19, 1798, in *PJM*, 17:113–15.

40. Stephen Moylan to James Madison, April 25, 1798, in ibid., 17:119.

CHAPTER 5. MONTPELIER TO WASHINGTON, DC

1. William Appleton Williams, *America Confronts a Revolutionary World, 1776–1976* (New York: William Morrow, 1976), pp. 28–31.

2. David McCants, *Patrick Henry: The Orator* (New York: Greenwood Press, 1990), p. 121; Jefferson notes in H. R. McIlwaine and J. P. Kennedy, *Journals of the House of Burgesses of Virginia* (Richmond, VA: Colonial Press, E. Waddy, 1905–1915), 9:xiii.

3. George Washington to Joseph Reed, February 10, 1776, in *The Writings of George Washington*, by George Washington, ed. John C. Fitzpatrick (Washington, DC: Government Printing Office, 1932) (hereafter cited as *GWW*), 4:321.

4. William Miller, *The Business of May Next: James Madison and the Founding* (Charlottesville: University Press of Virginia, 1992), pp. 8–9.

5. Fisher Ames to George Minot, May 3, 1789, in *The Works of Fisher Ames*, by Seth Ames (Boston: Little, Brown, 1854), 1:34–35.

6. Noble Cunningham Jr., *In Pursuit of Reason: The Life of Thomas Jefferson* (Baton Rouge: Louisiana State University Press, 1987), p. 176; Stuart Leibiger, *Founding Friendship: George Washington, James Madison and the Creation of the American Republic* (Charlottesville: University Press of Virginia, 1999), p. 120.

7. Charles Callan Tansill, *The Making of the American Republic: The Great Documents, 1774–1789* (New Rochelle, NY: Arlington House Press, 1972), p. 105.

8. Samuel Otis to Theodore Sedgwick, June 15, 1788, Sedgwick Family Papers, Massachusetts Historical Society.

9. J.-P. Brissot de Warville, *New Travels in the United States of America, 1788*, trans. M. S. Vamos and Durand Echeverria, ed. Durand Echeverria (London: J. E. Jordan, 1794), pp. 146–48.

10. Plumer's Memorandum, April 8, 1806, Plumer's biographical notes in the William Plumer Papers, Library of Congress, New Hampshire State Library, p. 478.

11. Hugh Grigsby, *The Virginia Convention of 1776* (Richmond, VA, 1855), p. 182.

12. Hamilton to Rufus King, October 30, 1794, in *James Madison*, by Irving Brant (Indianapolis, IN, Bobbs-Merrill), 1:416.

13. Ibid.

14. Ibid., 1:417.

15. Eugene Link, *Democratic and Republican Societies, 1790–1800* (New York: Columbia University Press, 1942), pp. 210–11.

16. George Washington to Timothy Pickering, July 27, 1795, in *GWW*, 34:251; George Washington, farewell address, September 19, 1796, in *GWW*, 35:226.

17. Theodore Sedgwick to Ephraim Williams, June 5, 1794, in Sedgwick Family Papers, Massachusetts Historical Society; Samuel Smith to O. H. Williams, March 30, 1794, in Otho Holland Williams Papers, no. 9, 866, Maryland Historical Society; Noble Cunningham Jr., *The Jeffersonian Republicans: The Formation of Party Organization, 1789–1801* (Chapel Hill: University of North Carolina Press, 1957), pp. 68–70.

18. Newspaper essay in several journals, September 22, 1792; Lance Banning, *The Sacred Fire of Liberty: James Madison and the Founding of the Federal Republic* (Ithaca, NY: Cornell University Press, 1995), p. 362; James Madison, "Government of the United States," essay, February 4, 1792, in *The Papers of James Madison: Secretary of State Series, Presidential Series, Retirement Series, Personal Papers*, ed. Robert Brugger et al. (Charlottesville: University Press of Virginia, 1986), 14:217–18.

19. Noel Gerson, *The Velvet Glove: A Life of Dolley Madison* (Nashville: Thomas and Nelson, 1975), p. 91.

20. Abigail Adams to Marcy Cranch, March 18, 1800, in *The New Letters of Abigail Adams, 1788–1801*, by Abigail Adams, ed. Stewart Mitchell (Boston: Houghton Mifflin, 1947), pp. 241–42.

21. Noble Cunningham Jr., "The Frances Few Diary," *Journal of Southern History* 29, no. 3 (August 1963).

22. Gerson, *Velvet Glove*, p. 94.

23. Ibid., p. 93.

24. Katherine Anthony, *Dolley Madison: Her Life and Times* (Garden City, NY: Doubleday, 1949), p. 118.

25. John Adams to Abigail Adams, February 11, 1796, in Adams Family Papers, Massachusetts Historical Society.

26. Sally McKean to Anna Payne, June 6, 1796, and September 3, 1796, in *Memoirs and Letters of Dolley Madison, Wife of James Madison, President of the United States*, by Lucia Cutts (1886; repr., Port Washington, NY: Kennikat Press, 1971), pp. 18–22.

27. Dolley Madison to Mrs. Zantzinger, sometime between 1808 and 1810, Dolley Madison Digital Edition, ed. Holly C. Shulman (Charlottesville: University of Virginia Press, Online Rotunda Edition, 2010--2013).

28. Dolley Madison to Benjamin Latrobe, March 17, 1809, in ibid.

29. Benjamin Latrobe to Dolley Madison, March 29, 1809, in ibid.; Benjamin Latrobe to Dolley Madison, March 17, 1809, in ibid.; Mary Latrobe to Dolley Madison, April 12, 1809, in ibid.; Benjamin Latrobe to Dolley Madison, April 21, 1809, in ibid.

30. James Longacre and James Herring, eds., "Mrs. Madison," in *National Portrait Gallery of Distinguished Americans* (New York: Herman Bancroft, 1836), pp. 4–5.

31. Sarah Gales Seaton Papers, January 1814, noted in Josephine Seaton, *William Winston Seaton of the 'National Intelligencer': A Biographical Sketch* (Boston: James Osgood, 1871), p. 113; Catherine Allgor, *A Perfect Union: Dolley Madison and the Creation of the American Nation* (New York: Henry Holt, 2006), p. 336.

32. Allgor, *Perfect Union*, pp. 245–47.

33. Anthony, *Dolley Madison*, p. 237.

34. Ibid., p. 197.

35. Margaret Bayard Smith, *A Winter in Washington; or, Memoirs of the Seymour Family* (New York: E. Bliss and E. White, 1824), pp. 43–44; Allgor, *Perfect Union*, p. 247.

36. Margaret Bayard Smith, *The First Forty Years of Washington Society*, ed. Gaillard Hunt (New York: Charles Scribner's Sons, 1906), pp. 61–63.

CHAPTER 6. A NEW WORLD

1. Lucia Cutts, *Memoirs and Letters of Dolley Madison, Wife of James Madison, President of the United States* (1886; repr., Port Washington, NY: Kennikat Press, 1971), p. 1.

2. *National Intelligencer*, March 5, 1801, and June 8, 1801.

3. *Alexandria Advertiser and Commercial Intelligencer*, February 28, 1800.

4. Ralph Ketcham, *James Madison: A Biography* (New York: Macmillan, 1971), p. 408.

5. Maud Goodwin, *Dolley Madison* (New York: Charles Scribner's Sons, 1940), p. 79.

6. Hetty Ann Barton, Diary of Hetty Ann Barton, May 1803, in Papers of Hetty Ann Barton, Historical Society of Pennsylvania.

7. Mary Bagot, *Exile in Yankeeland: The Journal of Mary Bagot, 1816–1819*, ed. David Hosford (Washington, DC: Historical Society of Washington, DC, 1984), p. 31.

8. US Census Bureau, 2nd–9th editions (Washington, DC: US Government Printing Office, 1800–1870).

9. Dolley Madison, *The Selected Letters of Dolley Payne Madison*, ed. David Mattern and Holly Schulman (Charlottesville: University Press of Virginia, 2003), pp. 40–41.

10. Constance McLaughlin Green, *Washington: Village and Capital, 1800–1878* (Princeton, NJ: Princeton University Press, 1962), pp. 27–28.

11. Ibid., p. 24.

12. Richard Griswold to Mrs. Fanny Griswold, December 6, 1800, in Griswold Manuscripts, Yale University Library.

13. Fawn Brodie, *Thomas Jefferson: An Intimate Portrait* (New York: W. W. Norton, 1974), p. 336.

14. Cutts, *Memoirs and Letters of Dolley Madison*, 2:1; Samuel Mitchill, "Dr. Mitchill's Letters from Washington: 1801–1813," *Harper's New Monthly Magazine* 58 (April 1879): 740–47.

15. Green, *Washington*, p. 46.

16. James Madison to Thomas Jefferson, April 33, 1801, in *The Papers of Thomas Jefferson*, by Thomas Jefferson, ed. Julian Boyd and Barbara Oberg (Princeton, NJ: Princeton University Press, 2007), 33:630.

17. Thomas Jefferson to James Madison, March 12, 1801, in ibid., 33:255–56.

18. Thomas Jefferson to James Madison, April 25, 1801, in ibid., 33:642.

19. Levi Lincoln to Thomas Jefferson, April 16, 1801, in ibid., 33:596–98.

20. Green, *Washington*, p. 26; James Madison to Thomas Jefferson, March 15, 1800, in *The Writings of James Madison*, by James Madison and Gaillard Hunt (New York: Russell and Russell, 1968), 2:155–56.

21. Dolley Madison to Anna Thornton, May 18, 1808, in Dolley Madison Digital Edition, ed. Holly C. Shulman (Charlottesville: University of Virginia Press, Online Rotunda Edition, 2010–2013) (hereafter cited as DMDE).

22. Ibid.

23. Cutts, *Memoirs and Letters of Dolley Madison*, p. 2.

24. Ralph Ketcham, *The Madisons at Montpelier: Reflections on the Founding Couple* (Charlottesville: University Press of Virginia, 2009), p. 1.

25. Nancy Isenberg, *Fallen Founder: The Life of Aaron Burr* (New York: Viking Press, 2007), pp. 148–49.

26. James Madison to Thomas Jefferson, January 10, 1801, in *The Republic of Letters: The Correspondence between Thomas Jefferson and James Madison, 1776–1826*, ed. James Smith (New York: W. W. Norton, 1995), 2:166–70.

27. Ron Chernow, *Alexander Hamilton* (New York: Penguin Press, 2004), p. 646.

28. Beckles Willson, *Friendly Relations: A Narrative of Britain's Ministers and Ambassadors to America (1791–1930)* (London: L. Dickson and Thompson, 1934), pp. 40–48.

29. Joseph Ellis, *American Sphinx: The Character of Thomas Jefferson* (New York: Alfred A. Knopf, 1994), p. 201.

30. James Madison to Thomas Jefferson, February 28, 1801, in Smith, *Republic of Letters*, 2:170–72.

31. James Madison to Thomas Jefferson, February 28, 1801, in Jefferson and Boyd (ed.) and Oberg (ed.), *Papers of Thomas Jefferson*, 33:99–100.

32. Thomas Jefferson to James Madison, March 12, 1801, in ibid., 33:255–56; Jefferson to Thomas Mann Randolph, June 4, 1801, in ibid., 34:256–57.

33. Paul Jennings, *A Colored Man's Reminiscences of James Madison* (Brooklyn, NY: G. C. Beadle, 1865), p. 19.

34. Hugh Howard, *Mr. and Mrs. Madison's War: America's First Couple and the Second War of Independence* (New York: Bloomsbury Press, 2012), p. 9.

35. James Monroe to James Madison, March 11, 1801, in *The Papers of James Madison: Secretary of State Series, Presidential Series, Retirement Series, Personal Papers,* ed. Robert Brugger et al. (Charlottesville: University Press of Virginia, 1986), 1:11.

36. Samuel Osgood to James Madison, April 24, 1801, in ibid., 1:113–14.

37. Dolley Madison to Anna Cutts, June 1804, in DMDE.

38. Thomas Jefferson to Meriwether Lewis, February 23, 1801, in Jefferson and Boyd (ed.) and Oberg (ed.), *Papers of Thomas Jefferson,* 33:51.

39. Thomas Jefferson to Mann Randolph, May 14, 1801, in ibid., 34:110–11.

40. Ibid., p. 409.

41. Katherine Anthony, *Dolley Madison: Her Life and Times* (Garden City, NY: Doubleday, 1949), p. 195.

42. Thomas Jefferson to Carlos Martinez de Irujo, March 24, 1801, in Jefferson and Boyd (ed.) and Oberg (ed.), *Papers of Thomas Jefferson,* 33:430.

43. Thomas Jefferson to T. M. Randolph Jr., November 16, 1801, in ibid., vol. 32; Thomas Jefferson to Albert Gallatin, September 18, 1801, in *Writings of Albert Gallatin,* by Albert Gallatin and Henry Adams (New York: Antiquarian Press, 1960), 1:55.

44. Abigail Adams to her daughter, 1800, in Goodwin, *Dolly Madison,* pp. 82–83.

45. Ibid., p. 93.

46. Anthony, *Dolley Madison,* p. 196.

47. Hetty Ann Barton, May 1803, in Papers of Hetty Ann Barton, Pennsylvania Historical Society.

48. Edward Coles to Hugh Blair Grigsby, December 23, 1854, Virginia Historical Society, in Ketcham, *James Madison,* p. 407.

49. John Quincy Adams, *The Diary of John Quincy Adams, 1794–1845: American Diplomacy, and Political, Social, and Intellectual Life, from Washington to Polk,* ed. Allan Nevins (New York: Frederick Ungar Publishing, 1928), p. 37.

50. Goodwin, *Dolly Madison,* p. 110.

51. Bagot, *Exile to Yankeeland,* April 3, 1816, and March 27, 1816, entries.

52. Ibid., March 9, 1817, entry.

53. Dr. Samuel Mitchill to his wife, January 4, 1892, in *Life and Letters of Dolley Madison,* by Allen Clark (Washington, DC: Press of W. F. Roberts, 1914), pp. 914, 50; Samuel Mitchill Papers, Museum of City of New York.

54. William Parker Cutler, *Life, Journals and Correspondence of Rev. Manasseh Cutler, LL.D.* (Cincinnati, 1888), 2:154n.

55. M. B. Smith, quoted in Clark, *Life and Letters of Dolley Madison,* pp. 64–65; Jeremiah Mason to Means Mason, December 12, 1813, in DMDE.

56. Margaret Smith to Susan Smith, July 31, 1806, in *Forty Years in Washington*

Society, by Margaret Bayard Smith, ed. Gaillard Hunt (New York: Charles Scribner's Sons, 1906), pp. 51–52.

57. Dolley Madison to Anna Thornton, August 26, 1807, in DMDE.

58. Smith, *Forty Years in Washington Society*, pp. 10–11.

59. *Washington Federalist*, December 18, 1806; Anthony, *Dolley Madison*, p. 121.

60. Anthony, *Dolley Madison*, p. 117.

61. Ibid., p. 123.

62. Madison, *Selected Letters of Dolley Payne Madison*, pp. 44–45.

63. Catherine Allgor, *A Perfect Union: Dolley Madison and the Creation of the American Nation* (New York: Henry Holt, 2006), pp. 50–51.

64. Virginia Moore, *The Madisons: A Biography* (New York: McGraw-Hill, 1979), p. 169; Martha Randolph to Thomas Jefferson, October 29, 1802, in Goodwin, *Dolly Madison*, p. 96; Dolley Madison to James Madison, November 13, 1805, in DMDE.

65. Dolley Madison to Anna Cutts, July 8, 1805, in Dolley Madison Papers, North American Women's Letters and Diaries, digital collection, doc. 13.

66. Dolley Madison to Anna Cutts, July 16, 1804, in Anthony, *Dolley Madison*, p. 164.

67. Thomas Jefferson to David Williams, January 31, 1806, in Noble E. Cunningham, *The Process of Government under Jefferson* (Princeton, NJ: Princeton University Press, 1978), pp. 41–44.

68. Dolley Madison to Anna Cutts, July 8, 1805, in Dolley Madison Papers, North American Women's Letters and Diaries, digital collection, doc. 13.

69. Noel Gerson, *The Velvet Glove: A Life of Dolley Madison* (Nashville: Thomas and Nelson, 1975), p. 100.

70. Ibid., p. 122.

71. Anthony, *Dolley Madison*, pp. 124–25.

72. Dolley Madison to Anna Cutts, May 22, 1805, in Cutts Family Papers, Library of Congress; Moore, *Madisons*, p. 186; Dolley Madison to Dolley Cutts, February 10, 1835, in DMDE.

73. T. M. Randolph to Harriet Randolph, December 7, 1804, in collection of letters of C. M. Storey, Papers of C. M. Storey, Massachusetts Historical Society.

74. Dumas Malone, *Jefferson and the Ordeal of Liberty* (Boston: Little, Brown, 1962), p. 394.

75. Cutts, *Memoirs and Letters of Dolley Madison*, 2:10; Dolley Madison to Phoebe Morris, August 16, 1812, in DMDE.

76. Cutts, *Memoirs and Letters of Dolley Madison*, 2:10.

77. Margaret Tinkcom, "Caviar along the Potomac: Sir Augustus John Foster's 'Notes on the United States,' 1804–1812," *William and Mary Quarterly* 3rd ser., 8 (January 1951): 155.

78. Isenberg, *Fallen Founder*, p. 235.

79. Plumer's Memorandum, in William Plumer Papers, Library of Congress, New Hampshire State Library, p. 208.

80. Dolley Madison to Anna Cutts, June 1804, in DMDE.

81. Anne Hollingsworth Wharton, *Social Life in the Early Republic* (Philadelphia, PA: J. B. Lippincott, 1903), p. 147.

82. H. B. Smith to Mrs. Kirkpatrick, January 13, 1804, in Smith, *First Forty Years of Washington Society*, pp. 45–47.

83. Dolley Madison to Anna Cutts, June 1804, in DMDE.

84. James Madison to Thomas Jefferson, April 22, 1801, in Jefferson and Boyd (ed.) and Oberg (ed.), *Papers of Thomas Jefferson*, 33:630.

85. William Thornton to James Madison, March 16, 1801, in Anthony, *Dolley Madison*, p. 111.

86. James Madison to Thomas Jefferson, January 10, 1800, in Madison and Hunt, *Writings of James Madison*, 2:167–70.

87. Thomas Jefferson to Dolley Madison, May 27, 1801, in Cutts, *Memoirs and Letters of Dolley Madison*, p. 28; Ketcham, *James Madison*, pp. 428–29.

88. Smith, introduction to *Forty Years in Washington Society*, pp. vii–viii.

89. *National Intelligencer*, March 9, 1800.

90. Ibid., June 8, 1801.

91. Ibid.

92. Ibid., October 26, 1801.

93. Ibid., December 6, 1802.

94. Ibid., December 10, 1802.

95. Moore, *Madisons*, p. 161.

CHAPTER 7. THE MADISONS AS SOCIAL LIONS

1. Ralph Ketcham, *James Madison: A Biography* (New York: Macmillan, 1971), p. 410.

2. Leonard White, *The Jeffersonian: A Study in Administrative History* (New York: Macmillan, 1951), pp. 187–88; James Madison to James Monroe, May 6, 1801, in *The Writings of James Madison*, by James Madison and Gaillard Hunt (New York: Russell and Russell, 1968), 6:419; James Madison to W. C. Nicholas, July 10, 1801, in Madison and Hunt, *Writings of James Madison*, 6:425.

3. Dolley Madison to Anna Cutts, July 8, 1805, in Dolley Madison Papers, North American Women's Letters and Diaries, digital collection, doc. 13.

4. Stanley Elkins and Eric McKitrick, *The Age of Federalism* (New York: Oxford University Press, 1993), pp. 74–75; Catherine Allgor, *A Perfect Union: Dolley Madison and the Creation of the American Nation* (New York: Henry Holt, 2006), p. 65.

5. *National Intelligencer*, March 4, 1801.

6. Margaret Smith to Susan Smith, March 4, 1801, in *The First Forty Years of Washington Society*, by Margaret Bayard Smith, ed. Gaillard Hunt (New York: Charles Scribner's Sons, 1906), pp. 25–26.

7. Thomas Jefferson to Joseph Priestley, March 21, 1804, in Madison and Hunt, *Writings of James Madison*, 2:7–8.

8. Willard Randall, *Thomas Jefferson: A Life* (New York: Henry Holt, 1993), p. 548; Jefferson's Inaugural Address, in *The Works of Thomas Jefferson* by Paul Ford (New York: G. P. Putnam's Sons, 1904), 33:139–52.

9. Thomas Jefferson to Governor Tom McKean of Pennsylvania, July 24, 1801, in Papers of Thomas Jefferson, Princeton University Library; Henry Adams, *History of the United States during the First Administration of James Madison* (New York: Literary Classics of the United States, Library of America, 1986), p. 319.

10. Thomas Jefferson to the heads of his departments, November 6, 1801, in *The Republic of Letters: The Correspondence between Thomas Jefferson and James Madison, 1776–1826*, ed. James Smith (New York: W. W. Norton, 1995), 2:1168.

11. Samuel Eddy, Jona. Russell, James Turder Jr., Levi Wheaton, and Henry Smith to Thomas Jefferson, March 5, 1801, in *Papers of Thomas Jefferson*, by Thomas Jefferson, ed. Julian Boyd and Barbara Oberg (Princeton, NJ: Princeton University Press, 2007), 33:187–88.

12. Thomas Jefferson to James Monroe, March 7, 1801, in *Writings of Thomas Jefferson*, by A. A. Lipscomb and A. E. Bergh (Washington, DC: Thomas Jefferson Memorial Association of the United States, 1903), 9:203.

13. Ibid., 9:204.

14. *American Citizen*, June 5, 1801.

15. James Madison to Dolley Madison, November 2, 1805, in Dolley Madison Digital Edition, ed. Holly C. Shulman (Charlottesville: University of Virginia Press, Online Rotunda Edition, 2010–2013).

16. Thomas Jefferson to James Madison, April 27, 1809, in Smith, *Republic of Letters*, 3:1585–86.

17. Letter to the *Federalist and New Jersey Gazette*, February 27, 1802.

18. *Alexandria Advertiser and Commercial Intelligence*, December 16, 1800.

19. Joseph Shulim, ed., *The Old Dominion and Napoleon Bonaparte: A Study in American Opinion* (New York: Columbia University Press, 1952), pp. 110–11.

20. James Madison to Thomas Jefferson, May 13, 1798, in *The Papers of James Madison: Secretary of State Series, Presidential Series, Retirement Series, Personal Papers*, ed. Robert Brugger et al. (Charlottesville: University Press of Virginia, 1986), 17:130.

21. Randall, *Thomas Jefferson*, pp. 562–63; *National Intelligencer*, June 8, 1801.

22. James Madison to Charles Pinckney, October 12, 1803, in Madison and Hunt, *Writings of James Madison*, 7:53–60, 71–74.

CHAPTER 8. THE LOUISIANA PURCHASE

1. J. Christopher Herold, *The Age of Napoleon* (New York: American Heritage Publishing, 1963), p. 144.

2. Thomas Jefferson, *Papers of Thomas Jefferson*, ed. Julian Boyd and Barbara Oberg (Princeton, NJ: Princeton University Press, 1950–2012), 36:21812; Joseph Shulim, ed., *The Old Dominion and Napoleon Bonaparte: A Study in American Opinion* (New York: Columbia University Press, 1952), p. 111.

3. *Richmond Examiner*, May 5, 1802; Shulim, *Old Dominion and Napoleon Bonaparte*, p. 121.

4. *New England Palladium*, April 12, 1803.

5. *Alexandria Advertiser and Commercial Intelligencer*, July 22, 1803, reprint of an October 19, 1802, letter from diplomat.

6. *Washington Federalist*, January 28, 1808.

7. Fawn Brodie, *Thomas Jefferson: An Intimate History* (New York: W. W. Norton, 1974), pp. 365–66; *National Intelligencer*, April 15, 1803, story about a February 3, 1803, letter.

8. Willard Randall, *Thomas Jefferson: A Life* (New York: Henry Holt, 1993), p. 566.

9. James Madison to James Monroe, January 8, 1785, in in *The Papers of James Madison: Secretary of State Series, Presidential Series, Retirement Series, Personal Papers*, ed. Robert Brugger et al. (Charlottesville: University Press of Virginia, 1986) (hereafter cited as *PJM*), 8:220.

10. Irving Brant, *James Madison* (Indianapolis, IN: Bobbs-Merrill, 1941–1946), 4:90.

11. *Washington Federalist*, February 3, 1808; *Washington Federalist*, January 19, 1806.

12. *Washington Federalist*, January 19, 1806.

13. *National Intelligencer*, February 18, 1803.

14. Harry Ammon, *James Monroe: The Quest for National Identity* (New York: McGraw-Hill, 1971), pp. 210–12; Herold, *Age of Napoleon*, p. 144.

15. John Quincy Adams, *Lives of Celebrated Statesmen* (New York: W. H. Graham, 1846), pp. 33–34.

16. Henry Adams, *John Randolph* (New York: Chelsea House, 1981; Armonk, NY: M. E. Sharpe, 1996), p. 121.

17. Thomas Jefferson to Samuel Kercheval, July 12, 1816, *Writings of Thomas Jefferson*, by A. A. Lipscomb and A. E. Bergh (Washington, DC: Thomas Jefferson Memorial Association of the United States, 1903), 7:9–17.

18. James Madison to James Monroe, summer 1803, in *The Writings of James Madison*, by James Madison and Gaillard Hunt (New York: Russell and Russell, 1968), 2:183–85.

19. Herold, *Age of Napoleon*, pp. 304–305.

20. Albert Gallatin to James Madison, February 7, 1803, in Madison and Hunt, *Writings of James Madison*, 2:179–80.

21. *Alexandria Advertiser and Commercial Intelligencer*, July 27, 1803.
22. *Washington Federalist*, December 3, 1806.
23. *Alexandria Advertiser and Commercial Intelligencer*, July 12, 1803.
24. Jefferson's second inaugural address, in *PJM*, 33:134–53.

CHAPTER 9. THE VETERAN SECRETARY OF STATE

1. Maud Goodwin, *Dolly Madison* (New York: Charles Scribner's Sons, 1940), p. 112; Dolley Madison to James Madison, November 2, 1805, in Dolley Madison Digital Edition, ed. Holly C. Shulman (Charlottesville: University of Virginia Press, Online Rotunda Edition, 2010–2013) (hereafter cited as DMDE).

2. Dolley Madison to Anna Cutts, July 31, 1805, in DMDE; Dolley Madison to Anna Cutts, June 3, 1804, in Dolley Madison Papers, North American Women's Letters and Diaries, digital collection; Goodwin, *Dolly Madison*, pp. 165, 108–109; Katherine Anthony, *Dolley Madison: Her Life and Times* (Garden City, NY: Doubleday, 1949), pp. 166–67.

3. James Madison to Thomas Jefferson, September 14, 1805, in *Republic of Letters: The Correspondence between Thomas Jefferson and James Madison, 1776–1826*, ed. James Smith (New York: W. W. Norton, 1995), 3:1384–86; Thomas Jefferson to James Madison, October 23, 1805, in *James Madison*, by Irving Brant (Indianapolis, IN: Bobbs-Merrill, 1941–1946), 4:289.

4. Dolley Madison to Anna Cutts, July 31, 1805, in DMDE.

5. Dolley Madison journal, October 24, 1805, in Anthony, *Dolley Madison*, pp. 169–70.

6. James Madison to Dolley Madison, October 31, 1805, in DMDE.

7. James Madison to Dolley Madison, November 1805, in DMDE.

8. Anthony, *Dolley Madison*, p. 210.

9. James Madison to Dolley Madison, December 14, 1826, in *James Madison's 'Advice to My Country,'* by James Madison, ed. David Mattern (Charlottesville: University Press of Virginia, 1997), p. 67.

10. Smith, *Republic of Letters*, 3:62–63.

11. Anna Cutts to Dolley Madison, May 1804, in Dolley Madison Papers, North American Women's Letters and Diaries, digital collection, doc. 5.

12. John Quincy Adams, *The Diary of John Quincy Adams, 1794–1845: American Diplomacy and Political, Social and Intellectual Life, from Washington to Polk*, ed. Allan Nevins (New York: Frederick Ungar Publishing, 1928), February 13, 1806 entry.

13. Dolley Madison to Eliza Rankin, 1807, in DMDE.

14. Dolley Madison to Anna Cutts, April 26, 1804, in Anthony, *Dolley Madison*, p. 147; Dolley Madison to Anna Cutts, July 26, 1806, in DMDE.

15. Dolley Madison to Anna Cutts, 1804, in Anthony, *Dolley Madison*, pp. 146–47.

16. Dolly Madison to Anna Cutts, April 26, 1804, in Dolly Madison Papers, North American Women's Letters and Diaries, digital collection, doc. 37; Dolley Madison to Anna Cutts, June 20, 1811, Cutts Family Papers, Library of Congress.

17. Henry Ward and Harold Greer Jr., *Richmond during the Revolution, 1775–83* (Charlottesville: University Press of Virginia, 1977), pp. 112–13.

18. *Richmond Daily Dispatch*, August 27, 1853.

19. *Pittsburgh Gazette*, November 28, 1833.

20. *Richmond Enquirer*, February 6, 1806; William Crawford, *Report on the Penitentiaries of the United States* (Montclair, NJ: Patterson Smith, 1969), p. 111; *Uniform Crime Statistics* (Washington, DC: Federal Bureau of Investigation, 2010), p. 2,011.

21. Jay Worrall, *Friendly Virginians: America's First Quakers* (unpublished manuscript, 1992), Virginia Historical Society.

CHAPTER 10. THE BATTLES WITH BRITAIN

1. Dumas Malone, *Jefferson and His Times* (Charlottesville: University Press of Virginia, 2005), 5:69–72; Jefferson inaugural, Paul Ford, *Works of Thomas Jefferson* (New York: G. P. Putnam's Sons, 1903), 9:193–200.

2. John Eppes to James Madison, January 18, 1810, in *The Papers of James Madison: Secretary of State Series, Presidential Series, Retirement Series, Personal Papers*, ed. Robert Brugger et al. (Charlottesville: University Press of Virginia, 1986) (hereafter cited as *PJM*), presidential ser. 2:189; Paul Hamilton to James Madison, May 23, 1810, in *PJM*, pp. 349–51.

3. *Washington Federalist*, January 21, 1808.

4. Ibid., January 23, 1808.

5. Ralph Ketcham, *James Madison: A Biography* (New York: Macmillan, 1971), pp. 463–64.

6. Albert Gallatin to Thomas Jefferson, December 18, 1807, in *Writings of Albert Gallatin*, by Albert Gallatin and Henry Adams (New York: Antiquarian Press, 1960), 1:368.

7. Wilson Nicholas to Thomas Jefferson, October 20, 1808, in *History of the United States during the First Administration of James Madison*, by Henry Adams (New York: Literary Classics of the United States, 1986), 4:345.

8. William Cullen Bryant, *The Embargo*, facsimile reproduction (Gainesville, FL, 1955), pp. 22–23.

9. Walter Wilson Jennings, *The American Embargo, 1807–1809* (Iowa City: University of Iowa Press, 1921), p. 128.

10. *Washington Federalist*, December 1808.

11. Ibid., May 4, 1808.

12. Ibid., December 1, 1808.

13. Matthew Lyons to a friend in Kentucky, reprinted in ibid., December 1808.

14. James Hillhouse letter in ibid., December 13, 1808.

15. Dolley Madison to Anna Cutts, June 3, 1808, in Dolley Madison Digital Edition, ed. Holly C. Shulman (Charlottesville: University of Virginia Press, Online Rotunda Edition, 2010–2013) (hereafter cited as DMDE); Dolley Madison to Mary Morris, August 20, 1805, in DMDE; Dolley Madison to Anna Cutts, June 18, 1807, in DMDE.

16. Joseph Story to Stephen White, December 24, 1808, in *The Life and Letters of Joseph Story*, ed. William Story (Boston: Charles Little and James Brown, 1851), 1:190–92.

17. *Aurora*, January 3, 1809.

18. Dolley Madison to Anna Cutts, March 1809, in *The Great Little Madison*, by Jean Fritz (New York: G. P. Putnam's Sons, 1989), p. 113.

19. Ketcham, *James Madison*, p. 498.

20. John Marshall to Rufus King, February 26, 1801, in *The Papers of John Marshall*, by John Marshall, ed. Charles Hobson (Chapel Hill: University of North Carolina Press, 1993) 6:82–83.

21. Thomas Jefferson to James Madison, March 11, 1808, in Ford, *Works of Thomas Jefferson*, 11:11–18.

22. *Aurora*, January 19, 1809; *Lexington Reporter* comments at beginning of January 1809, reprinted in *Aurora*, January 19, 1809.

23. Ketcham, *James Madison*, p. 465.

24. James Madison to William Pinckney, April 4 and 8, 1808, and May 1, 1808, Princeton University Library.

25. Katherine Anthony, *Dolley Madison: Her Life and Times* (Garden City, NY: Doubleday, 1949), p. 191.

26. Thomas Jefferson to the citizens of Anne Arundel County, Maryland, February 17, 1809, in *Aurora*, March 8, 1809.

27. Dolley Madison to Anna Cutts, August 28, 1808, in Lucia Cutts, *Memoirs and Letters of Dolley Madison, Wife of James Madison, President of the United States* (1886; repr. Port Washington, NY: Kennikat Press, 1971), pp. 65–66.

28. James Madison to correspondent, 1833, in *Selected Letters of Dolley Payne Madison*, by Dolley Madison, ed. David Mattern and Holly Schulman (Charlottesville: University Press of Virginia, 2003), p. 54.

CHAPTER 11. MISTER PRESIDENT

1. John Quincy Adams, *The Diary of John Quincy Adams, 1794–1845: American Diplomacy and Political, Social and Intellectual Life, from Washington to Polk*, ed. Allan Nevins (New York: Frederick Ungar Publishing, 1928), p. 58.

2. *Washington Federalist*, December 31, 1808; *Aurora*, January 18, 1809.

3. *Washington Federalist*, April 8, 1808.

4. Charles Ambler, *Thomas Ritchie: A Study in Virginia Politics* (Richmond: Bell, Book and Stationary, 1913), pp. 45–47.

5. John Randolph in the House of Representatives, June 1, 1809, quoted in *National Intelligencer*, June 21, 1809.

6. Samuel Smith to Cary Nicholas, April 1, 1806; Henry Adams, *History of the United States during the First Administration of James Madison*, condensed volume (New York: Literary Classics of the United States, Library of America, 1986), p. 170.

7. John Pancake, *Samuel Smith and the Politics of Business, 1752–1839* (Birmingham: University of Alabama Press, 1972), pp. 78–79.

8. Ibid., pp. 99–100.

9. Harry Ammon, *James Monroe: The Quest for National Identity* (New York: McGraw-Hill, 1971), p. 278.

10. Martin Zahniser, *Charles Cotesworth Pinckney: Founding Father* (Chapel Hill: University of North Carolina Press, 1967), p. 254; *Washington Federalist*, January 25, 1808.

11. *Washington Expositor*, March 1808.

12. Ibid., December 4, 1807.

13. *Aurora*, January 18, 1809; Dumas Malone, *Jefferson and His Time* (Charlottesville: University Press of Virginia, 2005), 5:99–101.

14. Samuel Mitchill, "Dr. Mitchill's Letters from Washington: 1801–1813," *Harper's New Monthly Magazine* 58 (April 1879): 752.

15. *Washington Expositor*, February 17, 1808.

16. *Aurora*, March 4, 1809.

17. Ralph Ketcham, *James Madison: A Biography* (New York: Macmillan, 1971), p. 428.

18. Ibid., p. 429.

19. John Quincy Adams, *Lives of Celebrated Statesmen* (New York: W. H. Graham, 1846), p. 37.

20. Ketcham, *James Madison*, p. 429; Noble Cunningham Jr., *Jeffersonian Republicans: The Formation of Party Organization, 1789–1801* (Chapel Hill: University of North Carolina Press, 1957), p. 232.

21. Maud Goodwin, *Dolly Madison* (New York: Charles Scribner's Sons, 1940), p. 118.

22. *National Intelligencer*, March 7, 1808.

23. Tom Abernathy, *The South in the New Nation, 1789–1819* (Baton Rouge: Louisiana State University Press, 1961), p. 313.

24. *Washington Federalist*, November 7, 1807.

25. Dolley Madison to Anna Cutts, June 18, 1807, in Dolley Madison Digital Edition, ed. Holly C. Shulman (Charlottesville: University of Virginia Press, Online Rotunda Edition, 2010–2013) (hereafter referred to as DMDE).

26. John Marshall to Charles Pinckney, October 19, 1808, in *The Papers of John Marshall*, by John Marshall, ed. Charles Hobson (Chapel Hill: University of North Carolina Press, 1993), 7:184.

27. William Plumer Jr., *The Life of William Plumer* (Boston: Phillips, Sampson, 1857), p. 362.

28. *Washington Federalist*, May 7, 1808.

29. James Madison, speech to the Constitutional Convention, July 11, 1787, in *The Papers of James Madison: Secretary of State Series, Presidential Series, Retirement Series, Personal Papers*, ed. Robert Brugger et al. (Charlottesville: University Press of Virginia, 1986) (hereafter cited as *PJM*), 10:98.

30. James Madison to Nicholas Trist, April 23, 1828, in *The Selected Letters of Dolley Payne Madison*, by Dolley Madison, ed. David Mattern and Holly Schulman (Charlottesville: University Press of Virginia, 2003), pp. 82–83.

31. Ketcham, *James Madison*, p. 435.

32. *Aurora*, January 5, 1809; Virginia Moore, *The Madisons: A Biography* (New York: McGraw-Hill, 1979), pp. 214–15.

33. Levi Lincoln to Thomas Jefferson, April 16, 1801, in *The Papers of Thomas Jefferson*, by Thomas Jefferson, ed. Julian Boyd and Barbara Oberg (Princeton, NJ: Princeton University Press, 2007), 33:596–99n.

34. Charles Cotesworth Pinckney to John Rutledge Jr., August 24, 1808, in Pinckney Cotesworth Harrington Papers, Southern Historical Collection, University of North Carolina; Zahniser, *Charles Cotesworth Pinckney*, p. 252.

35. Eliza Collins Lee to Dolley Madison, March 2, 1809, in DMDE.

36. Stella Sutherland, *Population Distribution in Colonial America* (New York: Columbia University Press, 1936), introduction charts; *National Gazette*, December 19, 1791.

37. James Madison, Letters of Helvidius, no. 3, September 1793, in *PJM*, 15:98.

38. *National Gazette*, February 18, 1792.

39. James Madison to Lafayette, November 25, 1820, in Madison, *Selected Letters of Dolley Payne Madison*, p. 14.

40. James Madison, inaugural address, March 4, 1809, in *The Writings of James Madison*, by James Madison and Galliard Hunt (New York: Russell and Russell, 1968), 8:47–50.

41. Margaret Bayard Smith, *The First Forty Years of Washington Society*, ed. Galliard Hunt (New York: Charles Scribner's Sons, 1906), p. 58.

42. Ibid., pp. 61–62.

43. Ketcham, *James Madison*, pp. 474–75.

44. Noble Cunningham Jr., "The Frances Few Diary," *Journal of Southern History* 29, no. 3 (August 1963), March 3, 1809 entry; Ketcham, *James Madison*, p. 476.

45. "Journal of Alexander Dick," March 1809, in *James Madison*, by Irving Brant (Indianapolis, IN: Bobbs-Merrill, 1941–1946), 5:33.

46. William Story, ed., *The Life and Letters of Joseph Story* (Boston: Charles Little and James Brown, 1851), 1:218; Abraham Hasbrouck to Severyn Bruyn, January 29, 1814, in DMDE.

47. Madison and Hunt, *Writings of James Madison*, 1:66–68, 269.

48. Robert Rutland, *The Presidency of James Madison* (Lawrence: University Press of Kansas, 1990), p. 21.

49. Ibid.

50. Harriet Martineau, *Society in America* (New York: Saunders and Otley, 1837), 1:60.

51. John Jackson to Dolley Madison, March 5, 1809, in DMDE.

52. *Washington Expositor*, March 12, 1809.

53. Thomas Jefferson to Levi Lincoln, August 26, 1801, in Paul Ford, *Works of Thomas Jefferson* (New York: G. P. Putnam's Sons, 1903), 4:406.

54. Fawn Brodie, *Thomas Jefferson: An Intimate History* (New York: W. W. Norton, 1974), p. 425; Katherine Anthony, *Dolley Madison: Her Life and Times* (Garden City, NY: Doubleday, 1949), p. 192.

55. *Aurora*, April 21, 1809.

56. Brodie, *Thomas Jefferson*, p. 381; Thomas Jefferson to James Madison, July 26, 1806, in Papers of Thomas Jefferson, Princeton University Library; James Madison to Nicholas Trist, July 6, 1826, in Papers of Thomas Jefferson, Princeton University Library.

57. Thomas Jefferson to Dupont Nemours, March 2, 1809, in *Writings of Thomas Jefferson*, by A. A. Lipscomb and A. E. Bergh (Washington, DC: Thomas Jefferson Memorial Association of the United States, 1903), 5:432–33.

58. James Madison to William Pinckney, March 17, 1809, in *PJM*, presidential ser. 1; Madison Papers, Princeton University Library.

59. James Madison to Thomas Jefferson, October 24, 1787, in *The Papers of Thomas Jefferson*, by Thomas Jefferson, ed. Julian Boyd and Barbara Oberg (Princeton, NJ: Princeton University Press, 2007), 12:276–77.

60. Garry Wills, *James Madison* (New York: Henry Holt, 2002), pp. 3–5.

61. Plumer's Memorandum, April 8, 1806, p. 478, William Plumer Papers, Library of Congress, New Hampshire State Library.

62. Ibid.

63. Albert Gallatin to Joseph Nicholson, December 16, 1808, New York Historical Society.

64. Dolley Madison to Anna Cutts, June 5, 1805, in Madison and Mattern (ed.) and Schulman (ed.), *Selected Letters of Dolley Payne Madison*, pp. 61–62.

65. Dolley Madison to Anna Cutts, May 25, 1804, in DMDE; Dolley Madison to Anna Cutts, June 4, 1805, in DMDE.

66. James Madison to James Monroe, December 26, 1803, in Madison and Hunt, *Writings of James Madison*, 2:189–91.

67. James Madison to William Claiborne, February 20, 1804, in ibid., 1:199–200.

68. Ethel Arnett, *Mrs. James Madison: The Incomparable Dolley* (Greensboro, NC: Piedmont Press, 1972), p. 253; "miscellany" notes in Dolley Madison Papers, North American Women's Letters and Diaries, digital collection.

69. Dolley Madison to Anna Cutts, May 22, 1804, in Anthony, *Dolley Madison*, p. 164.

70. Phoebe Morris to Dolley Madison, July 22, 1809, in DMDE.

71. Ibid.; Dolley Madison to Anna Cutts, October 27, 1810, in DMDE.

72. James Madison to Thomas Jefferson, August 9, 1805, and James Madison to Governor Claiborne, August 28, 1804, in *PJM*, secretary of state ser. 7:643–45.

73. James Madison to James Monroe, November 9, 1804, in Madison and Hunt, *Writings of James Madison*, 2:208–10; James Madison to Thomas Jefferson, May 22, 1808, in *The Republic of Letters: The Correspondence between Thomas Jefferson and James Madison, 1776–1826*, ed. James Smith (New York: W. W. Norton, 1995); Madison to Jefferson, July 28, 1806, in Smith, *Republic of Letters*, 3:1422, 1429.

74. James Madison to William Hayward, March 19, 1809, in Madison and Hunt, *Writings of James Madison*, 2:434–35.

75. Madison's political skills were evident in a letter to Jefferson on August 20, 1805, in Smith, *Republic of Letters*, 3:1379–80; Adrienne Koch, *Jefferson and Madison: The Great Collaboration* (Birmingham, AL: Palladium Press, 2005), pp. 126–27; *National Gazette*, December 20, 1792; Madison to Edmund Pendleton, January 21, 1792, in Madison and Hunt, *Writings of James Madison*, 1:546.

76. James Madison, Federalist No. 55, February 13, 1788, in *PJM*, 10:505.

77. Coles to Harold Grigsby, December 23, 1854, in Rives Papers, Library of Congress.

78. Charles Adams, "The Madison Papers," *North American Review* 53 (1841): 75.

79. *Aurora*, March 22, 1809.

80. James Madison to Thomas Jefferson, October 30, 1808, in Smith, *Republic of Letters*, 3:1554–57.

81. *Aurora*, March 10, 1809.

CHAPTER 12. A NEW ADMINISTRATION AND A NEW COUPLE

1. Kurt Leichtle and Bruce Carveth, *Crusade against Slavery: Edward Coles, Pioneer of Freedom* (Carbondale: Southern Illinois University Press, 2011), pp. 29–30.

2. Elbridge Gerry Jr., *The Diary of Elbridge Gerry Jr.* (New York: Brentano's, 1927), p. 179.

3. Benjamin Latrobe to Dolley Madison, March 20, 1809, in Dolley Madison Digital Edition, ed. Holly C. Shulman (Charlottesville: University of Virginia Press, Online Rotunda Edition, 2010–2013) (hereafter referred to as DMDE).

4. Catherine Allgor, *A Perfect Union: Dolley Madison and the Creation of the American Nation* (New York: Henry Holt, 2006), p. 153.

5. James Madison to Dolley Madison, November 1805, in DMDE; James Madison to Dolley Madison, December 2, 1799, in DMDE.

6. Maud Goodwin, *Dolly Madison* (New York: Charles Scribner's Sons, 1940), pp. 138–39.

7. *Washington Federalist*, March 3, 1808.

8. Ibid., March 19, 1809.

9. Ibid., March 12, 1809.

10. Ibid., October 1808.

11. *Washington Expositor*, May 4, 1808.

12. Virginia Moore, *The Madisons: A Biography* (New York: McGraw-Hill, 1979), pp. 202–203.

13. John Randolph to James Garnett, August 31, 1808, in Randolph-Garnett Letters, Library of Congress.

14. Albert Gallatin to James Madison, October 29, 1809, in *The Papers of James Madison: Secretary of State Series, Presidential Series, Retirement Series, Personal Papers*, ed. Robert Brugger et al. (Charlottesville: University Press of Virginia, 1986) (hereafter cited as *PJM*), presidential ser. 2:45.

15. James Dinsmore to James Madison, October 29, 1809, in ibid., presidential ser. 2:44.

16. James Madison to Thomas Jefferson, October 30, 1809, in ibid., presidential ser. 2:48–49; George Davis to Dolley Madison, July 12, 1806, in Moore, *Madisons*, p. 205; Lucy Washington to Anna Cutts, July 20, 1811, in Lucia Cutts, *Memoirs and Letters of Dolley Madison, Wife of James Madison, President of the United States* (Port Washington, NY: Kennikat Press, 1971).

17. Dolley Madison to John Payne, September 21, 1809, in DMDE; Dolley Madison to David Warden, March 8, 1811, in DMDE.

18. Charles Goldsborough to James Madison, November 9, 1809, in *PJM*, presidential ser. 2:62–64.

19. Dolley Madison to a friend, April 9, 1804, in Dolly Madison Papers, North American Women's Letters and Diaries, digital collection, doc. 8; Moore, *Madisons*, p. 188; Goodwin, *Dolly Madison*, pp. 121–23.

20. Dolley Madison to Eliza Collins Lee, February 26, 1808, in DMDE.

21. Dolley Madison to Anna Cutts, June 3, 1808, in ibid.

22. Ibid.

23. Dolley Madison to James Madison, October 23, 1805, in ibid.

24. *National Intelligencer*, October 15, 1801, and October 20, 1801; *Washington Federalist*, February 2, 1806.

25. *National Intelligencer*, October 30, 1801.

26. *Aurora*, February 11, 1809.

27. John Randolph to James Monroe, January 1, 1809, in *James Madison*, by Irving Brant (Indianapolis, IN: Bobbs-Merrill, 1941–1946), 5:22–27.

28. William Wirt, *Letters of a British Spy* (New York: 1803; Chapel Hill: University of North Carolina Press, 1970), in *James Monroe: The Quest for National Identity*, by Harry Ammon (New York: McGraw-Hill, 1971), p. 369.

29. Fawn Brodie, *Thomas Jefferson: An Intimate History* (New York: W. W. Norton, 1974), pp. 178–79; Ammon, *James Monroe*, p. 276; Thomas Jefferson to James Madison, March 30, 1809, and May 25, 1809, in *The Republic of Letters: The Correspondence between Thomas Jefferson and James Madison, 1776–1826*, ed. James Smith (New York: W. W. Norton, 1995), 3:1579–80.

30. Ammon, *James Monroe*, pp. 278–82.

31. Henry Adams, *History of the United States during the First Administration of James Madison* (New York: Literary Classics of the United States, Library of America, 1986), p. 369; Ammon, *James Monroe*, p. 246.

32. Jean Fritz, *The Great Little Madison* (New York: G. P. Putnam's Sons, 1989), pp. 107–108.

33. Goodwin, *Dolly Madison*, pp. 140–41.

34. David Ress, *Governor Edward Coles and the Vote to Forbid Slavery in Illinois, 1823–1824* (Jefferson, NC: McFarland, 2006), p. 37; Leichtle and Carveth, *Crusade against Slavery*, pp. 30–35; Preston, quoted in *Dolley Madison: Her Life and Times*, by Katherine Anthony (New York: Doubleday, 1949), p. 204.

35. Dolley Madison to Anna Cutts, May 25, 1804, in DMDE; Anne Hollingsworth Wharton, *Social Life in the Early Republic* (Philadelphia, PA: J. B. Lippincott, 1903), pp. 144–45.

36. William Preston, "Journal," in E. F. Eliet, *Court Circles of the Republic* (Hartford, CT: Hartford Publishing, 1869), p. 84.

37. William Parker Cutler, *Life, Journals and Correspondence of Rev. Manasseh Cutler, LL.D.* (Cincinnati, 1888), pp. 142–43.

38. George Watterston to Dolley Madison, in DMDE; Ethel Arnett, *Mrs. James Madison: The Incomparable Dolley* (Greensboro, NC: Piedmont Press, 1972), pp. 116–17; anonymous authors to Dolley Madison, July 14, 1811, in DMDE.

39. David Warden to Dolley Madison, July 19, 1811, in DMDE; George Washington Steptoe to Dolley Madison, March 10, 1809, in DMDE.

40. Lucia Cutts, *Memoirs and Letters of Dolley Madison, Wife of James Madison, President of the United States* (Port Washington, NY: Kennikat Press, 1971), vol. 2, date unknown.

41. Arnett, *Mrs. James Madison*, p. 118; Joseph Milligan to Dolley Madison, December 13, 1809, in DMDE.

42. Benjamin Latrobe to Dolley Madison, April 12, 1809, in DMDE; John Jacob Astor to Dolley Madison, February 20, 1811, in DMDE; Dolley Madison to John Jacob Astor, March 13, 1811, in DMDE; Joel Barlow to Dolley Madison, December 21, 1811, in DMDE; Dolley Beckwith to Dolley Madison, May 4, 1807, in DMDE.

43. Anthony, *Dolley Madison*, p. 120.

44. Harriet Martineau, *Retrospect on Western Travel* (1838; repr., New York: Greenwood Press, 1969), 1:193.

45. Dolley Madison to Anna Cutts, December 22, 1811, in DMDE.

46. Wharton, *Social Life in the Early Republic*, p. 153.

47. Goodwin, *Dolley Madison*, p. 142.

48. Dolley Madison to James Madison, November 1, 1805, and August 28, 1808, in DMDE.

49. Ibid.; William Thornton to James Madison, March 3, 1817, in *PJM*; Founding Era Collection, University of Virginia.

50. Dolley Madison to Elizabeth Ellicott, December 1788, in DMDE; Dolley Madison to Mary Cutts, March 1833, in DMDE; Dolley Madison to Anna Cutts, June 18, 1806, in DMDE; Dolley Madison to Anna Thornton, September 1808, in DMDE; Dolley Madison to James Madison, November 12, 1805, in DMDE.

51. Sally McKean to Dolley Madison, June 7, 1797, and August 3, 1797, in DMDE; Dolley Beckwith to Dolley Madison, May 4, 1807, in DMDE.

52. Dolley Madison to Anna Cutts, July 15, 1811, in ibid.

53. Edward Coles to Dolley Madison, June 10, 1811, in ibid.

54. Ibid.

55. Dolley Madison to Ed Coles, June 15, 1811, in ibid.

56. William Story, ed., *The Life and Letters of Joseph Story* (Boston: Charles Little and James Brown, 1851), p. 218.

57. Noel Gerson, *The Velvet Glove: A Life of Dolley Madison* (Nashville: Thomas and Nelson, 1975), pp. 125–26.

58. Margaret Bayard Smith, *The First Forty Years of Washington Society*, ed. Gaillard Hunt (New York: Charles Scribner's Sons, 1906), p. 26.

59. William Seale, *The President's House: A History* (Washington, DC: National Geographic Society, White House Historical Association, 1986), 1:129.

60. Goodwin, *Dolley Madison*, pp. 88–89.

61. Ibid., p. 140.

62. Gerson, *Velvet Glove*, pp. 150–51.

63. Dolley Madison to Anna Cutts, July 5, 1816, in DMDE.

64. Madison at the Republican Meeting of Cecil County, Maryland, March 5, 1810, in *PJM*, presidential ser. 2:263.

65. Baron de Montlezun, "A Frenchman Visits . . . Orange County," September 16, 1816, diary entry, in DMDE.

CHAPTER 13. THE NEVER-ENDING DISPUTE WITH GREAT BRITAIN

1. John Quincy Adams, *Lives of Celebrated Statesmen* (New York: W. H. Graham, 1846), p. 38.

2. Thomas Jefferson to James Madison, November 26, 1809, in *Republic of Letters: The Correspondence between Thomas Jefferson and James Madison, 1776–1826*, ed. James Smith (New York: W. W. Norton, 1995), 3:1607–1608.

3. Robert Livingston to James Madison, January 1810, in *The Papers of James Madison: Secretary of State Series, Presidential Series, Retirement Series, Personal Papers*, ed. Robert Brugger et al. (Charlottesville: University Press of Virginia, 1986) (hereafter cited as *PJM*), presidential ser. 2:166–68.

4. James Madison to the secretary of the Republican Meeting of South Carolina, October 17, 1809, in *PJM*, presidential ser. 2:16–17.

5. James Madison to Thomas Jefferson, May 25, 1810, in Smith, *Republic of Letters*, 3:1630–31.

6. James Madison to William Raynolds, October 20, 1809, in *PJM*, presidential ser. 2:23.

7. James Madison to William Pinkney, October 23, 1809, in ibid., pp. 27–28.

8. James Madison to Thomas Jefferson, November 6, 1809, in ibid., pp. 55–56.

9. William Duane to James Madison, December 1, 1809, in ibid., pp. 97–102.

10. John Jackson to James Madison, October 12, 1809, in ibid., pp. 13–14.

11. William Pinkney to James Madison, December 10, 1809, in ibid., pp. 121–24.

12. James Madison to Congress, November 29, 1809, in ibid., pp. 90–94.

13. *Aurora*, January 5, 1809.

14. North Carolina Assembly to James Madison, December 23, 1809, in *PJM*, presidential ser. 2:156.

15. John Adams letters, in *National Intelligencer*, April 4, 1809, and May 3, 1809.

16. *National Intelligencer*, April 21, 1810.

17. James Madison's message to Congress, May 23, 1809, in *PJM*, presidential ser. 1:75–100.

18. *National Intelligencer*, October 16, 1809.

19. *New York Commercial Advertiser*, July 12, 1809, and July 19, 1809; *National Intelligencer*, September 6, 1809.

20. *Aurora*, April 14, 1809.

21. Albert Gallatin to James Madison, September 5, 1810, in *The Writings of Albert Gallatin*, ed. Henry Adams (Philadelphia, PA: J. P. Lippincott, 1879), 1:485–86.

22. Thomas Jefferson to James Madison, April 17, 1809, in Smith, *Republic of Letters*, 3:1585–86; Albert Gallatin to James Madison, September 17, 1810, in ibid., 1:490–91.

23. *National Intelligencer*, April 19, 1809.

24. *National Intelligencer*, April 1809.

25. Thomas Jefferson to James Madison, April 19, 1808, and April 24, 1809, in Smith, *Republic of Letters*, 3:1582–84, 1584–85.

26. James Madison to Thomas Jefferson, August 3, 1809, and Thomas Jefferson to James Madison, September 12, 1809, in Smith, *Republic of Letters* 3:1596–97, 1602.

27. Caesar Rodney to James Madison, October 17, 1809, in *PJM*, presidential ser. 2:16–17.

CHAPTER 14. THE EVER-CHANGING AMERICA

1. *National Intelligencer*, June 3, 1801.

2. Robert Kapsch, *The Potomac Canal* (Morgantown: West Virginia University Press, 2007), back cover quote; Robert Payne, *The Canal Builders: The Story of Canal Engineers through the Ages* (New York: MacMillan, 1959), p. 140.

3. Robert McClellan, *The Delaware Canal: A Picture Story* (New Brunswick, NJ: Rutgers University Press, 1967), introduction.

4. George Washington to James Madison, December 3, 1784, in *The Writings of George Washington*, by George Washington, ed. John Fitzpatrick (Washington, DC: Government Printing Office, 1932), 2:165–68; Kapsch, *Potomac Canal*, pp. 50–51.

5. George Washington to Benjamin Harrison, in *The Writings of Thomas Jefferson*, by Thomas Jefferson, ed. Paul Ford (New York: 1892–1899), 10:406; Wayland Dunaway, *History of the James River and Kanawha Co.* (New York: Columbia University Press, 1922), pp. 14–17.

6. Payne, *Canal Builders*, pp. 142–45.

7. Jefferson's annual message to Congress, December 2, 1806, in *Political Writings of Thomas Jefferson*, ed. Merrill Peterson (Charlottesville, VA: Thomas Jefferson Memorial Foundation, 1993), 2:529.

8. Christy Borth, *Mankind on the Move: The Story of Highways* (Washington, DC: Automotive Safety Foundation, 1969), p. 148.

9. Madison speech to Congress, April 1792, in *The Papers of James Madison: Secretary of State Series, Presidential Series, Retirement Series, Personal Papers*, ed. Robert Brugger et al. (Charlottesville: University Press of Virginia, 1986) (hereafter cited as *PJM*), 7:304; *National Gazette*, March 3, 1792; John Quincy Adams, *The Diary of John Quincy Adams, 1794–1845: American Diplomacy, and Political, Social, and Intellectual Life, from Washington to Polk*, ed. Allan Nevins (New York: Frederick Ungar Publishing, 1928), p. 47.

10. Joseph Macasek, *Guide to the Morris Canal in Morris County* (Mendham, NJ: Morris County Heritage Commission, 1996), p. 50.

11. James Madison to Thomas Jefferson, May 15, 1808, in James Madison Papers, Library of Congress.

12. Noel Gerson, *The Velvet Glove: A Life of Dolley Madison* (Nashville, Thomas and Nelson, 1975), p. 178; Walter Jones to Dolley Madison, sometime in 1811, in Dolley Madison Digital Edition, ed. Holly C. Shulman (Charlottesville: University of Virginia Press, Online Rotunda Edition, 2010–2013) (hereafter referred to as DMDE).

13. Dolley Beckwith to Dolley Madison, May 4, 1807, in DMDE.

14. James Madison to Dolley Madison, December 4, 1826, in ibid.

15. Borth, *Mankind on the Move*, pp. 120, 122, 126.

16. George Bernard and others to James Madison, October 1809, in *PJM*, presidential ser. 2:1–2.

17. Thomas Jefferson to Congress, December 2, 1806, in Peterson, *Political Writings of Thomas Jefferson*, p. 539.

18. *Washington Federalist*, February 6, 1805.

19. Philip Jordan, *The National Road* (Indianapolis, IN: Bobbs-Merrill, 1948), pp. 76–79.

20. Merrit Ierley, *Traveling the National Road: Across the Centuries on America's First Highway* (Woodstock, NY: Overlook Press, 1990), pp. 54–56.

21. J. L. Ringwalt, *Development of Transportation Systems in the United States* (Philadelphia, 1888), p. 31; Jordan, *National Road*, p. 86.

22. Jeremiah Young, *A Political and Constitutional Study of the Cumberland Road* (Chicago: University of Chicago Press, 1902), p. 106.

23. Jordan, *National Road*, pp. 106–107.

24. Ierley, *Traveling the National Road*, pp. 113–14.

25. Ibid., pp. 73–75.

26. Ibid., p. 48.

27. *New York Columbian*, June 19, 1812.

28. James Madison to Congress, "Special Message to Congress," December 23, 1811, in *The Writings of James Madison*, by James Madison and Gaillard Hunt (New

York: Russell and Russell, 1968), 8:172–73; Richard Brookhiser, *Gentleman Revolutionary: Gouverneur Morris, the Rake Who Wrote the Constitution* (New York: Free Press, 2003), p. 190.

29. Payne, *Canal Builders*, p. 146.

30. Ann Bartholomew, ed., *The Delaware and Lehigh Canals* (Easton, PA: Center for Canal History, 1989), introduction.

31. James Madison to Albert Picket, September 1821; David Mattern and Holly Schulman, *The Selected Letters of Dolley Payne Madison* (Charlottesville: University Press of Virginia, 2003), p. 109.

32. Ralph Ketcham, *James Madison: A Biography* (New York: Macmillan, 1971), pp. 472–73.

33. Madison speech at Virginia ratifying convention for the Constitution, June 20, 1788, in *PJM*, p. 163.

34. Madison's annual message to Congress, December 5, 1810, in *PJM*, presidential ser. 3:52.

35. James Longacre and James Herring, eds., "Mrs. Madison," in *National Portrait Gallery of Distinguished Americans* (New York: Herman Bancroft, 1836), 1:21.

CHAPTER 15. WAR LOOMS EVERYWHERE OVER AMERICA

1. *Washington Federalist*, January 9, 1808.

2. *Washington Expositor*, April 16, 1808; *Aurora*, April 23, 1809.

3. *Washington Federalist*, February 20, 1808.

4. *Albany Register*, May 1809, reprinted in *Aurora*, May 23, 1809; William Pinkney to James Madison, December 20, 1809, in *The Papers of James Madison: Secretary of State Series, Presidential Series, Retirement Series, Personal Papers*, ed. Robert Brugger et al. (Charlottesville: University Press of Virginia, 1986) (hereafter cited as *PJM*), presidential ser. 2:121–22.

5. *Spirit of Seventy Six*, January 16, 1810, and January 26, 1809.

6. James Madison to the Vermont General Assembly, December 26, 1809, in *PJM*, presidential ser. 2:145–46.

7. J. C. A. Stagg, *Mr. Madison's War: Politics, Diplomacy and Warfare in the Early American Republic, 1783–1830* (Princeton, NJ: Princeton University Press, 1983), pp. 177–87.

8. Thomas Jefferson to John Armstrong, March 5, 1809, in Cutts Family Papers, Library of Congress.

9. James Madison to Dolley Madison, August 7, 1809, in Dolley Madison Digital Edition, ed. Holly C. Shulman (Charlottesville: University of Virginia Press, Online Rotunda Edition, 2010–2013) (hereafter cited as DMDE).

10. Dolley Madison to Anna Cutts, December 20, 1811, Dolley Madison Papers, North American Women's Letters and Diaries, digital collection, doc. 24.

11. Francis Jackson to his mother, October 7, 1809, and Francis Jackson to George Jackson, October 14, 1809, in *The Bath Archives: A Further Selection from the Diaries and Letters of Sir George Jackson,* ed. Lady Jackson (London, 1873), 1:17, 26; Lady Jackson to George Jackson, November 22, 1809, in Jackson, *Bath Archives,* 1:28.

12. James Madison to William Pinkney, October 23, 1809, in Madison Papers, Princeton University Library.

13. Ezekiel Bacon to Joseph Story, November 27, 1809, in Papers of Joseph Story, Library of Congress; Virginia Moore, *The Madisons: A Biography* (New York: McGraw-Hill, 1979), p. 231; Ralph Ketcham, *James Madison: A Biography* (New York: Macmillan, 1971), pp. 499–500.

14. Thomas Jefferson to Walter Jones, March 5, 1810, in *Writings of Thomas Jefferson,* by A. A. Lipscomb and A. E. Bergh (Washington, DC: Thomas Jefferson Memorial Association of the United States, 1903), 9:274.

15. Dolley Madison to a friend, March 27, 1812, in Dolley Madison Papers, North American Women's Letters and Diaries, digital collection, doc. 26.

16. Edward Coles to John Coles, November 30, [year unknown], in David Ress, *Governor Edward Coles and the Vote to Forbid Slavery in Illinois, 1823–1824* (Jefferson, NC: McFarland, 2006), p. 39.

17. Moore, *Madisons,* p. 249; Dolley Madison to Anna Cutts, July 15, 1811, in DMDE.

18. Dolley Madison to a friend, March 27, 1812, in Dolley Madison Papers, North American Women's Letters and Diaries, digital collection, doc. 26.

19. James Madison on Dolley Madison, in Cutts Family Papers, Library of Congress; Moore, *Madisons,* p. 231.

20. John Pancake, *Samuel Smith and the Politics of Business, 1752–1839* (Birmingham: University of Alabama Press, 1972), p. 85.

21. *Aurora,* June 2, 1809.

22. *Aurora,* June 6, 1809; *Baltimore American,* May 1809.

23. Connecticut congressman Roger Nelson resolution in the House of Representatives, December 26, 1808, as reported in *National Intelligencer,* December 29, 1808.

24. *Washington Federalist,* November 7, 1807.

25. Ketcham, *James Madison,* p. 499.

26. James Madison to William Pinkney, October 10, 1810, in *The Writings of James Madison,* by James Madison and Galliard Hunt (New York: Russell and Russell, 1968), 8:121–22.

27. James Madison to Thomas Jefferson, October 19, 1810, in Madison and Hunt, *Writings of James Madison,* 8:109; Ketcham, *James Madison,* pp. 504–506.

28. Henry Clay to C. A. Rodney, August 17, 1811, in *Roger Brown, 1812: The Republic in Peril*, by Roger Brown (New York: Columbia University Press, 1964), pp. 30–31; Ketcham, *James Madison*, pp. 508–509.

29. James Madison to William Raynolds, October 20, 1809, in *PJM*, presidential ser. 2:23.

30. James Madison to William Pinkney, October 23, 1809, in ibid., presidential ser. 2:27–28.

31. Vermont General Assembly to James Madison, November 1809, in ibid., presidential ser. 2:68–71.

32. Thomas Jefferson to James Madison, November 26, 1809, in ibid., presidential ser. 2:84–85.

33. William Duane to James Madison, December 1, 1809, in ibid., presidential ser. 2:97–98.

34. James Madison to Congress, November 29, 1809, in ibid., presidential ser. 2:90–95.

35. James Madison to Pierre Samuel DuPont de Nemours, December 3, 1809, in ibid., presidential ser. 2:104.

36. Henry Clay to W. Worsley, May 24, 1812 in *James Madison*, by Irving Brant (Indianapolis, IN: Bobbs-Merrill, 1941–1946), 5:469.

CHAPTER 16. THE FIRST DAYS OF THE WAR OF 1812

1. Thomas Jefferson to James Madison, March 26, 1812, in *The Republic of Letters: The Correspondence between Thomas Jefferson and James Madison, 1776–1826*, ed. James Smith (New York: W. W. Norton, 1995), 3:1690–91; *New York Columbian*, June 19, 1812.

2. Dolley Madison to Anna Cutts, 1812, in Dolley Madison Papers, North American Women's Letters and Diaries, digital collection, doc. 27.

3. *New York Columbian*, special edition, June 21, 1812.

4. James Madison to Congress, November 1, 1812, in *Messages and Papers of the President*, comp. James Richardson (Washington, DC: US Government Printing Office, 1897–1917), 2:505.

5. Ibid.

6. John Calhoun to James McBride, April 4, 1812, in *Papers of John C. Calhoun*, ed. Robert Meriwether (Columbia: University of South Carolina Press, 1959), pp. 99–100.

7. John Keemle to James Madison, January 11, 1810, in *The Papers of James Madison: Secretary of State Series, Presidential Series, Retirement Series, Personal Papers*, ed. Robert Brugger et al. (Charlottesville: University Press of Virginia, 1986) (hereafter cited as *PJM*), presidential ser. 2:172–74.

8. John Stark to James Madison, January 21, 1810, in ibid., pp. 200–201.

9. George Washington Parke Custis to James Madison, May 31, 1810, in ibid., presidential ser. 2:363–65.

10. Alfred Madison to James Madison, January 13, 1810, in ibid., presidential ser. 2:176–77.

11. John Tyler to James Madison, January 15, 1810, in ibid., p. 179.

12. Caesar Rodney to James Madison, January 16, 1810, in ibid., presidential ser. 2:181–87.

13. *National Intelligencer*, February 5, 1810.

14. *New York Columbian*, June 22 and 23, 1812.

15. *National Intelligencer*, June 27, 1812.

16. Republican Meeting of Cecil County, Maryland, to James Madison, February 21, 1810, in *PJM*, presidential ser. 2:252–53.

17. *New York Columbian*, June 23, 1812; *Aurora*, July 1, 1812.

18. *New York Columbian*, June 27, 1812.

19. Ibid.

20. Ibid., June 30, 1812.

21. *Palladium*, June 30, 1812.

22. Ibid., June 19 and July 28, 1812.

23. Ibid., June 23, 1812.

24. Ibid.

25. Ibid.

26. Ibid.

27. George Logan to James Madison, January 10, 1810, in *PJM*, presidential ser. 2:169–72.

28. Mrs. William Gale to her mother, spring 1812 in *Social Life in the Early Republic*, by Anne Hollingsworth Wharton (Philadelphia, PA: J. B. Lippincott, 1903), pp. 159–60.

29. *Palladium*, July 3, 1812.

30. Ibid., July 1812; Irving Brant, *James Madison* (Indianapolis, IN: Bobbs-Merrill, 1941–1946), 6:24–31; *Boston Evening Post*, July 31–August 10, 1812.

31. *Palladium*, July 3, 1812.

32. Ibid., July 7, 1812.

33. Ibid., July 10, 1812.

34. Ibid., July 21, 1812.

35. Ibid., July 21 and 31, and August 7, 1812; *Salem Gazette*, June 23, 1812.

36. *Palladium*, August 14, 1812.

37. Ibid., August 11, 1812.

38. Letter of Edwin Gray, in ibid., July 10, 1812.

39. Virginia Moore, *The Madisons: A Biography* (New York: McGraw-Hill, 1979), p. 244.

40. *New York Columbian,* July 1, 1812.

41. Ibid., July 3, 1812.

42. *Palladium,* July 24, 1812.

43. Paul F. Boller Jr., *Presidential Campaigns* (New York: Oxford University Press, 2004), p. 27.

44. *National Intelligencer,* July 1, 1812; *New York Columbian,* July 3, 1812.

45. Katherine Anthony, *Dolley Madison: Her Life and Times* (New York: Doubleday, 1949), pp. 222–23.

46. Daniel Barnard, *Lecture on the Character and Services of James Madison* (Albany, NY: Power Press of Hoffman and White, 1837), pp. 42–43.

CHAPTER 17. THE WAR YEARS

1. Rexford G. Tugwell, *The Enlargement of the Presidency* (Garden City, NJ: Doubleday, 1960), pp. 63–65; Dolley Madison to Phoebe Morris, March 6, 1813, in Dolley Madison Digital Edition, ed. Holly C. Shulman (Charlottesville: University of Virginia Press, Online Rotunda Edition, 2010–2013) (hereafter referred to as DMDE).

2. Dolley Madison to Phoebe Morris, October 17, 1812, in DMDE.

3. Dolley Madison to Mrs. Joel Barlow, November 15, 1811, in ibid.

4. Katherine Anthony, *Dolley Madison: Her Life and Times* (Garden City, NY: Doubleday, 1949), pp. 235–36.

5. Dolley Madison to Phoebe Morris, October 17, 1812, in DMDE.

6. Anne Hollingsworth Wharton, *Social Life in the Early Republic* (Philadelphia, PA: J. B. Lippincott, 1903), p. 163.

7. James Madison to Congress, February 24, 1813, in *The Papers of James Madison: Secretary of State Series, Presidential Series, Retirement Series, Personal Papers,* ed. Robert Brugger et al. (Charlottesville: University Press of Virginia, 1986) (hereafter cited as *PJM*), presidential ser. 6:61–62.

8. James Madison to John Nicholas, April 2, 1813, in ibid., presidential ser. 6:175–76.

9. James Madison to Isaac Shelby, August 12, 1813, in ibid., presidential ser. 6:513.

10. James Madison to John Armstrong, September 8, 1813, in ibid., presidential ser. 6:602–604.

11. Henry Dearborn to James Madison, April 7, 1813, in ibid., presidential ser. 6:179–80.

12. James Madison to William Plumer, April 14, 1813, in ibid., presidential ser. 6:197–98.

13. Tench Coxe to James Madison, April 20, 1813, in ibid., presidential ser. 6:217–18.

14. Daniel Webster to various friends, June 1813, in Webster Papers, New Hampshire Historical Society.

15. James Monroe to Thomas Jefferson, June 28, 1813, in *Writings of Monroe*, by Stanislaus Hamilton (New York: G. P. Putnam's Sons, 1898–1903), 6:271–73; Louis Serrurier to Hugues Bassano, June 21, 1813, in *James Madison*, by Irving Brant (Indianapolis, IN: Bobbs-Merrill, 1941–1946) 6:184; Ralph Ketcham, *James Madison: A Biography* (New York: Macmillan, 1971), p. 561.

16. Phoebe Morris to Dolley Madison, June 24, 1813, in DMDE.

17. Noel Gerson, *The Velvet Glove: A Life of Dolley Madison* (Nashville: Thomas and Nelson, 1975), p. 213.

18. Dolley Madison to Anna Cutts, April 8, 1812, in DMDE.

19. Thomas Jefferson to James Madison, July 13, 1813, in *PJM*, presidential ser. 6:434–35; Jonathan Dayton to James Madison, in *PJM*, presidential ser. 6:436–38.

20. Dolley Madison to Phoebe Morris, October 17, 1812, in DMDE.

21. Anthony, *Dolley Madison*, p. 205.

22. Dolley Madison to Edward Coles, June 15, 1811, in DMDE; Dolley Madison to Anna Cutts, June 8, 1811, in DMDE; Dolley Madison to Phoebe Morris, July 29, 1812, in DMDE.

23. Phoebe Morris to Dolley Madison, May 6, 1811, in ibid.; Dolley Madison to Phoebe Morris, May 10, 1811, in ibid.

24. Elisha Scott to Dolley Madison, April 1, 1813, in ibid.; Stephen Sayre to Dolley Madison, March 8, 1809, in ibid.; Aaron Palmer to Dolley Madison, March 3, 1811, in ibid.; Lucy Rummey to Dolley Madison, July 10, 1813, in ibid.; Deborah Stabler to Dolley Madison, sometime in 1813, in ibid.

25. Molly Randolph to Dolley Madison, June 6, 1809, in ibid.

26. Dolley Madison to Hannah Gallatin, July 29, 1813, in ibid.; Dolley Madison to Mary Cutts, February 21, 1812, in ibid.

27. Anthony, *Dolley Madison*, pp. 200–201.

28. Jonathan Roberts to M. Roberts, November 17 and 25, 1811, Historical Society of Pennsylvania.

29. Dolley Madison to John Payne, September 21, 1809, in DMDE.

30. Dolley Madison to Anna Cutts, June 8, 1811, and April 8, 1812, in ibid.

31. Dolley Madison to Anna Cutts, December 22, 1811, and April 8, 1812, in ibid.

32. Edward Coles to Dolley Madison, June 10, 1811, in ibid.; Dolley Madison to Edward Coles, June 15, 1811, in ibid.

33. Dolley Madison to Phoebe Morris, April 24, 1813, and May 6, 1813, in ibid.; Dolley Madison to Anna Cutts, July 15, 1811, in ibid. (italics in the original).

34. Dolley Madison to Anna Cutts, April 8, 1812, in ibid.

35. Ibid.

36. Catherine Allgor, *A Perfect Union: Dolley Madison and the Creation of the American Nation* (New York: Henry Holt, 2006), pp. 230–31; Dolley Madison to (presumably) John J. Astor, June 3, 1810, in DMDE.

37. Wharton, *Social Life in the Early Republic*, p. 253.

38. Mason Weems to Dolley Madison, July 22, 1813, in DMDE.

39. Dolley Madison to Anna Cutts, March 20, 1812, in Dolley Madison Papers, North American Women's Letters and Diaries, digital collection, doc. 25.

40. Lucy Todd to Dolley Madison, May 29, 1812, in DMDE.

41. Dolley Madison to Anna Cutts, April 8, 1812, in ibid.

42. Dolley Madison to Phoebe Morris, January 14, 1813, and March 6, 1813, in ibid.

43. Dolley Madison to James Taylor, March 13, 1811, in ibid.; Dolley Madison to Edward Coles, May 13, 1813, in ibid.

44. *London Courier*, December 5, 1811.

45. Anthony, *Dolley Madison*, p. 202.

46. Richard Rush to John Binns, February 1812, Historical Society of Pennsylvania; Richard Rush to C. J. Ingersoll, February 26, 1812, and March 15, 1812, Historical Society of Pennsylvania.

47. Dolley Madison to Anna Cutts, May 12, 1812, in Dolley Madison Papers, North American Women's Letters and Diaries, digital collection, doc. 28; Dolley Madison to James Taylor, November 10, 1810, in DMDE.

48. C. C. Moore to his mother, June 4, 1812, Museum of the City of New York; Brant, *James Madison*, 6:73.

49. Dolley Madison to Anna Cutts, May 12, 1812, in Dolley Madison Papers, North American Women's Letters and Diaries, digital collection, doc. 28.

50. Sally d'Yrugo to Dolley Madison, June 20, 1812, in ibid., doc. 39.

51. Dolley Madison to Edward Coles, May 12, 1813, in ibid., doc. 31.

52. Ibid.

53. Elbridge Gerry Jr., *The Diary of Elbridge Gerry Jr.* (New York: Brentano's, 1927).

54. Wharton, *Social Life in the Early Republic*, pp. 212–13; *The War* (newspaper), December 10, 1812.

55. Dolley Madison to Payne Todd, August 6, 1814, in DMDE.

56. Dolley Madison to Hannah Gallatin, 1814, in ibid.; Wharton, *Social Life in the Early Republic*, p. 216.

57. Maud Goodwin, *Dolly Madison* (New York: Charles Scribner's Sons, 1940), pp. 162–65.

58. Josephine Seaton, *William Winston Seaton: A Biographical Sketch* (Boston: J. R. Osgood, 1971), p. 141.

CHAPTER 18. THE EARLY YEARS OF THE WAR

1. Irving Brant, *James Madison* (Indianapolis, IN: Bobbs-Merrill, 1941–1946), 6:60.
2. Richard Rush to Ralph Ingersoll, August 19, 1812, Historical Society of Pennsylvania.
3. Ralph Ketcham, *James Madison: A Biography* (New York: Macmillan, 1971), pp. 535–42; *Boston Chronicle*, November 22, 1813; Isaac Brock to George Provost, July 12, 1812, in *Select British Documents of the Canadian War of 1812*, ed. William Wood (Toronto: Champlain Society, 1920–1928), 1:352; Louis-Marie Turreau to Charles Talleyrand, July 1805, in *The Madisons: A Biography*, by Virginia Moore (New York: McGraw-Hill, 1979), p. 275.
4. Albert Gallatin to James Madison, October 11, 1812, in *Writings of Albert Gallatin*, by Albert Gallatin and Henry Adams (New York: Antiquarian Press, 1960), 1:526–31.
5. Donald Hickey, *The War of 1812: A Forgotten Conflict* (Chicago: University of Illinois Press, 1990), p. 76; Paul Jennings, *A Colored Man's Reminiscences of James Madison* (Brooklyn, NY: George C. Beadle, 1865), p. 8.
6. Louis Serrurier to Hugues Bassano, January 8, 1813, in Brant, *James Madison*, 6:126; Richard Rush to Ralph Ingersoll, January 13, 1813, in Historical Society of Pennsylvania.
7. Richard Rush to Ralph Ingersoll, October 18, 1812, and November 17, 1812, sent to Madison later, Historical Society of Pennsylvania.
8. Ketcham, *James Madison*, p. 556.
9. Brant, *James Madison*, 6:158–63.
10. Ketcham, *James Madison*, p. 546; Thomas Jefferson to James Madison, February 8, 1813, in *The Republic of Letters: The Correspondence between Thomas Jefferson and James Madison, 1776–1826*, ed. James Smith (New York: W. W. Norton, 1995), 3:1714–15.
11. Thomas Jefferson to James Madison, February 21, 1813, in Smith, *Republic of Letters* 3:1715–17.
12. Dolley Madison to Edward Coles, August 31, 1812, in Dolley Madison Digital Edition, ed. Holly C. Shulman (Charlottesville: University of Virginia Press, Online Rotunda Edition, 2010–2013) (hereafter cited as DMDE); Richard Rush to Charles Ingersoll, August 29, 1812, in Papers of Thomas Jefferson, Firestone Library, Princeton University; Thomas Jefferson to James Madison, November 6, 1812, in *The Papers of James Madison: Secretary of State Series, Presidential Series, Retirement Series, Personal Papers*, ed. Robert Brugger et al. (Charlottesville: University Press of Virginia, 1986), presidential ser. 3:440–41.
13. Donald Hickey, *The War of 1812: A Forgotten Conflict* (Chicago: University of Illinois Press, 1990), p. 90.

14. Ketcham, *James Madison*, p. 562.

15. James Madison to Thomas Jefferson, June 22, 1812, Historical Society of Pennsylvania; Richard Rush to Ralph Ingersoll, July 23, 1812, Historical Society of Pennsylvania.

16. Richard Rush to Alexander Ingersoll, September 15, 1812, in ibid.

17. Dolley Madison, *The Selected Letters of Dolley Payne Madison*, ed. David Mattern and Holly Schulman (Charlottesville: University Press of Virginia, 2003), p. 340.

CHAPTER 19. WAR

1. Stephen Van Rensselaer to Daniel Tompkins, August 31, 1812, and Henry Dearborn to Stephen Van Rensselaer, September 2, 1812, and September 26, 1812, in *History of the United States during the First Administration of James Madison*, by Henry Adams (New York: Literary Classics of the United States, Library of America, 1986), 6:342–45.

2. *London Times*, January 12, 1813.

3. Donald Hickey, *The War of 1812: A Forgotten Conflict* (Chicago: University of Illinois Press, 1990), p. 156.

4. Harry Coles, *The War of 1812* (Chicago: University of Chicago Press, 1965), pp. 86–88.

5. Hickey, *War of 1812*, p. 165.

6. Ibid., pp. 95–96.

7. *Essex Register*, December 16, 1812 (reprint from a Halifax paper); *London Times*, January 1, 1813.

8. Hickey, *War of 1812*, pp. 132–33.

9. *London Times*, January 6, 1813.

10. Ralph Ketcham, *James Madison: A Biography* (New York: Macmillan, 1971), p. 566.

11. Ibid.

12. Ibid.

13. Coles, *War of 1812*, pp. 116–17; Hickey, *War of 1812*, p. 154; John Elting, *Amateurs, to Arms!* (New York: DaCapo Press, 1995), pp. 80–81.

14. James Madison to Congress, December 7, 1813, in *Annals of Congress: Debates and Proceedings in the Congress of the United States, 1789–1824* (Washington, DC: US Government Printing House, 1834–1856), 13:538–44.

15. Coles, *War of 1812*, p.152.

16. Ketcham, *James Madison*, p. 572; Louis Serrurier to Antoine LeForest, June 27, 1814, in *James Madison*, by Irving Brant (Indianapolis, IN: Bobbs-Merrill, 1941–1946), 6:268–69.

17. Ibid., pp. 170–71.

18. *Lexington Reporter,* August 7, 1813.

19. *Niles Register,* April 22, 1815.

20. *London Courier,* January 1814.

CHAPTER 20. THE MONTPELIER OF THE PRESIDENT

1. George Shattuck, *Diary,* 1834–1842, Massachusetts Historical Society, Boston.

2. Charles Ingersoll, "A Visit to Mr. Madison at Montpelier, May 2, 1836," in *The Madisons at Montpelier: Reflections on the Founding Couple,* by Ralph Ketcham (Charlottesville: University Press of Virginia, 2009), p. 165.

3. Harriet Martineau, *Retrospect on Western Travel* (1838; repr., New York: Greenwood Press, 1969), 2:233–40.

4. Catherine Allgor, *The Queen of America: Mary Cutts's Life of Dolley Madison* (Charlottesville: University of Virginia Press, 2012), pp. 160–61; Anna Thornton, *Diary of Anna Marie Thornton,* 1793–1863, in Dolley Madison Digital Edition, ed. Holly C. Shulman (Charlottesville: University of Virginia Press, Online Rotunda Edition, 2010–2013) (hereafter referred to as DMDE).

5. Ketcham, *Madisons at Montpelier,* pp. 4–12.

6. Dolley Madison to Anna Cutts, August 1811, in DMDE.

7. Margaret Bayard Smith, *The First Forty Years of Washington Society,* ed. Gaillard Hunt (New York: Charles Scribner's Sons, 1906), p. 81.

8. Ibid., p. 82; Anna Thornton to Dolley Madison, August 24, 1802, in DMDE.

9. Nelly Willis to Dolley Madison, June 8, 1813, in ibid.

10. Matthew Hyland, *Montpelier and the Madisons: House, Home and American Heritage* (Charleston, SC: History Press, 2007), p. 28.

11. Dolley Madison to Anna Cutts, August 19, 1811, in DMDE.

12. Virginia Moore, *The Madisons: A Biography* (New York: McGraw-Hill, 1979), p. 393.

13. Hyland, *Montpelier and the Madisons,* pp. 51–52.

14. James Madison to James Monroe, December 11, 1798, in *The Papers of James Madison: Secretary of State Series, Presidential Series, Retirement Series, Personal Papers,* ed. Robert Brugger et al. (Charlottesville: University Press of Virginia, 1986) (hereafter cited as *PJM*), 17:73–75; Robert Livingston to James Madison, November 10, 1798, in *PJM,* 17:161–62.

15. Dolley Madison to Anna Cutts, August 19, 1811, in DMDE.

16. Anna Thornton to Dolley Madison, August 21, 1809, in ibid.

17. Dolley Madison to Anna Cutts, July 15, 1811, in ibid.

18. Margaret Smith to a friend, August 4, 1809, in ibid.

19. Dolley Madison to Anna Cutts, December 22, 1811, in ibid.

20. Anna Thornton Diary, September 5, 1802, entry, Montpelier Archives.

21. James Madison to Thomas Jefferson, June 19, 1793, in *PJM*, 15:33–34.

22. Hyland, *Montpelier and the Madisons*, p. 38.

23. Ibid., p. 39.

CHAPTER 21. INTO THE WAR'S STRETCH

1. Gaillard Hunt, *The Life of James Madison* (New York: Doubleday, Page, 1902), pp. 350–51.

2. Robert Rutland, *The Presidency of James Madison* (Lawrence: University Press of Kansas, 1990), pp. 184–85.

3. *Alexandria Gazette*, September 15, 1814; Margaret Bayard Smith, *The First Forty Years of Washington Society*, ed. Gaillard Hunt (New York: Charles Scribner's Sons, 1906), pp. 101–15.

4. William Wirt to Elizabeth Wirt, October 14, 1814, in Wirt Papers, Maryland Historical Society, and in *Marriage in the Early Republic: Elizabeth and William Wirt and the Companionate Ideal*, by Anya Jabour (Baltimore: Johns Hopkins University Press, 1998); Catherine Allgor, *A Perfect Union: Dolley Madison and the Creation of the American Nation* (New York: Henry Holt, 2006), pp. 319–20.

5. Dolley Madison to Mary Latrobe, December 3, 1814, in Dolley Madison Digital Edition, ed. Holly C. Shulman (Charlottesville: University of Virginia Press, Online Rotunda Edition, 2010–2013) (hereafter referred to as DMDE).

6. Anthony Pitch, *The Burning of Washington: The British Invasion of 1814* (Annapolis, MD: Naval Institute Press, 1998), p. 215.

7. Francis Gilmer, quoted in *The Abbe Correa in American, 1812–1820*, ed. Richard Davis (Philadelphia, PA: American Philosophical Society, 1955), p. 101.

8. Smith, *Forty Years of Washington Society*, p. 105.

9. *Corbett's Weekly Register*, May 7, 1814.

10. Hugh Howard, *Mr. and Mrs. Madison's War: America's First Couple and the Second War of Independence* (New York: Bloomsbury Press, 2012), p. 256.

11. Pitch, *Burning of Washington*, p. 162.

12. Allgor, *Perfect Union*, p. 323.

13. Paul F. Boller Jr., *Presidential Wives: An Anecdotal History* (New York: Oxford University Press, 1988), p. 43.

14. *National Intelligencer*, September 7, 8, and 28, 1814; *National Intelligencer*, October 28, 1814.

15. *Federal Republican*, January 12, 1815.

16. Dolley Madison to Hanna Gallatin, December 26, 1814, in DMDE.

17. Howard, *Mr. and Mrs. Madison's War*, p. 271.

18. Thomas Johnson to Dolley Madison, January 19, 1815, in DMDE.

19. Allgor, *Perfect Union*, p. 332.

20. Paul Jennings, *A Colored Man's Reminiscences of James Madison* (Brooklyn, NY: George C. Beadle, 1865), p. 17.

21. Charles Ingersoll, *Historical Sketch of the Second War between the United States and Great Britain* (Philadelphia, PA: Lea and Blanchard, 1849), 2:65.

22. Jennings, *Colored Man's Reminiscences*, pp. 17–18.

23. Rutland, *Presidency of James Madison*, p. 187.

24. Constance McLaughlin Green, *Washington: Village and Capital, 1800–1878* (Princeton, NJ: Princeton University Press, 1962), 1:75–80.

25. *London Times*, April 1817.

26. Rutland, *Presidency of James Madison*, pp. 192–93.

27. Henry Adams, *History of the United States during the First Administration of James Madison* (New York: Literary Classics of the United States, 1986), 9 vol. edition, 9:220–21, 240–41.

CHAPTER 22. HOME TO MONTPELIER

1. James Smith, ed., *The Republic of Letters: The Correspondence between Thomas Jefferson and James Madison, 1776–1826* (New York: W. W. Norton, 1995), 2:1167.

2. Margaret Bayard Smith to Mrs. Kirkpatrick, March 13, 1814, in ibid., p. 94.

3. Margaret Bayard Smith to Susan Bayard Smith, February 26, 1809, in ibid., pp. 54–57.

4. William Eustis to James Madison, 1823, in *The Writings of James Madison*, by James Madison and Gaillard Hunt (New York: Russell and Russell, 1968), 9:135.

5. Ralph Ketcham, *James Madison: A Biography* (New York: Macmillan, 1971), p. 355.

6. Federalist No. 14, in *The Papers of James Madison: Secretary of State Series, Presidential Series, Retirement Series, Personal Papers*, ed. Robert Brugger et al. (Charlottesville: University Press of Virginia, 1986) (hereafter cited as *PJM*), 10:288.

7. Irving Brant, *James Madison* (Indianapolis, IN: Bobbs-Merrill, 1941–1946), 6:420; James Paulding, "An Unpublished Sketch of James Madison," *Virginia Magazine of History and Biography* 67 (October 1959): 435.

8. Gaillard Hunt, *Life in America One Hundred Years Ago* (New York: Harper Brothers, 1914), p. 19.

9. John Quincy Adams to James Madison, December 6, 1816, in Washburn Papers, Massachusetts Historical Society, 9:12.

10. Eliza Collins Lee to Dolley Madison, March 4, 1817, in Dolley Madison Papers,

North American Women's Letters and Diaries, digital collection, doc. 40; William Johnson Jr., to Dolley Madison, 1817, in Dolley Madison Digital Edition, ed. Holly C. Shulman (Charlottesville: University of Virginia Press, Online Rotunda Edition, 2010–2013) (hereafter referred to as DMDE).

11. Lucia Kantzow to Dolley Madison, June 26, 1818, in DMDE.

12. Ketcham, *James Madison*, p. 619.

13. Katherine Anthony, *Dolley Madison: Her Life and Times* (New York: Doubleday, 1949), p. 268.

14. Ibid.

15. Dolley Madison to Anthony Morris, August 20, 1839, in DMDE.

16. Ibid.; Margaret Bayard Smith to Mrs. Boyd, August 17, 1828, in *The First Forty Years of Washington Society*, by Margaret Bayard Smith, ed. Gaillard Hunt (New York: Charles Scribner's Sons, 1906), pp. 232–37; H. D. Gilpin to his father, September 16, 1827, in *Virginia Magazine of Biography and History* 86 (October 1968): 449–70.

17. Paulding, "Unpublished Sketch of James Madison," pp. 432–37.

18. Dolley Madison to a niece, in Anthony, *Dolley Madison*, p. 264.

19. Ibid.

20. Matthew Hyland, *Montpelier and the Madisons: House, Home and American Heritage* (Charleston, SC: History Press, 2007), p. 83.

21. James Madison to Thomas Jefferson, July 18, 1793, and July 20, 1793, in *PJM*, 15:113.

22. Ralph Ketcham, *The Madisons at Montpelier: Reflections on the Founding Couple* (Charlottesville: University Press of Virginia, 2009), pp. 36–37.

23. Abigail Mayo to Dolley Madison, February 23, 1804, in DMDE; Dolley Madison to her niece Dolley Madison, March 10, 1830, in DMDE; Dolley Madison to Judith Smith, March 1, 1800, in DMDE.

24. Robert Scott, *Diary of Robert Scott*, October 26, 1829, private collection, Versailles, Kentucky; Ketcham, *James Madison*, p. 637.

25. Catherine Allgor, *The Queen of America: Mary Cutts's Life of Dolley Madison* (Charlottesville: University of Virginia Press, 2012), p. 162.

26. Ketcham, *Madisons at Montpellier*, pp. 32–33.

27. Hyland, *Montpelier and the Madisons*, p. 50.

CHAPTER 23. A NEW LIFE AMID THE FORESTS

1. Phoebe Morris to Dolley Madison, September 1824, in Dolley Madison Digital Edition, ed. Holly C. Shulman (Charlottesville: University of Virginia Press, Online Rotunda Edition, 2010–2013) (hereafter referred to as DMDE).

2. Dolley Madison to John Jackson, November 27, 1824, in ibid.; Frances Wright to Dolley Madison, July 26, 1825, in ibid.

3. Noel Gerson, *The Velvet Glove: A Life of Dolley Madison* (Nashville: Thomas and Nelson, 1975), p. 235; Matthew Hyland, *Montpelier and the Madisons: House, Home, and American Heritage* (Charleston, SC: History Press, 2007), p. 59.

4. Eliza Collins Lee to Dolley Madison, March 30, 1819, in DMDE.

5. Dolley Madison to Edward Coles, September 5, 1819, in Dolley Madison Papers, North American Women's Letters and Diaries, digital collection, doc. 33.

6. Dolley Madison to Mary Cutts, March 13, 1833, in DMDE.

7. Dolley Madison to Mary Cutts, August 1, 1833, in ibid.

8. Dolley Madison to Mary Cutts, November 4, 1833, in ibid.

9. Dolley Madison to Richard Cutts, August 11, 1833, in ibid.

10. Dolley Madison to Mary Cutts, March 1833, in ibid.

11. James Paulding, "An Unpublished Sketch of James Madison," *Virginia Magazine of History and Biography* 67 (October 1959): 432–37.

12. Virginia Moore, *The Madisons: A Biography* (New York: McGraw-Hill, 1979), p. 393.

13. Dolley Madison to Mary Cutts, August 1, 1833, in DMDE.

14. Dolley Madison to Richard Cutts, 1824, in ibid.

15. Dolley Madison to Anna Cutts, June 6, 1829, in ibid.

16. James Madison to Thomas Jefferson, February 24, 1826, in *The Writings of James Madison*, by James Madison and Gaillard Hunt (New York: Russell and Russell, 1968), 9:244.

17. Dolley Madison to Richard Cutts, August 16, 1832, in DMDE.

18. James Madison to Thomas Jefferson, June 1831, in Madison and Hunt, *Writings of James Madison*, 4:565.

19. Ibid.

20. James Madison to J. K. Paulding, April 1831, in ibid., 4:173–77.

21. Dolley Madison to Payne Todd, July 6, 1826, in DMDE.

22. Ralph Ketcham, *The Madisons at Montpelier: Reflections on the Founding Couple* (Charlottesville: University Press of Virginia, 2009), pp. 133–39.

23. Dolley Madison to Sarah "Sally" Coles Stevenson, February 20, 1820, in DMDE.

24. Dolley Madison to Anna Cutts, August 22, 1820, in ibid.

25. Dolley Madison to Anna Cutts, April 3, 1818, in ibid.

26. Margaret Page to Dolley Madison, August 19, 1817, in ibid.

27. Jackie Blount to Dolley Madison, July 28, 1817, in ibid.

28. Kitty Rush to Dolley Madison, November 24, 1820, in ibid.

29. Maria Scott to Dolley Madison, August 30, 1820, in ibid.; Ellen Coolidge to Dolley Madison, April 24, 1820, in ibid.; Dolley Madison to Eliza Collins Lee, August

27, 1820, in ibid.; Dolley Madison to Eliza Collins Lee, April 21, 1819, in ibid.; Dolley Madison to Caroline Eustis, January 22, 1819, in ibid.

30. Ellen Coolidge to Dolley Madison, April 24, 1820, in ibid.

31. Dolley Madison to Sarah "Sally" Coles Stevenson, February 1820, in ibid.

32. Eliza Longueville to Dolley Madison, November 15, 1823, in ibid.

33. Dolley Madison to her niece Dolley, March 30, 1830, in ibid.

34. General James Taylor to Dolley Madison, January 2, 1831, in ibid.; Dolley Madison to Anna Cutts, June 6, 1829, in ibid.

35. Dolley Madison to Anna Cutts, April 23, 1827, in ibid.

36. James Smith, ed., *The Republic of Letters: The Correspondence between Thomas Jefferson and James Madison, 1776–1826* (New York: W. W. Norton, 1995), pp. 233–37.

37. Harriet Martineau, *Retrospect of Western Travel* (1838; repr., New York: Greenwood Press, 1969), 1:150–51, 189–99.

38. Ibid.

39. Ibid.

40. Ibid.

41. Ibid.

42. Ibid.

43. James Madison to Ed Coles, August 27, 1834, in Madison and Hunt, *Writings of James Madison*, 9:542.

44. Martineau, *Retrospect of Western Travel*, 1:150–51.

45. James Madison to Hubbard Taylor, August 15, 1835, in Madison and Hunt, *Writings of James Madison*, 4:577–584; Ketcham, *Madisons at Montpelier*, pp. 156–57.

46. Dolley Madison to Mary Cutts, March 10, 1835, and October 1835, in DMDE.

47. Charles Ingersoll, "A Visit to Mr. Madison," in Ketcham, *Madisons at Montpelier*, pp. 165–71.

48. Ibid.

49. Catherine Allgor, *A Perfect Union: Dolley Madison and the Creation of the American Nation* (New York: Henry Holt, 2006), p. 357; Dolley Madison to Edward Coles, April 16, 1834, in DMDE; Dolley Madison to Anna Cutts, May 15, 1832, in DMDE.

50. Hyland, *Madisons at Montpelier*, p. 59.

51. Sally d'Yrugo to Dolley Madison, June 20, 1812, in Dolley Madison Papers, digital, North American Women's Letters and Diaries, doc. 39.

52. Dolley Madison to Anna Cutts, May 1812, in DMDE.

CHAPTER 24. PAYNE TODD

1. Dolley Madison to Payne Todd, April 12, 1823, in Dolley Madison Digital Edition, ed. Holly C. Shulman (Charlottesville: University of Virginia Press, Online Rotunda Edition, 2010–2013) (hereafter referred to as DMDE).

2. John Quincy Adams, *Memoirs of John Quincy Adams* (Philadelphia, PA: J. P. Lippincott, 1874–1877), note on September 18, 1814, 3:32; Catherine Allgor, *The Queen of America: Mary Cutts's Life of Dolley Madison* (Charlottesville: University of Virginia Press, 2012), p. 183.

3. Ralph Ketcham, *James Madison: A Biography* (New York: Macmillan, 1971), pp. 600–601; Katherine Anthony, *Dolley Madison: Her Life and Times* (Garden City, NY: Doubleday, 1949), pp. 251–55.

4. Anthony, *Dolley Madison*, p. 252.

5. Eliza Collins to Dolley Madison, July 15, 1817, in DMDE; Fanny Rose to Dolley Madison, March 19, 1822, in DMDE.

6. Anthony, *Dolley Madison*, pp. 361–63.

7. Ibid., p. 251.

8. Virginia Moore, *The Madisons: A Biography* (New York: McGraw-Hill, 1979), p. 380.

9. A. Morris to Dolley Madison, July 14, 1820, in DMDE.

10. Phoebe Morris to Dolley Madison, July 15, 1820, in ibid.

11. Dolley Madison to Payne Todd, July 20, 1832, in ibid.

12. Dolley Madison to Payne Todd, May 24, 1821, in ibid.

13. Ibid.; Edward Coles to Dolley Madison, February 22, 1832, in DMDE.

14. Sophie Bache to Dolley Madison, September 25, 1825, in ibid.

15. Dolley Madison to Payne Todd, April 27, 1828, in ibid.

16. Sarah "Sally" Coles Stevenson to Dolley Madison, December 1820, in ibid.

17. Edward Coles to Dolley Madison, February 22, 1816, in ibid.

18. Dolley Madison to Payne Madison, December 2, 1824, in ibid.

19. Dolley Madison to Anna Cutts, December 1822, in ibid.; Dolley Madison to Payne Todd, December 2, 1834, in ibid.

20. Dolley Madison to Payne Todd, July 16, 1827, in ibid.

21. Land records, Orange County, November 12, 1838, and March 29, 1839, in ibid.

22. James Madison to Payne Todd, November 13, 1825, in Anthony, *Dolley Madison*, pp. 274–75.

23. James Madison to Payne Todd, February 15, 1826, in DMDE.

24. James Madison to Payne Todd, April 26, 1826, in James Madison Papers, Library of Congress.

25. Dolley Madison to Dolley Cutts, July 30, 1826, in DMDE.

26. Dolley Madison to Anna Cutts, Jun, 1821, in ibid.

27. John Coles Payne to Payne Todd, October 12, 1836, in ibid.

28. Ibid.; Dolley Madison to Payne Todd, May 24, 1821, and April 9, 1823, in ibid.

29. Dolley Madison to Thomas Parke, May 9, 1809, in ibid.

30. Ketcham, *James Madison*, pp. 614–16.

31. Dolley Madison to Payne Todd, July 20, 1834, in DMDE.

32. Dolley Madison to Payne Todd, May 28, 1821, in ibid.

33. Edward Coles to W. C. Rives, 1857, in Rives Papers, Library of Congress.

CHAPTER 25. THE MADISONS

1. David Brion Davis, *Slavery in the Age of Revolution, 1770–1823* (Ithaca, NY: Cornell University Press, 1975), pp. 106, 125, 128.

2. James Madison to Edmund Randolph, March 10, 1784, in *The Writings of James Madison*, by James Madison and Gaillard Hunt (New York: Russell and Russell, 1968), 2:31.

3. James Madison to John Parrish, June 6, 1790, in Cox-Parrish-Wharton Papers, Historical Society of Pennsylvania; Ralph Ketcham, *James Madison: A Biography* (New York: MacMillan, 1971), p. 315.

4. Patrick Henry to Robert Pleasants, January 18, 1773, in *Friend Anthony Benezet*, by George S. Brookes (Philadelphia, PA: University of Pennsylvania Press, 1937), pp. 443–44; Patrick Henry to Anthony Benezet, January 18, 1773, in Benezet Letters, Friends House, London; Davis, *Slavery in the Age of Revolution*, pp. 196–97; Thomas Jefferson, *The Life and Selected Writings of Thomas Jefferson*, ed. Adrienne Koch and William Peden (New York: Modern Library, 1993), pp. 278–79.

5. Dolley Madison to Dolley Cutts, July 30, 1826, in Dolley Madison Digital Edition, ed. Holly C. Shulman (Charlottesville: University of Virginia Press, Online Rotunda Edition, 2010–2013) (hereafter referred to as DMDE).

6. Sarah "Sally" Coles Stevenson to Dolley Madison, June 21, 1833, in ibid.

7. Edward Coles to Thomas Jefferson, July 31, 1814, in *Governor Edward Coles* (Springfield: Trustees of the Illinois State Historical Library, 1920), pp. 158–60.

8. Davis, *Slavery in the Age of Revolution*, p. 204.

9. *Virginia Gazette*, July 24, 1774.

10. Davis, *Slavery in the Age of Revolution*, p. 197.

11. Samuel Allinson to Patrick Henry, October 12, 1774, in Rutgers University special collections (general revolutionary papers collection); Davis, *Slavery in the Age of Revolution*, p. 398; Thomas Paine, "African Slavery in America," in Davis, *Slavery in the Age of Revolution*, p. 279.

12. Max Farrand, ed., *The Records of the Federal Convention of 1787* (New Haven, CT: Yale University Press, 1937), 3:256.

13. David Rice, *A Kentucky Protest against Slavery: Slavery Inconsistent with Justice and Good Policy—Proved by a Speech, Delivered in the Convention, Held at Danville, Kentucky* (New York, 1812), p. 13.

14. Memorial from Benjamin Rush and others, Pennsylvania Abolitionist Society, February 12, 1813, in *The Papers of James Madison: Secretary of State Series, Presidential Series, Retirement Series, Personal Papers*, ed. Robert Brugger et al. (Charlottesville: University Press of Virginia, 1986) (hereafter cited as *PJM*), presidential ser. 6:13–14.

15. Farrand, *Records of the Federal Convention of 1787*, 3:211.

16. *Connecticut Courant*, December 12, 1796.

17. Davis, *Slavery in the Age of Revolution*, p. 336.

18. James Madison to his father, September 8, 1783, in *PJM*, 7:304.

19. Harriet Martineau, *Retrospect of Western Travel* (1838; repr., New York: Greenwood Press, 1969), 1:192.

20. Paul Jennings, *A Colored Man's Reminiscences of James Madison* (Brooklyn, NY: G. C. Beadle, 1865), pp. 17–18; James Madison to Edward Coles, October 3, 1834, in James Madison Papers, University of Virginia.

21. Ralph Ketcham, *The Madisons at Montpelier: Reflections on the Founding Couple* (Charlottesville: University Press of Virginia, 2009), pp. 41–43.

22. James Madison to Frances Wright, September 1, 1825, in Madison and Hunt, *Writings of James Madison*, 3:224–29.

23. James Madison to Robert Walsh, November 27, 1819, in ibid., 8:443.

24. Dolley Madison to Eliza Law, October 17, 1804, in DMDE; John Tayloe III to Dolley Madison, December 29, 1808, in DMDE; Francis Scott Key to Dolley Madison, June 30, 1810, in DMDE.

25. James Madison to Edward Coles, October 3, 1834, in *The Last of the Fathers: James Madison and the Republican Legacy*, by Drew R. McCoy (New York: Cambridge University Press, 1989), p. 258.

26. James Madison to Henry Clay, June 1833, in James Madison Papers, Library of Congress.

27. Spotsylvania County Order Book, September 6, 1832 entry, p. 151.

28. James Madison to Mordecai Collins, November 5, 1790, in *PJM*, 13:302–303.

29. James Madison Jr. to James Madison Sr., July 28, 1787, in *PJM*, 10:118.

30. Jennings, *Colored Man's Reminiscence*, pp. 17–18.

31. Davis, *Slavery in the Age of Revolution*, p. 419.

32. Ketcham, *Madisons at Montpelier*, pp. 45–46; Dolley Madison to Anna Cutts, July 23, 1818, in DMDE.

33. Dolley Madison to Anna Cutts, December 1822, in DMDE; Dolley Madison to Anna Cutts, May 3, 1806, in DMDE.

34. Presumed Dolley Madison note, 1837, in DMDE; Matthew Hyland, *Montpelier and the Madisons: House, Home, and American Heritage* (Charleston, SC: History Press, 2007), p. 92.

35. Henry Moncure to Anna Cutts, June 17, 1843, in Dolley Madison Papers, Library of Congress.

36. Catherine Allgor, *A Perfect Union: Dolley Madison and the Creation of the American Nation* (New York: Henry Holt, 2006), p. 369.

37. Ketcham, *Madisons at Montpelier*, p. 164; Ellen Coolidge to Thomas Jefferson, August 1, 1825, in *The Family Letters of Thomas Jefferson*, by Thomas Jefferson, ed. Edna Betts and James Bear Jr. (Columbia: University of Missouri Press, 1966), pp. 454–55.

38. Peter Force, "Scrapbook about James Madison," special collections, Alderman Library, University of Virginia.

39. Martineau, *Retrospective of Western Travel*, 2:150–51.

CHAPTER 26. DOLLEY

1. Ralph Ketcham, *The Madisons at Montpelier: Reflections on the Founding Couple* (Charlottesville: University Press of Virginia, 2009), p. 140.

2. Harry Coles, *The War of 1812* (Chicago: University of Chicago Press, 1965), pp. 268–69.

3. Dolley Madison to General James Taylor, January 29, 1834, in Dolley Madison Digital Edition, ed. Holly C. Shulman (Charlottesville: University of Virginia Press, Online Rotunda Edition, 2010–2013) (hereafter referred to as DMDE).

4. Dolley Madison to Judith Rives, May 24, 1832, in ibid.; Dolley Madison to Lucy Todd, May 1836, in ibid.; Dolley Madison to Fanny Lear, October 27, 1835, in ibid.

5. Katherine Anthony, *Dolley Madison: Her Life and Times* (Garden City, NY: Doubleday, 1949), p. 325.

6. Ibid., p. 326.

7. James Madison memo, April 1826, in DMDE.

8. Irving Brant, *James Madison* (Indianapolis, IN: Bobbs-Merrill, 1941–1946), 6:516–20; Ralph Ketcham, *James Madison: A Biography* (New York: Macmillan, 1971), pp. 669–70; Paul Jennings, *A Colored Man's Reminiscences* (Brooklyn, NY: G. C. Beadle, 1865), pp. 20–21.

9. Dolley Madison to Charles Ingersoll, June 15, 1836, in DMDE.

10. Margaret Smith to her husband, March 12, 1829, in *The First Forty Years of Washington Society*, by Margaret Bayard Smith, ed. Gaillard Hunt (New York: Charles Scribner's Sons, 1906), pp. 299–300.

11. Jennings, *Colored Man's Reminiscences*, p. 17.

12. Wyndham Robertson to Dolley Madison, July 1, 1836, in DMDE; George Smith, chair, Madison, Virginia, city council, to Dolley Madison, July 1836, in DMDE; Martha Jefferson to Dolley Madison, July 1, 1836, in DMDE; Andrew Stevenson to Dolley Madison, September 16, 1836, in DMDE.

13. John Coles Payne to Edward Coles, March 15, 1837, in ibid.

14. Anthony, *Dolley Madison*, pp. 330–31.

15. Dolley Madison to Henry Clay, November 8, 1836, in DMDE; Dolley Madison to Eliza Collins Lee, July 26, 1836, in DMDE; Septima Meikleham, "Montpelier: Quiet Home Life of Mr. and Mrs. Madison," in Meikleham-Randolph-Trist-Coolidge Family Papers, Alderman Library, University of Virginia.

16. Dolley Madison to Margaret Smith, 1838, in Smith, *First Forty Years of Washington Society*, p. 379.

17. Dolly Madison to General B. Peyton, July 13, 1840, in DMDE; Dolley Madison to A. A. H. Palmer, May 12, 1842, in DMDE.

18. Matthew Hyland, *Montpelier and the Madisons: House, Home, and American Heritage* (Charleston, SC: History Press, 2007), pp. 92–93; C. G. Chamberlayne, *Ham Chamberlayne—Virginian; Letters and Papers of an Artillery Officer in the War for Southern Independence 1861–1865* (Richmond, VA: Deitz Press, 1932), p. 188.

19. Anthony, *Dolley Madison*, p. 374.

20. Payne Todd to James Madison Hite, May 10, 1837, in DMDE.

21. George Tucker to Dolley Madison, August 23, 1836, in ibid.; James Paulding to Jared Sparks, September 11, 1836, in ibid.; William Rives to Judith Rives, November 29, 1836, in ibid.

22. John Coles Payne to William Rives, December 24, 1836, in ibid.

23. United States Senate, *Journal of the Senate*, July 1, 1836, in ibid.

24. Payne Todd to Dolley Madison, 1844 note, in ibid.

25. Eugene Exman, *The Brothers Harper: A Unique Publishing Partnership and Its Impact upon the Cultural Life of America, 1817–1853* (New York: Harper and Row, 1965), p. 200.

26. Dolley Madison to Payne Todd, May 26, 1838, in DMDE; Dolley Madison to Payne Todd, January 22, 1844, in DMDE.

27. Ibid.

28. Dolley Madison to Andrew Jackson, September 2, 1836, in ibid.

29. Anna Payne to Payne Todd, September 14, 1836, in ibid.

30. Dolley Madison to Payne Todd, March 23, 1837, in ibid.

31. Ibid.

32. John Campbell to William Rives, April 5, 1837, in ibid.; George Featherstonhaugh to William Rives, April 10, 1837, in ibid.

33. Dolley Madison to Ann Maury, October 9, 1836, in ibid.

34. John Payne to Edward Coles, January 27, 1837, in ibid.

35. Dolley Madison to unknown correspondent, April 3, 1838, in ibid.

36. Dolley Madison to Dolley Cutts, December 1831, in ibid.; Phoebe Morris to Dolley Madison, January 19 , 1824, in ibid.

37. Judith Rives to Dolley Madison, January 26, 1829, in ibid.

38. Judith Rives to Dolley Madison, February 1829, in ibid.

39. Edward Coles to Dolley Madison, February 22, 1832, in ibid.

40. Anthony, *Dolley Madison*, pp. 333–34; Noel Gerson, *The Velvet Glove: A Life of Dolley Madison* (Nashville: Thomas and Nelson, 1975), p. 238.

41. Dolley Madison to Richard Cutts, October 1837, in DMDE.

42. Dolley Madison to Anthony Morris, September 2, 1837, in ibid.

43. Lucy Todd to James Todd, October 5, 1842, in ibid.; Dolley Madison to Payne Todd, July 20, 1832, in ibid.

44. Dolley Madison to Richard Cutts, 1841, in ibid.

45. Edward Coles to Sally Stevenson, November 12, 1836, in ibid.

46. J. Eastman Johnson, in *Life and Letters of Dolley Madison*, by Allen Clark (Washington, DC: Press of W. F. Roberts, 1914), p. 506.

47. Letter by slave Sarah, in Papers of Dolley Madison, Library of Congress.

48. Lucia Cutts, *Memoirs and Letters of Dolley Madison, Wife of James Madison, President of the United States* (1886; repr. Port Washington, NY: Kennikat Press, 1971), p. 206; Meikleham, "Montpelier."

49. Ethel Arnett, *Mrs. James Madison: The Incomparable Dolley* (Greensboro, NC: Piedmont Press, 1972), p. 348–49.

50. Lucy Todd to James Todd, October 5, 1842, in DMDE.

51. George Spotswood to Payne Todd, September 15, 1841, in ibid.

52. Anthony, *Dolley Madison*, p. 325.

53. Dolley Madison to Anna Cutts, July 1819–1822, in DMDE; Dolley Madison to Margaret Smith, in Smith, *First Forty Years of Washington Society*, p. 380; Dolley Madison to Mary Cutts, May 28, 1835, in DMDE.

54. Dolley Madison to Anna Thornton, September 1, 1808, in DMDE; Dolley Madison to Lucy Cutts, August 29, 1807, in DMDE.

55. Adams Diary, October 24, 1837 entry, in Anthony, *Dolley Madison*, pp. 348–49.

56. Anthony, *Dolley Madison*, p. 351.

57. Gerson, *Velvet Glove*, pp. 240–41.

58. Philip Hone to a friend, in Anthony, *Dolley Madison*, p. 352.

59. Ketcham, *Madisons at Montpelier*, p. 179.

60. Anthony, *Dolley Madison*, p. 387.

61. Dolley Madison to Betsy Coles, February 21, 1838, in DMDE.

62. Anthony, *Dolley Madison*, pp. 361–63.

63. Dolley Madison to Anthony Morris, September 3, 1838, in DMDE.

64. Dolley Madison to Anthony Morris, August 20, 1839, in ibid.

65. *National Intelligencer*, January 2, 1839; *New York Express*, January 2, 1839.

66. William Kemble Sr. to William Kemble Jr., January 26, 1839, in DMDE.

67. William Preston to Dolley Madison, July 4, 1839, in ibid.

68. Richard Rush to Dolley Madison, December 22, 1837, in ibid.

69. Anthony, *Dolley Madison*, p. 393.

70. Ibid.

71. *National Intelligencer*, July 17, 1849.

SELECT BIBLIOGRAPHY

Madison, Dolley. *Dolley Madison Digital Edition*. Edited by Holly C. Shulman. Charlottesville: University of Virginia, 2004–.

Washington, George. *The Writings of George Washington*. Edited by John C. Fitzpatrick. Washington, DC: US Government Printing Office, 1932.

BOOKS

Abernathy, Tom. *The South in the New Nation, 1789–1819*. Baton Rouge: Louisiana State University Press, 1961.

Adams, Abigail. *The New Letters of Abigail Adams, 1788–1801*. Edited by Stewart Mitchell. Boston: Houghton Mifflin, 1947.

Adams, Henry. *History of the United States during the First Administration of James Madison*. Condensed vol. New York: Literary Classics of the United States, Library of America, 1986.

———. *John Randolph*. Boston: Houghton-Mifflin, 1898. Reprint, Armonk, NY: M. E. Sharpe, 1996.

Adams, John Quincy. *The Diary of John Quincy Adams, 1794–1845: American Diplomacy and Political, Social and Intellectual Life, from Washington to Polk*. Edited by Allan Nevins. New York: Frederick Ungar Publishing, 1928.

———. *Lives of Celebrated Statesmen*. New York: W. H. Graham, 1846.

Allgor, Catherine. *A Perfect Union: Dolley Madison and the Creation of the American Nation*. New York: Henry Holt, 2006.

Ambler, Charles. *Thomas Ritchie: A Study in Virginia Politics*. Richmond: Bell, Book and Stationary, 1913.

Ames, Seth. *The Works of Fisher Ames*. 2 vols. Boston: Little, Brown, 1854.

Ammon, Harry. *James Monroe: The Quest for National Identity*. New York: McGraw-Hill, 1971.

Annals of the Congress of the United States, 1789-1824. Washington, DC: US Government Printing House, 1834–1856.

419

Anthony, Katherine. *Dolley Madison: Her Life and Times.* Garden City, NY: Doubleday, 1949.

Arnett, Ethel. *Mrs. James Madison: The Incomparable Dolley.* Greensboro, NC: Piedmont Press, 1972.

Bagot, Mary. *Exile in Yankeeland: The Journal of Mary Bagot, 1816–1819.* Edited by David Hosford. Washington, DC: Historical Society of Washington, DC, 1984.

Banning, Lance. *The Sacred Fire of Liberty: James Madison and the Founding of the Federal Republic.* Ithaca, NY: Cornell University Press, 1995.

Barnard, Daniel. *Lecture on the Character and Services of James Madison, Delivered before the "Young Men's Association for Mutual Improvement in the City of Albany," February 28, 1837.* Albany, NY: Power Press of Hoffman and White, 1837.

Bartholomew, Ann. *The Delaware and Lehigh Canals.* Easton, PA: Center for Canal History, 1989.

Boller, Paul, Jr. *Presidential Campaigns.* New York: Oxford University Press, 2004.

———. *Presidential Wives: An Anecdotal History.* New York: Oxford University Press, 1988.

Borth, Christy. *Mankind on the Move: The Story of Highways.* Washington, DC: Automotive Safety Foundation, 1969.

Brant, Irving. *James Madison.* 6 vols. Indianapolis, IN: Bobbs-Merrill, 1941–1946.

Brodie, Fawn. *Thomas Jefferson: An Intimate History.* New York: W. W. Norton, 1974.

Brookes, George S. *Friend Anthony Benezet.* Philadelphia: University of Pennsylvania Press, 1937.

Brookhiser, Richard. *Gentleman Revolutionary: Gouverneur Morris, the Rake Who Wrote the Constitution.* New York: Free Press, 2003.

Brown, Roger. *The Republic in Peril: 1812.* New York: Columbia University Press, 1964.

Brugger, Robert, and Robert Rutland, Robert Crout, Jeanne Sisson, Dru Dowdy, William Hutchinson, William Rachel, eds. *The Papers of James Madison: Secretary of State Series, Presidential Series, Retirement Series, Personal Papers.* 36 vols. Charlottesville: University Press of Virginia, 1986.

Bryant, William Cullen. *The Embargo.* Facsimile reproduction. Gainesville, FL, 1955.

Calhoun, John C. *Papers of John C. Calhoun.* Edited by Robert Meriweather et al. Columbia: University of South Carolina Press, 1959.

Chamberlayne, C. G. *Ham Chamberlayne—Virginian; Letters and Papers of an Artillery Officer in the War for Southern Independence 1861–1865.* Richmond, VA: Deitz Press, 1932.

Chernow, Ron. *Alexander Hamilton.* New York: Penguin Press, 2004.

Clark, Allen. *Life and Letters of Dolley Madison.* Washington, DC: Press of W. F. Roberts, 1914.

Coles, Harry. *The War of 1812.* Chicago: University of Chicago Press, 1965.

Crawford, William. *Report on the Penitentiaries of the United States.* Montclair, NJ: Patterson Smith, 1969.

Cunningham, Noble, Jr. *In Pursuit of Reason: The Life of Thomas Jefferson.* Baton Rouge: Louisiana State University Press, 1987.

———. *The Jeffersonian Republicans: The Formation of Party Organization, 1789–1801.* Chapel Hill: University of North Carolina Press, 1957.

———. *The Process of Government under Jefferson.* Princeton, NJ: Princeton University Press, 1978.

Cutler, William Parker. *Life, Journals and Correspondence of Rev. Manasseh Cutler, LL.D.* 2 vols. Cincinnati, 1888.

Cutts, Lucia. *Memoirs and Letters of Dolley Madison, Wife of James Madison, President of the United States.* 2 vols. Port Washington, NY: Kennikat Press, 1971. Reprint, 1886.

Davis, David Brion. *Slavery in the Age of Revolution, 1770–1823.* Ithaca, NY: Cornell University Press, 1975.

De Warville, J.-P. Brissot. *New Travels in the United States of America, 1788.* Translated by M. S. Vamos and Durand Echeverria. Edited by Durand Echeverria. London: J. S. Jordan, 1794.

Dunaway, Wayland. *History of the James River and Kanawha Company.* New York: Columbia University Press, 1922.

Eberlein, Harold, and Cortlandt Van Dyke Hubbard. *Historic Houses of George-Town and Washington City.* Richmond, VA: Dietz Press, 1958.

Elkins, Stanley, and Eric McKitrick. *The Age of Federalism.* New York: Oxford University Press, 1993.

Ellet, E. F. *Court Circles of the Republic.* Hartford, CT: Hartford Publishing, 1869.

Ellis, Joseph. *American Sphinx: The Character of Thomas Jefferson.* New York: Alfred A. Knopf, 1994.

Elting, John. *Amateurs, to Arms! A Military History of the War of 1812.* New York: Da Capo Press, 1995.

Ewell, James. *The Planter's and Mariner's Medical Companion.* 3rd ed. Philadelphia: Anderson and Meehan, 1816.

Farrand, Max, ed. *The Records of the Federal Convention of 1787.* 4 vols. New Haven, CT: Yale University Press, 1937.

Ford, Paul. *Writings of Thomas Jefferson.* 10 vols. New York: G. P. Putnam's Sons, 1892–1899.

Fritz, Jean. *The Great Little Madison.* New York: G. P. Putnam's Sons, 1989.

Gallatin, Albert, and Henry Adams. *Writings of Albert Gallatin.* 3 vols. New York: Antiquarian Press, 1960.

Gerson, Noel. *The Velvet Glove: A Life of Dolley Madison.* Nashville: Thomas and Nelson, 1975.

Goodwin, Maud. *Dolley Madison.* New York: Charles Scribner's Sons, 1940.

Green, Constance McLaughlin. *Washington: Village and Capital, 1800–1878.* Princeton, NJ: Princeton University Press, 1962.

Greene, Jack, ed. *The Ambiguity of the American Revolution.* New York: Harper and Row, 1968.

Grigsby, Hugh. *The Virginia Convention of 1776.* Richmond, VA, 1855.

Hamilton, Alexander. *The Papers of Alexander Hamilton.* Edited by Harold Syrett. Vol. 11. New York: Columbia University Press, 1961–1987.

Herold, J. Christopher. *The Age of Napoleon.* New York: American Heritage Publishing, 1963.

Hickey, Donald. *The War of 1812: A Forgotten Conflict.* Urbana: University of Illinois Press, 1990.

Howard, Hugh. *Mr. and Mrs. Madison's War: America's First Couple and the Second War of Independence.* New York: Bloomsbury Press, 2012.

Hunt, Gaillard. *Life in America One Hundred Years Ago.* New York: Harper and Brothers, 1914.

Hyland, Matthew. *Montpelier and the Madisons: House, Home and American Heritage.* Charleston, SC: History Press, 2007.

Ierley, Merritt. *Traveling the National Road: Across the Centuries on America's First Highway.* Woodstock, NY: Overlook Press, 1990.

Ingersoll, Charles. *History of the Second War between the United States of America and Great Britain Declared by Act of Congress, the 18th of June, 1812, and Concluded by Peace, the 15th of February, 1815.* 2 vols. Philadelphia: Lea and Blanchard, 1845–1849.

Isenberg, Nancy. *Fallen Founder: The Life of Aaron Burr.* New York: Viking Press, 2007.

Jackson, George. *The Bath Archives: A Further Selection from the Diaries and Letters of Sir George Jackson, from 1809–1816.* Edited by Lady Catherine Charlotte Jackson. London, 1873.

Jefferson, Thomas. *The Papers of Thomas Jefferson.* Edited by Julian Boyd and Barbara Oberg. 37 vols. Princeton, NJ: Princeton University Press, 2007.

Jennings, Walter Wilson. *The American Embargo, 1807–1809.* Iowa City: University of Iowa Press, 1921.

Jordan, Philip. *The National Road.* Indianapolis, IN: Bobbs-Merrill, 1948.

Kapsch, Robert. *Potomac Canal: George Washington and the Waterway West.* Morgantown: West Virginia University Press, 2007.

Ketcham, Ralph. *James Madison: A Biography.* New York: Macmillan, 1971.

———. *The Madisons at Montpelier: Reflections on the Founding Couple.* Charlottesville: University Press of Virginia, 2009.

Koch, Adrienne. *Jefferson and Madison: The Great Collaboration.* Birmingham, AL: Palladium Press, 2005.

Koch, Adrienne, and William Peden. *The Life and Selected Writings of Thomas Jefferson.* New York: Modern Library, 1944.

Leibiger, Stuart. *Founding Friendship: George Washington, James Madison and the Creation of the American Republic.* Charlottesville: University Press of Virginia, 1999.

Leichtle, Kurt, and Bruce Carveth. *Crusade against Slavery: Edward Coles, Pioneer of Freedom.* Carbondale: Southern Illinois University Press, 2011.

Link, Eugene. *Democratic and Republican Societies, 1790–1800.* New York: Columbia University Press, 1942.

Lipscomb, A. A., and A. E. Bergh. *Writings of Thomas Jefferson.* 20 vols. Washington, DC: Thomas Jefferson Memorial Association of the United States, 1903.

Lloyd, Alan. *The Scorching of Washington: The War of 1812.* Washington, DC: Robert B. Luce, 1974.

Longacre, James, and James Herring, eds. "Mrs. Madison." In *National Portrait Gallery of Distinguished Americans.* New York: Herman Bancroft, 1836.

Macasek, Joseph. *Guide to the Morris Canal in Morris County.* Morristown, NJ: Morris County Heritage Commission, 1996.

Madison, Dolley. *The Selected Letters of Dolley Payne Madison.* Edited by David Mattern and Holly Schulman. Charlottesville: University Press of Virginia, 2003.

Madison, James. *James Madison's 'Advice to My Country.'* Edited by David Mattern. Charlottesville: University Press of Virginia, 1997.

Madison, James, and Gaillard Hunt. *The Writings of James Madison.* 9 vols. New York: Russell and Russell, 1968.

Malone, Dumas. *Jefferson and His Time.* 6 vols. Charlottesville: University Press of Virginia, 2005.

———. *Jefferson and the Ordeal of Liberty.* Boston: Little, Brown, 1962.

Marshall, John. *The Papers of John Marshall.* 12 vols. Edited by Charles Hobson. Chapel Hill: University of North Carolina Press, 1993.

Martineau, Harriet. *Retrospect on Western Travel.* London: Saunders and Otley, 1838. Reprint, New York: Greenwood Press, 1969.

———. *Society in America.* 2 vols. New York: Saunders and Otley, 1837.

McCants, David. *Patrick Henry: The Orator.* New York: Greenwood Press, 1990.

McClellan, Robert. *The Delaware Canal: A Picture Story.* New Brunswick, NJ: Rutgers University Press, 1967.

McGregor, James. *Washington from the Ground Up.* Cambridge, MA: Belknap Press, 2007.

McIlwaine, H. R., and J. P. Kennedy. *Journals of the House of Burgesses of Virginia.* 13 vols. Richmond, VA: Colonial Press, E. Waddey, 1905–1915.

Miller, William. *The Business of May Next: James Madison and the Founding.* Charlottesville: University Press of Virginia, 1992.

Moore, Virginia. *The Madisons: A Biography.* New York: McGraw-Hill, 1979.

National Geographic Society. *The Capital of Our Country.* Washington, DC: National Geographic Society, 1923.

Pancake, John. *Samuel Smith and the Politics of Business, 1752–1839.* Birmingham: University of Alabama Press, 1972.

Payne, Robert. *The Canal Builders: The Story of Canal Engineers through the Ages.* New York: Macmillan, 1959.

Peterson, Merrill, ed. *Political Writings of Thomas Jefferson.* Charlottesville, VA: Thomas Jefferson Memorial Foundation, 1993.

Pitch, Anthony. *The Burning of Washington: The British Invasion of 1814.* Annapolis, MD: Naval Institute Press, 1998.

Plumer, William, Jr. *The Life of William Plumer.* Boston: Phillips, Sampson, 1857.

Randall, Willard. *Thomas Jefferson: A Life.* New York: Henry Holt, 1993.

Ress, David. *Governor Edward Coles and the Vote to Forbid Slavery in Illinois, 1823–1824.* Jefferson, NC: McFarland, 2006.

Rice, David. *A Kentucky Protest against Slavery: Slavery Inconsistent with Justice and Good Policy—Proved by a Speech, Delivered in the Convention, Held at Danville, Kentucky.* New York, 1832.

Richardson, James. *A Compilation of the Messages and Papers of the Presidents 1789–1902.* Washington, DC: Washington Bureau of National Literature and Art, 1897–1917.

Ringwalt, J. Luther. *Development of Transportation Systems in the United States.* Philadelphia, 1888.

Shulim, Joseph, ed. *The Old Dominion and Napoleon Bonaparte: A Study in American Opinion.* New York: Columbia University Press, 1952.

Skeen, C. Edward. *Citizen Soldiers in the War of 1812.* Lexington: University of Kentucky Press, 1977.

Smith, Sir Harry. *Autobiography of Lieutenant-General Sir Harry Smith.* London: John Murray, 1903.

Smith, James, ed. *The Republic of Letters: The Correspondence between Thomas Jefferson and James Madison, 1776–1826.* 3 vols. New York: W. W. Norton, 1995.

Smith, Margaret Bayard. *The First Forty Years of Washington Society.* Edited by Gaillard Hunt. New York: Charles Scribner's Sons, 1906.

———. *A Winter in Washington; or, Memoirs of the Seymour Family.* New York: E. Bliss and E. White, 1824.

Stagg, J. C. A. *Mr. Madison's War: Politics, Diplomacy and Warfare in the Early American Republic, 1783–1830.* Princeton, NJ: Princeton University Press, 1983.

Steiner, Bernard. *The Life and Correspondence of James McHenry, Secretary of War under Washington and Adams.* Cleveland: Burrows Brothers, 1907.

Story, William, ed. *The Life and Letters of Joseph Story.* 2 vols. Boston: Charles Little and James Brown, 1851.

Sutherland, Stella. *Population Distribution in Colonial America.* New York: Columbia University Press, 1936.

Tansill, Charles Callan. *The Making of the American Republic: The Great Documents, 1774–1789.* New Rochelle, NY: Arlington House Press, 1972.

Tugwell, Rexford. *The Enlargement of the Presidency*. Garden City, NY: Doubleday, 1960.

Ward, Henry, and Harold Greer Jr. *Richmond during the Revolution, 1775–83*. Charlottesville: University Press of Virginia, 1977.

Wharton, Anne Hollingsworth. *Social Life in the Early Republic*. Philadelphia: J. B. Lippincott, 1903.

White, Leonard. *The Jeffersonian: A Study in Administrative History*. New York: Macmillan, 1951.

Williams, John. *History of the Invasion and Capture of Washington, and the Events Which Preceded and Followed*. New York: Harper and Brothers, 1857.

Williams, William Appleton. *America Confronts a Revolutionary World, 1776–1976*. New York: William Morrow, 1976.

Wills, Garry. *James Madison*. New York: Henry Holt, 2002.

Willson, Beckles. *Friendly Relations: A Narrative of Britain's Ministers and Ambassadors to America (1791–1930)*. London: L. Dickson and Thompson, 1934.

Wirt, William. *The Letters of a British Spy*. New York, 1803.

Wood, William, ed. *Select British Documents of the Canadian War of 1812*. Toronto: Champlain Society, 1920–1928.

Worrall, Jay. *Friendly Virginians: America's First Quakers*. Athens, GA: Iberian Publishing, 1999.

Young, Jeremiah. *A Political and Constitutional Study of the Cumberland Road*. Chicago: University of Chicago Press, 1902.

Zahniser, Martin. *Charles Cotesworth Pinckney: Founding Father*. Chapel Hill: University of North Carolina Press, 1967.

PAPERS

Adams Family Papers, Massachusetts Historical Society.

Anna Maria Brodeau Thornton Papers, Library of Congress.

Cutts Family Papers, Library of Congress.

George Shattuck Papers, Massachusetts Historical Society.

Hunter Family Papers, New York Historical Society.

Meikleham-Randolph-Trist-Coolidge Family Papers, Alderman Library, University of Virginia.

Otho Holland Williams Papers, Maryland Historical Society.

Papers of Anthony Benezet, Quaker and Special Collections, Haverford College, Haverford, Pennsylvania.

Papers of Hetty Ann Barton, Historical Society of Pennsylvania.

Papers of Joseph Story, Library of Congress.

Sedgwick Family Papers, Massachusetts Historical Society.
Samuel Latham Mitchill Papers, Museum of the City of New York.
William Plumer Papers, Library of Congress, New Hampshire State Library.

JOURNALS

Adams, Charles. "The Madison Papers." *North American Review* 53 (1841).
Cunningham, Noble, Jr. "The Frances Few Diary." *Journal of Southern History* 29, no. 3 (August 1963).
Mitchill, Samuel. "Dr. Mitchill's Letters from Washington: 1801–1813." *Harper's New Monthly Magazine* 58 (April 1879).
Smith, James Morton. "Sedition in the Old Dominion: James T. Callender and 'The Prospect before Us.'" *Journal of Southern History* 20, no. 2 (May 1954).
Tinkcom, Margaret. "Caviar along the Potomac: Sir Augustus John Foster's 'Notes on the United States,' 1804–1812." *William and Mary Quarterly* 3rd series, 8 (January 1951).

NEWSPAPERS

Albany Register, May 1809.
Alexandria Advertiser and Commercial Intelligencer, February 28, 1800; December 16, 1800; July 12, 1803; July 22, 1803; July 27, 1803.
Alexandria Gazette, September 15, 1814.
American Citizen, June 5, 1801.
Aurora, May 15, 1799; January 3, 1809; January 5, 1809; January 18, 1809; January 19, 1809; February 11, 1809; March 4, 1809; March 8, 1809; March 10, 1809; March 22, 1809; April 14, 1809; April 21, 1809; April 23, 1809; May 23, 1809; June 2, 1809; June 6, 1809; July 1, 1812.
Baltimore American, May 1809.
Baltimore Patriot, August 31, 1814.
Boston Chronicle, November 22, 1813.
Boston Evening Post, July 31–August 10, 1812.
Connecticut Courant, December 12, 1796.
Corbett's Weekly Register, May 7, 1814.
Essex Register, December 16, 1812.
Federal Republican, January 12, 1815.
Gazette of the United States, April 24, 1798.

Lexington Reporter, January 1809; August 7, 1813.

London Courier, December 5, 1811; January 1814.

London Times, January 1, 1813; January 6, 1813; January 12, 1813; April 1817.

National Gazette, December 19, 1791; February 18, 1792; March 3, 1792.

National Intelligencer, March 9, 1800; March 4, 1801; March 5, 1801; June 3, 1801; June 8, 1801; October 15, 1801; October 20, 1801; October 26, 1801; October 30, 1801; December 6, 1802; December 10, 1802; February 18, 1803; April 15, 1803; March 7, 1808; December 29, 1808; April 1809; April 4, 1809; April 19, 1809; May 3, 1809; June 21, 1809; September 6, 1809; October 16, 1809; February 5, 1810; April 21, 1810; June 27, 1812; July 1, 1812; August 20, 1814; September 7, 1814; September 8, 1814; September 28, 1814; October 28, 1814; January 2, 1839; July 17, 1849.

New England Palladium, April 12, 1803.

New York Columbian, June 19, 1812; June 21, 1812; June 22, 1812; June 23, 1812; June 27, 1812; June 30, 1812; July 1, 1812; July 3, 1812.

New York Commercial Advertiser, July 12, 1809; July 19, 1809.

New York Express, January 2, 1839.

Niles Register, April 22, 1815.

Palladium, June 19, 1812; June 23, 1812; June 30, 1812; July 1812; July 3, 1812; July 7, 1812; July 10, 1812; July 21, 1812; July 24, 1812; July 28, 1812; July 31, 1812; August 7, 1812; August 11, 1812; August 14, 1812.

Pittsburgh Gazette, November 28, 1833.

Richmond Daily Dispatch, August 27, 1853.

Richmond Enquirer, February 6, 1806.

Richmond Examiner, May 5, 1802.

Salem Gazette, June 23, 1812.

Spirit of Seventy-Six, January 26, 1809; January 16, 1810.

Virginia Gazette, July 24, 1774.

Washington Expositor, December 4, 1807; February 17, 1808; March 1808; April 16, 1808; May 4, 1808; March 12, 1809.

Washington Federalist, February 6, 1805; January 19, 1806; February 2, 1806; December 3, 1806; December 18, 1806; November 7, 1807; January 9, 1808; January 21, 1808; January 23, 1808; January 25, 1808; January 28, 1808; February 3, 1808; February 20, 1808; March 3, 1808; April 8, 1808; May 4, 1808; May 7, 1808; October 1808; December 1, 1808; December 13, 1808; December 31, 1808; March 12, 1809; March 19, 1809.

INDEX